A TRIAL SEPARATION

A TRIAL SEPARATION

Australia and the Decolonisation
of Papua New Guinea

DONALD DENOON

E PRESS

Published by ANU E Press
The Australian National University
Canberra ACT 0200, Australia
Email: anuepress@anu.edu.au
This title is also available online at http://epress.anu.edu.au

National Library of Australia Cataloguing-in-Publication entry

Author: Denoon, Donald.

Title: A trial separation : Australia and the decolonisation of Papua New Guinea / Donald Denoon.

ISBN: 9781921862915 (pbk.) 9781921862922 (ebook)

Notes: Includes bibliographical references and index.

Subjects: Decolonization--Papua New Guinea.
            Papua New Guinea--Politics and government

Dewey Number: 325.953

All rights reserved. No part of this publication may be reproduced, stored in a retrieval system or transmitted in any form or by any means, electronic, mechanical, photocopying or otherwise, without the prior permission of the publisher.

Cover: Barbara Brash, *Red Bird of Paradise*, Print

First published by Pandanus Books, 2005
This edition © 2012 ANU E Press

For the many students who taught me so much about Papua New Guinea,
and for Christina Goode, John Greenwell and Alan Kerr,
who explained so much about Australia.

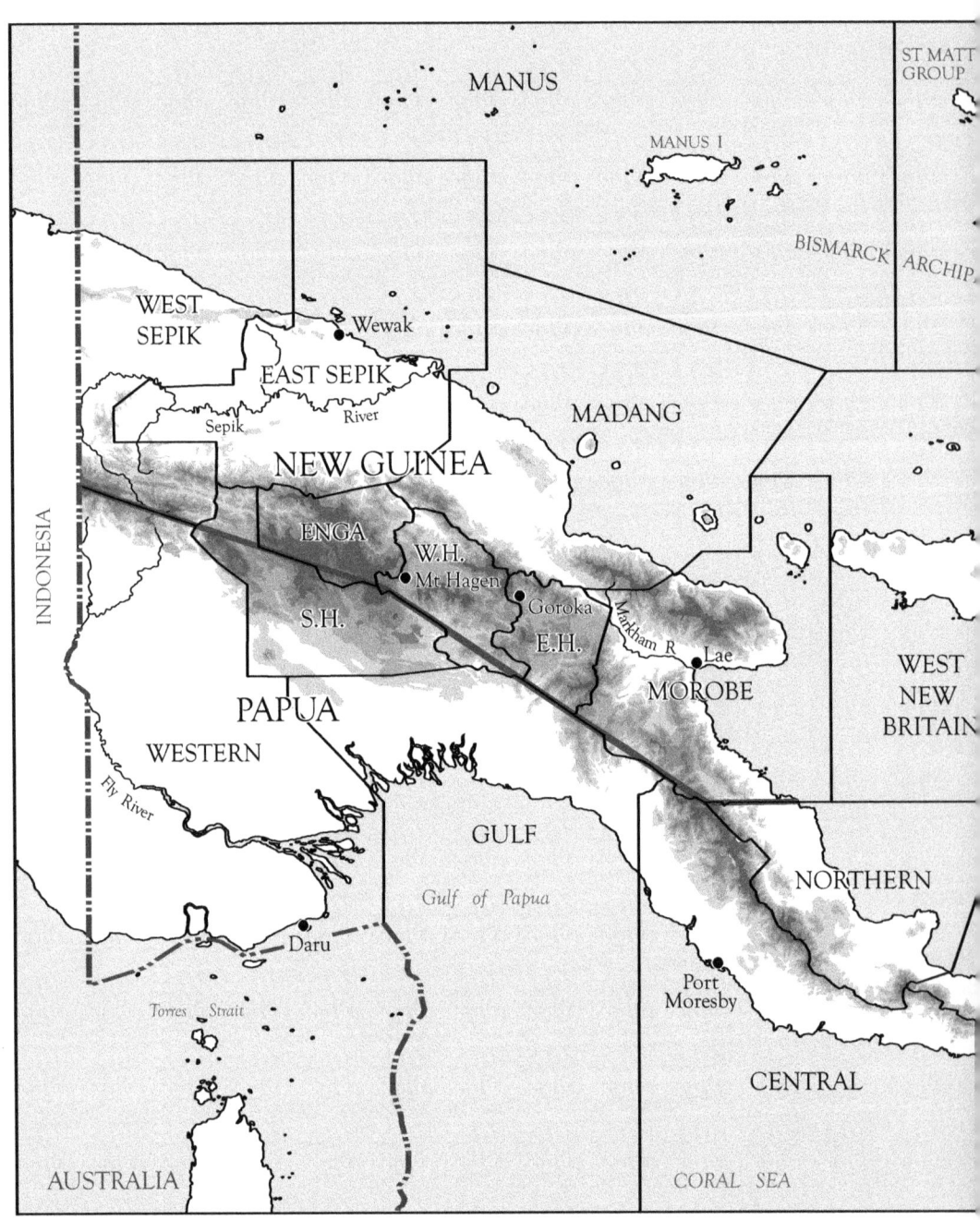

Map 1: The provinces of Papua New Guinea

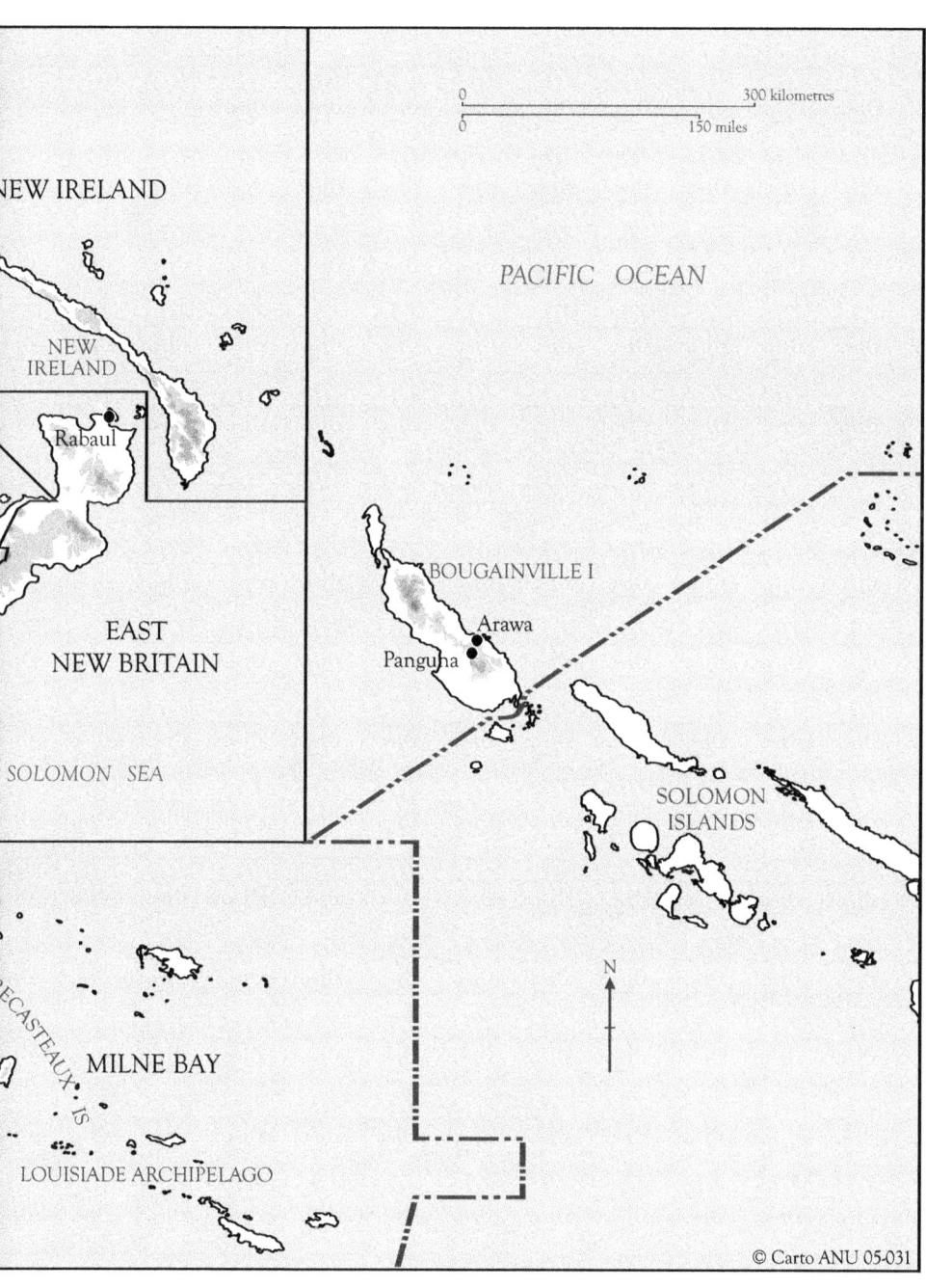

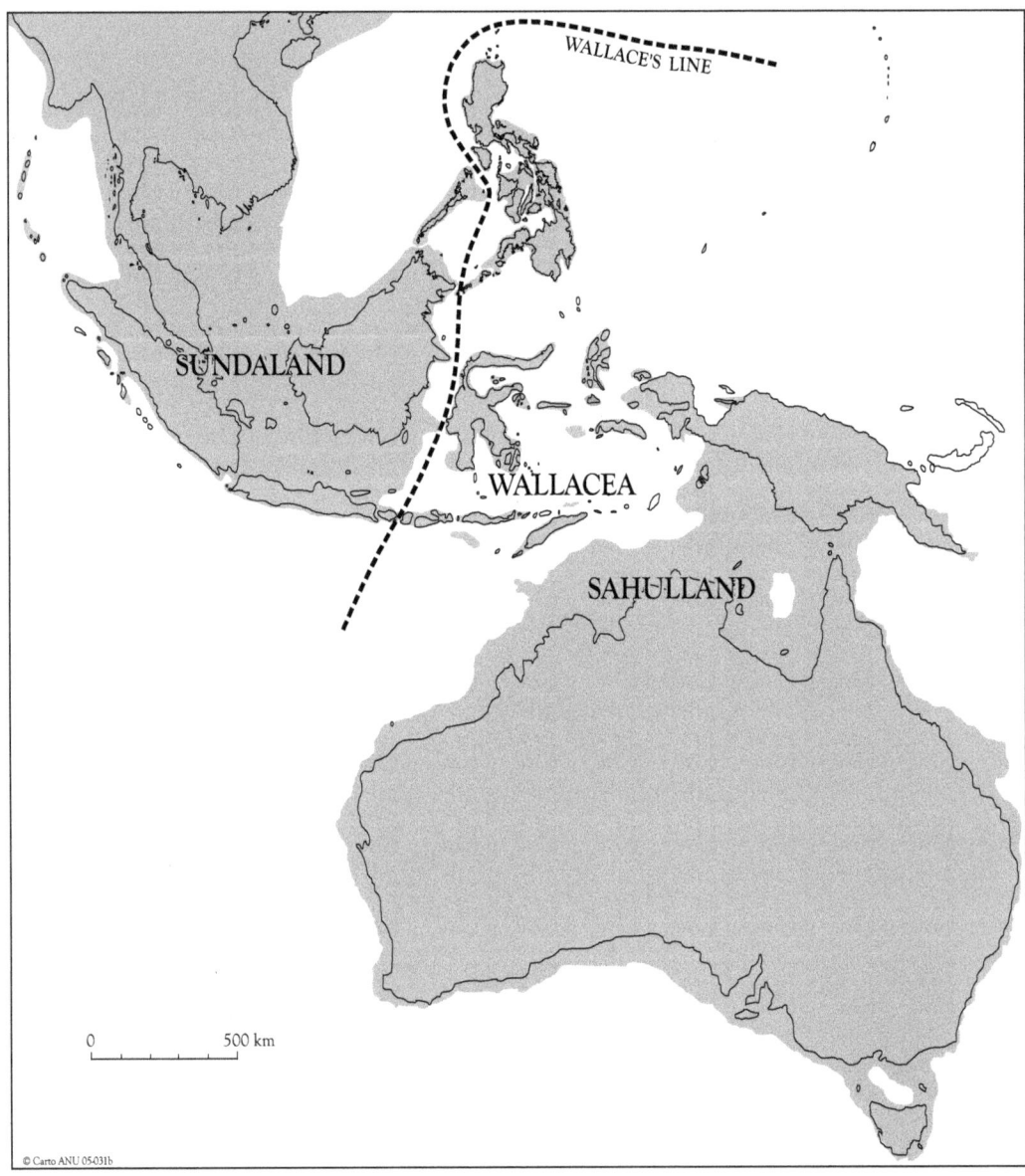

Map 2: The prehistoric continent of Sahul consisted of the continent of Australia and the islands of New Guinea and Tasmania.

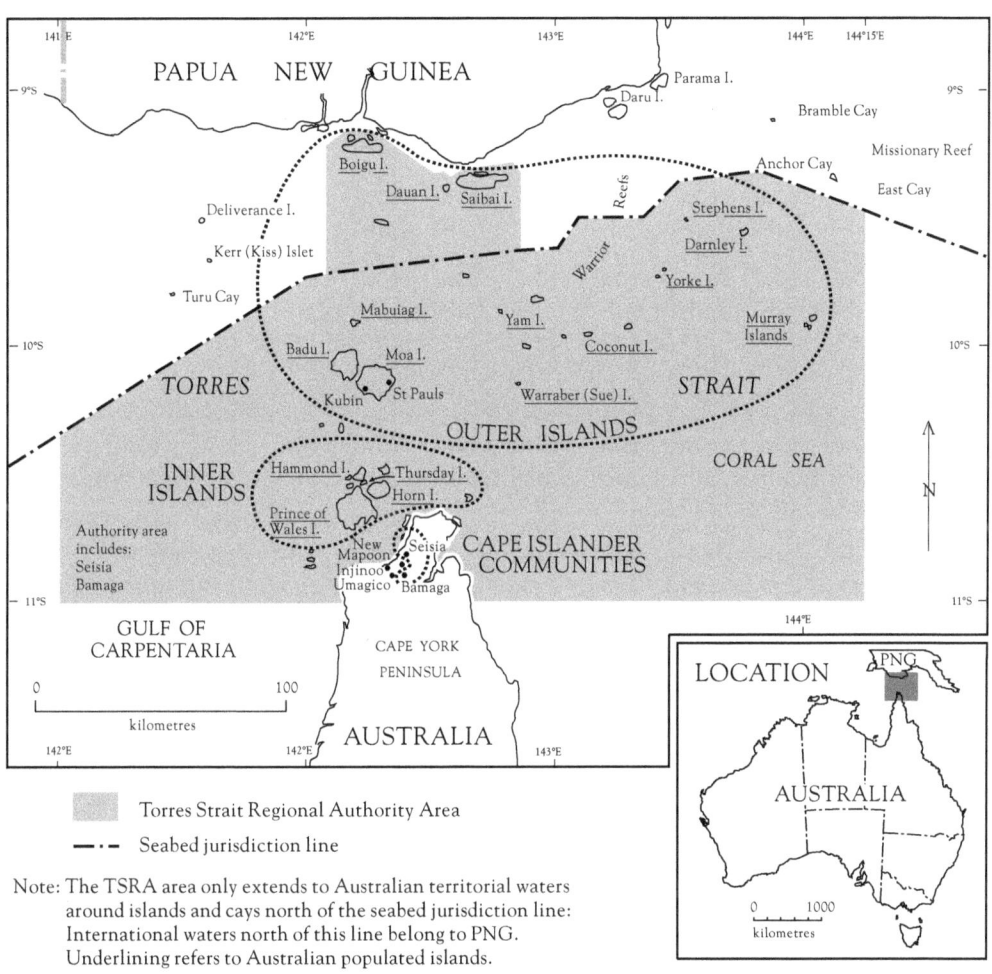

Map 3: The seabed jurisdiction line between Australia and Papua New Guinea.

Preface

I knew little of Papua New Guinea when my family and I arrived in 1972 from Idi Amin's Uganda. One colleague at Makerere University had told us about cargo cults[1] and another had shown us *Gardens of War*,[2] the photo-essay on the Dugum Dani in Irian Jaya. These books portray cultural complexity and physical vigour, but no 'modern' politics or economics, so we were ill-prepared for the realities of Melanesian societies, Australian rule and the interactions between them.

Formal political life focused on Port Moresby, a dusty town of 100,000 people in a shadow that shielded it from the rains that drenched the rest of the country. It was obviously the administrative centre, whose distinct segments illustrated social and political relations in the dependent Territory. Along the Coral Sea coast and around Fairfax Harbour lived the first-comers, Motu-speaking villagers, whose stilted houses and walkways jutted over the water. They were the first to weigh the costs and benefits of interacting with Europeans. British and Polynesian evangelists brought unfamiliar infections, and later new therapies. Destroyed during the Pacific War, the villages had been rebuilt. They were the first villages to be formed into local government councils and cooperatives; and their young men and women worked in the first clerical and para-professional jobs opened to Melanesians. Looking down on these villages were the homes of missionaries and the hot little offices of public servants in Konedobu, the centre of administration.

The Owen Stanley Range largely isolated Port Moresby from the rest of island New Guinea, whereas Fairfax Harbour allowed easy access for Australian shipping. Inland from Konedobu and Korobosea Village was Boroko, a shopping centre and suburb for middle-ranking public servants. Their houses were raised above the ground and were cooled by ceiling fans and louvred windows. Boroko expanded as Port Moresby's population grew in step with the other Australian capital, Canberra. Inland from Boroko, in June Valley and Waigani, new buildings foreshadowed an independent country: the Administrative College, the university and offices for bureaucrats moving from Konedobu. Around them clustered the houses of their staff and the squatter settlements of migrants from the countryside, labourers, servants and their families.

There was little explicit hostility between these communities, although elderly Papuan men often stepped off the pavement to avoid colliding with white women.[3] More evident than this residue of colonial racism were tensions between settled coastal communities and migrants in the new suburbs and squatter settlements. That tension expressed suspicions between Papuans and New Guineans, and between coastal people and Highlanders.[4]

Shortly before we arrived, the territory held its third election under adult suffrage. Out of many parties and factions, the young Michael Somare built a majority coalition for early self-government and independence, edging out the conservative United Party. In Australia, the Liberal Government shared Somare's ambition, and the young Minister for Territories, Andrew Peacock, enjoyed warm relations with Papua New Guinea's leaders. The Labor Party was even more eager. When Gough Whitlam became Prime Minister of Australia at the end of 1972, he declared that independence should be celebrated (or at any rate achieved) within two years. This scenario seemed fanciful while all major decisions were still made in Canberra, the territory lacked any capacity to make policy, the House of Assembly was a rubber stamp and there were only a handful of Papua New Guinean graduates.

This alignment of forces was baffling to anyone — such as myself — brought up in the violence of apartheid and electrified by the drama of *uhuru* in Kenya, *ujamaa* in Tanzania[5] and the murderous anarchy of Idi Amin. Roles were surely confused? But no: Australians were united in their desire to decolonise, although Papua New Guineans were nervous of independence. Equally startling was the optimism of my new colleagues, who expected Papua New Guineans to learn from, and avoid, the violence, the autocracy and the corruption that they saw in newly independent Africa. But events seemed to justify that wide-eyed confidence. Within three years, Somare's coalition reorganised the Public Service, negotiated an aid package and renegotiated an important mining agreement. They drafted, debated and enacted a constitution, and created a planning capacity, a defence force and all the other limbs of a modern state. Secession was averted in Bougainville and in Papua, an explosive land dispute was defused around Rabaul, anxious Highlanders were mollified and the fragile coalition held together. Pessimists had expected bloodshed, perhaps on the scale of Congo. With peaceful independence, the optimists were vindicated: the coup that overthrew a government took place not in Port Moresby but in Canberra.

In the euphoria of 1975, decolonisation was a triumph. Ten years later, some of the gloss had worn off[6] and, by the 1990s, there were doubts about the capacity of the State to function. The army was mired in civil war, an economic crisis had been precipitated by the closure of the Panguna copper mine, several provincial governments had failed, Parliament was unstable, the Public Service was politicised and demoralised, and scandals circulated around squandered resources. Long before the civil war ground to a halt in 1997, the optimists were routed. Commissions of inquiry routinely reported confusion and peculation. In 2004, Australia and Papua New Guinea negotiated an increased aid bill and an Enhanced Cooperation Package. Australians once again work in Papua New Guinea's government departments, the police and the army.

It is now commonplace for Australians to declare that Australia departed too soon or too fast. Allan Patience, Professor of Politics at the University of Papua New Guinea, attributes Australian worries about Papua New Guinea's 'failing state' partly to 'the frankly horrifying rise in crime' and corruption. But he also denounces 'Australia's abysmal record as a colonial power and as an incompetent decoloniser'.[7] Some Papua New Guineans make the complementary point: in a letter to the *Post-Courier* newspaper,

'Grassroots' of Goroka asks if the people must 'keep suffering at the hands of the 109 MPs and cronies? Let the Australians come back and manage the country as part of Australia and let us, the bulk of the population, enjoy the basic services'.[8]

But today's pessimism is just as unbalanced as yesterday's optimism.[9] Europeans took centuries to weld their weak sovereigns, powerful churches and local fight-leaders into the kinds of state that we now take for granted. Corruption and mismanagement might be quite normal in state-formation. Despite immense problems, Papua New Guinea was well governed for at least a decade after 1975. We cannot assume that longer Australian tutelage would have produced better Melanesian governance, and Australians might have had less freedom of choice in the 1970s than the critics now suppose. Papua New Guinea did become independent in 1975, but I now see this as a phase in a much longer relationship, rather than the end of a turbulent story.

In tracing the evolution of Australian policy, I have enjoyed generous support. The Australian Department of Foreign Affairs and Trade allowed me access to closed archives, and archivists in Australia and Papua New Guinea have been helpful. I owe an immense debt to lively students and patient colleagues at the University of Papua New Guinea. But my greatest debts are to participants in the decolonisation project, who shared their time, their memories and their mellow second thoughts. Many talked to me and many contributed to a 'Hindsight' workshop.[10] And Hank Nelson's studies of Papua New Guinea are absolutely indispensable.

Footnotes
1. Peter Worsley, *The Trumpet Shall Sound*, Schocken, New York, 1968; Peter Lawrence, *Road Belong Cargo: a study of the cargo movement in the southern Madang district*, Manchester University Press, 1964.
2. Robert Gardner and Karl Heider, *Gardens of War: Life and Death in the New Guinea Stone Age*, Random House, New York, 1968.
3. Amirah Inglis, *'Not a White Woman Safe': Sexual Anxiety and Politics in Port Moresby, 1920–1934*, ANU Press, 1974.
4. Although Papua and New Guinea were administered jointly after the Pacific War, Papua (the southeastern quadrant of the island of New Guinea) has been an Australian Territory since 1907, whereas New Guinea (the northeastern quadrant and the Bismarck Archipelago) had been a German colony until 1914 and was administered by Australia as a League of Nations Mandate from 1922 until the Pacific War.
5. In Swahili, 'uhuru' means freedom; 'ujamaa' means rural collectives.
6. Sione Latukefu (ed.), *Papua New Guinea: A Century of Colonial Impact, 1884–1984*, Port Moresby, 1985.
7. Allan Patience, 'What is Australia Really Up To?', *Post-Courier*, July 5, 2004.
8. *Post-Courier*, July 1, 2004.
9. Interview with Alan Kerr, who wonders what scandals the BBC might have reported when the Tudors were creating the English State, or when Napoleon was imposing a new order on France.
10. 'Hindsight: a Retrospective Workshop for Participants in the Decolonisation of Papua New Guinea', Australian National University, November 3–4, 2002, rspas.anu.edu.au/pah/publications/php

Contents

Introduction ... 1

Part 1: Australian Rule

Chapter 1: Miss Tessie Lavau Discovers Australia ... 7
  Natives ... 9
  Planters and Peasants ... 10
  Missionaries and Millenarians ... 13
  Government ... 16

Chapter 2: Emulating Australia ... 21
  Political Education ... 21
  Hasluck's Vision ... 24
  The Australian Context ... 30

Chapter 3: Guided Democracy ... 35
  The Gunther Select Committee and a House of Assembly ... 35
  Barnes and Warwick Smith ... 40
  The Paternalistic State ... 44
  Appendix: The First House of Assembly ... 48

Chapter 4: Impasse ... 52
  The Guise Select Committee ... 52
  The Second House of Assembly ... 57
  Nation-Building and the Sceptics ... 59
  Appendix: The Second House of Assembly ... 66

Chapter 5: New Directions ... 70
  Managing Social Change ... 70
  New Australians and New Papua New Guineans ... 73
  Whitlam Intervenes: Gorton Responds ... 78
  The Gorton Reforms ... 80

Part 2: Decolonisation

Chapter 6: Gearing Up 85
   The Arek Select Committee 85
   The Gearing-Up Program 88
   Security Issues 94
   Appendix: Commonwealth Acts Applying to Papua New Guinea 97

Chapter 7: New Men, New Visions 100
   Andrew Peacock and Michael Somare 100
   Gough Whitlam and Bill Morrison 103
   The Papua New Guinea Office and the Liaison Unit 106
   Appendix: The Third House of Assembly and the First Cabinet 110

Chapter 8: Creating a Constitution 112
   The Constitutional Planning Committee 112
   The CPC Recommendations 117
   The Compromise Constitution 120
   Discharging the United Nations Trust 124

Chapter 9: A National Economy 128
   Economic Strategy 128
   Land 131
   Minerals 133
   Aid 136
   A National Economy? 140
   Appendix: The 'Eight Aims' 141

Chapter 10: Creating a State 143
   A National Bureaucracy 144
   The Uniformed Forces 145
   The Judicial System 151

Chapter 11: Defining the State 158
   National Unity and Decentralisation 159
   Borders with Australia and Indonesia 163
   Projecting Independence 166

Part 3: The Limits of Independence

Chapter 12: Independence and its Discontents 171
   A Failing State? 171
   Measuring Independent Papua New Guinea 179

Chapter 13: The Continuing Connection 186

Bibliography 199
Index 210

Introduction

Independence in Papua New Guinea was marked by flurries of activity and stately rites, anxiety as well as elation. Formal celebrations were muted, even nervous, in Port Moresby. Hubert Murray Stadium commemorates a long-serving proconsul. There, on the eve of independence, the Australian flag was lowered with solemn respect. Michael Somare, Prime Minister-designate, hosted a dinner in a house above Fairfax Harbour, to watch the midnight fireworks. Speaking without notes and with rare passion, he paid tribute to his colleagues and his subordinates, then he turned to the Prime Minister of Australia. The two were at loggerheads over Australian aid but Somare ignored that issue to extol Gough Whitlam's role in bringing Australia's colonial role to a close. His praise was much more than courtesy required: Whitlam — an orator never lost for words — astounded his audience when they saw him weep.[1] For many in that room and elsewhere, the separation of Australia and Papua New Guinea was cathartic.

Across town, negotiations had to be completed before midnight to secure the future of the Ok Tedi copper mine. At midnight, judges and the Governor-General were sworn in, and the Finance Minister, Julius Chan, became the first naturalised citizen.[2] Overnight an out-of-season shower provided ambiguous omens. Next morning, the Southern Cross and Bird of Paradise flag was raised near the new Parliament House. With the lowering of one flag and the raising of another, Australia's Governor-General became almost as foreign as Imelda Marcos of the Philippines (whose ostentatiously late arrival caused the cancellation of a fly-past). Papua New Guinea was no longer an Australian Territory but a sovereign state.

To decolonise is to dismantle foreign control: independence is the achievement or recovery of sovereignty. These portentous words aligned Australia with European colonial powers and they added Papua New Guinea to the register of emancipated colonies. The rites of passage to independence had become familiar long before their reprise in Port Moresby. On the surface, this was a mere postscript to a global narrative.

But this uncoupling was unique. For one thing, these rituals decolonised both countries. Whitlam held broad objections to colonial relationships, including Australia's residual links to imperial Britain. Believing that colonialism demeaned the coloniser as well as the colonised, he later reflected that 'Australia was never truly free until Papua New Guinea became free'.[3] Such freedom, however, implied a degree of separation that was unlikely in view of the history, the geography and the economies of the two neighbours. For millennia, Australia and New Guinea formed one continent with distinctive flora and marsupial animals, links that survived the drowning of Torres Strait. These ancient ties were explained by Alfred Russel Wallace in *The Malay Archipelago: The Land of the Orang Utan and Bird of Paradise*.[4] Scholars refuse to call this lost continent Greater Australia (or Greater New Guinea), so the obscure 'Sahul' is its usual name (see Map 2).[5]

The partition of Sahul is incomplete. Torres Strait, which separates New Guinea from Australia, is narrower and shallower than Bass Strait, which makes Tasmania an island. Islands and shoals jeopardise east-west navigation through Torres Strait, but they assist north-south movement. Some of the connections between Australia and the islands were expressed in the term 'Australasia'. In 1828, Sydney politician W. C. Wentworth published his survey of *Australasia* and called himself an Australasian. Edward Gibbon Wakefield, the propagandist of planned colonisation, defined Australasia as 'Australia and all the smaller islands in its neighbourhood'.[6] Queensland planters saw the islands as a source of cheap labour, and a Queensland magistrate tried to annex eastern New Guinea in 1883. In 1890, the Victorian Parliament treated Australasia as the mainland, New Zealand, Tasmania, Fiji 'and any other British Colonies or possessions in Australasia, now existing or hereafter to be created'.[7] The term expressed a British and colonial state of mind as well as a geographical entity, and it embraced the south-eastern quarter of the island of New Guinea, which became a British Protectorate in 1884.

Despite these links, a popular Australian account in 1965 saw the island of New Guinea as 'the last unknown'.[8] Tortuous terrain, malaria and the absence of obvious resources had delayed European exploration until the 1880s (and the densely populated Highlands were mapped only in the 1930s). A rash publisher printed the record of an expedition to New Guinea in 1872 that found kingdoms, fabulous wealth and a mountain higher than Everest. David Glen judges that such fantasies were informed by the traditions of European exploration, which saw New Guinea 'somewhere between the harsh and wild African interior and a softer Pacific vision of tropical paradise'.[9] In the next few decades, outsiders' images did evolve, but they always emphasised the 'otherness' of New Guinea — physical as well as social. The dry, flat Australian continent was mainly temperate, while the wet tropical territory crumpled into mountain ranges that fed tumultuous rivers.

When the Australian colonies federated in 1901, the name first proposed for that federation was Australasia. Fiji had been part of the Federal Councils of the 1880s, but none of Britain's island possessions were invited to the negotiations, and New Zealand backed out. Australasia survived as a scientific term but withered in political discourse.[10] The Federal Constitution mentions a responsibility for Pacific Islands, but close relations did not develop between Australians and Melanesians (as they began to be called). When Commonwealth governments began to define Australians, they were inspired by the vision of a 'white Australia', peopled by Europeans, so most islanders were expelled.[11] Prospectors scoured the islands for gold but the usual focus of Australian interest was strategic, especially when Russian, French or German ships crossed the horizon. Hunger for gold and fear of foreigners shaped Australian policies.

The first Attorney-General of Australia, Alfred Deakin, told readers of the London *Morning Post* that 'the Australian' looked at French and German colonies in the region 'nearly in the light of an intrusion on his property'. Deakin's typical Australian was so self-assured that he 'views the Continent behind him … as too contracted for his operations, and by no means as confining his sphere of influence'.[12] This, says Hank Nelson, was the voice of

> a young Australia confident of its right to expand influence beyond the continent, resentful of those who had got there first, and beginning to assert a national, rather than an empire, perspective.[13]

Once the Australians federated, Britain was keen to hand over British New Guinea. When Prime Minister Edmund Barton agreed, he spoke of 'the long centuries for which I hope New Guinea is to be a territory, perhaps, a State of this Commonwealth', and he thought other islands might also be acquired.[14] Deakin was more realistic about an enduring contradiction: 'A "White Australia" may exist, across the straits, but a "Black New Guinea" the territory now is and must always remain.'[15]

Despite the grandiloquence, it was left to a handful of missionaries, planters and miners to embody Australians' flickering interest in the Territory of Papua (the new name of British New Guinea), under the frail protection of an embryonic state. Australia's ambition was little more than strategic denial — the exclusion of other European powers — and the Great War allowed an expeditionary force to realise this ambition by expelling Germans from New Guinea. Ex-German New Guinea was administered separately from ex-British New Guinea, but both were Australian Territories. The War in the Pacific, from 1941 to 1945, underlined their importance to Australian security. When peace returned, Australia created a joint administration over Papua and New Guinea, and devoted a great deal more attention to it.

Australians and Melanesians seldom met. Australians enjoyed easy access to the Territory, while Melanesians visited Australia only as servants or students. In the little towns of the Territory, segregation was the organising principle, and the two populations might as well have inhabited different worlds.[16] Melanesians were the least urban people on Earth; Australians the most urbanised (neither group saw itself as urbane). Australians expected high incomes, democratic and bureaucratic structures and values, publicly funded schools, hospitals and transport. Unlike their neighbours, they were monolingual and monocultural and their diet was rich in protein. If they thought about Melanesians, they saw them as 'primitive' at worst and always 'natives'. Natives spoke primitive lingoes and worshipped ancestors or idols. They did not need, nor could they appreciate, the benefits of modernity. Contrasting ways of living seemed to justify the application of Australian law to Australians and simple Native Regulations to 'natives'.

Australian economists were dismayed when they began to quantify the lives of Papua New Guinea's two million people. After half a century of Australian influence, in the early 1960s the World Bank recorded less than £20 million worth of exports and imports worth £30 million. Australian grants covered three-quarters of official receipts. Plantations needed few skilled workers. Only half of each cohort went to school, and they did not stay long.[17] People were barred from visiting town, wearing Western clothes, drinking alcohol, or emulating Australians. The thrust of policy was not to bridge difference but to preserve it. 'The Territory' was not yet a country. Although the law defined its people as Australians, they were not citizens. As J. D. B. Miller pointed out, the Territory's development posed every possible difficulty:

> The obvious features ... are the lack of anything approaching national unity; the lack of a local elite; an economy with little to sell; a government which is necessarily expensive; a heavy dependence upon Australian subsidies; [and] an incalculable neighbour in the shape of Indonesia.[18]

There were few challenges to Australian rule. Ambiguity shrouded the Territory's destiny, since the term implied that (like the Northern Territory) it might evolve into a state of the Commonwealth. Its future was clarified only in 1966 when a Papua New Guinean delegation asked if they could become Australia's seventh state. That was unthinkable; white and black Australians were not equal before the law, the goal of 'White Australia' governed migration, and a welfare state cosseted white citizens. Cabinet recoiled from the vision and resolved that Papua New Guinea's destiny was separation, so the goal of Papua New Guinea's independence was stated first as an Australian rejection.

The pace of change quickened when Whitlam, as Leader of the Labor Party, began to advocate independence. By 1970, Prime Minister John Gorton was converted. Conservatives on both sides of Torres Strait doubted that Papua New Guinea was ready for independence. So did separatists. When Cabinet ruled out statehood, the Territory House of Assembly splintered. Papua's members sought a separate status, and so did some Bougainvilleans and some Tolai around Rabaul.

Papua New Guinea was still an Australian Territory. Responsibility lay with a minister in Canberra, and services were provided by Commonwealth agencies. The largest bloc in the Territory House of Assembly, the United Party, feared devolution — and an obstructive House could paralyse change. To the chagrin of the United Party and the delight of Australians, however, Territory elections in February 1972 yielded a coalition committed to devolution, led by Michael Somare and Julius Chan. Somare became de facto Chief Minister and an enthusiastic partner in the transfer of powers.

The direction of change was settled, but not the pace. When Labor came to power in Australia later that year, Whitlam confirmed his insistence on unity and 1974 as his target date for independence.[19] With internal self-government in 1973, Bill Morrison, as Minister for External Territories, abolished his department, transferring its residual powers to the Department of Foreign Affairs.

Somare was the focus of huge and contrary pressures from Australia, from his own coalition and from a Constitutional Planning Committee. Placating impatient Australians, reassuring anxious Highlanders and holding an angular coalition together, the fledgling Cabinet also negotiated a constitution, defused secession, created policy and planning capacity, and transformed the Public Service. This took longer than Whitlam expected, but the goal was reached, breathlessly, in September 1975.

Or was it? Many people say that independence came too soon; others accept that the timing was about right, and a few insist that it was overdue. However, developments in the past 30 years beg the question: is 'independence' the appropriate term for what happened in 1975?

Footnotes
1. Interview, Mark Lynch.
2. Interview, Ross Garnaut.
3. 'Freedom for Australia too', *The Australian*, September 16, 1975.
4. Alfred Russel Wallace, *The Malay Archipelago: The Land of the Orang Utan and Bird of Paradise*, London, 1874; and *The Geographical Distribution of Animals*, London, 1876.
5. Chris Ballard, 'Stimulating Minds to Fantasy? A Critical Etymology for Sahul', in M. A. Smith, M. Spriggs and B. Fankhauser (eds), *Sahul in Review*, ANU, 1993.
6. These usages are cited in *The Australian National Dictionary*, Melbourne, 1988.
7. Edward Morris, *Austral English: a dictionary of Australasian words, phrases and usages*, London, 1898.
8. Gavin Souter, *New Guinea: the last unknown*, Sydney, 1965.
9. David Glen, 'The Last Elusive Object', MA thesis, ANU, 2000, chapter 1, referring to John A. Lawson, R. N., *Wanderings in the Interior of New Guinea*, Chapman Hall, London, 1875.
10. John Hirst, *Sentimental Nation: the Making of the Australian Constitution*, Melbourne, 2000; James Belich, *Paradise Reforged: A History of the New Zealanders from the 1880s to the Year 2000*, Penguin, Auckland, 2001, p46ff.
11. Clive Moore, *Kanaka: A History of Melanesian Mackay*, Port Moresby, IPNGS, 1985.
12. Hank Nelson, 'Frontiers, Territories and States of Mind', in D. Denoon (ed.), *Emerging from Empire?*, citing Alfred Deakin, *Federated Australia: Selections from Letters to the* Morning Post *1900–1910*, Melbourne University Press, 1968, edited and introduced by J. A. La Nauze, pp. v, xv. Quotation from *Morning Post*, March 19, 1901.
13. Hank Nelson, 'Frontiers, Territories and States of Mind'.
14. *Australian Parliamentary Debates*, House of Representatives, Vol. 6, 1901–02, pp. 7079–91.
15. Alfred Deakin, *Federated Australia*, p. 85; *Morning Post,* December 31, 1901.
16. Amirah Inglis, *'Not a White Woman Safe': Sexual Anxiety and Politics in Port Moresby, 1920–1934*, ANU Press, 1974.
17. International Bank for Reconstruction and Development [the 'World Bank'], *The Economic Development of the Territory of Papua and New Guinea*, Johns Hopkins Press, Baltimore, 1965; John Langmore, 'A Critical Assessment of Australian economic policy for Papua New Guinea between 1945 and 1970', mimeo, Department of Economics, University of Papua New Guinea, 1972; Donald Denoon, 'Capitalism in Papua New Guinea', *Journal of Pacific History*, Vol. XX, No. 3–4, 1985, pp. 119–34.
18. J. D. B. Miller, 'Australia's Difficulties in New Guinea', ANU seminar paper, November 1965, reprinted in *Journal of Pacific History*, 2005.
19. Whitlam's speech is cited by David Hegarty in the January-April 1973 section of Clive Moore with Mary Kooyman (ed.), *A Papua New Guinea Political Chronicle 1967–1991*, Bathurst, NSW, 1998.

PART 1: AUSTRALIAN RULE

Chapter 1

Miss Tessie Lavau Discovers Australia

Like a handful of other Papuans and New Guineans in the 1950s, Miss Tessie Lavau of Iokea Village in Kerema District of Papua visited Australia as a nursemaid with her employers on their vacation 'down south'. Most Australians in the Territory employed a servant, but few brought them to Australia. These household relations must have been friendly: when Miss Lavau moved on to be a public service typist, the family offered her a place to stay if she ever visited Australia. In 1958, she acted on their suggestion and made her application. That very ordinary action startled Australian officials on both sides of Torres Strait, and forced them to think about relations between the Territory and people of Papua and New Guinea and the Commonwealth and people of Australia.

Lacking direct experience, most Australians relied on stereotypes of the Territory and its people. In 1964, the Australian journalist Keith Willey toured the Territory from the Indonesian border to Bougainville, recycling stereotypes that were already on their last legs:[1]

> Remote from the surge and flow of human endeavour, [New Guinea] slumbered; yet it, too, had a kind of history … Dawn men, forced from the jungles of Asia by stronger races to the north and west, straggled through the chain of islands which is now Indonesia to find refuge here in the southern ocean. The result is a people bewildering in diversity, sundered by 750 languages and a thousand tribes.
>
> Lumped together under the name of Melanesian are negritos, small and woolly-haired; and tall, slender warriors who show links with the Aboriginal Australians. The Kiwais of the Fly estuary could be one of the lost tribes of Israel. The Bukas are as handsome — and as black — as the Somalis. Pigmies with a life expectancy of less than thirty years range the swamps of the western Sepik. In the Highlands are strains even of the so-called Hairy Ainus …

> Among the coastal tribes cannibalism was universal and several missionaries went into the cooking pots …

Willey was reporting the first election for 'a Stone Age parliament'.

> To transform a living museum into nationhood within a generation is a task of giant proportions. Twenty years ago it would have seemed an impossible dream; yet in New Guinea today, dream is becoming reality.

It would be hard to assemble more clichés per page, yet the liberal Willey based them on his own observations and on talks with Territory residents.

Another Australian, Gavin Souter, described New Guinea as 'the last unknown',[2] but the converse was just as true. Tight rules governed the 'Removal of Native People from the Territory'.[3] Melanesians entered Australia under supervision in parties of uniformed forces, as crew of Territory vessels, as servants, for schooling, medical treatment, conferences or Scouting jamborees. (The Administration fostered Boy Scouts and Girl Guides for character-building.[4]) What were misleadingly called 'educational tours' were also permitted. In 1927, the Government was scandalised to discover two New Guineans at school in rural New South Wales. Their headmaster attested that 'no white boys have given me so much satisfaction'; these 'fine lads' were popular, courteous, punctual — and good cricketers. Nevertheless, the Australian Minister for Territories decided to prevent the Administrator of New Guinea from sending any other youngsters to Australian schools. After all, as the *Rabaul Times* pointed out, that exposure might provoke such lads to ask for higher wages, or even to go on strike.[5] That prohibition prevailed until the 1950s, when a selective scheme was introduced under tight supervision.

After the Pacific War, the Territory Administration proposed to bring groups of Papua New Guineans to Australia for short courses in technical subjects:

> native leaders would see the hard and continuous work of Australians to produce the means and articles of commerce … and they would gain a clear realisation that there is no miracle or royal road in production.

Territories Minister Eddie Ward conceded that much good would result — but 'it would be premature'.[6] Few Papua New Guineans saw Australia at all. During 1957, five men were brought south by their employers; for everyone else, Australia was unknowable. In 1954, an inquisitive 'native teacher' asked to see the Australian way of life. Before the Director of Education and the Director of Native Affairs had reviewed his request, however, he withdrew it.

So Miss Lavau's application startled the authorities, who referred it up through the ranks to the desk of the Administrator. He mulled it over and decided that:

> The girl is a mature type who has adopted European dress and living standards and has saved sufficient money to pay her fare both ways …

> I can see no objection to granting permission for a native person to leave the Territory in these circumstances, provided that the bona fides of the applicant stand up to close examination and that each application is dealt with on its individual merits following a close investigation into the character, background and motives of those concerned with it and to the relationship between the applicant and the persons in Australia who are to be visited …

Applications would be rare, since few could afford the trip or had friends to house them.[7]

Miss Lavau's character survived scrutiny (and so did her sponsors) and the proposal satisfied the Administrator's ideas of seemly race relations. Sir Donald Cleland earnestly desired that 'individual native people build up personal contacts with individual Australian citizens' — under the sleepless eye of authority, which would assess character and motive. A District Commissioner would vet each applicant, officers in Australia would conduct random checks, and each visit would be limited to three months.

A decision of this weight required the support of the Minister for Territories. Sir Paul Hasluck endorsed Cleland's advice and referred the matter to the Minister for Immigration, Sir Alexander Downer. Two governments, two Commonwealth departments, two Cabinet ministers and many police studied the case, which might seem absurd for a visit to a police inspector's family by a law-abiding tourist. But the entry of any non-European to Australia was problematic. Miss Lavau was not only testing the racial conventions of the Territory; she was questioning the nexus between the Territory and the rest of Australia, and picking at the seams of White Australia.

The application uncovered a paradox. On what legal basis could Australian citizens be excluded from Australia? The Minister for Immigration unearthed this anomaly:

> The Migration Act permits the exclusion from Australia of any 'immigrant'. [Decisions and observations by the High Court suggested] that any person may be regarded as an immigrant who is not a constituent member of the Australian community — whatever his national status may be.
>
> On this basis, legal power exists to prevent the entry to Australia of either natives of Papua, whose national status is that of Australian citizens, or natives of the Trust Territory of New Guinea, who are Australian protected persons (Nationality and Citizenship Act and Citizenship Regulations).[8]

He did not need to explain that 'constituent members of the Australian community' was a euphemism for 'white'. It was not nationality but race that separated Miss Lavau from her friends, and the Australian Territory from the Australian Commonwealth.

Natives

Australians described Papua and New Guinea as a dependent Territory, inhabited by two million natives and a few thousand non-natives, most of them from Australia. Natives were, of course, born in the Territory, but the term groaned under a weight of colonial history and ideology. Since 'native' and 'stranger' first met on Pacific beaches,[9] the balance of power had tilted: the stranger became the settler and the native became a subordinate.

The term brought people under Native Regulations, which were simpler and more oppressive than the laws governing Australians. 'Natives' had been evangelised and colonised, so they were no longer 'savages', but they were not yet citizens, a conversion that would occur if and when the Territory evolved into a State. Meanwhile, they were legally incompetent. In Stewart Firth's view, the concept of the native was a device to create social distance and keep control.[10] Whites expected each other to remain aloof from natives. Almost all believed that they were in every way superior to their servants. Rhetorically, the native was masculine and singular, a device that homogenised hundreds of languages, living styles and production systems, matriliny and patriliny, coast and highland. The term 'native' melted varied humanity down to a pitiable stereotype. Of such a poor creature no one would expect social complexity, political acumen, intellectual vigour, artistry or science.

Miss Lavau was rare in being discussed in her own name. The Administration had a Central Advisory Committee for the Education and Advancement of Women. Lady Rachel Cleland, the formidable wife of the Administrator, was one member; but the chair and three of the 14 members were men, and only two or three were indigenes. The committee had no vision beyond women's clubs, Girl Guides, water supply and welfare officers.[11] These were irrelevant to most women. Paula Brown recorded this statement from a Simbu woman:

> What we women do is very difficult. 1) We cook for our family every day ... 2) Go to the garden every day ... 3) Clean the grass in the garden and plant the food crops. 4) Look after pigs ... 5) Look after our babies while we are doing the other jobs ... The work that men do is very simple ... They break firewood, cut grass or clear the bush, dig the garden drains, build houses only. They do not do it every day. Men spend most of their time doing nothing and talking.

Simbu men insisted that they worked just as hard;[12] but neither view imagined common ground with the agenda of the committee.

The committee hesitated to 'advance' educated women. Two went to a Melbourne meeting of the Associated Country Women of the World in 1962 and made such a good impression that the ACWW voted funds for 'the advancement of the women of the Territory', and asked how to do this. Six months later the Administration confessed that the file was lost. The ACWW persisted, offering support to women training as nurses in Australia. The Health Department knew of none, although there were in fact seven.[13]

Planters and Peasants

The territory was anomalous among tropical colonies in the limited impact of its plantations. When Australians annexed Papua in 1907 and occupied New Guinea in 1914, they expected plantations to be the engine of development. As early as the 1920s, Papuan officials despaired of the planters and instead began to coerce villagers to produce copra on village land. Plantation prospects were brighter in New Guinea, where Germans had developed estates. After World War I, these were expropriated and sold to Australian ex-servicemen, just in time to break their hearts in the 1930s Depression. The planters blamed the Australian companies Burns Philp and W. R. Carpenter, which enjoyed a near monopoly of trade, or the laws that required all cargoes to be shipped in white-crewed and expensive Australian vessels.[14]

The plantation strategy resurfaced after the Pacific War when ex-servicemen were again placed on the land. But few Australians ever had capital and those who did could enjoy more secure title in Australia.[15] The most promising development occurred in the Highlands, where Australians pioneered coffee estates in alliance with Big Men, who mobilised labour for them. But even these plantations were limited. In 1960, New Guinea's production was:[16]

Crop	*Holdings*	*Acres*	*Production (tonnes)*
Cocoa	355	78,441	4,520
Copra	474	219,549	70,596
Coffee	171	7,415	1,726

By then, agricultural extension officers (*didimen*) and cooperatives officers had helped villagers to grow cocoa, mainly on the Gazelle Peninsula around Rabaul, and Highlanders had planted more coffee than had Australians.[17]

In 1953, scholars from The Australian National University reviewed development and reached a common conclusion:[18]

> An economist [Trevor Swan] reports that … European industry on the whole is making little if any headway, and may even be in a state of slow decline … The running-down of copra and gold is scarcely balanced by development in new directions …
>
> An anthropologist [Cyril Belshaw] argues that native society offers a basis for economic organisation for productive purposes, through individual enterprise, native co-operatives, and looser forms of community development …
>
> A geographer [the chairman of the review committee, Oskar Spate] points out that the New Guinea terrain does not lend itself to widespread European settlement, but does present many opportunities for the development of native crops …
>
> *Our central thesis, then, is that a prosperous New Guinea economy can be built on the foundations of native society, and that this is not only socially the most desirable but economically the most feasible …*

European agriculture flourished only in a few places where soil, topography and anchorages favoured it; whereas 'native agriculture' had evolved for 6,000 years.[19] Adapting to climates and soils, people grew taro, sweet potato, sago or yam; they cleared bush, selected varieties, inter-planted, mulched and irrigated. These staples also sustained pigs, the main store of wealth. Highland production was spurred by elaborate exchanges of pigs, shells, feathers and other valuables, such as the *moka* of the Melpa people.[20] Coastal production sustained maritime expeditions such as the *kula* that so impressed Malinowski.[21] These rituals and adventures were sustained by hard work and years of planned surplus, but these skills were barely visible to Australians. Archaeologists did not reveal the antiquity of New Guinea agriculture until the 1960s; swidden seemed inefficient to Europeans, pigs and cassowaries could not be herded like cattle, and benefits from exchange relations were invisible to casual observers. Officials saw only backwardness, especially when steel tools displaced stone axes. Mass-produced pottery, long-range sailing vessels (such as the *lagatoi*, which survived only on Papuan postage stamps) and most of the coastal trading systems were also superceded by imports.

Economists grappled with these issues when Sir John Crawford, Australia's leading economic policy-maker, became Director of The Australian National University's Research School of Pacific Studies in 1961. Encouraged by Crawford, Ernest Fisk visited the Highlands. Goroka town dismayed him: 'This was not under-development as I had known it. It seemed to be an earlier stage in the process of economic evolution.' But in the countryside he struck a paradox:

> These people seemed to have more leisure, more adequate food supplies, and generally to be considerably better off than quite a lot of villagers in South and East Asia whose average incomes were recorded as being very much higher.[22]

This economy defied conventional economics, so Fisk turned to anthropology. Richard Salisbury had analysed the introduction of metal tools, which triggered a reordering of work and leisure, and Scarlett Epstein had contrasted *Capitalism, Primitive and Modern* in East New Britain.[23] Fisk coined the term 'subsistence affluence', best described in his doggerel:

The Song of the Tribal Economist [24]

> The primitive farmer says Cash
> Is unsatisfactory trash;
> It won't keep off the rain
> And it gives me a pain
> If I use it to flavour my hash ...
> If I act in a rational way
> I'll just sit on my backside today.
> When I want a good feed
> I've got all I need

> Piping hot, and there's nothing to pay.
> Cash cropping is all very well
> If you've *got* to have something to sell;
> But tell me sir, why,
> If there's nothing to buy
> Should I bother? You can all go to hell.

When Fisk's 'primitive affluence' (softened to 'subsistence affluence' by Ron Crocombe) escaped from academia into colonial society, it helped to justify low wages. A World Bank mission stated that view with less finesse than Fisk: 'Subsistence agriculture is relatively easy and has bred an agricultural [labour] force that has not had to acquire disciplined work habits.'[25]

Economists and administrators believed that land tenure was communal and that this was an obstacle to progress. If so, the obstacle was adamant: land was the source not only of people's food and crops, but also of their identities. The 800 languages of Papua New Guinea articulate an ancient tradition of isolated communities whose attachment to particular pieces of land narrowed their horizons, but made the attachment correspondingly intense. At the end of the colonial era in Papua, less than two million acres out of 55 million had been alienated: of those two million acres, only 24,000 were owned as freehold, and the balance remained in Crown ownership. The situation in New Guinea was similar, but there were areas of intense production, such as the Gazelle Peninsula, where ownership was contested.[26]

In 1952, a Native Land Commission began to record native title rights and to identify 'ownerless land'. Their task was complicated because 'there are many different rights in any one parcel of land and they are often held by different parties'.[27] Some people had rights of way to their own gardens; others needed access to water; some held rights to cultivate, and others to hunt or gather wild produce. Working against that tradition, the commission became bogged down. Ten years later, a Land Titles Commission was asked to determine and register customary rights and also found itself involved in disputes. From a bureaucratic point of view, arguments over land rights were a problem, but for Papua New Guineans such wrangles were normal: tenure always had to be adjusted to take account of migration, succession and marriage.[28] The people and their cultures — not to mention their convoluted economic relations — were evidently the major obstacle to development and modernisation.

Missionaries and Millenarians

If culture was the problem, Christianity and schooling might provide a solution. Firth notes that colonial governments in Melanesia were rudimentary, whereas Christian missions exercised wide powers. Many missions came earlier and provided more services than the State. During Japanese occupation in World War II, many missionaries stayed with their flocks when other foreigners fled. Indeed, 'the outside world was embodied not in government but in the mission station with its plantations, workshops, schools and gardens, and with missionaries who came to stay, and learned the language of their congregations'.[29] Christianity became 'traditional' for many people. In Bougainville in 1939, anthropologist Douglas Oliver counted 65 missionaries shepherding 30,000 souls, or two out of every three villagers. By 1968, Australian officials counted 57,000 Catholics, with a priest for every 1,426 people:

> The forty priests, 442 catechists, 96 sisters, 50 brothers, 58 seminarians, 39 catechist trainees, 17 lay missionaries, 386 certified teachers give the Catholic Mission in Bougainville contact in depth with the people, which the Administration cannot match.

The United Church also had 10,000 members and there were 3,000 Seventh-Day Adventists.[30] In most parts of the territory, there was a dominant mission - often Catholic, but Lutherans in much of the Highlands and Anglicans in the Northern District of Papua. The United Church prevailed in most of coastal Papua once the London Missionary Society (Congregational) and the Methodists joined forces. Missions offered almost all the schooling. In Bougainville in 1967, administration schools enrolled 2,105 pupils compared with the missions' 15,000. Until the University of Papua New Guinea and the Institute of Technology opened in 1967, missions monopolised higher education, and most of the indigenous leaders of the 1960s and 1970s were products of the seminaries.[31] In consequence, few people recognised

> the overall role of the central government in creating such things as the framework of arrangements under which Bougainville exists, has relations with the rest of the Territory and the rest of the world, and enjoys the basic public services ...[32]

Christians and 'pagans' do not account for all faiths. Colonialism, Christianity and commerce required ideological as well as material adjustment. Many thinkers coopted European customs, and some revived their own. These innovations were branded 'cargo cults', a pejorative term for any movement that relied on ritual action, especially if it doubted the wisdom of the missions or the Administration. They were most often seen after the Pacific War, when the phrase 'cargo cult' was coined. In an influential book of 1957, Peter Worsley — barred from Papua New Guinea because of his radical politics — represented these movements as proto-nationalist responses to colonialism, forerunners of modern politics.[33] Other scholars argue that cults were not desperate reactions but creative enterprises. Lamont Lindstrom observes that Melanesians often seek economic advantage through ritual action and they presume that knowledge is the product of revelation. Social activists must be (and must be seen as) prophets.[34] What is clear is that their adherents desired not only Western goods, but harmony among themselves and in relation to Europeans.

It was a millenarian episode that revived Australian politicians' interest. In 1956, the Administration proposed Local Government Councils for Buka, the smaller island of Bougainville District. The officials then imposed a tax on adult men, whether or not they joined the councils. In opposition, the Hahalis Welfare Society emerged in 1960, to advance the interests of Hahalis, Ielelina and Hanahan villagers. Like the councils, the society promoted cash-cropping and formed a work collective, but its members shunned the councils and official cooperatives. Self-help and hard work lifted production, allowed capital formation and raised consumption; but the Administration and missions still disapproved. According to the Territory's Intelligence Committee, the society

> degenerated into a cargo cult in which there was no longer any semblance of individual ownership; one result of this being sexual promiscuity, practised through the establishment of 'baby gardens'. Believing in their own self-sufficiency, they totally rejected the Mission and the Administration and refused to conform to any Local Government Council requirements, including the payment of tax.[35]

As in this case, 'cargo cult' became a shorthand term for irrationality, superstition — and opposition. How could members be brought back to the fold? Confrontation backfired. When the Catholics excommunicated some leaders, they founded their own congregation.[36] In 1962, when society leaders advised their followers not to pay the tax, the Administration flew in 400 police and more than 400 protesters were arrested.[37] But in the longer-term, opposition seemed to pay off. The Administration built roads, clinics and schools, which were used by society members and council adherents alike. And, although missionaries condemned the society's morals, they invested in projects that everyone enjoyed.[38] Over time, tempers cooled. By 1968, Hahalis members were cooperating with officialdom, and even with the council.[39]

On the larger island of Bougainville, millenarian ideas seemed endemic. In 1968, an investigator deduced that cultists hoped for

> a period of no Government, with no police force or army, when people can live as they do now, with their same worldly goods, with no internal strife and in universal brotherhood. The majority of people … are distrustful of the Administration, and prefer to have as little contact with it as possible … The Marist Mission is in a similar position.[40]

In a similar vein, Eugene Ogan reported a Nasioi man's narrative in 1962–63, complaining to the United Nations Visiting Mission:

> When my grandfather was alive and my father just a little boy, the Germans came. They gave us steel axes and laplaps. Then the Australians came and drove away the Germans. Then the Japanese came and drove away the Australians. Then the Americans came and drove away the Japanese so the Australians could come back. Now my grandfather is dead, my father is an old man, and I am a grown man. And what do we have? Nothing more than steel axes and laplaps.[41]

Government

The physician Ian Maddocks saw the Territory as a series of largely self-sufficient villages, each with narrow horizons:

> [The villager] did not read newspapers, the majority did not hear the radio. His sources of information were government officials who may have been infrequent visitors, rumours passed on by returning workers, or by those adventurers who travelled outside of the local boundaries.[42]

To villagers in such isolation, 'Papua and New Guinea' was a mere abstraction. The major centres of government were Port Moresby, the capital, Lae, at the mouth of the Markham River and the terminus of the Highlands Highway, and Rabaul, the commercial and government centre of New Guinea until a volcano and the war wrecked it. Each district had a township as its headquarters. Indigenous people seldom ventured into these Australian enclaves, which were almost as baffling and menacing as the territory of other language groups. The officials whom people met most often were *kiaps* — field officers of the Department of District Administration and Native Affairs, from District Commissioners (DCs) to cadet Patrol Officers. Sam Alasia, in the nearby Solomon Islands, sums up the general experience of Melanesians. A visit by the DC provoked a flurry of anxious activity:

> The village was cleaned, pigs were fenced, cultural items were prepared for performances, elders, teachers and church leaders were invited. The DC was 'the government' ... Most Islanders perceived the government as represented by an individual ... because it resembled the traditional system.[43]

On the other side of the border, in Bougainville, Douglas Oliver reported that:

> [Some *kiaps*] may be liked personally and others are undoubtedly hated, but as representations of an all-powerful 'Force' ... they are all more or less feared. In some cases this fear is exacerbated by dislike, distrust or contempt, in others it is tempered by genuine respect and even liking. But even in cases of the latter, natives ... know by experience that postings are brief and that the next *Kiap* will probably be a wholly different kind of individual.[44]

Kiaps exercised control mainly by foot patrols. Their village visits were brief and they had to rely on *Tok Pisin* to communicate so they had limited insight into village affairs. A *kiap* relied on what he could see (pit latrines, swept courtyards, fenced-off pigs, tidy houses, records in the Village Book) and whatever village officials told him. Village officials (*luluais* in New Guinea, Village Constables in Papua) were government appointees who might — or might not — be Big Men with authority of their own. Only in the 1950s did local councils begin to replace this personal link between the State and society. In 1963,

Local and District Courts were created, gradually displacing the *kiap* courts. These innovations, designed to introduce an impartial justice system, stripped the *kiaps* of many of their sanctions and rewards.[45] Until then, however, the *kiaps* relied on the personal authority of 'native leaders' as 'traditional' Big Men or 'modern' office-bearers. The Local Government Councils were intended to build democratic processes. In practice, councils often served to entrench and enlarge the powers and authority of individual Big Men. [46]

Invisible to villagers, the Territorial Government was housed in offices in the suburb of Konedobu in Port Moresby. After the Pacific War, the Australian Government appointed Colonel J. K. Murray as Administrator, then left him and his embryonic regime to get on with it. Little was achieved in the next six years, and, in 1951, Territories Minister Hasluck replaced Murray with Donald Cleland, a political colleague from Western Australia, and incited heads of territory departments to propose and implement projects. This approach unleashed a great deal of energy. As Director of Public Health, Dr John Gunther doubled the number of government hospitals in a dozen years and funded the missions to do the same. Dr Bill Groves wrought a similar miracle in schools, yet failed to satisfy Hasluck. All development was to be achieved from the top down. Cash-crop cultivation must be supervised by *didimen* or organised through cooperative societies guided by Australian officials.[47] Political participation should be channelled through Local Government Councils, which must accept expert guidance. These scenarios allowed little initiative by the *kiaps*, and almost none by Papua New Guineans, who (as in Buka) were coopted into official structures or discouraged from expressing their views.

Equally invisible to village people was a Legislative Council, inaugurated in 1951. Sixteen of its 28 members were officials, bound to support the Administrator's proposals. Three others were appointed to represent the missions, another three to represent planters, three more for commerce, and three — Merari Dickson from Milne Bay, Aisoli Salin from the New Guinea Islands, and Pita Simogun from the New Guinea mainland — represented indigenous interests. Indigenous membership grew to seven in 1961. The official members were now a minority, but the council was more decorative than effective. The Administrator could ignore its advice and so could the Minister. Occasionally, the Administration consulted council members, but these opinions were hardly independent. Concerning the Hahalis affair, a Native Member apologised that he must again

> ask the Administration to forgive our New Guinean indigenes for the misunderstanding and selfishness they have, and to do what it considers to help us until the day comes when our people will appreciate all the things very much.

He complained that *kiaps* were too lenient, issuing cautions rather than stamping out bad behaviour. A colleague, who had travelled to Buka on behalf of the Administration, observed: 'It will be better for the Government to step in immediately to stop this sort of native cult business so it will not spread.' A third grumbled that young people who had more education than their elders 'want to spoil the whole place'.[48] Before sending in the police, the Administration sent two councillors to persuade Hahalis members to pay tax, but they failed. The deference of Native Members gave rise to strange alignments. Australian members saw that they had nothing to fear from more Papua New Guinean members, whose presence would inhibit the Minister from exercising his controlling powers.[49] No one thought that they would develop agendas of their own.

People like Tessie Lavau had no role in these bodies: the institutions and traditions of paternal, rural governance could not accommodate them. The Government did oppose racism, at least formally, and in the 1950s legal drafting began cleansing the laws of odious terms. But politically correct language did not abolish the disabilities that people endured on account of their native condition. If the countryside was ruled by *kiaps* and Big Men, the towns were enclaves of Australian suburbia, where villagers were unwelcome. Indigenous people could expect paternalism at best — service at the side door of shops and trade stores, drinks served in plastic rather than glasses — and overt racism on occasion.

Ugly incidents were increasingly frequent as the dichotomy between colonial towns and native countryside eroded: even 'native leaders' objected to discrimination in cinemas, sports clubs and shops, and the treatment of young educated people was often much worse. When Julius Chan returned from school in Queensland, joined the Public Service and applied to join the public servants' Aviat Club in Port Moresby, he was blackballed in a move that was widely seen as racism.[50] To avoid such disgraceful incidents, Hasluck wondered if businessmen might be required to endorse 'the Government's policy against racial discrimination'.[51] This was not an acute insight: policy did discriminate, and Australian residents did little more than reflect and articulate that fact.

Tessie Lavau and Julius Chan crossed the boundary between Natives and Citizens, but boundaries of many kinds continued to define the life chances of whole categories of people. Australians moved freely into the Territory, unless (like Peter Worsley and Jeremy Beckett) they were seen as radical and were deemed to be security risks. Although Papuans were Australian citizens in law, and New Guineans were Australian protected persons, neither had a right to enter Australia, as they were not 'constituent members of the Australian community'.[52] The way forward from statelessness was to transform the Territory into a State, within or beyond the Australian federation. That event would alter the identity of Australia as well as Papua New Guinea.

Footnotes
1. Keith Willey, *Assignment New Guinea*, Jacaranda Press, Brisbane, 1965, pp. 1–15.
2. Gavin Souter, *New Guinea: the Last Unknown*, London, 1963.
3. Australian Archives, Department of Territories. A 452/1, file 60/8329, Administrator to Department, September 8, 1958.
4. Eg., Rachel Cleland, *Grass roots to independence and beyond: the contribution by women in Papua New Guinea 1951-1991*, Claremont, W. A., 1996.

5. A518, B818/1/3. Discussion initiated by Minister's cable to Administrator, Rabaul, August 18, 1927. Headmaster Schilling to Collector of Customs, Sydney, March 7, 1929. *Rabaul Times,* January 25, 1929.
6. A518, B818/1/3, Administrator to Minister, July 31, 1948, and reply, September 24, 1948.
7. A452/1, file 60/8329, Administrator to Department, September 8, 1958.
8. Ibid., Minister A. R. Downer to W. C. Wentworth MP, October 27, 1959.
9. Greg Dening, *Islands and Beaches: Discourses on a Silent Land, Marquesas, 1774-1880,* University of Hawai'i Press, 1980.
10. Stewart Firth, 'Colonial Administration and the Invention of the Native', in Donald Denoon, Stewart Firth, Jocelyn Linnekin, Karen Nero and Malama Meleisea (eds), *The Cambridge History of The Pacific Islanders,* Melbourne, 1997.
11. Papua New Guinea National Archives, Department of Information and Extension Services (DIES) file ES/59/103, minutes of the Central Advisory Committee for the Education and Advancement of Women, ninth meeting, October 8, 1959. Rachel Cleland, *Pathways to Independence: Story of Official and Family Life in Papua New Guinea from 1951 to 1975,* Perth, 1983.
12. Paula Brown, 'Gender and Social Change: New Forms of Independence for Simbu Women', *Oceania,* XIX (1988), p. 128.
13. PNG Archives, DIES file ES/59/103, desultory correspondence during 1963.
14. Maxine Dennis, 'Plantations', in D. Denoon and C. Snowden, *A Time to Plant and a Time to Uproot: A History of Agriculture in Papua New Guinea,* Port Moresby, 1979. Ken Buckley and Kris Klugman, *The History of Burns Philp: the Australian company in the South Pacific,* Burns Philp, Sydney, 1981.
15. G. T. Harris, 'Papuan Village Agriculture', in *A Time to Plant and a Time to Uproot.*
16. Maxine Dennis, 'Plantations' in Ibid.
17. M. J. Donaldson and Ken Good, *Articulated agricultural development: traditional and capitalist agriculture in Papua New Guinea,* Sydney, 1988.
18. Oskar Spate, Cyril Belshaw and Trevor Swan, 'Some Problems of Development in New Guinea', March 1953, typescript, Division of Pacific and Asian History, ANU.
19. Jack Golson, 'Agriculture in New Guinea: The Long View', 'Agricultural Technology in New Guinea', and 'New Guinea Agricultural History: a Case Study', in Denoon and Snowden, *A Time to Plant and a Time to Uproot.*
20. *Ongka: A selfaccount by a New Guinea bigman,* translated by Andrew Strathern, London, 1979.
21. Bronislav Malinowski, *Argonauts of the Western Pacific,* London, 1922.
22. E. K. Fisk, *Hardly Ever a Dull Moment,* History of Development Studies Monograph 5, National Centre for Development Studies, Australian National University, 1995, pp. 230-1.
23. R. F. Salisbury, *From Stone to Steel: economic consequences of a technological change in New Guinea,* Melbourne, 1962. T. S. Epstein, *Capitalism, Primitive and Modern: Some Aspects of Tolai Economic Growth,* Canberra, 1968.
24. Fisk, *Hardly Ever a Dull Moment,* p. 236. See also his 'Planning in a Primitive Economy: special problems of Papua New Guinea', *The Economic Record,* Vol. 38, No. 40, December 1962; 'Planning in a Primitive Economy: from pure subsistence to the production of a market surplus', *The Economic Record,* Vol. 40, No. 90, June 1964; and 'Labour absorption capacity of subsistence agriculture', *The Economic Record,* Vol. 47, No. 119, September 1971.
25. World Bank Report, cited in D. Denoon, 'New Economic Orders', in Denoon et al., *The Cambridge History of the Pacific Islanders.*
26. W. A. Lalor, Public Solicitor, 'Land Law and Registration', in B. J. Brown and G. Sawer (eds), *Fashion of Law in New Guinea,* Butterworths, Sydney, 1969.
27. R. G. Crocombe, 'Land Tenure in the South Pacific', in R. G. Ward, *Man in the Pacific Islands: essays on geographical change in the Pacific Islands,* Oxford, 1972, p. 220.
28. Alan Ward, in 'Hindsight'.
29. Stewart Firth, 'Colonial Administration and the Invention of the Native', in Denoon et al., *The Cambridge History of the Pacific Islanders.*
30. 68/4999, 'Bougainville Situation', October 2, 1968.

31. 69/2217, undated report on the impact of Bougainville copper on wages.
32. David Elder, 'Bougainville Background', cited in Donald Denoon, *Getting Under the Skin: the Bougainville copper agreement and the creation of the Panguna Mine*, Melbourne University Press, 2000.
33. Peter Worsley, *The Trumpet Shall Sound: a Study of 'Cargo' Cults in Melanesia*, London, 1957.
34. Lamont Lindstrom, 'Custom Remade', in Denoon et al., *The Cambridge History of the Pacific Islanders*; and Peter Lawrence, *Road Belong Cargo: a study of the cargo movement in the southern Madang district*, Manchester, 1964, p. 31.
35. 68/4999, Territory Intelligence Committee Paper 3/68, September 12, 1968.
36. J. T. Griffin, 'Bougainville — Secession or Just Sentiment?', *Current Affairs Bulletin*, 48 (9), 1972.
37. Douglas Oliver, *Bougainville: a Personal History*, Melbourne, 1973, pp. 150–3; Alexander Mamak and Ahmed Ali (eds), *Race, Class and Rebellion in the South Pacific*, Sydney, 1979.
38. Max and Eleanor Rimoldi, *Hahalis and the Labour of Love: a social movement on Buka Island*, Oxford, 1992; Oliver, *Bougainville: a Personal History*, Chapter 8; Elder, 'Bougainville Background'.
39. 67/3861, Assistant District Commissioner's report to his Director, October 18, 1968.
40. 68/4999, Territory Intelligence Committee Paper 3/68, September 12, 1968.
41. Eugene Ogan, 'Some Historical Background to the 1989 unrest in Bougainville', seminar paper, Department of Political and Social Change, ANU, June 1989.
42. Ian Maddocks, 'Udumu a-hagaia' (Motu, meaning open your mouth), Inaugural Lecture, University of Papua New Guinea, 1968.
43. Sam Alasia, 'Party Politics and Government in Solomon Islands', Discussion Paper 1997/7, State, Society and Governance in Melanesia Project, ANU.
44. Douglas Oliver, 'Some Social-Relational Aspects of CRA Copper Mining on Bougainville: a Confidential Report to Management', 1968, cited in Denoon, *Getting Under the Skin*.
45. Sinclair Dinnen, *Law and Order in a Weak State: crime and politics in Papua New Guinea*, University of Hawai'i Press, 2001.
46. Ibid.; and Bill Gammage, *The Sky Travellers: Journeys in New Guinea, 1938-1939*, Melbourne University Press, 1998.
47. Catherine Snowden, 'Cooperatives', in Denoon and Snowden (eds), *A Time to Plant and a Time to Uproot*.
48. Text of House of Assembly debates, cited in Denoon, *Getting Under the Skin*.
49. Ian Downs, *The Australian Trusteeship: Papua New Guinea 1945–75*, AGPS, Canberra, 1980, p. 215.
50. *South Pacific Post*, April 6, 1962.
51. Eg., A 452 62/1850, Minister's note, February 14, 1962.
52. A452/1, 60/8329.

Chapter 2

Emulating Australia

Political Education

Tessie Lavau's curiosity was widely shared but seldom satisfied until 1962 when 'native leaders', including nominated members of the Legislative Council, asked to visit Australia to see how government worked.[1] Their interest delighted the officials who were planning to create an elected legislature: a tour might produce 'men who know what we are talking about when we ask them to consider further changes'. All official thinking accepted that Papua New Guineans must understand the workings of Australian government, not that Australians should understand Papua New Guinea society.

Selecting a party was tricky. Each district should send one person and David Fenbury (Secretary of the Administrator's Department) told DCs that the tourists must have 'the basic education or the native intelligence to absorb the lessons they will learn' about Australian institutions. They need not be election candidates but they must be 'the sort of people who would naturally be associated … with any discussions about constitutional reform'. Fenbury — years ahead of his time — noted that 'use of the pronoun "him" is not intended to preclude consideration of females'. But this was mere rhetoric: no women were considered.

If gender was a barrier, opposition to the Administration was not. Antagonism — in moderation — might even attract favour.[2] *Kiap* Johnston was in two minds about Lukas Chauka of Mouk Village in Manus. Chauka was a kinsman of the soldier and 'cargo cult' leader Paliau Maloat, and served as Vice-President of Baluan Council in Manus. He was illiterate and spoke no English, but was fluent and self-assured in Tok Pisin.

> He would not be afraid of speaking his mind in public and he has on several occasions shown that he can mix reasonably well with Europeans.

He did make 'radical statements' and sometimes denounced the Administration, 'but I don't believe that he believes the truth of these statements'. For United Nations visitors, he staged a play to dramatise how the missions and private enterprise 'wanted to do everything to help the natives but were prevented … by the Administration'. Afterwards, however, 'he was quite pleasant and adopted an entirely different attitude, blaming the sloth and ignorance of the people for their standard of living, etc.'.

Shallow antagonism might be just the ticket. Chauka had surely been helpful; he was obviously intelligent, he had 'sound ideas' and he wanted progress for his people — but might he 'go to extremes'? He was related to Paliau Maloat, the charismatic ex-serviceman whose independent spirit and ideas worried officials. Chauka got the nod but most *kiaps* favoured men whose attitudes were well known. All were in their prime, with more than average exposure to government and missions. They all owed their selection to the patronage of a DC. Some were public servants or teachers. Bin Arawaki was visiting Port Moresby to observe the Legislative Council. Kup Ogut had a son at school in Queensland (and needed permission to visit him). Vin ToBaining quit to join the committee that was reforming the legislature.

The Touring Party

Papua	Address and District	Age	Occupation
Gabriel Ehava	Gulf	45	farmer and Ministerial Member
Robert Tabua	P&T Daru, Western	42	public servant [clerical]
Oala Oala Rarua	Konedobu, Central	34	teacher seconded to Administrator's Department
Leatani Baloiloi	Esa'ala, Milne Bay	36	public servant [interpreter]
Timaeus Sambubu	Saiho Hospital, Northern	40+	public servant [lab assistant]
New Guinea			
Vin ToBaining	Vunamami, East New Britain	40+	farmer
Simogen Pita	District Office, Wewak	40+	farmer
Lukas Chauko	Baluan, Manus	43	villager
Paul Lapun	Mariga Village, Bougainville	36	farmer
Eritus Hitter	Lualul Village, Kavieng, New Ireland	37	agricultural field worker
Yakutung Saki	Finschhafen, Morobe	42	farmer
Stahl Mileng	Marup Village, Karkar, Madang	40	mission teacher
Bin Arawaki	Okuyufa Village, Eastern Highlands	35+	farmer
Kup Ogut	District Office, Mt Hagen, Western Highlands	40	entrepreneur

[none from Southern Highlands]

The head of Information and Extension Services, L. R. Newby, led the group. Since travel was governed by rules for the Removal of Natives, Newby had to extract from the Director of Native Affairs 'a General Exemption under his Circular 53/63 of 17th April 1961, to permit the members of the party to proceed to Australia for special studies'.[3] He and *kiap* P. J. Walsh then assembled the party for a fortnight's preparation, bought them warm clothes to cope with Canberra's chilly spring, and escorted them through Australia.

Their curriculum was decided by the Territories Minister himself.[4] It was typical of Sir Paul Hasluck to supervise his officers in detail. In doing so, he revealed how limited was the constitutional change he expected.

> I would not puzzle them at this stage with Federal problems … and would keep them away from any State Parliament …
>
> Give concentrated attention to the Federal Parliament. What they want to learn is about —
> a elections
> b parties – the role of Government and Opposition
> c how the Parliament works – how it does things – and they need time with officers of the House to see how the business is prepared …
> d they need to get the idea of argument according to rules
> e they need to learn from members how they look after their constituents
> f they need to see how joint parliamentary committees work
> g they need to learn how Cabinet works
> h they need to learn how Ministers work and the relationship between Ministers and their departments, leading to the role of the public service
> i they should spend a good deal of time seeing departments at work …
> j they should appreciate, too, the working of the press gallery and the broadcasting system and the reason for the attendance of people in the public gallery.

Lest his officials miss the point, he added:

> Costs can be cut, the joy-ride element reduced and the purpose of the visit better served if you concentrate the visit on Canberra. Consequently cancel all the planning you have done and work along the lines indicated above.

The members were given 10 shillings (approximately five dollars in today's terms) a day and clothing, but no one organised afternoon tea (the approved form of interracial socialising) before they left Port Moresby. Their days were devoted to instruction and their evenings to Australian films and discussions.

They spent 19 cool days in Canberra, then a planned town of 60,000 people that offered few distractions from daily briefings, visits to institutions and important people, and debriefing sessions. They met Prime Minister Menzies, the Leader and Deputy Leader of the Opposition, the President of the Senate, the Speaker of the House of Assembly, the Knight-at-Arms and the Usher of the Black Rod, Hasluck himself, the Chief Electoral Officer, and many public servants. Their relaxation was no joyride either: the War Memorial, the American Embassy, the New Guinea Association, the Canberra Club and Rotary. They spent three days in the Snowy Mountains, an evening with the Queanbeyan Council, and a day with a shire council. They did no shopping. The Australia they saw was the Australia the Minister selected for them to see — and emulate.

Hasluck had little interest in party politics (see below) and his tour program was heavily weighted towards government, mainly the formal and even ritual elements of governing. What did they make of their crash course? Oala Oala-Rarua alone reported at length in writing, a guarded account that dwelt on matter-of-fact issues and which thanked the organisers. He was impressed by the 'amount of money needed for the Parliament, the parliamentarians, the officers, clerks and typists, and all the people who work behind the scenes — the public servants'. He quoted Menzies' lofty view of the Opposition — 'It keeps me and my ministers on our toes' — not an alternative government but a stimulant for those in office. He and his colleagues were startled by the oppositional role of parties and they thought the Territory 'too immature' for them. The relations between a minister and his department fascinated him. Only on the subject of the Senate did he criticise Australian practice, observing that its original function (a house of review) had been displaced (and devalued) by party politics.

Evidently the party had
— agreed to be selective in telling of their experiences and will, inter alia, mention:
— the importance of an opposition,
— the inevitability of parties and the risk of having too many,
— minister's responsibility to parliament for his department's actions,
— minister's accountability to parliament,
— a member can be voted out of his seat, but only at elections,
— the Senate has been captured by party politics & is no longer a watchdog,
— [and] governmental operations similar at state and federal level.

Newby urged DCs to promote meetings, and required the tourists to convene discussions and report. A few obliged, including the ultra-reliable Lukas Chauka, who must have misheard the party line: instead of the agreed agenda, he exhorted his compatriots to work hard — just like Australians.[5] Nowhere in Canberra did they see that 'the State' needed more to make it work than the observance of parliamentary rituals.

Hasluck's Vision

The martinet who knew exactly what Papua New Guineans needed to know was Paul Hasluck, a patrician Liberal from Perth. Then in his fifties, he had been a journalist, a historian and a diplomat before he entered Parliament. He became minister in 1951 in a new Territories portfolio, which was separated from External Affairs and added the Northern Territory to Nauru and Papua and New Guinea.[6] He was determined to master the issues and formulate policies himself. He abhorred the trappings of a colonialism which he conflated with British practice. On his first visit to the territory, he was 'revolted at the imitation of British colonial modes and manners' by officials who imagined wrongly that 'such was the way in which one ruled dependent peoples'.[7] His revulsion embraced Administrator Colonel J. K. Murray, an agronomist by training — and a Labor Party appointee.[8]

Hasluck was fastidious about the language of policy and (in 1956) reminded his staff

> not to use 'native' as a noun ... [T]here are undoubtedly many unpleasant associations ... and a suggestion of inferiority, and these terms are undoubtedly objectionable to maladjusted people like the Indians.[9]

Alas, the mind-set was more stubborn than the word. The Territory evolved from Papua and New Guinea into Papua-New Guinea and then shed the hyphen, but 'Papuan or New Guinean' was clumsy, so the people dangled semantically between an unacknowledged colonial past and an unspecified future. The future was unclear because Hasluck also eschewed 'colony' (which implied eventual independence) and preferred the less precise 'territory', which let him duck the question of destiny. 'Self-determination' was the slippery term used in discussing possible futures: a path that might lead to independence, or to incorporation into Australia, or to a status not yet invented.

Hasluck relished being 'virtually the Premier and the whole of a state Cabinet'.[10] A better description was that of the French statesman who likened him to an inspector-general. For a politician, Hasluck had little stomach for politics. He was lucky that his portfolio was in effect non-political, which might explain why he stayed in it for 12 years. Cabinet had scant interest in his work and the Labor Party exempted Territories issues from criticism. The journalist Peter Hastings exaggerated only slightly when he called Australian policy a 'bipartisan meeting of closed minds'![11] Hasluck belonged in the 'progressive' tradition that despised compromising politics and pinned its faith on technical expertise to achieve material advance. He was keen to deliver services, especially health and schools, and he was good at extracting government grants for them. He hectored the officers of his department and he kept a tight rein on Territory government in frequent visits and direct talks with the heads of its departments.[12] He saw himself as the most distinguished intellectual in Cabinet. In 1967, when Prime Minister Harold Holt drowned, Hasluck made his bid to be Prime Minister — by telling colleagues that he was available, and passively awaiting their judgment.[13] Sir Paul ended his career as Governor-General, a position in which he ran a high risk of being 'revolted at the imitation of British colonial modes and manners'.

Once he had appointed his own administrator (Cleland) and remade the department, he focused on the extension of government reach and the gradual spread of education. A decade later he was pursuing the same goals, which he restated in a public address in Port Moresby in 1960. He would not permit more elected members of the Legislative Council: there would be no more European elected members 'until we could get native elected members', and he wanted 'increased native membership to be effective and not a sham'. For years it had been his policy 'to prepare the native people' for such a role. But he was at pains to distinguish an enhanced role from real self-government. Before the Territory could become self-governing:

> it has to see great social advances (i.e. changes in the way people live and in their relationships to one another and to the community at large). It has to see great economic changes so that the people can earn a living at a decent standard and so that the country can support its services even if other countries still finance its development. It has to see the growth of local administration and political capacity.

These changes are not made by a stroke of the pen or by the passing of a resolution but by hard work year by year.
And ,'social, economic and political change 'will only come with the help of Australians'.[14]

Hasluck's intellectual strength and political frailty emerge in an exchange in 1961 provoked by the United Nations. He always refused to set target dates for self-government, much less for independence. On the other hand — to soften that refusal — he was willing to set and meet educational, social and economic goals. In 1961, the department proposed these targets for the next five years. The plans went from Cabinet to an interdepartmental committee, with 12 pages of Hasluck's commentary, which explained 'where we are going and what is the best way to get there' and computed the necessary 'scale and direction of our effort'.[15]

This quintessential statement of Hasluck's program began by delineating Australia's interests. Foremost was

> a sense of trust towards the people [of the Territory] and [Australia's] national self-respect and pride, derived both from past history and a present wish to succeed before the eyes of the world ...

There were strategic interests, 'mainly to deny the use of the area to any other power'. There were potential economic interests in agriculture (to complement rather than rival Australia's produce). There was also a need to ensure stable government.

Since Australia's tasks could never be fully accomplished, 'we will be perpetually fighting for time and perpetually called on to justify our actions'.

> If we are to carry this job through 'to the end', two questions we have to ponder are: (1) What is the point in the progress of the country and its people which we would regard as 'the end' so far as our efforts are concerned; (2) is it best to try to reach that point of time more quickly or more slowly ... ?

> Our thesis has been that social and economic advancement is the only sound foundation for political advancement and that a system of justice and competent and honest public service are just as important for self-government as an elected legislature or indigenous political leadership.

This meant the creation of something like the institutions, the values and the personnel of an Australian State. That extraordinary ambition implied nearly infinite resources over a very long time, but external pressures and internal change made self-government likely long before the Territory was ready. Self-government would happen

> before the economic and social advancement has gone far enough for the Territory to support itself financially, provide food and work for its people from its own resources at the higher standards they are seeking, staff its public services, and protect the individual through the Courts, to say nothing of assuming the responsibility for foreign affairs and defence.

Since constitutional advance might outstrip institutions and personnel, Hasluck proposed 'degrees in self-government' on the model of Australia's own constitutional history. He recalled that the eastern Australian colonies had enjoyed limited autonomy for decades after 1851 (when Britain delegated certain powers to colonial law-makers): they gained more powers with Federation in 1901, more again with Dominion status between the two world wars, leading to virtual independence in the present. Hasluck hoped that Australia might supervise a self-governing Papua New Guinea in much the same way that Britain had overseen the Australian colonies a century earlier, delegating powers gradually and cautiously.

This was a very different scenario than was being played out in Britain's African colonies, where independence came only months after self-government. How could this heterodox strategy survive misunderstanding and denunciation?

> Our only hopes of doing that lie in geographical propinquity, economic ties to the Australian market, the undoubted feeling of loyalty to the Throne which the indigenes at present have, and the possibility that through our diplomacy, aided by ANZUS, the United States may help us to do in our situation what the British Navy did in the nineteenth century for the Australian colonies.

The 30-year horizon was chosen deliberately. Papua New Guinea would need judicial and other specialists, budget support, defence aid and marketing assistance for at least that long.

Would Australia want to share this staggering load? And should progress be as swift as possible, or deliberate and slow? Present policy aimed at a sound rather than a swift result:

> It will need courage, skill and patience under insult to maintain that in the face of international pressure and segments of opinion among Australian 'intellectuals'. I suggest we should still try to maintain it.

Hasluck anticipated the need to double Australia's grant in the next five years. Even so, the Administration would achieve much less than it should in land management and agriculture, health services and schools. This work could be supplemented by international agencies, but only technical (and 'non-political') bodies such as the South Pacific Commission, the World Health Organisation and the Food and Agriculture Organisation. Several pages of calculations canvassed ways to save money, but the funds sought were the least that would suffice for this grand design.

The Territory's itemised needs suggest how much Hasluck hoped to achieve, how little had been done and how few resources were available. He wanted to double the size of the Public Service in order to:
— raise school enrolments from 150,000 to 350,000;
— enrol 10,000 secondary scholars, 2,000 technical students and 2,000 teacher trainees;
— build or rebuild 70 smaller hospitals (base hospitals were already in place);
— provide antenatal care to 60 per cent of women (compared with the current 20 per cent);
— survey 40-50,000 people each year, for tuberculosis, to cover half of the population;
— extend government influence to the whole population by 1963, and control by 1966;
— extend Local Government Council coverage from 350,000 to 800,000 people;
— raise production of cocoa and coffee by 100 per cent;
— raise production of rubber, logs and sawn timber by 50 per cent;
— create 7,500 land blocks, inspecting 250,000 acres 'for those native farmers who do not have access to suitable land under customary native land tenure'; and
— double the mileage of roads.

Even if all programs succeeded, the Territory would remain an archipelago of insular societies, linked by an over-stretched administration and funded by a minute cash economy. But each tentative step would lead in the direction of Australian ways of doing things.

In the usual rhythm of government, the submission was sent to an interdepartmental committee, which endorsed its analysis but thought that self-government might arrive in 20 years, or even 10. They were amazed by the Territory's backwardness. Some areas were not yet under regular administration: only 73,000 people (12 per cent of those of working age) earned wages, 17,000 in government and 56,000 in private enterprise (mainly plantations). Of the half-million children of school age, only one-quarter were at school, including 3,000 in post-primary education. The committee agreed with Hasluck that there must be balance — and therefore linkage — between economic, social and constitutional change. Since they could imagine no way to speed up the lethargic pace of economic development, they assumed that political change must also be glacial. They therefore followed each step of Hasluck's argument and endorsed his targets, suggesting only that grants or loans might be sought from a wider range of sources.[16]

Alas, this proposal failed to capture the attention of Hasluck's colleagues. Four months later, he wrote to Menzies more in anger than in sorrow:

> You will recall that the Government has undertaken to give to the United Nations target dates for social, educational and economic advancement ... and that ... a great deal of work was done by my department in preparing papers for Cabinet ...
>
> In the event Cabinet did not choose to consider these papers.[17]

His argument failed to impress his colleagues, but it does explain what is otherwise anomalous in his public statements. After he left office (as Nelson points out)[18] Hasluck claimed that he had always envisaged self-government as the outcome of his policies; but as minister, he had said that he could not foresee

> the day when Papua and New Guinea will become a member of the Australian Commonwealth on exactly the same terms and in exactly the same constitutional relation as the six States ... There is no reason whatsoever why they should not enter into relation with the Commonwealth on terms to be negotiated ... when Papua and New Guinea can speak as one people.[19]

His imagined future embraced self-government and a 'permanent constitutional link' because of his — unique — belief that the UN would accept decades of self-government. If the UN knew any Australian history, it was unmoved. If Hasluck had known less constitutional history and more of international relations, he would not have devised that scenario.

There was more obvious consistency in Hasluck's demand that the Territory's destiny was singular. To knit its peoples into one community and one polity required 'even development' so as to equalise economic conditions and opportunities. In Downs's words: 'policies of gradualism were pursued ... to allow the more backward areas to "catch up".'[20]

A peculiarity of this submission was the importance attributed to the UN. Australia reported to the Trusteeship Committee of the Security Council in respect of New Guinea (but not for Papua). The Trusteeship Committee sent a mission every three years. These friendly meetings usually proposed minor reforms, but, in 1960, the UN General Assembly created a parallel Decolonisation Committee (the Committee of 24) to help dismantle all colonial relationships. The Committee of 24 embodied African and Asian sentiment, and was surprised that colonial rule in the Pacific was seldom challenged. Only a handful of member states of the South Pacific Commission were independent, and the Commission (unlike the Organisation for African Unity) was a mainly technical body, exchanging information and insights among the colonial powers.

The Committee of 24's bark was fierce but its bite was toothless. What mattered (as Hasluck knew well) was the view of the Western powers, and especially the United States. When the US and Britain withdrew support from the Netherlands, for example, Dutch rule in West Papua came to an abrupt end: as Irian Jaya, the territory became a province of Indonesia.[21] In a revealing encounter with Whitlam, the French statesman

Couve de Murville told him that the enthusiasts would eventually get round to Papua New Guinea,

> 'but it depends on whom else they have to eat first.' He referred to Rhodesia and to British African territories ... next, he said, the attack would be concentrated on Portuguese and Spanish African territories; it might take another four or five years for them to be 'digested'; after that attention would no doubt turn to New Guinea.[22]

That level of Western cynicism blunted UN resolutions. Foreign Affairs reassured the Department of Territories in 1961 that

> It would not be surprising if so long as we are able to tell the same story about our territories as we can today and stand firmly by it the [Trusteeship] Council becomes a bore to many members. The Africans are plainly not interested in New Guinea, more enlightened Asians realise already that it presents special problems ... [23]

The UN Visiting Mission of 1962, chaired by Sir Hugh Foot, was unusually effective. Nevertheless, when they insisted on discussing self-government and target dates, Hasluck would not be pushed either.[24] In respect of political targets, he had made his position clear to the Secretary of the Department: 'You know my views about target dates. I recognise that we have to supply [to the UN] some appropriate eye-wash from time to time and we can provide it on request.'[25] That splenetic statement also reveals Hasluck's scepticism about most planning. Downs quotes him saying that 'I regard social planning in any except the immediate and visible situation or the specific social task as revealing the arrogance of the feeble or the self-deception of the dreamer'.[26]

It was in this spirit that Hasluck adopted Foot's advice and invited the World Bank to survey the Territory. That survey found less than £20 million of exports and imports worth £30 million. The terms of trade were surging the wrong way and there was no sign of new sources of revenue (the World Bank ruled out mining). Australian grants provided three-quarters of government receipts and only one-fifth of that was designed to create income.[27] Spate, Belshaw and Swan had reached that conclusion a decade earlier, but they believed that 'native agriculture' was a basis for development, whereas the World Bank could not conceive such a strategy. They proposed that economic development be given priority, ignoring Hasluck's preference for even development in favour of 'concentration of effort'. 'Native agriculture' would not be the foundation of this strategy.[28]

The Australian Context

Because Papua New Guinea was an Australian territory, several Commonwealth departments had branches there. The more important were Army and Navy, Attorney-General's, Civil Aviation, Meteorological Bureau, National Development, Prime Minister's (for the Public Service Board and the Auditor-General), Shipping and Transport, and Works. There were also half a dozen agencies, including airlines, the Reserve Bank and the Australian Broadcasting Commission.[29] In theory, they could ignore the Minister for Territories and even defy the Administrator, although they seldom did.

To develop his ideas into policies and programs, the Minister for Territories had a department of Commonwealth public servants. Hasluck wielded rare influence over them because he had largely created the department. The 1930s department had been swept aside by war and its peace-time revival was threatened by the Army's Directorate of Research and Civil Affairs (DORCA), a clutch of scholars in uniform. DORCA reported to the Minister, Eddie Ward,[30] but Ward was distracted. He had to divide his time between Territories and his other portfolio, Transport; and he spent much of his political capital defending himself from a Royal Commission. By 1949, there were 78 staff in the department, but they clung to passive traditions so that policy and programs languished.[31] Downs regrets the waste, with 'Administration committees considering prospects and objectives, an isolated Administrator waiting for decisions from Canberra and a Minister preoccupied by political events'.[32]

Matters improved in 1949 when the Liberal-Country Party coalition won office. Territories gained a high-profile minister in Percy Spender, but it was submerged in the more prestigious Department of External Affairs. Little attention was given to Papua New Guinea before Hasluck became minister in 1951 of a portfolio that split from External Affairs. He seized the chance to rebuild the department with C. R. (Esky) Lambert as secretary. When he left a dozen years later, few officials could recall any other minister. In principle, the department developed policy while the Administration carried out programs. That gave immense authority to Hasluck. His searching visits made him the sole point of coordination, because heads of Territory departments often reported directly to him. Like every commentator on these years, Downs calls them 'the Hasluck period'.

No other minister enjoyed (or endured) such disinterest from Cabinet. The fact that the Territory did not elect anyone to the Commonwealth Parliament helps to explain this. Any debate on Melanesians was uncomfortable since one base of Australian identity was the aspiration of 'White Australia' — continental apartheid. Commitment to White Australia was reinforced by the Pacific War, during which fear of invasion was intensified by resonances of half a century's lurid fiction about the yellow hordes. White Australia justified discrimination among immigrants, which produced an increasingly 'white' society:

Non-Europeans in Australia, 1901–47[33]

Year	*Country of Origin*			
	China	*Melanesia*	*India*	*Japan*
1901	32,997	9,654	7,637	3,593
1933	14,249	3,098	3,098	2,466
1947	12,094	1,638	2,898	335

In anxious isolation from other cultures, official Australia saw no need to modify its antique notions of racial hierarchy. Prime Minister Menzies — Knight of the Thistle, Warden of the Cinque Ports and devoted monarchist — reviewed his ideas about colonial rule only when British Tories began to devolve power in Africa.[34] Meanwhile, he was smugly deaf to the racism that informed his government's policies:

> *It is our national desire to develop in Australia a homogeneous population in order that we may avert social difficulties which have arisen in many other countries. [And] we are ... a friendly people not given to making distinctions among people on grounds of race or religion.*[35]

His myopia was widely shared. His Minister for External Affairs, Richard Casey, was a patrician who had served Australia in Washington and the Raj in Bengal, without denting his ethnic self-assurance. To win friends and disarm critics, he wanted to project this cosy image — which inadvertently listed the Government's sensitivities:

> the absence of racial prejudice in Australia, the idea of Australia as a waterless land unsuitable for mass settlement, ... our progressive social reforms and the egalitarian nature of Australian society, ... the primitive nature of our aborigines and of the New Guinea peoples, and even the beneficial aspects of colonial regimes.[36]

The causes of anxiety were communism and Asian nationalism. Together, they made 'Asia' almost as menacing in the 1950s as it was in the 1850s. By contrast, the Territory posed resolvable problems rather than moral dilemmas. Although its undeveloped state was almost as embarrassing as the survival of Aboriginal Australians, the place and the people could be managed by paternal officials.

Many of Hasluck's policies survived his departure. Papua New Guinea must be one entity and its cultural divisions must not be exacerbated by uneven development. The task of modernisation was immense; it was Australia's task; and it would take many skilled people, a very long time, and huge resources. The outcome would be a society, an economy and a bureaucracy that increasingly resembled Australia's. At an unhurried pace, Melanesians would be initiated into Australian-style representative government, beginning with local councils. To the philosopher-minister, this was quite consistent with decades of patient tutelage leading to — and beyond — self-government.

Hasluck maintained that Australia's relations with Papua New Guinea were unique. That assertion helped to nullify British precedents and blunt UN resolutions – but it was also true. These polities were linked — and divided — by Torres Strait. It was therefore apt that the government of the Territory was shared by two agencies. Relations between Konedobu and Canberra were usually cool and often tetchy, yet each needed the other. The Administration was not an embryonic state: it had no capacity to make policy. Rather, it was a colonial regime whose officers served out their careers in the Territory, interacted with Melanesians and were often touched by them. The department was part of the Commonwealth, whose officers moved to and from other departments, and they might never visit the Territory. This awkward complementarity mirrored the difficulty of their mission: to mediate radically different economies, societies and cultures that were, and would forever remain, close neighbours.

Footnotes
1. Papua New Guinea Archives, DIES file ES/59/53, Political Education Tour, 1962. D. M. Fenbury [Secretary, Department of the Administrator] to District Commissioners, July 5, 1962.
2. Ibid., W. J. Johnston (acting DO, Lorengau, Manus District) to DC, Lorengau, August 20, 1962, and DC to Fenbury, August 21. I am indebted to Stephen Pokawin for information about Lukas's family.
3. Ibid., T. W. Ellis (DC, Mount Hagen) to DIES; L.R . Newby to DCs, September 4, 1962.
4. A 452 62/1850, Political Education of Native Leaders, Hasluck's minute of May 22, 1962.
5. Ibid., Newby to DCs, October 24, 1962; and Newby to party members, November 19, 1962, and responses gradually petering out by the middle of 1963.
6. I use the term 'Department of Territories' throughout, although it often had other names, such as the Department of External Territories.
7. Paul Hasluck, *A Time for Building: Australian Administration in Papua and New Guinea 1951-1963*, Melbourne University Press, 1976, p. 14.
8. Brian Jinks, 'Papua New Guinea I942–1952: policy, planning and J. K. Murray', PhD, University of Sydney, 1975.
9. A 452, 62/3210, Minister's minute, January 27, 1956.
10. Paul Hasluck, *A Time for Building*, p. 6.
11. Interview, Jim Byth.
12. Ian Downs, *The Australian Trusteeship: Papua New Guinea 1945–75*, AGPS, Canberra, 1980; Jinks, 'Papua New Guinea I942–1952'. Couve de Murville described Hasluck as his own inspector-general; Hasluck, *A Time for Building*, p. 407.
13. Ian Hancock, *John Grey Gorton: He Did It His Way*, Melbourne University Press, 2002.
14. A 452/1 61/3897. Hasluck's address of July 10, 1960, sent to External Affairs on July 14, 1960.
15. A 452 61/1785, Hasluck to Prime Minister Menzies, May 5, 1961.
16. A 452 61/1785, External Affairs to Territories, June 2, 1961, enclosing the report.
17. A 452 61/1785, Hasluck to Menzies, October 20, 1961.
18. Hank Nelson, 'The Talk and the Timing', in D. Denoon (ed.), *Emerging from Empire? Decolonisation in the Pacific Islands*, Department of Pacific and Asian History, ANU, 1997.
19. Hasluck, *A Time for Building*, pp. 86, 239.
20. Ibid., pp. xviii-xix; and Hasluck, 'Australia's Task in PNG', cited in Downs, *The Australian Trusteeship*, p. 93.
21. C. L. M. Penders, *The West New Guinea Debacle: Dutch Decolonisation and Indonesia, 1945-1962*, Crawford House, Adelaide, 2002; Stuart Doren, 'Western Friends and Eastern Neighbours: West New Guinea and Australian self-perception', PhD thesis, ANU, 1999. In 1963, Dutch New Guinea became the Indonesian province of Irian Barat, renamed Irian Jaya in 1973. From 1998 until 2003, it was permissible to use the names Papua or Irian Jaya; now the region has been divided into two provinces: one is Irian Jaya Barat and the other is Papua or Irian Jaya.
22. A 452/1 62/1161, External Affairs to Territories, July 6, 1962. De Murville is talking to Whitlam.
23. A 452/1 61/3817, Australian Mission to UN cable, November 21, 1961.
24. A 452/1 62/1161,summary record of meeting on May 18, 1962.
25. Ibid.; 60/374, minister's minute of January 28, 1960.
26. Downs, *The Australian Trusteeship*, p. 93.
27. International Bank for Reconstruction and Development [World Bank], *The Economic Development of the Territory of Papua and New Guinea*, Johns Hopkins Press, Baltimore, 1965.
28. R. G. Crocombe, 'That Five Year Plan', *New Guinea*, December 1968/January 1969; H. Arndt, R. Shand and E. K. Fisk, 'An Answer to Crocombe – I, II, III', *New Guinea*, June/July 1969; R. G. Crocombe, 'Crocombe to his critics', *New Guinea*, September/October 1969.
29. A 452 T29, 70/3045, discussions on the implications of self-government, 1970.
30. Downs, *The Australian Trusteeship*, pp. 11–13.
31. Denoon, 'Capitalism in Papua New Guinea', *Journal of Pacific History* Vol. XX, No. 3–4, 1985; Downs, *The Australian Trusteeship*, pp. 11–3, 82–3.

32. Downs, *The Australian Trusteeship*, pp. xviii.
33. Andrew Markus, *Australian Race Relations 1788-1993*, Allen & Unwin, Sydney, 1994.
34. R. G. Menzies, *Afternoon Light: Some Memories of Men and Events*, Penguin, Melbourne, 1969; and David Goldsworthy, 'Menzies, Britain and the Commonwealth', in Frank Cain (ed.), *Menzies in War and Peace*, Sydney, 1997.
35. Ibid., p. 172.
36. Casey to Holt, August 14, 1959, External Affairs Archives, cited by Daniel Oakman in *Facing Asia: A History of the Colombo Plan*, Pandanus Books, 2004.

Chapter 3

Guided Democracy

The Gunther Select Committee and a House of Assembly

After half a century of patrolling coastal villages and half a generation of police rule in the Highlands, government in the 1950s still relied on 'native leaders' to relay their purposes to isolated villages and report back. The middlemen could act as 'traditional' Big Men, such as Bin Arawaki from the Eastern Highlands and Kup Ogut from the Western Highlands (Chapter 2), or as 'modern' office-bearers such as Lukas Chauka in Local Councils.

Less personal arrangements were in the wind. After a report by the Melbourne Law Professor David Derham in 1960, the new policy was to remove police from the *kiaps'* control,[1] while Local and District Courts would eventually displace *kiap* courts. Elected Local Councils began to emerge, replacing the *luluais* and *tultuls* — village officials appointed and answerable only to the *kiaps*. Rural Progress Associations and Cooperative Societies were introduced or beefed up to boost production.[2] In Weber's terms, these reforms would move governance from its charismatic to its bureaucratic stage.

The Administration relied on rural 'native leaders' even in the Legislative Council. From three of 12 non-official members, the number of 'native members' grew to seven in 1961, but they were still deferential. Young Ilinome Tarua listened to Murari Dickson from Kwato Mission in Milne Bay. 'He never talked about what happened' in Council, preferring his real interests, 'evangelical work and cricket'. In 1961, Alice Wedega, also from Kwato, became the first woman member and flew to Sydney to learn parliamentary procedures.

> John Gunther instructed them that when it comes to voting, they had to vote in the Administration. However … I think Auntie Alice would have voted against the government view allowing Papua New Guineans to take alcohol … [because] a missionary at Kwato had told us that alcohol is evil.[3]

Alice and her colleagues usually did support the Administration, but tinkering with land tenure antagonised even the most compliant. Since 1952, a Native Land Commission had struggled to simplify and record native title. After 10 baffled years, Hasluck lost patience and proposed to convert land from customary tenure into a new form of title to encourage investment and inheritance from fathers to sons (gender equity being far from his mind). A Land Titles Commission would determine rights and register them under a Land Registration (Communally Owned Land) Ordinance, or in individual title under the Land (Tenure Conversion) Ordinance.[4] When the bills came to the Council, however, speakers demanded more protection for customary owners. It took a year to amend the legislation to meet this demand, and the amendments made the law unworkable.[5] This was a Damascus Road moment when expatriates saw that indigenous members could stymie the Minister.[6]

Unknown to these crafty converts to democracy, the Minister was leaning the same way. In 1960, the UN created a Decolonisation Committee and Harold Macmillan asserted that 'winds of change' were making African independence inevitable. The Dutch departure from West Papua was imminent, and Sukarno's unstable and destabilising Indonesia would share a land border with Australian territory. Prime Minister Menzies announced a new view of decolonisation: 'If in doubt you should go sooner, not later.' To counter anti-colonial critics, the Territory's indigenous representatives must become more visible and audible.[7] In brief, Hasluck needed Native Members to shield him from the UN; Australian-elected members needed Native Members to shield them from the Minister; and official members expected Native Members to shield them from importunate expatriates.

To represent democratic reform as a Territory initiative, the Legislative Council was told to create a select committee on constitutional change. To ensure that this committee's advice matched the Minister's vision, it was chaired by the chunky and punchy John Gunther. After studying medicine in Sydney and practicing in the Solomon Islands, he had 'a good war' in which he ran important field trials on Manus Island. After the war, he was appointed Director of Health.[8] When Hasluck gave him free rein and a liberal budget, he built hospitals and clinics across the country and enlisted dozens of ex-army medical orderlies. Lacking doctors, he recruited European refugees from Australia, where non-British doctors were barred from working. He launched military-style campaigns against specific diseases, armed with the magic bullets of penicillin, sulfa drugs, quinine and DDT. The epitome of paternalism, his officers sprayed villages, treated Highlanders for TB before working on the coast, and created maternal and child health services. In 1956, Hasluck shifted Gunther and his fierce charisma to the job of Assistant Administrator and manager of the Legislative Council.

The Gunther Committee's Interim Report in 1962 admitted frankly that its proposals, 'though largely based on the freely expressed wishes of the people, *in fact go well beyond* the conservative proposals which they themselves put forward'.[9] The Report recommended a House of Assembly, most of whose 54 members would be elected from a common roll. The Administrator would preside alongside 10 other officials, and 10 elected seats would be reserved for expatriates. Indigenous people's representatives would predominate. Quizzed by Menzies, Gunther guaranteed that he would control this House and steer administration business through it.[10] This was no empty boast: he could count on the 'Native Leaders'.

Gunther's committee was suspended during the tour of a remarkable UN Visiting Mission, led by the astute British diplomat Sir Hugh Foot. As Director of Education, Leslie Johnson could see what the mission was doing. Its Principal Secretary (James Lewis) held talks with officers of the Administration and endorsed the reforms that they were planning. This mission not only 'made positive, firm and constructive proposals on matters of magnitude', but tried to impose a timetable for their achievement. They did not change the direction of policies, but accelerated them. Publicly, the Gunther Committee responded to Foot's initiatives. Behind the scenes, the shoe might have been on another foot.[11] At any rate, Gunther's interim report was so well received in Canberra that he never wrote a final report.

The dawn of democracy required a great effort to enrol voters, organise the poll and explain the procedures. Maddocks watched as Local Government Councils disseminated unreliable information:

> the villager's only hard source was the electoral education patrols which set out to instruct him in his duties as an elector, which distributed informational material and later recorded his vote. He saw and heard the candidates before the election, though often not all of them, and afterwards he occasionally saw and heard his member, though some never did enjoy this privilege.[12]

This democracy did not bubble up from below but trickled down from on high to protect the status quo.[13] And the electors vindicated Gunther's judgment by picking candidates likely to support the Administration (see Appendix). Nine Australians and the missionary Percy Chatterton won reserved seats, and six other Australians won open seats. Seven of the Australians were *kiaps*, including John Pasquarelli, who also traded in artefacts.[14]

The 38 Papua New Guineans outnumbered the 26 expatriates. Mission networks helped: 14 winners professed to be Catholic and 12 Lutheran. (Only Pasquarelli ever criticised the missions, and he was not re-elected.) Nineteen members had never been to school (18 were Highlanders) and only four had studied beyond primary school. Perhaps 20 were illiterate and only 11 were fluent in English. Most were comfortable in Tok Pisin, but Handabe Tiaba — a Southern Highland fight-leader — shared no language with any other member: after double translation, an official summarised proceedings for him.[15] Koitago Mano from Ialibu had not realised that Port Moresby was on the same island as the rest of the country. Few members had any idea of the structure of the Government, or how an assembly might affect it.

A seminar introduced members to Westminster procedures — naturally, no attempt was made to modify arcane precedents. The language of business was English so, despite interpreters, 'there was a totally inadequate exchange of ideas'. Johnson suspected that some officers tolerated this mystification because it reinforced their control.

When the Assembly met, bizarre precedents were set:

> Proceedings commenced with the Speaker … reading a total of 18 messages from the Administrator, informing the House that he had assented to 19 ordinances, and had reserved 7 ordinances for the Governor-General's pleasure, that the Governor-General had assented to 10 ordinances and had not disallowed a further 32 ordinances [of the old Legislative Council]. Minutes later, an Official Member (Secretary for Law), speaking in English and using legal and parliamentary jargon, introduced the Explosives Bill 1964 [which] passed all stages (including insertion of an official amendment in committee) in less than ten minutes. In a sense the tone was set, and it altered relatively little during the ensuing four years.[16]

The introductory seminar allowed leaders to emerge — within limits. J. K. McCarthy had spent his adult life in New Guinea, and he spoke well and wittily in Tok Pisin. The elected members wanted him as Speaker and he was keen to serve; but, as he was an official, the Administrator could (and did) veto that choice and the post fell to Horrie Niall, formerly DC of Morobe. The seminar also selected indigenous undersecretaries to explain government business to other elected members. Although officials briefed them each morning on the day's business, they were merely decorative. Simogun Pita — policeman and war hero — complained that 'the Government has made me an Undersecretary but I do not know what I am supposed to do and my Department has not shown me'. Most were puzzled and so were the heads of the departments to which they were attached, since undersecretaries had no formal powers. Even for garnering support, the device was clumsy. In total, undersecretaries cast 289 votes for administration motions but 123 against. Paul Lapun was interested only in Bougainville and voted more often against (28) than for (20) the Administration. Like Lapun, Nicholas Brokam was seldom seen in his department. Lepani Watson was often absent and voted often against the Administration, whereas Robert Tabua was seldom absent and rarely opposed the Administration.

In 1966, Johnson succeeded Gunther as manager of government business. Calmer than Gunther, he had a more detached manner and he was a perceptive observer of the House and its ill-assorted members. He recognised and tried to address the frustrations of the undersecretaries. He shifted Matthias ToLiman, the teacher, to Education, Sinake Giregire, the coffee grower to Agriculture and Lepani Watson, the Cooperatives Officer, to Trade. The benefits of this reshuffle were few and undersecretaries' initiatives rare: Giregire did carry a bill to ban playing cards, but Tabua failed in an attempt to control crocodile hunting.

The House met in a modest building in downtown Port Moresby. Some meetings lasted a week; a fortnight (the budget session of 1967) was the longest. Members were paid and undersecretaries received a bonus. Most expatriates stayed at a hotel, while most Papua New Guineans stayed with *wantoks* (kin) — one lodged with the Johnsons' servant. Eventually, John Guise's and Lepani Watson's houses became 'political salons', but the salons were isolated from the electors. The exception — Tony Voutas — shows why. Voutas was unusual, not least in having a degree in Political Science before he became a *kiap*. As a candidate in a 1966 by-election, he ran 'a long, arduous, novel and sophisticated campaign in his mountainous electorate' and created a network with a representative in each of 250 villages. He could not reform the House, but he held regular electorate meetings.[17] No other member followed his exhausting example.

Political reality bore little relation to the law. The only formal curbs on law-makers were the assent of the Administrator or the Governor-General, and a ban on introducing money bills. More effectual was Canberra's provision of two-thirds of the budget. Official members were not allowed to vote or speak independently[18] and few others had the confidence to try. But there were flickers of mutiny. In the life of the old Legislative Council, only six of 856 bills had been introduced by private members (and four passed). In the first 12 meetings of the new House, 40 of the 252 bills were introduced by private members, who also circulated draft bills to provoke the Administration to introduce its own.[19]

Gunther's control was helped by divisions among elected members. He sat at one end of the horseshoe of seats. Directly opposite sat Ian Downs, the irascible former DC. Johnson mused that a forum including the very articulate Downs, Stuntz, Gunther and McCarthy 'provided limited opportunity for self-expression by others'. In any case several members merely brought forward their electors' requests. The rowdiest member was Peter Lus from the Sepik; the most mystical was Koriam Urekit from East New Britain who showed his electors a large iron key, 'explaining that it was the key to the House of Assembly, which could not begin work until he got there'. Tei Abal, a medical orderly from Enga, and the teacher Matthias ToLiman, from East New Britain, did use the House as a springboard for national leadership, both on the conservative wing of opinion.

During the second meeting, an elected members' group formed around Guise (who resigned as undersecretary) and ToLiman, but the group imploded. Johnson surmised that expatriates were ambivalent about indigenous leaders, that they jostled for the role of power-behind-the-throne, and that most indigenous members had only parochial interests.

These manoeuvres revealed Guise as the likeliest popular leader. As a police sergeant major, he had represented the Territory at the Queen's coronation, and he had the ambivalent advantage of mixed-race status. He was older and more fluent in English than most others. 'By virtue of experience, ability, personality and political nous he was the outstanding indigenous member,' thought Johnson. 'He spoke, wrote and read English well and was fluent in Pidgin and Motu.' He seemed more calculating than passionate, and he channelled his great political ambitions into another Select Committee on Constitutional Development, chaired by himself, with Brokam, Giregire, Pita, Downs, William Bloomfield and John Stuntz (elected members), and Gunther, W. W. Watkins and Johnson (officials). They then coopted Lapun, Abal, Wegra Kenu and Dirona Abe. The young West Australian Fred Chaney was secretary.

Alas, its modest outcomes created no role for him (Chapter 4) and the docile House fulfilled the role scripted by Hasluck, providing cover for paternalism. When the UN Decolonisation Committee advocated target dates for self-government, ToLiman moved that only Papua New Guineans should determine the timing. All 22 indigenous speakers supported him. The same alliance supported Abal's Development Capital Guarantee Declaration to protect overseas investment.

Gunther and Johnson made the House toe the line, but the official members paid a high price in frustration. Johnson recalls that:

> we were too often faced with policies originating in Canberra and about which we had not had opportunities to advise our views. Further we were conceded little room for manoeuvre in gaining acceptance of these policies.

He told Warwick Smith — the Secretary of the Department — that officials must be able to compromise within broad policy, but

> *the policy ... of insisting that we adhere closely to their rigid interpretation of policy, required us to devote so much of our energies to getting approved legislation through the House unchanged that we had little time for the more important task of educating and involving members in the democratic process.*

To secure the votes, Johnson had to rely on dubious tactics. He would pass business on the first day of a sitting, before elected members could form another view. Later in the week, and especially at night, a quorum melted away. So well did he play these games that only one bill was vetoed and one other returned for a technical amendment.

Barnes and Warwick Smith

An elected House implied devolution, but Canberra's control tightened, partly through better communications but largely because of changes in personnel. The Hasluck era ended in 1963 when Sir Paul was promoted to Defence. Territories fell to the lean, taciturn and courtly Charles Barnes, a Country Party backbencher from Queensland.[20] It is not clear why the Country Party wanted this portfolio: possibly to prevent the Territory from undercutting Australian farmers.[21] Barnes had prospected for gold and flown planes on Cape York before he settled down to breed horses. Now in his sixties, he had sat in Parliament for five quiet years and he was amazed by his elevation. His party leader, 'Black Jack' McEwen, explained,

> 'I couldn't put one of my younger men there. I know you are not ambitious (self-seeking) and you can never win in this portfolio' ... The expression, 'no-win situation' became more and more obvious during the next eight years.[22]

This was the only office Barnes ever held. A subordinate described him as kind and honourable, loyal to God, Queen and Country — and inarticulate. Another resented the time needed to protect Barnes from questions in Parliament, and all were nervous when he spoke in public.[23] In 1965, for example, he read a prepared address quoting the Derham Report: 'At the present time to speak of self-government is unreal. There is no *self* to govern or to be governed.' During Question Time he strayed beyond his brief, implying that self-government might be 20 years away, that most people did not want it, and that the UN Trusteeship Council was half-hearted.[24] While none of this was untrue, it was all impolitic.

Barnes had no interest in policy, so McEwen advised him to appoint George Warwick Smith as Departmental Secretary. In his 40s, Warwick Smith was hard-driving and hard-nosed. He operated in this structure:

> Secretary (George Warwick Smith)
> No Deputy Secretary (unlike most departments)
> Three First Assistant Secretaries each heading a Division
> Three or Four Sections per Division, each headed by a Director.

Senior officers — all men — thought well of themselves. Their later careers justify this estimate but at the time they often seemed bumptious.[25] Warwick Smith often left posts empty until the ideal candidate appeared, which intensified pressure on his staff. He drove people so hard that some broke, but, his subordinates conceded, he was 'an excellent policy-man'.[26] That was just as well: he assumed Hasluck's policy-making mantle. His style fostered rivalries, as Patrick Galvin noticed when he joined Territories in 1967 as Section Head in International Relations, having met Warwick Smith's criterion that he was under 40. Two of the First Assistant Secretaries were the Englishman John Ballard and the Dunera Boy Gerry Gutman. In the next few years, Gutman was outmanoeuvred by his junior, Tim Besley, who was 'highly skilled in picking up other people's ideas'. The intellectual Gutman was clumsy in office politics and quit when it became clear (through an acting appointment) that Besley had overtaken him.[27]

Warwick Smith was detested throughout Konedobu. He argued that the Minister was responsible to Parliament for every action taken in his name, and it was the Secretary's task to protect this authority from usurpers. While he might have delegated power to elected Territory leaders, he flatly refused to pass responsibility from an elected minister in Canberra to non-elected officials in Konedobu. An admiring subordinate conceded that 'that relationship was … especially irksome … at the Port Moresby end because there seemed to be this brake always in Canberra'.[28] His obituary concedes that his 'proclivity to intervene in day-to-day matters … was the source of much irritation and frustration within the administration and the Territory'.[29]

So the style changed but in most respects policy continued. Minister and Secretary were of one mind — the Secretary's — that political change 'could not be divorced from economic development', which was a 'long hard road'.[30] Warwick Smith was pleased to find Papua New Guineans as conservative as himself. Reporting a meeting with another of the political education tours initiated in 1962 (Chapter 2), he told the Administrator:

> No Member suggested any further political advance and many reiterated the view that they wanted no more political changes until economic and social development had caught up with the present political situation. Several members were critical of [the moderate nationalist group] Pangu and one … said he thought that the initiative

for this party had come from Australia … Their general attitude was one of considerable conservatism as concerned political advance and there was no little touch of doubt whether the Territory … was not being pushed along at too fast a rate.[31]

This might have been what rural dignitaries thought, but it perfectly describes Warwick Smith's own views.

Barnes's visits to the Territory were brief, but Warwick Smith kept control and ensured that the Administration did not think beyond today, and telex allowed ever-closer oversight. Officers in Konedobu, and even District Officers, were losing their autonomy. Tight control provoked challenge. Gunther had expected to become Secretary of the Department if Hasluck had remained minister. In the new dispensation

> he thought with some justice that his judgement of both the desirable and the possible was at least as good as that of officers in Canberra. He rejected in his forthright way the detailed oversight to which we were all subjected. He stalked out of a meeting between the official members of the [Select] Committee and Warwick Smith in Port Moresby, and shortly afterwards resigned from the Administration altogether …[32]

His colleagues remained but they shared his indignation:

> We felt irritation at the close surveillance of our parliamentary activities but by and large we did not disagree too much with the thrust of established policy except as it may have restricted the activities of our individual departments.[33]

When Sir Donald Cleland retired as Administrator in 1966, Barnes plucked David Hay from Foreign Affairs to succeed him. Warwick Smith spelt out Hay's tasks so precisely that there could be no doubt about Canberra's control. Hay's job was:

> to maintain law and order; to contribute his suggestions and advice towards the formulation of policies … and to carry out these policies in such a way, and in harmony with the Government's long-term objectives in relation to the Territory, that the process of change is a smooth one and that a program of balanced development can be progressively achieved without divisive effects.[34]

At 50, Hay had enjoyed a fine career in peace and war. Courteous, courtly and conservative, he favoured gradual change. His devotion to order made him prefer officers who were loyal rather than innovative. His inaugural address in 1967 confirmed Australia's promise 'to support PNG so long as that is what they want'. He restated the standard pledge 'to defend PNG as if it were part of the Australian mainland'. He explained Australia's commitment to fund economic and social development; and spoke of gradual moves towards self-government. He wanted 'to create something new without first having to destroy existing institutions. This means that the movement can proceed at a pace you want and in an atmosphere of calm.'[35]

And he was determined to bring departmental heads to heel.

> In the early days you had pirates like Gunther ... who had been inclined to take no notice of the Canberra instructions, but in my day I took the view that as senior officers you just had to do what you were told.

The demotion of Gunther from minister's favourite to administrator's bête noire is a measure of the new control. To head the Administrator's department, Hay defied advice by appointing the tough-minded DC Tom Ellis rather than the independent-minded David Fenbury. Equally, he was irritated by the Public Solicitor's Office and its head, Peter Lalor, who 'acted as a kind of legal adviser to the opposition to the government'.

But Hay chafed under many restraints. As in Australia, the Public Service Commission enjoyed statutory power over appointments. The Territory Commissioner, Gerry Unkles, applied rules strictly, reported to the Minister and to the Commission in Canberra, and tried to avoid Hay. The same paralysis was produced by rules of financial delegation, which meant that every proposal was costed first in Port Moresby, and again in Canberra.

In Konedobu, potential policy-making centres emerged. One was the Central Policy and Planning Committee. Hasluck strangled it at once: that committee 'is quite inappropriate as an embryo Cabinet: ... members have a totally wrong conception of its function if they have views entertaining the idea for a moment'. If decisions were to be made locally, they were the province of an Interdepartmental Coordinating Committee in which the Administrator, his assistants and heads of departments met only once a month. The Administrator's Council could conceivably devise policy, especially after 1968 when elected members of the House were added. However, a majority of elected members on the Council

> was meaningless unless their advice was sought and heeded on a much wider range of issues than in the past. Also, despite the fact that all Councillors were Members of the House of Assembly, there was no other relationship between the Administrator's Council and the House.

Coordination might also have been possible through financial oversight. After the World Bank report, Alan McCasker was seconded from the Australian Treasury as Economic Adviser in 1965. A bluff, seasoned and professional analyst of great ability but little political flair, he was imprisoned in a subordinate role that made minimal use of his talents.[36]

Policy shifts were less dramatic than changes in personnel and management style. The most marked was a new emphasis on economic development. In Downs's analysis, the new era differed from the old in its commitment to economic development to reduce dependence on Australia. The blueprint was the World Bank report which emphasised:

overseas investment and continued European participation in development strategies. Political gradualism was seen by the Minister as a necessary restraint to encourage investment from overseas and gain time for a measure of economic independence to be achieved.[37]

This strategy provoked hot debate,[38] and it deepened the authoritarianism of relations between Canberra and Konedobu, and between Konedobu and the *kiaps*.

The Paternalistic State

Based on *kiaps* and patrols, the Administration was essentially rural. Officials were comfortable with 'native leaders' but suspicious of 'educated natives'. When the Hahalis Welfare Society (Chapter 1) tried to act independently, for example, they were briskly brought to book. Their methods scandalised missionaries and *kiaps*; but it was their independence of mind that really affronted Church and State.[39]

This climate inhibited the emergence of tertiary study. In Hasluck's view, education (like democracy) must grow from the bottom up. Primary education must be widely spread before secondary education, and tertiary training must await widespread secondary schooling. But he did appoint a committee to consider tertiary education and it did recommend a university. Two members of the committee died in 1962, and no action eventuated until the Foot Committee revived the issue. In response, the Currie Commission (comprising George Currie, Gunther and Oskar Spate) was launched in March 1963, and proposed a university and a technical institute.[40] The need was urgent as there were only three Papua New Guinean graduates (Henry ToRobert, John Natera and Joseph Aoae), and yet the report 'shuffled around Canberra for almost a year until pressures on the Department and the Minister finally elicited authority for us to proceed'.[41]

As late as 1966 therefore, the Territory's only higher education was provided by the Catholic Holy Spirit Regional Seminary in Madang. When seminarians launched a journal, *Dialogue*, officials bridled. The DC read the second issue with anxiety. He was annoyed that the first issue was welcomed by Spate at the ANU, Gunther as Vice-Chancellor-designate of the University of Papua New Guinea, and two bishops. This material, the DC warned Cleland, 'merits the immediate attention of the Internal Security Authorities'. Cleland, who agreed, assumed that the editorial and an article on Bougainville must have been ghost-written, probably by Father Wally Fingleton. They 'come close to inciting subversion. They are probably the most inflammatory items on Administration/indigenous relationships yet published by a non-Communist organisation', although it was rumoured that another Catholic publication might be 'even more strident'.[42]

The editorial was signed by Leo Hannett. His later career allows no doubt that he wrote his own material. His essay was a critique of administration paternalism, and especially the recent mining legislation. Citing impeccably non-socialist sources (Winston Churchill, Pope John XXIII and President Kennedy), he urged the House to protect the people's rights. After Daniel Tsibim's article on Bougainville, John Momis argued that theology should be taught at the University of Papua New Guinea, Michael

Lugabai considered the moral effects of urbanisation, Michael Aike wondered if the Church could insist on celibacy, Ignatius Kilage sought ways to graft baptism onto ancestral rites, Leo Mek pondered the outcome of the impending election, and Theodore Miriung asked if Papuans and New Guineans possessed a sense of gratitude.

Dialogue published a high proportion of the country's intelligentsia.[43] To the DC and Administrator, however, already in dispute with the Church, their articles were indefensible:

> following on the astonishingly frank attack mounted by Bishop Lemay of Bougainville against the mining legislation, [they] may indicate the commencement of a new phase in Administration/Catholic Mission relationships.

Distrust of 'educated natives' is even clearer in Barnes's reaction when he inaugurated Tos Barnett's course for Native Magistrates at the Administrative College. He had not been briefed on the nature of the course, and arrived to find a moot in progress, with roles played by Papua New Guineans — the accused and the police, of course, but also the prosecutor and the magistrate. Barnes turned to Barnett in shock and whispered, 'But they're all natives!'[44]

Suspicion of higher education was widespread. In 1970, the University of Papua New Guinea's Waigani Seminar assembled a lively collection of politicians, economists, political scientists, anthropologists and public servants.

> With unbelievable obtuseness the Administration discouraged public servants from attending the seminar and in one or two cases actively forbade them to do so ... The seminar ended with a paper presented by George Warwick Smith ... The lifeless delivery and content of the paper itself and the low-keyed and soporific filibuster which followed ... dramatically illustrated the great gap between the lively potential of this country and the prosaic ... approach of Canberra and Konedobu.[45]

An issue that excited educated Papua New Guineans was the regulation of mining. Since public debate was discouraged, the main forum was the House of Assembly. Even here debate was limited, as officials were never allowed to deviate from positions laid down in Canberra. When prospectors of Conzinc Riotinto (CRA) found payable copper ores, the House had to pass legislation (drafted in Canberra) to regulate the large-scale enterprises that had evolved in recent years. There was resistance by direct landowners and unease among many others when the Crown insisted that it owned all sub-surface ores. Bougainville's member, Paul Lapun, proposed to divert 20 per cent of royalties to landowners. When other members failed to support him, he scaled down his proposal to 5 per cent. He still lost the vote by 22 to 30.

Lapun's intervention provoked 'a sharp difference of opinion' between Canberra and Konedobu on the (correct) assumption that Lapun would return to the charge when the House met again. The department wanted to invoke Standing Orders to prevent the revival of an issue so soon after it had been settled, whereas the Administration thought it only fair to ventilate the issue. In the reprise, Lapun won by 31 to 21 and the Administration had to dissuade the department from disallowing the amendment.

But this was a sideshow. Real negotiations were conducted entirely between the company and the department, and the agreement was enacted by the House pro forma.[46] *Kiaps* did discuss the project with villagers but, as James Griffin put it:

> The people were not *consulted* as to whether they wanted the mine or not; but at least after a time it was *explained* to them what was involved ... As [DC Ashton] said to this writer: 'Explain to them! Why we've explained it to them till we're blue in the face.'[47]

The closest that Papua New Guineans came to negotiating was in an ad hoc meeting in Canberra, when CRA sponsored a fact-finding tour by five Bougainvilleans. They had two hours of talks with department officials who had been debating what (if any) benefit should go to landowners. The officials took the opportunity to test opinion.[48] The Bougainvilleans made three points: the Administration should increase its development funding in Bougainville; landowners should receive some share of royalties; and developers 'should allocate a proportion of their profits to a local development fund ... A figure of 25% of profits was mentioned'. The minute-taker noted that:

> 1 A promise has been given in general terms.
> 2 There is no legal obligation for payments to the indigenous people ...
> 3 A case can be made for an ex gratia or extra legal payment ... for what amount to political reasons but it would be preferable for the provision to be made through the normal programme of public works ...
>
> If a Special Development Fund were considered, payment could take the form of:
> a contribution ... from the royalties ...
> a payment from the mining company ... is not considered impractical if the amount is not too large, e.g. £10,000 per annum or up to 2% of profits ...
> a payment of royalties or profits to individual landowners. This ... would create an undesirable precedent.
> additional Administration funds ...

Later, the minute-taker was more circumspect, pointing out that

> the views expressed by departmental officers were sympathetic and the delegation ... seems to have assumed, of course quite wrongly, that this sympathetic view was tantamount to a promise that [their] proposals would be accepted.[49]

So the delegation believed that its claim had been accepted, until Barnes declared — in Kieta — that all benefits should flow to 'Papua New Guinea as a whole'.

In the House, expatriates were harder to control than Papua New Guineans. It was Downs, not Guise, who led a campaign to reshape the budget. It was the ex-*kiap* Barry

Holloway who proposed ministerial government — in the Parliamentary Executive (Interim Provisions) Bill 1965. In the last session (1967), Voutas, another ex-*kiap*, tried to mandate equal pay for women. Guise was much less radical. He proposed to merge church and state schools. Johnson noted that this measure would benefit mission schools, so it was supported by members who 'had an eye on the Church's influence on the minds of voters'.

But the first dispute to overturn Canberra policy was squarely a concern of Papua New Guineans. In almost all respects — labour relations, court procedures, parliamentary practice, access to alcohol, clothes and books and mineral rights — the Territory was being made to conform with Federal Australia (see Chapter 5). The exception was the wage structure. Papua New Guinea's bureaucrats were deployed in the three Australian Public Service grades, with a Territory supplement: Division One for departmental heads; Division Two required a High School Leaving Certificate; Division Three required a trade certificate. In a rare recognition of local circumstances, a Fourth Division (Auxiliary) was added 'for Papua New Guineans who did not have appropriate qualifications to enter the high ranks'.[50] By 1962, 30 Papua New Guineans were in Division Two. In the long run, an indigenous public service might be paid slightly more than their counterparts in Australia. To avert this outcome, Hasluck resolved to create a Territory public service, with salaries geared to the local economy, and expatriates shifted into an auxiliary division. The bill was passed on the last day of the Legislative Council, while officials held a majority. The new salary scale was not specified.

When the local salary scale was finally published in September 1964, Teachers' College students rallied behind Ebia Olewale, President of the Students' Council, who had been briefed by his Australian lecturers. The students readily agreed to 'go down to Konedobu to talk to the Administrator and the Education Department'. However, the protest was limited:

> I asked students from other colleges, like Admin College, where Michael Somare and Albert Maori Kiki were, from Posts and Telegraphs and from PNG Medical College to come along with us but they retracted because they were already public servants and they were being paid, and they would be sacked if they marched with us …
>
> So we marched on Konedobu … Dr Gunther met us … and the Director of Education came, and they assured me that yes, they were going to review our case …

When the Tertiary Students' Federation resolved that Olewale visit all the colleges in the Territory, he turned again to Gunther: 'Dr Gunther must have discussed it with Sir Donald Cleland, they gave me a ticket and accommodation warrants.'[51]

Having internalised the principle of equal pay for equal work, public servants and students faced not only a denial of that principle but a drastic pay cut. When the matter came to the House, 24 elected members spoke. All accepted the need for a salary scale geared to the economy, but all objected to the figures proposed. Downs proposed some local control over the Public Service Commission. The department was shocked, and the official members resisted the push, but the motion was carried the same day, with no elected member opposing it.

Villagers still ignored the House but public servants — Australian as well as Papua New Guinean — saw that they could make it their forum. Although Canberra continued to treat the House merely as an instrument for carrying out orders, this coup hinted that it might become a rival centre of power.

Appendix: The First House of Assembly

Open

John Pasquarelli (Australian)	Angoram
Paul Lapun	Bougainville (Undersecretary, Forests)
Waiye Siune	Chimbu
Uauwi Wauwe	Chuave
Pita Lus	Dreikikir
Koriam Michael Urekit	East New Britain
Lepani Watson	Esa'ala Losuia
Zure Zurecnuoc	Finschhafen (Undersecretary, Treasury)
Robert Tabua	Fly River (Undersecretary, Public Works)
Sinake Giregire	Goroka (Undersecretary, Assistant Administrator, Services)
Keith Tetley (Australian)	Gulf
Graham Pople (Australian)	Gumine
Keith Levy (Australian)	Hagen
Ugi Biritu	Henganofi
Koitaga Mano	Ialibu
Barry Holloway (Australian)	Kainantu
William Bloomfield (Australian)	Kaindi (died, succeeded by Tony Voutas)
Siwi Kurondo	Kerowagi
Tambu Melo	Kutubu
Singin Pasom	Lae
Poio Iuri	Lagaip
Ehava Karava	Lakekamu
Makain Mo	Lumi
Suguman Matibri	Madang
Paliau Maloat	Manus
Pita Tamindei	Maprik
Gaudi Mirau	Markham
Momei Pangial	Mendi
John Guise*	Milne Bay (Undersecretary, DIES)
Kaibelt Diria	Minj
Eriko Rarupu	Moresby
Nicholas Brokam*	New Ireland (Undersecretary, Assistant Administrator, Economic)
Muriso Warebu	Okapa
Edric Eupu	Popondetta (Undersecretary, Lands)
Matthias ToLiman	Rabaul (Undersecretary, Administrator's Department)
Stoi Umut	Rai Coast
Meanggarum James	Bamu

Dirona Abe   Rigo-Abau (Undersecretary, Public Health)
Handabe Tiaba   Tari
Wegra Kenu   Upper Sepik
Tei Abal   Wabag
Leine Iangalo   Wapenamanda
Paul Manlel   West New Britain
Simogen Pita*   Wewak-Aitape (Under Secretary, Police)

Special Electorates
Percy Chatterton   Central
John Stuntz*   ex-*Kiap*   East Papua
Ian Downs*   ex-*Kiap*   Highlands
Frank Martin   Madang-Sepik
Oriel Ashton   New Britain
William Grove   New Guinea
Horace Niall*   ex-*Kiap*   North Markham
Graham Gilmore   South Markham
Donald Barrett*   West Gazelle
Ronald Neville   West Papua

Officials
1964   November 1967
John Gunther, Assistant Administrator (Services)   -   Leslie Johnson
Harold Reeve, Assistant Administrator (Economic)   -   Frank Henderson
W. W. Watkins (Law)   -   Watkins
A. P. J. Newman (Treasurer)   -   Newman
W. F. Carter (Posts & Telegraphs)   -   Carter
Frank Henderson (Agriculture, Stock & Fish)   -   William Conroy
J. K. McCarthy (Native Affairs)   -   Tom Ellis
Leslie Johnson (Education)   -   Roy Scragg (Health)
Noel Mason (Labour)

* formerly a member of the Legislative Council

Administrator's Council
Gunther, Reeve and McCarthy; Guise, Brokam, ToLiman, Tabua, Zurecnuoc, Downs and Stuntz.

Source: Johnson, "Westminster in Moresby".

Footnotes
1. Bill Gammage, *The Sky Travellers: Journeys in New Guinea 1938–1939*, Melbourne, 1998; Sinclair Dinnen, *Law and Order in a Weak State: Crime and Politics in Papua New Guinea*, University of Hawai'i, 2001; August Kituai, *My Gun, My Brother*, Honolulu, University of Hawai'i, 1998.
2. Catherine Snowden, 'Cooperatives', in Denoon and Snowden (ed.), *A Time to Plant and a Time to Uproot*.
3. Ilinome Frank Tarua, in 'Hindsight'. See also Alice Wedega, *Listen My Country*, Sydney, 1981.
4. Alan Ward, 'Land Reform', in 'Hindsight'.
5. Leslie W. Johnson, 'Westminster in Moresby: Papua New Guinea's House of Assembly, 1964–1972', undated, annotated typescript in the possession of Christine Goode.
6. Ian Downs, *The Australian Trusteeship*, p. 217.
7. James Griffin, Hank Nelson and Stewart Firth, *Papua New Guinea: A Political History*, Melbourne 1979, chapter 11; and Johnson, "Westminster in Moresby".
8. Denoon with Dugan and Marshall, *Public Health in Papua New Guinea, 1884–1984: Medical Possibility and Political Constraint*
9. Ian Downs, *The Australian Trusteeship*, p. 237.
10. Hank Nelson, Personal Communication.
11. Johnson, 'Westminster in Moresby'.
12. Ian Maddocks, 'Udumu a-hagaia'.
13. Johnson, 'Westminster in Moresby'.
14. John Pasquarelli, *The Pauline Hansen Story by the man who knows*, New Holland, Frenchs Forest, NSW, 1998.
15. Mark Lynch, 'Communication and Cargo: some roles performed by Members of Papua New Guinea's House of Assembly, 1964–1972', MA thesis, Sussex University, 1972; Hank Nelson, 'Our Great Task', in *Meanjin*, Vol. 62 (3), 2003, pp. 123–35; Johnson, 'Westminster in Moresby'.
16. Lynch, 'Communication and Cargo', p. 41.
17. Ibid., and A. C. Voutas, 'Elections and Communications', in Marion Ward (ed.), *The Politics of Melanesia*, Waigani Seminar Papers, 1970.
18. Sir David Hay's memoirs, National Library of Australia Oral History Collection.
19. C. J. Lynch, 'A Description of Aspects of Political and Constitutional Development and Allied Topics', in B. J. Brown and G. Sawer (eds), *Fashion of Law in New Guinea*, Butterworths, Sydney, 1969. Lynch was the parliamentary draftsman. This was his presentation to the International Commission of Justice in Port Moresby in September 1965, updated to October 1968.
20. E. P. Wolfers, 'January–April 1967', in Moore and Kooymans, *A Papua New Guinea Political Chronicle 1967–1991*.
21. See comments by E. G. Whitlam and E. P. Wolfers in 'Hindsight'.
22. Loraine Nott, *CEB: exploits of an uncommon man*, Pioneer Press, Warwick, Qld, 1989, p. 62.
23. Interviews with Don Mentz and Sir Frank Espie.
24. A 452/1 62/1161, Barnes's address to the Melbourne Junior Chamber of Commerce, August 27, 1965, and correspondence with the Australian mission to the UN.
25. Interviews, Tim Besley and Don Mentz.
26. Interviews, Don Mentz, John Greenwell and Paul Kelloway.
27. Interview, Pat Galvin.
28. Pat Galvin, in 'Hindsight'.
29. John Farquharson, 'George Warwick Smith', *Sydney Morning Herald*, December 31, 1999.
30. House of Representatives, March 31, 1966, pp. 805-6; and May 2, 1968, pp. 1059; Downs, *The Australian Trusteeship*, pp. 368-76.
31. A 452/1 67/6847, Warwick Smith to Hay, undated (but 1967 or later).
32. Johnson, 'Westminster in Moresby'.
33. Ibid.
34. Downs, *The Australian Trusteeship*, p. 286.
35. This and the following quotes are from Sir David Hay's interviews, National Library of Australia, 1973.

36. Interviews, Ross Garnaut and John Langmore.
37. Downs, *The Australian Trusteeship*, p. xix.
38. R. G. Crocombe, 'That Five Year Plan', *New Guinea*, December 1968/January 1969; H. Arndt, R. Shand and E. K. Fisk, 'An Answer to Crocombe – I, II, III', *New Guinea*, June/July 1969; R. G. Crocombe, 'Crocombe to his critics', *New Guinea*, September/October 1969.
39. Max and Eleanor Rimoldi, *Hahalis and the Labour of Love*; Denoon, *Getting Under the Skin*.
40. The University of Papua New Guinea grew up in Port Moresby while the other institution went to Lae, where it eventually became the University of Technology.
41. Ian Howie-Willis, *A Thousand Graduates: conflict in university development in Papua New Guinea, 1961-1967*, Australian National University, 1980.
42. 66/5311, Administrator to Department, enclosing DC Hicks to Administrator, November 3, 1966, enclosing Vol. 1, section II of *Dialogue*.
43. John Momis was elected to the House in 1972 and has represented Bougainville ever since. Ignatius Kilage became an intellectual and Ombudsman. Theodore Miriung became a lawyer and led Bougainville's interim provincial administration when he was assassinated, probably by the PNG Defence Force.
44. Interview, Tos Barnett.
45. Robert Waddell, 'May-August 1970', in Moore and Kooymans, *A Papua New Guinea Political Chronicle 1967–1991*.
46. Denoon, Getting Under the Skin.
47. James Griffin, 'Bougainville', Australia's Neighbours, 68, 1970.
48. 66/458, Ahrens's note, dated September 30, 1965.
49. 66/458, Lattin's minute and draft response, February 10, 1966.
50. Johnson, 'Westminster in Moresby'.
51. Sir Ebia Olewale, in 'Hindsight'.

Chapter 4

Impasse

The Guise Select Committee

John Guise's Select Committee was scarcely more democratic than Gunther's. Not only did it contain three expatriate elected members of the House, but also three officials, one of whom (W. W. Watkins, the abrasive Law Officer) became deputy chair, while Fred Chaney was its secretary. Watkins argued for 'certain matters to be the subject of talks between the Commonwealth Government and the Committee'.[1] As members were keen to protect the Australian connection, they consulted Canberra on the following agenda before they consulted the people.

Matters for Discussion

1   In the event of the people deciding that they wish Papua and New Guinea to be one country, the following alternatives arise —
    a   that Papua becomes a Trust Territory [with] New Guinea and Papuans become Australian protected persons rather than Australian citizens; or
    b   that New Guinea become[s] an Australian Territory and New Guineans acquire Australian citizenship rather than a status of Australian protected persons; or
    c   that there be a Papuan and New Guinean citizenship.
[In any event] there would also be a desire to continue close association with Australia. The Commonwealth Government's view as to the extent of such an association is sought.

2   Could a statement be made on the application of Commonwealth migration provisions [in each of these cases].

3   Does the Commonwealth Government consider that a period of internal self-government is desirable … ?

4   [If so,] has the Commonwealth Government any views on [how … any such system should ensure that the best advice possible … is still available to the Administrator who remains responsible for the administration of the Territory

> and the carrying out of Commonwealth Government policy so long as Australia provides major financial assistance.
> 5 Has the Commonwealth Government any views as to whether there should be a form of Ministerial Government … or … some pattern akin to the American system …
> 6 In the event of the people attaining self-government …
>   a Would Australia be prepared to continue to provide major financial assistance … and under what conditions.
>   b What would be the nature of the links between Australia and the Territory at Government level.
> It is the desire of the Committee to assure the Commonwealth Government that the people of Papua and New Guinea will accept the principles of the Rule of Law …

This extravagant deference may be the product of Watkins' pen as much as the committee's wishes. Buried in the humble language, however, was an explosive question — could the Territory become Australia's seventh state? Certainly not! If the department had little interest in devolution, it was positively alarmed by integration. They stage-managed the meeting with private talks with officials beforehand, and they reinforced Barnes with high-powered colleagues. The committee therefore met Treasurer William McMahon, Attorney-General Bill Snedden and Minister for Immigration Hubert Opperman.[2]

Through Marjorie Crocombe, Guise knew of the 'free association' agreement between New Zealand and Cook Islands. Cook Islanders enjoyed partial independence and they could live and work in New Zealand.[3] Guise might have wanted a similar relationship with Australia, or even statehood, or he might have hoped only to clarify choices. In any event, Barnes and his colleagues scotched the idea. Such a breach of White Australia would — as J. D. B. Miller put it — prove political suicide for the party that proposed it.[4] Neither Papuan Australian citizens nor New Guinean Australian Protected Persons could be treated as 'constituent members of the Australian community'.

Barnes's sanitised report (the talks 'took place in an atmosphere of cordiality and frankness') repeated the formula that the Territory had the right to determine its own direction and pace. While the people could opt for independence, any continuing association with Australia 'would require the agreement of the Australian Government of the day'. But ambiguity persisted. The meeting agreed that Papua New Guineans could be asked

> whether they wanted constitutional development to take a course directed towards separation from Australia or … towards evolution of an association or relationship with Australia which will endure after self-determination …

And constitutional change was still shackled to economic development:

> Until the Territory has moved further forward economically and the people are able through the spread of education to understand better the issues involved, the Government was willing to see the Territory continue in its present relationship…

The meeting consented also to the continued exclusion of Papua New Guineans from the mainland. Although the White Australia Policy had been relaxed and 400 Papua New Guineans were now studying in Australian schools, skilled Papua New Guineans should live and work in their own land.[5]

But even now Barnes dreamed of a seventh state, asserting that 'possible further forms of association' should not be ruled out. For his own reasons, Guise ran a similar line, 'complaining that Federal Ministers had been vague about the possibility of Papua and New Guinea becoming a seventh State'.[6] This was hot air. Barnes agreed to nothing except to increase the membership of the House, and to extend the powers of undersecretaries.

This reform was modest — but so were the committee's ambitions, as is clear from the narrow questions they put to the people:[7]

1 Do the people consider that the present composition of the House meets the needs of the Territory … ?
2 … are there enough electorates or too many or too few?
3 Should there be more rigid qualifications for candidates, eg., ability to read and write English or Pidgin or Motu, specified standard of education, etc.?
4 Do you think it is necessary we should still have Special Electorates?
5 Should all positions in the House … be open to all persons regardless of race … ?
6 Should there be official members in the House … ?
7 These are the important questions but have you any other views on other matters … ?

Most of the people were content with this agenda, but there were other views. The boldest, over the signatures of 10 to 13 men, proposed a non-racial democracy exercising real autonomy. They sought immediate but limited responsible government, in which elected members of the House would form a Cabinet and exercise authority 'in all domestic affairs'. A Public Service Board would replace the Public Service Commission, to foster local officers who lacked 'rigid academic qualifications'. The Administrator would be replaced by an Australian High Commissioner and an indigenous deputy.

The department harrumphed that 'the statement is "anti-colonial" in tone and appears to be the work of Cecil Abel'.[8] In a sense they were right. The only people with the vision and drafting skills to compose such proposals were public servants and students. Cecil Abel, son of the missionary Charles Abel and inheritor of Kwato Mission, was teaching at the Administrative College where he met the (now-legendary) Bully Beef Club — a discussion group of trainees. Despite their national vision, they described themselves in regional terms:

Albert Maori Kiki	Gulf	Mike Somare	Wewak
Oala Rarua	Port Moresby	Elliott Elijah	Trobriands
Sinaka Goava	Hanuabada	Cecil Abel	Milne Bay
Kamona Waro	Hula	Karl Nombri	Chimbu
Ebia Olewale	Daru	Ilomo Batton	Sepik
Gerai Asiba	Daru	Reuben Taureka	Marshall Lagoon
Pen Anakapu	Suau		

The Political Scientist Ted Wolfers noted that Abel was the only Australian, Nombri the only Highlander, and only three (Somare, Batton and Nombri) were New Guineans.[9] Hay was quick to point out that they were 'in no sense leaders and represent their own views and possibly those of a section of the Tertiary student population'.[10] The irascible Watkins was blunter: these 'impertinent' men showed 'absolute disregard for what has been done in the Territory'.[11] But they were not alone in their disgraceful ingratitude: two former *kiaps* in the House — Voutas and Holloway — made similar submissions. Their ideas were also ignored.

The contrasts between the Gunther and the Guise Committees are instructive. Supported by the Minister, Gunther secured large changes without public support. Guise enjoyed access to all parties, but not their trust.[12] Johnson summed him up like this:

> Guise was never prepared to put his [mixed-race] status at risk to grasp at the prize. Had he unequivocally put himself in the van of those demanding early self-government he would have been far in front of all possible rivals, but he equivocated and was passed by others who had less to lose by a radical stance.[13]

The planter and politician Tom Leahy admired Guise's intelligence and his vision but he 'was never really sure what road he would be on or who he should follow. He could never make up his mind whether he was native or white.'[14] Guise's ambivalence was a strength as he balanced the views of Australian officials, expatriates, worried Papua New Guineans and public service cadets. But balance sounded like equivocation, and ruled out a bold scenario such as that of the '13 angry men' — or the two excited ex-*kiaps*.

Nor did the committee misrepresent the public. Hay's analysis of public meetings describes the narrow range of debate. Attendance was good and interest evident. Few men spoke, and no women. Apart from a few young educated men, most speakers claimed to be formulating community views, and these were conservative.

> Most expressed a wish for some further constitutional progress but within strict limits. There was no criticism at all of existing arrangements ... The young men ... had more radical views but there was nothing very extreme. There was not a good knowledge of the existing arrangements nor of the powers of the present House ...
>
> The name Under-Secretary was not popular. The word Minister was commonly suggested though this did not imply Ministerial status in the Australian sense ...
>
> There was widespread criticism of the failure of Under-Secretaries to combine successfully their representative duties with their Ministerial responsibilities ...
>
> No-one knew much about the function of the Administrator's Council ... [15]

Not only did the department manage the House: it managed its attempts to reform itself. Warwick Smith reminded Cabinet that Territory opinion should determine the pace of change, and that the best test of opinion was the Select Committee itself and the House. Their credibility would suffer 'if the Government appeared to have influenced the Select Committee to the exclusion of the Territory people'.

> On the other hand it would be advantageous if the recommendations made by the Select Committee were of such a nature that the Government could accept these without embarrassment. [If Cabinet were to articulate its views] it might be possible for some influence to be exercised towards an acceptable result, for example, by 'floating' suggestions through the official members of the Select Committee or by informing the Select Committee of the Government's attitude …

To help Cabinet form a view, Warwick Smith drafted one:
- Although authority would be devolved, the Commonwealth would remain responsible and 'the Minister would retain the right to direct policy or to question any action'.
- Authority would *not* be devolved in relation to 'reserved' subjects, including internal security, external affairs, defence, constitutional advance, law and information.
- Constitutional change must be balanced by the need to preserve standards of administration.
- In view of the Territory's extreme economic dependence, 'the Commonwealth must determine the strategy of the Budget'.

Within those parameters, 'quasi-ministers' might exercise powers 'within defined limits for certain selected departments dealing with matters of immediate electoral concern such as Education, Health and Works'. There was a good case for abolishing the racial qualification for the 10 special electorates and relying instead on an educational qualification. There was also a case for enlarging the membership of the House and of the Administrator's Council.[16]

To keep the Select Committee on the rails, Warwick Smith required reports from official members, to an extent that Guise could not have guessed. This enabled him, for example, to defeat a plausible proposal that the House take control of revenue raised locally. By describing the effects (in his view, dire) of two budgets and divided authority, he repelled the reformists.[17] He could readily accept other ideas arising from community meetings: doubling the number of elected members, not requiring formal education in candidates, and scrapping the racial criterion for special electorates. So the Guise Committee achieved only the little advances scripted for it.

On these bases, the second House of Assembly was elected in 1968 and declined to exercise even the powers delegated to it. The House had a majority of elected members and even the Executive Council was dominated — numerically — by seven elected members sitting with the Administrator and three officials.[18] Either body could therefore have used its numbers to resist or deflect Australian policy, but no such rebellion occurred because most members were content to be appendices to the Administration. They had no mandate — nor had they asked for one — from an uninterested electorate. Instead, they had a mandate from Canberra.

The Second House of Assembly

The House was full of Papua New Guineans, but it was still an Australian legislature. It accepted, for example, that members should wear suits, so an enterprising outfitter imported a hundred. Many were too long in the sleeve and leg for owners who — especially after drinks — had trouble navigating. They accepted other precedents with the same docility. As before, members began with a week's seminar, when Guise surprised them by choosing to be Speaker. Newly elected Tom Leahy wondered how a Cabinet would operate. He found out in his role as interpreter for the Secretary to the Australian Cabinet, Sir John Bunting, who flew in to explain. 'By the time he finished we were in no doubt as to what a Cabinet was.' However, 'in that first Cabinet I don't think there was an English speaker'.[19]

Twenty-one of 54 members of the House were re-elected, and again some were ex-kiaps. Mission links were still valuable: 29 elected members were Catholic, 11 Anglican and six Lutheran, besides several other Protestants. Twenty-six had never been to school, but all now claimed to speak Tok Pisin, if not English. Most spoke only for their constituencies: even the Mataungan radical Oscar Tammur, the most fluent and voluble speaker in English and Tok Pisin, focused on the turbulent affairs of the Gazelle peninsula. A few expatriates had wider interests: the retired missionary Percy Chatterton made himself a human rights ombudsman.[20]

Party attachments fluctuated, but several Members were affiliated with the Papua And New Guinea Union (Pangu) which favoured early self-government. Pangu formed in June 1967 when the '13 angry men' won support from the radical ex-*kiaps* Holloway and Voutas and seven other members of the First House — Lapun, Lus, Brokam, James Meanggarum, Paliau Maloat, Wegra Kenu and Siwi Kurondo. Pangu's leader was 32-year-old Michael Somare, a generation younger than Guise and born at the opposite end of the Territory, in the Sepik District. Guise had been a policeman, Somare was the son of a policeman, and he won support from public servants, students and academics. But he had a rough ride in the House, where a majority

> was determined to put the Pangu Pati firmly in its place by rejecting that party's initiatives irrespective of their merit. It seemed too, that [many] white elected members ... were endeavouring to orchestrate their black colleagues to crush political initiatives that might accelerate any movement towards self-government.[21]

Downs had been a trenchant debater in the First House, but he did not recontest. A year later he complained to Hay that the Administration seemed to oppose every Pangu proposal. Hay denied this, but he conceded that several European members did oppose every Pangu proposal, and:

> Perhaps some of this rubbed off on to some Official Members. It was not, however, the Administration's policy ... I added that Pangu complicated the situation by reason of the fact that they regarded themselves as the opposition and behaved as such.[22]

Somare used his first speech as leader to position Pangu as a 'loyal opposition', but the exchange between Downs and Hay captures the increasing ill-temper of proceedings. In 1971, for instance, when *kiap* Jack Emanuel was murdered in East New Britain, several members denounced the Mataungans and hurled abuse at Tammur. And Pangu could give as good as it got. Somare once dismissed Tei Abal as a stooge, and dredged up the settlers' term of abuse, 'rock-ape'.[23]

In the second House, the preponderance of elected members was even greater than before; but they were no more likely than the first to assert themselves. The Select Committee wanted undersecretaries to be called ministers. The department compromised with 'Ministerial Members', but they were even more docile than the old undersecretaries. To get things going, five bills passed through all stages in half an hour.[24]

White members formed an Independent Group, comprising Lussick, Leahy, Buchanan, Watts, Neville, Fielding and Middleton, and drew in Abal and Giregire. They could often muster 50 votes and they helped (with Pangu) to polarise the House. Independent in name, they supported the Administration. The official members in the first House were 'always nervous' about the passage of the budget. To Johnson's relief:

> In the second House we could always count on majority support, for it was now Ministerial Members who presented their Departments' estimates and defended their deficiencies.[25]

In 1969, Voutas initiated a Select Committee on Parliamentary Procedures, which tabled 80 proposals to clarify members' confusion. Interpretation remained a problem, relieved partly by Highland *kiaps* appointed for the purpose, and by more officials speaking Tok Pisin. The most effective outcome of the Voutas Committee was standing committees, in which members could study bills before they came into the House. Still, most members floundered in Westminster traditions in parliamentary papers, procedures and speeches.

There were some heated exchanges. A Public Order Bill, provoked by Prime Minister Gorton's visit to Rabaul (see below), proposed some emergency powers. Academics protested but the House enacted the bill over the protests of Chatterton, Somare and Tammur. An issue that galvanised public servants was the Public Service Commission's rash attempt to rename the Administrative College. When Pangu moved to restore the old name, two ministerial members crossed the floor and five abstained, so Pangu's motion was carried.

More typical of the House, in 1969 a committee looked into education. ToLiman, as Ministerial Member for Education, endorsed its advice to merge mission and government schools into a national system. This was a popular proposal, yet Donatus Mola from North Bougainville denounced it as 'a Communist type policy', since 'the Missions are teaching only for spiritual needs while the Administration teaches only for material needs'. Mercifully, his objection was ignored, and six months later the legislation came to the House. When Mola's Bougainville colleague Lapun moved to protect the right of missions to maintain their own fees, ToLiman told him that the Catholic representative in Port Moresby had helped draft the legislation. It was, said Johnson, 'ToLiman's finest hour'. Perhaps it was: but it was brief. It is also the only clear case of a ministerial member shaping policy. As a school for parliamentary procedures, the House was inept. As a school for the government of an independent country, it was grotesque.

Nation-Building and the Sceptics

The best nation-building was done in real schools at a time of great expansion. Sir Alkan Tololo, the first national Director of Education, recalled that 'we helped to organise the competition to have a flag and surprisingly it was one of the girls from a school in the Gulf Province who designed our flag'. Equally important was the choice of English as the medium of instruction. 'We opted for English, a uniting factor: that is why we brought in the English-speaking teachers from Australia. Let's unite the country.'[26]

As Speaker at the opening of the House, Guise appealed for national unity; and the Governor-General asserted that 'national unity is essential'. (The prospects were bleak: the next weekend a riot followed a rugby league match between Papua and New Guinea.) Guise wanted the House to adopt a name, a flag and an anthem. Oddly, the Department chose 'to dissuade this premature effort to short-circuit the orderly process of decolonisation':

> There is a danger … if the adoption of common symbols is used by some people to force the pace of political development beyond what the majority of people wish to see it.[27]

But most resistance to national unity came from within.

The House was usually a spectator in separatist conflicts because so many members were local activists, ambivalent about national unity. One of the most critical debates was to endorse a management regime for the Panguna copper mine in Bougainville.[28] This would be an immense open-cut, larger than any in Australia. It would be hugely expensive, and investors wanted security, so Panguna needed specific legislation as well as the basic law discussed in Chapter 3. The lead company was Conzinc Riotinto Australia (CRA), the Australian branch of the London-based giant, Rio Tinto. The agreement had been negotiated between the department and the company and, although resisted by landowners, it was vital that the House not amend it. The Administration's problem was to maximise benefits for the whole Territory, whereas members of the House focused on the interests of their immediate constituents. Before the bill came to the House, therefore, Hay discussed it with his executive councillors, who 'showed great interest in the means of making the Agreement well known to other Members of the House'.[29]

The second-reading speech spelt out the benefits for the Territory. On benefits for Bougainville it was vague: after Lapun's amendment to the mining law, landowners would receive 5 per cent of royalties — but this meant only 5 per cent of 1.25 per cent of the value of the ore. More stress was placed on education, health, services and jobs. In reality, most skilled and semi-skilled work would be done by expatriates, and the company would import most of its supplies. Only slowly did members see what landowners grasped at once: the laws claimed the ores for the Crown. In gauging landowners' views, the officials ignored their elected representatives. The opinions of the *kiaps* and CRA's research persuaded Hay that the people would acquiesce, and the House bowed to the seemingly inevitable: the Mining (Bougainville Copper Agreement) Ordinance 1967 became law on November 30. *Kiaps* could now tell landowners that the deal had the approval of the people, through their elected assembly.

That was obtuse. Papua New Guinea was a remote abstraction and Bougainvilleans did not accept that the House represented them.[30] Secession began to be debated and Lapun, the meat in this terrible sandwich, read this resolution to the June 1969 session:

> We, the Nasioi and Rorovana people in general have been wronged by the Australian Administration's desire to force its will upon we people in the matter of resuming native held lands and the Arawa plantation … at no time has the Government given us cause to have confidence in it or caused us to trust it.

Lapun implored the officials: 'Do not take the people's rights away. Do not attack them when they freely express their political views on secession.' Joseph Lue (Bougainville regional) floated the popular but surprising view that self-government was divisible: 'These groups on the Gazelle Peninsula and in Bougainville want something now … Give them self-government tomorrow. All others shall receive self-government as they are ready.'[31]

More important than the debates in the House were events on the ground, when Rorovana and Arawa villagers organised passive resistance to surveyors, and provided great copy for Australian reporters. James Griffin recalled:

> [The *Sydney Sun*] carried on the front page a picture of a helmeted policeman with a truncheon lifting aside a bare-breasted woman … The *Sydney Daily Mirror* … referred to 'Bloody Thugs' and 'Australia's Bullies in New Guinea', and asked, 'Where the hell are we heading?' There was also a companion photograph of riot squad police wearing gas masks, carrying batons and looking very intimidating.[32]

The ABC reported that the story 'hit the Australian Press like a baton charge'.[33] Five morning papers led with it, and it made the front page of four others (but not the Hobart *Mercury*, more excited by a 'Rise in Devil Population in Tasmania'). The *Canberra Times* described the events as a disaster. When Barnes declared that force would to be used to maintain law and order, the Melbourne *Age* (August 7, 1969) sniped:

> If Mr Barnes had more tact, understanding and skill, The Age might suggest that he travel to the island and attempt to settle the dispute in talks with the Bougainvilleans. But his past performances suggest that he would be better advised to stay in Canberra.

Most severe was the *Australian*. On the morning of the first protest, it grieved: 'The ineptitude of the Administration … is a matter of the deepest concern.' Six days later, it complained that: 'Even now, incredibly, the implications of what is happening on Bougainville do not seem to have seeped through to the Australian Government.'

By comparison, public protests were lame. In Canberra, Leo Hannett addressed a meeting of 90 people, including Jim Davidson, the Professor of Pacific History at the ANU. Next day, 30 ANU students demonstrated. In Brisbane, the Revolutionary Socialist Students Alliance printed a fiery pamphlet by the Trobriand Island poet John Kasaipwalova,[34] but it was the media that disturbed the Minister. The Administrator denounced an ABC television program as 'a clever piece of propaganda aimed at undermining the Australian public's confidence in the Government and its Papua New Guinea policy'.[35] The Government was proceeding to acquire land that the landowners refused to yield, but they had lost control of the public relations agenda. As the head of the *kiaps*, Tom Ellis feared that enemies were massing under Paul Lapun, not to halt the mining operation but to attack the Administration and gain more compensation. 'There is only one prime target being attacked in Bougainville at the present moment by anyone and this is the Administration.'[36] And when the department reviewed its options, it recognised that a House of Assembly Committee would be counterproductive and might provoke secession.[37]

Bypassing the House, Lapun flew to Australia with another local leader, Raphael Bele, ostensibly to seek High Court intervention.[38] Papua New Guineans had always been escorted (Chapter 1), but these men travelled alone. In Melbourne, they met Sir Maurice Mawby of the mining company. CRA could count the costs of delay and the benefits of compromise, so they soon found common ground. When Lapun and Bele met Barnes and Prime Minister Gorton, they could offer an alternative to Barnes's strategy, and one that was acceptable to CRA. Gorton agreed at once and Barnes had to announce his own backdown: the Government would welcome negotiations with the people, CRA and the local company, Bougainville Copper Limited (BCL), would negotiate directly with landowners, and discussion could range widely. Gorton insisted that CRA not only negotiate but be *seen* to do so.[39] So agreement was reached *despite* the House. Highlanders thought the Administration was 'pussyfooting' around protestors. Pangu's Voutas and Somare wanted the mine as revenue for the nation. From 1967 until production began in 1972, therefore, the House was split.

During his campaign to reconcile people to this development, Hay preached the virtues and benefits of unity. As the academic Robert Parker put it,

> Ten Bougainville leaders were conducted to other parts of the Territory to see the benefits of economic development while five indigenous ministerial office holders were sent to Bougainville to put the Administration's case.

Incensed by Parker's draft entry for *Australia in World Affairs* — 'polemic journalism rather than history' — Hay persuaded the editor to change the last words to:

> And five indigenous members of the AEC [Australian Executive Council] went to Bougainville at the Council's request to explain Administration policy.[40]

This was manipulation. It was also an under-count: seven (Lue, Tore Lokoloko, Abal, Paul Langro, Oala Oala-Rarua, Somare and Voutas) had visited Bougainville.

In hindsight, Hay had two regrets. One was the development of Panguna.[41] The other was his acceptance of a disputed election in Rabaul. The tension that disrupted local government grew out of land, the most emotive issue anywhere in the Pacific. Mainly through alienation in the German era, much of the best land in the Gazelle had been lost to the Tolai.[42] In the 1920s, Australians began to convert land in German ownership into Torrens title, which is indefeasible. Native claims could be heard, but in that high-colonial era they were probably discounted. Then the land register was lost during the Japanese occupation, so fresh investigations began in 1951. Nick O'Neill observed the attempts of Tolai to establish claims, beginning with Varzin Plantation. When Tedep and others claimed 'native customary rights' over the land, the Commissioner of Titles rebuffed them and ordered the title to be placed on the new register. Tedep appealed to the Territory Supreme Court, which upheld his claim. So far so good, but the matter was taken to the High Court of Australia, which held that the loss of the register did not destroy existing title. Secondary evidence would be enough to establish that registration had probably taken place. 'There could be no enquiry into whether or not the land was properly obtained from its traditional owners in the first place.' These arguments offended the Tolai, and yet the traditional owners of Japlik and Vunapaladig land lost a similar claim:

> They claimed that they had a right to be on the land because from time immemorial they owned the land which had never been used by others. The Supreme Court decided that because there was a restored title to the land, no claim of right could be made to the land contrary to that title.[43]

Against this background, many Tolai mistrusted the 1969 proposal to replace their Local Government Council with a Multiracial Council for Rabaul town. Many saw this as a device to allow Chinese and Australians undue influence. Land and race issues were a toxic brew, and the Mataungan Association organised a boycott of the council election. So popular was the boycott that fewer than one in five voted, but the officials refused to yield. When Hay and other dignitaries attended the opening of the council, a Mataungan protest drowned out proceedings.

They were now locked into an impasse. To maintain services, the council had to collect taxes, which many refused to pay. To prosecute them would be inflammatory. To ignore them would reward subversion. Seeking a resolution, DC Jack Emanuel would 'go out for whole nights, sitting in the villages, listening and talking'. So did *kiap* Ross Allen.[44] These struggles dragged on until Emanuel was murdered and the police retaliated violently.

The House was again irrelevant because it could not form a view, and the officials were divided. The hawks were led by Tom Ellis. Hay recalls that

> Ellis, with all his faults, was an expert in how to arrest people — that is what he loved doing better than anything else — and in the kind of field work that comes naturally to the [Department of District Affairs] staff.

Ellis treated the Mataungans as 'the enemy'. Hay did try to resolve issues: he and Barnes (with Kim Beazley of the Labor Party) enlisted Moral Rearmament as peacemakers. On police matters though, Hay trusted Ellis more than Ray Whitrod, the progressive Chief of Police. Ellis was not alone: Toliman (a non-Mataungan Tolai), Pangu members and the AEC were all gung-ho for firm action. So, it seemed, were other Local Government Councils. Nor was the department flexible. When Hay tried to buy two plantations to redistribute, Warwick Smith insisted that this be done (at glacial speed) as a commercial deal by the Development Bank.

Weeks of tension followed until September 1, when leading Mataungans Damien Kereku and Melchior Tomot walked into the council offices, stole the keys and made threats. Hauled before the magistrate, they were well represented by Ikenna Nwokolo, the first African at the Territory Bar. The magistrate found the accused guilty but, to the dismay of the prosecution, imposed no penalty and berated the Administration! That judgment led to a Commission of Inquiry into the best form of government for the Gazelle. Hay welcomed the commission and named the anthropologist Scarlett Epstein as a consultant to it. But his hope of resolution was dashed when Barnes appointed as commissioner a Queensland mate, Peter Connolly QC, who rejected conciliation and applauded the Administration's hard line. This fanned the flames. In sporadic outbursts of temper, council members were assaulted — and so was *kiap* Fenton, when Tomot swung a hay-maker at Hay. But direct action was not a Mataungan monopoly: Ellis began (in Hay's delicate phrase) 'a period of intensive and active patrolling in which — well, you can put it in various ways — the rule of law was restored'.

The victims of 'intensive and active patrolling' won little sympathy in the House. In 1970 Tammur moved that Australia grant self-government by the end of 1972, with the usual proviso that 'those parts of the Territory which do not wish to have self-government may continue under the present system'. If the House had known that Gorton also wanted self-government, they might have accepted Tammur's motion, but Gorton's shift was still a secret, so the motion failed by 14 to 51. That lopsided vote, thought Johnson, was because Tolai

> were the most affluent of Papua New Guineans, had the best education facilities and occupied many senior posts in the Administration. Members thought that they had little to complain about.

These grievances festered. At the end of 1971, the head of the Territories Department's Government and Law Division concluded that the main security problem was 'how to deal with the Gazelle'. Land disputes would intensify and litigation would usually fail because:

> [traditional owners] will only succeed now where there is some defect in title and it will be purely coincidental if this coincides with some legitimate claim to ownership according to their customs.

Three hundred disputes were outstanding. Tolai would occupy the land as squatters and 'if the law is to be enforced action should be taken to remove the squatters'. There was no chance of conciliation.[45]

As these crises deepened, the House grew perverse. Pangu nationalists found common ground with anti-colonial separatists, while the United Party conservatives favoured national unity. But even the United Party had doubts. As Abal put it, 'Unity depends on some equalisation of standards of education, economic and social development.' When Brere Awol introduced a motherhood motion in favour of national unity, Somare defended the separatists, and Lapun asked:

> How are we going to promote unity in this country when certain areas are getting all the benefits while others are being neglected? It seems to me that the neglect of the people of the New Guinea islands has been the cause of their desire to secede … I believe that the best solution would be to ask Canberra for a referendum.

Papua was the third threat to unity, again invoking uneven funding. Bert Counsel, an Australian married to a Papuan, was the leading advocate for separation:

> A fat lot of use it is for a Papuan member to stay in the House. All he is ever asked to do is to approve development expenditure for New Guinea. [And] there is no way in the world that we in Papua will ever be happy at the prospect of being told what to do by a bunch of Highlanders.

To quash this sentiment, Johnson authorised a statement in the House that it was Australian policy to move Papua New Guinea to self-government 'as a united country'. Any difference in legal status between New Guinea and Papua 'has been of little consequence since the approval by the United Nations of the administrative union in 1947'. A motion was proposed by Pangial and carried 30 to 25, seeking a committee to test Papuan wishes. The majority was an unholy alliance of all Papuan members, Pangu and Julius Chan's new People's Progress Party (PPP). Although the motion was carried, it had little popular support. When the Territories Minister invited Papuan ministerial members to Canberra, they 'went in hope and returned in disappointment' with nothing more than the promise of a study.

When the second House rose, Johnson claimed much too much merit for its members:

> We have grown to think of Papua New Guinea as one country ... This has been a national parliament and it has been the genesis of national feeling.

> In 1964 the House had very considerable powers but the people of Papua New Guinea did not think of government as something belonging to them. The Government is now free to grow from the will of the people ...[46]

On the other hand, members had not helped to pacify Bougainville, they had shown no sympathy for the Mataungans and they divided over relations between New Guinea, Papua and Australia. To blame the members is easy, but they did not betray the values of their constituents. Tested in the 1972 election, they emerged quite well. Most expatriates lost their seats, but Neville, Middleton, Ward and Chan were returned, while Chatterton and Voutas retired. Of 63 indigenous members, 38 were re-elected.

The Second House had been ineffectual, but much responsibility for this sad condition must lie with the Territories Department, which insisted on Westminster forms, determined the House's structure, limited its functions and manipulated its will.

Appendix: Members of the Second House of Assembly (First Session)

Open

John Guise*	Alotau	Discreetly Pangu
Nauwi Sauinambi	Ambunti-Yangoru	
Peter Johnson	Angoram	
Meanggarum James*	Bogia	Pangu
Karigi Bonggere	Chimbu	
Uauwi Wauwe Moses*	Chuave	
Sinake Giregire*	Daulo	Ministerial Member, Posts & Telegraphs
Kokomo Ulia	Dreikikir	
Norman Evenett	Esa'ala	Died, replaced by Timothy Ward
Meck Singilong	Finschhafen	Assistant Ministerial Member, Rural Development
Matthias ToLiman*	Gazelle	Ministerial Member, Education
Louis Sebu Mona	Goilala	
Sabumei Kofikai	Goroka	
Ninkama Bomai	Gumine	
Pena Ou	Hagen	
Boino Azanifa	Henganofi	
Toua Kapena	Hiri	Ministerial Member, Labour
Michael Kaniniba	Huon Gulf	Pangu
Turi Wari	Ialibu	
Paulus Arek	Ijivitari	
Kaura Duba	Jimi	Died, replaced by Thomas Kavali, NG National
Rauke Gam	Kabwum	
Yano Belo	Kagua	
Noel Casey	Kainantu	
Anani Maino	Kaindi	
Koitaga Mano*	Kandep-Tambul	
Koriam Michael Urekit*	Kandrian-Pomio	
Daniel Bokap	Kavieng	
Tore Lokoloko	Kerema	Ministerial Member, Public Health
Siwi Kurondo*	Kerowagi	Assistant Ministerial Member, Forests, NG National
Tom Koraea	Kikori	
Oscar Tammur	Kokopo	
Taimya Kambipi	Kompiam-Baiyer	
Andrew Wabiria	Koroba	Assistant Ministerial Member, Surveys & Mines
Lepani Watson*	Kula	Assistant Ministerial Member, Cooperatives
Poio Iuri*	Lagaip	
Pupune Aruno	Lufa	
Angmai Bilas	Mabuso	Ministerial Member, Trade & Industry
Paliau Maloat*	Manus	Pangu
Pita Lus*	Maprik	Pangu
Thomas Leahy	Markham	
Momei Pangial*	Mendi	
James McKinnon	Middle Ramu	
Percy Chatterton*	Moresby	
Mek Nugintz	Mul-Dei	
Mangobing Kakun	Munya	Pangu
Julius Chan	Namatanai	
Patik Nimanbor	Nawae	
Tegi Ebei'al	Nipa	

Donatus Mola	North Bougainville	Additional Asst. Ministerial Member, DIES
Warren Dutton	North Fly	
Muriso Warebu*	Okapa	
Epineri Titimur	Rabaul	
John Poe	Rai Coast	
Nathaniel Uroe	Rigo-Abau	
Katigame Endekan	Sobe	
Paul Lapun*	South Bougainville	Pangu
Ebia Olewale	South Fly	Pangu
John Middleton	Sumkar	
John Maneke	Talasea	
Matiabe Yuwi	Tari	
Wesani Iwoksim	Upper Sepik	
Tei Abal*	Wabag	Ministerial Member, Agriculture, Stock & Fish
Kaibelt Diria*	Wahgi	Assistant Ministerial Member, Local Government
Yakob Talis	Wapei-Nuku	
Leine Iangalo*	Wapenamanda	
Brere Awol	West Sepik Coastal	
Beibi Yambanda	Wewak	

Regional

Joseph Lue	Bougainville	Assistant Ministerial Member, Technical Education
Oala Oala-Rarua	Central	Pangu, Asst. Ministerial Member, Treasury
Eric Pyne	Chimbu	Died, replaced by John Nilles
Dennis Buchanan	Eastern Highlands	
Oriel Irving Ashton*	East and West New Britain	Ministerial Member, Public Works
Michael Somare	East Sepik	Pangu
Jason Garrett	Madang	
Walter Lussick	Manus and New Ireland	
Cecil Abel	Milne Bay	Pangu
Tony Voutas*	Morobe	Pangu
William Fielding	Northern	
Ron Neville*	Southern Highlands	
Virgil Counsel	Western and Gulf	
John Watts	Western Highlands	
Paul Langro	West Sepik	Assistant Ministerial Member, DIES

* members of first House of Assembly

Official members

Frank Henderson	– Asst. Administrator (Economics) who died and was replaced by James Ritchie, who resigned and was replaced by Harry Ritchie
Leslie Johnson	– Asst. Administrator (Services) who became Administrator and was not replaced.
W. W. Watkins	– Law, who retired and was replaced by Lindsay Curtis, who resigned and was replaced by Bill Kearney
A. P. J. Newman	– Treasurer
Tom Ellis	– Director, District Administration
Donald Grove	– Lands, Surveys and Mines
Charles Littler	– Inspector, District Administration
Stanley Foley	– DC Chimbu
Ronald Galloway	– DC Port Moresby
Herbert Seale	– DC Lae, who resigned and was not replaced

Footnotes
1. A 452/1 66/2960. Draft questionnaire in Watkins to Cleland, March 11, 1966, enclosed in Cleland to Department, March 11, 1966.
2. Ibid., Department to Administrator, telex, April 14, 1966.
3. Ron Crocombe, personal communication, December 2003.
4. J. D. B. Miller, 'Australia's New Guinea Problem', seminar paper, International Relations, ANU, reprinted in *Journal of Pacific History*, 2005.
5. A 452/1 66/2960, text of Barnes's statement on April 21, 1966.
6. Johnson, 'Westminster in Port Moresby', quoting ABC radio broadcast, April 25, 1966.
7. 66/2960, Administrator to Department, May 20, 1966.
8. Ibid., enclosed in Administrator to Department, August 13, 1966.
9. Edward P. Wolfers, 'January-April 1967', in Moore and Kooyman, *A Papua New Guinea Political Chronicle 1967-1991*.
10. 66/2960, Administrator to Department, March 23, 1967.
11. Wolfers, 'January-April 1967', p. 11.
12. 66/2960, Administrator to Department, enclosing Assistant Administrator to Administrator, March 31, 1967.
13. Johnson, 'Westminster in Port Moresby', p. 8.
14. Tom Leahy, *Markham Tom: Memoirs of an Australian Pioneer in Papua New Guinea*, Crawford House, Adelaide, 2002, p. 152
15. 66/2960, Administrator to Secretary, February 23, 1967.
16. A 452/1 66/943, Draft of Cabinet Submission 1194 of January 27, 1966.
17. A 452/1 66/2960, notes and correspondence with Cleland, Dick and Watkins.
18. Ibid., folio 271, and Secretary to Administrator, July 9, 1966. The officials were the Administrator, two assistants and the Director of District Administration. Members from the House were Nicholas Brokam, Ian Downs, John Guise, John Stuntz, Robert Tabua, Matthias ToLiman and Zure Zurecnuoc.
19. Leahy, *Markham Tom*, pp. 155-6.
20. Percy Chatterton, *Day that I have Loved*, Sydney, 1974.
21. Johnson, 'Westminster in Port Moresby'.
22. 68/5563, Part II, Administrator to Department, June 2, 1969.
23. David Hegarty, 'September–December 1971', in Moore and Kooyman, *Papua New Guinea Political Chronicle 1967–1991*.
24. Mark Lynch, 'Communication and Cargo'.
25. Johnson, 'Westminster in Port Moresby': the source of the quote and of the following paragraphs.
26. Sir Alkan Tololo in 'Hindsight'.
27. Johnson, 'Westminster in Port Moresby', quoting a message on file 69/3605, undated.
28. Denoon, *Getting Under the Skin*
29. 67/1104, Part 2, Administrator to Department, May 15, 1967.
30. Hay, interview, National Library of Australia.
31. Johnson, 'Westminster in Port Moresby'.
32. Jim Griffin, 'Bougainville', *Australia's Neighbours*, January–February 1970.
33. Text in 68/5448.
34. 69/3671, Hannett's address, Canberra, August 5, demonstrations: see also 70/1623.
35. 68/5448, Minutes of October 22, 23, 30 and 31; Department to ABC, October 28; Administrator to Department, January 16, 1969; and (undated) reply.
36. 69/4123, Ellis's notes for the Administrator, August 9, 1969.
37. 69/3687, minute of August 14, 1969.
38. *Post Courier*, August 11, 1969.
39. 69/3687, 'Notes for Prime Minister and Minister ...', August 20, 1969; 69/4453, record of discussions, 2pm, Thursday August 21, 1969; and 69/4453, FAS note for file, August 22, 1969, and appendices.
40. Ibid.
41. Ibid., and Greenwell's comments in 'Hindsight'.

42. Nick O'Neill, in 'Hindsight'.
43. Administration of TPNG v Blasius Tirupia [197-72] PNGLR 229. See also William Kaputin, 'Indefeasibility and Justice', in Peter Sack, *Problem of Choice — Land in Papua New Guinea's future*, ANU Press, 1974, pp. 159–60.
44. Trevor Shearston's vivid historical novel, *Straight Young Back*, brings these skirmishes to life.
45. A452 T29, 1971/3088, John Greenwell's minute, December 7, 1971, on an interdepartmental committee.
46. Johnson, 'Westminster in Port Moresby'.

Chapter 5

New Directions

Managing Social Change

After 14 years as Administrator, Sir Donald Cleland retired in 1967 and used his final speech to take stock. Ted Wolfers glossed his address:

> Strong Australian control, the stress on the long distance still remaining before self-determination, the assumption that inter-racial cooperation was still a viable proposition, were the principal points of Cleland's speech, as they had been the hallmarks of Hasluck's career and policy.[1]

There was no sign of faster change. Cleland even suggested that constitutional matters would be better handled by lawyers than by political processes. When Hay took over, he accepted the glacial pace but wanted to consult 'Papua New Guinean institutions'. To improve relations with the Administrator's Council, he slowed its procedures so that members could grasp what they were doing. He believed that they were grateful, but that did not transform them into an engine of policy-formation, or even a reliable sounding board.

Hay consulted a public relations expert who advised him to extend the broadcasting service and to form a conservative party 'to counter some of the radical elements'. That idea lapsed but, consistent with his focus on public relations, Hay prepared three introductory speeches: one to the public (in Tok Pisin), another to the Administrator's Council, and a third to his heads of departments. Once settled in Konedobu, he tried to appoint Terry White as his liaison officer, a move that introduced him to a persistent frustration: the Public Service Commission could not move quickly, when it moved at all. (It took Hay a year to appoint a press secretary.) Eventually, Terry White managed Hay's liaison with 'opinion-formers … student groups, Members of the House of Assembly, the business world — but mostly the Papua New Guinea elements'.[2]

Was this the democratic way to test opinion? When mining company CRA needed to assess opposition among Bougainvilleans, their managing director, Frank Espie, went to Harvard to engage the anthropologist Douglas Oliver. Oliver had done research in

Bougainville and agreed to revisit the island and to mobilise young scholars to work there independently.[3] Espie respected Oliver's advice, but when the Territories Department saw his report, its response was merely defensive:[4]

> formal liaison and exchange of information [between Canberra, Konedobu and CRA] could have altered some of the recommendations regarding the collection of information (surely the responsibility of government rather than the company).
>
> [This report] fails to achieve its purpose. The psychological material is probably correct but the recommendations appear to support further psychological study and information collection rather than to provide the answers sought by the company or to utilise existing avenues of information.

This was preposterous. To find out what villagers were thinking, CRA sought the best advice that money could buy. Hay was keen to debrief experts who visited the territory:[5] otherwise officials relied on 'existing avenues of information' — a polite term for untrained *kiaps*. No one treated elected politicians as representatives of their constituents.

But the reference to psychology is odd. It was not Oliver but the department's own experts who claimed the insights of social psychology. In 1966, the Minister was impressed by a report on 'Communication of Government Policy to the People of Papua and New Guinea', which proposed an advisory committee to advise him on:

i the social changes likely to result from new Government policies,
ii the nature and intensity of the resistance likely to be shown …
iii methods of minimizing such resistance.

The paper was commended to senior officers, and Barnes established a Social Change Advisory Committee to advise him on social change, official policy and 'problems of communication between "government" and the native people'.[6] The committee's core members were Brigadier Edward Campbell, former Director of Psychology for the Army and author of the paper that impressed the Minister, and Dr Alex Sinclair, a psychiatrist who had surveyed the mental health of Papua New Guineans.

The committee presented a low profile. Meetings were rare, but members were consulted individually and the agenda was wide: in 1967, Bougainville prospecting, public servants' wages and land in the Gazelle. In 1968, they addressed national unity, localisation, the defence force and Bougainville; and, in 1969, land legislation, Bougainville (again), unity (yet again), trade unions, family planning and manpower planning.[7] Given the backgrounds of the members and the recent emergence of colonial social psychology,[8] their analyses were predictable. Western behaviour was the goal, indigenous values the obstacle and paternal administration the solution. They cited no empirical evidence to flesh out this formula. Addressing the vexed issue of land, for instance, they ignored all reports of actual land use[9] and accepted without question that the proper goal was the 'ultimate achievement of individual tenure, replacing the traditional communal tenure'. The committee asked itself 'how best to take into account the cultural change for and the views of indigenes in assessing what system of tenure is most suitable, and educate indigenes to accept change'.[10]

Describing the general dilemma of governance, they repeated their earlier advice:

> Any administrative authority attempting to implement a process of cultural change in an immature preliterate social group is in the unenviable position of a parent attempting to guide a family of not very co-operative adolescents towards adulthood.

This parent could exercise authority 'at three levels of maturity': first, authoritarian, then paternal, and eventually, 'he may set definite limits to areas of behaviour, and within these limits, allow the adolescent complete freedom'.

> This is the precise situation in which the Administration finds itself in Bougainville… deciding to what degree it can relax its paternalistic control and encourage permissive risk taking. If it remains paternalistic it will be resented. If it is permissive, its new attitude may be perceived as weakness.

> The only solution … appears to be the application of a masked and subtle form of directiveness which will give the native people greater control and responsibility.

Reviewing the difficulty of communicating with 'native peoples' in general, and especially with Bougainvilleans, the committee declared that Bougainville was 'ready-made for the application of a psychological operation aimed at manipulating public attitudes in the Administration's favour'. Part of that plan was

> a full scale propaganda campaign having
> 1 the OVERT aim of advancing the people's political education and so enabling them to make a more reasoned decision on their future.
> 2 The COVERT aims of exploiting the lines of fission [described in the report] and providing factual information which the supporters of the Administration can use in argument.[11]

The committee's bark was more alarming than its bite. The members never consulted the people; they ignored other disciplines; they avoided the ANU's New Guinea Research Unit; and only in 1969 did they meet scholars with real expertise — the political scientist Charles Rowley and the anthropologist Ralph Bulmer. Eventually, Hay asked the obvious question:

> I have some doubts as to whether the Committee ought to be continued at all: … over a large part of Government activity communication with the people is now a responsibility of Ministerial Members to be carried out by their Departments.[12]

For the same reasons, he questioned the rationale of the Public Relations Advisory Committee that he had created as administrator. When Tim Besley in Canberra proposed to extend the role of the SCAC, he found only one instance of cross-cultural communication. At its most recent meeting, the committee had at last included a Papua New Guinean, to discuss censorship. For Besley, this was useful in giving firsthand information, feeling and attitudes to the committee, and impressing the public servant with the Australians' concern for 'the social and cultural issues involved in carrying out our responsibilities'.[13]

SCAC's advice implied — what Barnes, his department and the Administration also expected — that relations between the governors and the governed would change very little. Government would evolve as an Australian Territorial Administration while Papua New Guineans were initiated into Australian governance. But developments in the territory were undermining this scenario.

New Australians and New Papua New Guineans

As funds flowed from Canberra, governance was less influenced by the frontier and 'modern' agencies emerged. *Kiaps* were still recruited but their instruction changed. When Philip Fitzpatrick was training at the Australian School of Pacific Administration in Sydney, his lecturers told cadets that they were 'social misfits':

> who else would enjoy sitting out on a lonely patrol post in a swamp by themselves …
> but they convinced me the discomfort would be worth the spectacle of watching the dying days of a colonial empire.[14]

Australian programs and procedures crossed Torres Strait and brought a leaven of Australians and others, shattering the formula that all white people were missionaries, *kiaps* or planters. Many were graduates, whereas *kiaps* were commonly recruited from school. Many were from Melbourne or South Australia; hitherto rural Queensland and New South Wales had been the main sources. Many old-timers saw themselves as bearers of order and civilisation to backward natives, but urban graduates saw themselves as critics, reformers or opponents of colonialism. This was an aspect of a broader change in Australia. During the 1960s, Australians were conscripted to fight in Vietnam, provoking a vigorous anti-war movement. The mistreatment of Aboriginal people on the land and in country towns was brought vividly to the attention of a wider public. Apartheid became an Australian issue when racially selected rugby teams represented South Africa. The Labor Party opposition was still wedded to White Australia and to the long-term occupation of Papua New Guinea, but there were enough liberal responses in and around government to justify the title of Donald Horne's overview, *Time of Hope*.[15] To many, Australian rule in the territory was indefensible. Decolonisation was the only honourable way to remove a blot on Australia's democratic reputation and an unfair impost on Melanesians.

Liberal ideas were slow to travel north. Jim Byth, an astute observer at Melbourne University Press and then in Port Moresby, insists that 'if you wanted to meet The Ugly

Australian in full howl for the whole 1950–75 period, in was in PNG that you were most likely to find him. And, let's be clear about it, her!'[16] But the new men were not bound by 'the white man's burden': they opposed the Vietnam War and hoped for better lives for Aboriginal people. There were new women too, who did not feel bound by the White Women's Protection Ordinance. Women and men alike could imagine, and work towards, self-government. John Langmore, for example, grew up in a Melbourne protestant family with links to the Kwato Mission in Milne Bay, so Papuan students visited his home in school holidays. He graduated in economics and social work — development economics being a modern form of mission. Coming to Port Moresby in 1963, he found kindred spirits when he joined Boroko United Church and the multiracial Contact Club.[17]

Langmore worked in the new Labour Department which was extending industrial relations beyond the straitjacket of indenture, and raising 'modern' issues such as Occupational Health and Safety. Alan McCasker, as Economic Adviser, relayed the ideas of the Australian economic strategist John Crawford.[18] Thinking outside old paradigms involved analyses of urban and rural minimum wages. These inquiries drew in the new Council for Social Service and activists such as Rachel Cleland, who had retired locally with her husband.[19] This network encouraged the efforts of freethinkers such as David Fenbury, *kiap* and 'renegade philosopher-bureaucrat'. Voutas and Holloway would raise awkward issues in the House. Their impact on policy was minimal, but non-conformists were clustering and supporting each other.

A critical forum was the ANU's New Guinea Research Unit in Waigani. As economists, anthropologists and geographers from the Research School of Pacific Studies began sustained field research, the Unit accommodated them and hosted debates with authorities. Directors Ron Crocombe and Ron May ran seminars and circulated papers that attracted everyone (except the Social Change Advisory Committee) with an interest in public policy.

Industrial relations also came under scrutiny. By the 1960s, Australia's industrial relations regime was probably the most complex in the world. Wages were negotiated in a three-cornered manner, in which the State was a third party between employers and unions. Each party was highly organised, and they negotiated in a regime of compulsory arbitration and conciliation in specialist courts. This sophisticated regime required workers to form unions to engage with employers in a quasi-judicial forum. If workers did not form unions, the system could not operate. But unions in Papua New Guinea were usually local, informal, ad hoc bodies that formed for the duration of a wage crisis. Rather than adapt to this reality, the State propped up the unions, ignoring their procedural irregularities and enabling them to present a façade in the tribunals. The new system was conducted in the name of Papua New Guinean workers but was managed by Australian experts.[20]

The transfusion of new men and women certainly animated the judicial system.[21] Until the 1960s, the legal establishment was four judges and a registrar, six magistrates, 15 lawyers in the Law Department, six in the Public Solicitor's Office and eight small private firms. Judicial institutions were shaken up when David Derham reviewed them. His report and Hasluck's selective response affirmed Australian principles and procedures, including independent magistrates and judges. Hasluck endorsed many of Derham's ideas: *kiaps* began to pass their judicial work to magistrates, and the constabulary began to look like a police force. But Derham also proposed a system of Village Courts, partly independent of Australian judicial principles. Hasluck's liberal principles would not tolerate a two-tiered court system, so courts became increasingly Australian in their personnel, principles and procedures.[22]

The influence of Melbourne was diffuse and stimulating. The Supreme Court was led by Chief Justice Sir Alan Mann, a Victorian appointed (he said) to create 'an independent system of courts of a much higher level of proficiency'. Smithers, Minogue QC and Frost QC followed from Melbourne. Ollerenshaw was the lone non-Victorian. John Greenwell, a barrister who was interested in the Territory through his friendship with the judges, applied to be Assistant Secretary (Legal) in the department, and took over in August 1970.[23]

More usual was the lure of the territory itself. Thomas Barnett was close to quitting law after purgatory in articles when his mentor, Derham, encouraged him to apply for a post as Judge's Associate. Arriving in 1961, he was kidnapped at the airport by the new Public Solicitor, Peter Lalor, as the office's first Defence Counsel. Lalor had studied law after a serious accident derailed his career as a *kiap*. As hard as his Eureka Stockade namesake, he inspired subordinates, made enemies — and defined the Public Solicitor's role as defending the people from the Government. Under his influence, Barnett assumed the mantle of crusader, and defeated so many prosecutions that he became 'Tossim Out Barnett'. He did notice that defendants might regret their acquittal if they were then killed in retaliation (or 'payback', as people called it). Some defendants happily admitted guilt for this reason: the corpse of one who took a contrary view was thrown onto the court verandah.[24]

The Public Solicitor's Office offered sophisticated remedies to the least sophisticated. A case often rested on irregularity: the *kiap* or policeman was unfair; the interpreter erred; the witness was bribed or was trying to please officials; the prosecution was over-zealous. The office represented everyone charged before the Supreme Court, often ingeniously. The office acted for land claimants against the Administration. In the Era Taora (Newtown, Port Moresby) land case, they argued that the Crown lacked the capacity, during the British Protectorate, to buy land at all (the claimants ultimately lost in the High Court of Australia). Even more radical was an attempt to invalidate the entire mining regime for inconsistency with the Australian Constitution.[25]

These are the memories of Geoffrey Dabb, who arrived in 1962, aged 23, from a Melbourne criminal law practice. A conversation with his mentor, Derham, propelled him to the Territory and his trial expertise took him on court circuits. Like Barnett for the defence, his prosecutions made him query his role. When he prosecuted two women in Enga who had strangled a younger wife, they insisted, 'We didn't use an axe. We only used a rope.' They had heard Justice Smithers insisting that 'This killing of people with axes is very wrong'.[26]

Another lawyer from that stable was John Ley: Wesley College, Melbourne Law School, bored as a solicitor.[27] A major influence was John Guise speaking on the ABC radio program *Guest of Honour*, explaining that Papua New Guinea was on the road to self-government and needed Australians of good will. (Langmore was moved by the same talk.) After six months in Crown Law, Ley moved to the Public Solicitor's Office. His colleagues were liberal, close-knit and at odds with their elders: they all resigned from the Aviat Club, for example, when Julius Chan was blackballed (Chapter 1).

By 1966, Ley was Deputy Public Solicitor in Rabaul, with Mataungan clients. In 1970, he studied African law in London and toured Africa, meeting Peter Bayne (also from Melbourne) in Dar es Salaam. By the time he returned to Papua New Guinea, there was a university with a Law Faculty headed by A. B. Weston and including Bayne, Abdul Paliwala from Tanzania and the Nigerian Ikenna Nwokolo. Bayne had studied in London and America before going to the University of Dar es Salaam. He followed Weston to Papua New Guinea, partly from interest in law and development, but also because he expected his Tanzanian wife to be happier in Port Moresby than in Australia.[28]

Most Supreme Court work was criminal trials, mainly when a judge, his associate, a prosecutor and a defence lawyer travelled on circuit. These were all-Australian parties until 1968 when Joseph Aoae became a prosecutor. In 1970, he was joined by Buri Kidu and Bernard Narokobi.[29] Violent crime was the main business, and the Highlands generated a great number — Dabb conducted six trials for murder in one day at Wabag.

The Public Solicitor wanted the autonomy that Australian courts took for granted. Mann also demanded an independent judiciary. He meant that judges should come from outside the Territory, that most government officers should be barred from exercising power in the lower courts, that the court was equal with the Administration in status, and that they should control their own resources. These aspirations irritated the *kiaps* and, in 1964, Mann came across a summary of criticisms made by DCs, who alleged that in some areas 'even the Supreme Court' was 'regarded with contempt'.

> Defence Counsel and officers of the Public Solicitor's office should have made clear to them that their duty is to ensure justice, and not to attempt to enhance their reputations and defeat justice by employing legal chicanery.

Mann was so incensed that he complained, successfully, to Barnes. The judges also sought international support, joining the International Commission of Jurists as a Territory branch.

A byproduct of the new diversity of views was a vogue for the African precedents that Hasluck had discouraged. Fenbury was rare in having been allowed to study British colonial practice.[30] In African analogies he was helped by Nigel Oram, town-planner from Uganda, now in the New Guinea Research Unit at the ANU. After 1967, several lawyers travelled to London to study African law, but there they learned that native courts were unlikely to survive, since they involved a differentiation between the administration of justice to Africans and that to non-Africans'.[31] The popularity of African precedents was intense but brief.

The Territory also attracted economists. ANU economists enjoyed personal links with government, often through Crawford and Professor Swan. Gerry Gutman, in the

Territories Department, attended seminars, and undergraduates could attend research seminars and meet policy-makers. Many graduate students had international interests. Ross Garnaut won a scholarship to the ANU in 1963 and continued to a PhD on South-East Asia, but first he detoured into the New Guinea Research Unit on vacation, working alongside the promising Papua New Guinean student Rabbie Namaliu (who went on to be a vacation scholar at the ANU).[32]

These networks were reinforced when the University of Papua New Guinea opened in Waigani. Vice-Chancellor Gunther fought cannily with the Territories Department for funding, and for the right to ignore the White Australia immigration policy in staffing (the New Guinea Research Unit had been the only exempt agency).[33] At the university's annual Waigani Seminars, international scholars inspired staff and students. The Law Faculty offered courses in constitutional law; Ulli Beier organised the publication and performance of students' poetry, novels and theatre; students and politicians organised campaigns; and political topics were ventilated in *New Guinea* magazine and in the *Australian Journal of Politics and History*.[34]

Gunther himself maintained an open house. Arriving from Nigeria, Ulli and Georgina Beier were startled to meet Kauage — a labourer, not yet an artist — when he dropped in for a beer on his way home from work. The first professors —Ken Inglis, the historian, Bulmer and Rowley — were scholars of vision who attracted keen lecturers who devised imaginative programs. To make up the first intake, the university combed the Public Service, seminaries, schools in Australia and Territory high schools. The future novelist Vincent Eri was a public servant; Hannet had been expelled from his long-suffering seminary; John Waiko flew in from Popondetta with an axe and a spare shirt; Namaliu arrived from Rabaul; and John Kasaipwalova brought with him the radical politics of Queensland University. As the first graduates, they could expect glittering careers: meanwhile, they animated a lively campus.

Beier was allowed to devise an entirely new approach to the teaching of literature:

> it is best to start by analysing a text from their own tradition. Students come out of mission schools with the notion that poetry is an English invention. 'Civilised' countries produce 'literature' while 'primitive' peoples produce 'folklore'.

Since English was no longer the preserve of the English people, a course in New English Writing from Africa revealed

> how African writers treated the language with a healthy disrespect, broke its back and welded it into a useful tool for themselves. Courses on new writing from Africa and India … corresponded to issues which preoccupied our students: colonialism, conflict between generations, the search for traditional values, problems of identity, the struggle for independence and post-independence disillusion …

> This was a moment in Papua New Guinea's history when a man had to be highly articulate and capable of formulating ideas.

By evoking a confident voice, Creative Writing enabled many students to do just that. At school, Waiko began to doubt the folk-knowledge he had learned as a child, when he assumed that the purpose of education was to learn European lore. That judgment was shaken by Hank Nelson and Inglis in courses on Papua New Guinea history; then he rebuilt his confidence in the wisdom of his Binandere people through Creative Writing and by staging a play.

To understand the response to this voice, we must recall the silence that preceded it. Most Australians met Melanesians as servants, policemen or villagers. They were an inert problem to be doctored, analysed, instructed, converted, disciplined or civilised. Missionaries and *kiaps* spoke for them. That they had a voice at all was a revelation. By the end of 1968, there was a series of *Papuan Pocket Poets. Kovave* published stories, poems and plays. These serials, with Albert Maori Kiki's autobiography, *Ten Thousand Years in a Lifetime*, Eri's novel *Crocodile*, and Ulli's work with Kiki — *Hohao* — suddenly comprised a serious body of literature.

The books addressed English-speakers but the plays reached wider audiences. Hannet's *The Ungrateful Daughter* makes an anti-colonial parable of the tale of a Melanesian girl adopted by Australians and promised in marriage to a prospector. Waiko's *Unexpected Hawk* uses Binandere images to convey the turmoil of colonialism; Kasaipwalova's *Reluctant Flame* uses the rhetoric of negritude to dissect Port Moresby. Plays were staged in an amphitheatre where gardeners and cleaners mingled with academics and students; families came, children joining in the hum of conversation; and the plays exploited slapstick satire and solemn dance-drama. Beier is not surprised that the first book by a Papua New Guinean was written by Kiki, the secretary of Pangu, 'because the birth of Literature was part of political awakening'. The new literature and the Tok Pisin plays linked young politicians with Highlander and other workers in Port Moresby. The writers enjoyed wider influence when Al Butovicius's Prompt Theatre took three of their plays to Canberra in 1970. In a vain attempt to negate their message, Barnes sent officers to explain that real Papua New Guineans were grateful to a paternal administration.

This intervention helped to promote — and to feed — a quickening Australian interest in the Territory. The media needed a crisis to focus its attention, preferably one that revealed the Government as incompetent. That requirement was met in 1969 when Bougainville landowners resisted the developers of Panguna mine (Chapter 4). The Australian media could not sustain their intense interest for long, but the silence had been broken, and for the next few years — until independence, in fact — Australian reporters lived in Port Moresby in order to report events for Australian newspapers. Similarly, the young writers dispersed into politics, government or business; yet a generation with something urgent to say was able to say it trenchantly. In doing so, they savaged Keith Willey's stereotypes (Chapter 1) of a land without history, populated by primitives.

Whitlam Intervenes: Gorton Responds

Yeast was working, but the dough had to be stirred. The chef de cuisine was Edward Gough Whitlam, patrician, lawyer and self-conscious man of destiny. In his ascent to the leadership of the Labor Party, he challenged policies dear to the party: White Australia, Hasluck's paternalism and Australia's colonial heritage. He knew the Highland pioneer Mick Leahy and, in a long parliamentary career — beginning in 1953 — he visited the Territory more often than any other backbencher. From 1960, as Deputy Leader, he opposed his leader on Territory issues. As he saw it, 'Calwell condoned Hasluck's leisurely programs because he believed the Territories were a *cordon sanitaire* for White Australia.' It was a struggle to convert the party. Frontbenchers Kim Beazley and Gordon Bryant were closer to Calwell — and to Hasluck and Barnes — than to Whitlam. Only in 1971 did the Party Conference declare that Labor would 'ensure the orderly and secure transfer to PNG of self-government and independence in its first term of office'.[35] Whitlam exercised more influence on the affairs of the Territory while in opposition than he did later as Prime Minister. In Goroka in 1965, he predicted that Australia might have only five more years in charge. The next year, he proposed that the Papua New Guinea Act be amended to become 'the constitution of an independent republic'.[36] In 1967, as party leader, he began talks on decolonisation with Bill Morrison, diplomat and (from 1969) Member of Parliament.[37] After the 1969 election that brought Labor in sight of victory, they toured Papua New Guinea 'to propagate and develop the ALP's policy'. In Whitlam's opinion, this intervention not only changed government policy, but helped to unseat Prime Minister Gorton.[38] In Rabaul, they were welcomed by Catholic and Methodist choirs 'and cheered by a congregation of 11,000, the largest in the Territory's history'. In Port Moresby, Whitlam insisted that independence was an Australian decision:

> it is either misleading or meaningless to assert that the decision for independence is one for the people of New Guinea alone. The form of independence is certainly for them to decide for themselves. The fact of independence has already been decided.[39]

If Labor won office, Papua New Guinea would gain early 'home rule', controlling everything except foreign affairs and defence.

> Whitlam relishes the contrast between his visit and Gorton's a few months later:

> John Gorton, who had never visited Papua New Guinea ... and David Hay ... were greeted in Rabaul by an audience of 10,000 who were as hostile as our 11,000 had been enthusiastic. [So hostile that Ellis] gave Gorton a handgun. In a panic, on Sunday 19 July, Gorton called a cabinet meeting which, without a written submission, agreed on the precautionary step of an Order in Council calling out the Pacific Islands Regiment. Tension between Gorton and Malcolm Fraser, the Minister for Defence, over this proposal was a factor in the resignation of Fraser on 8th March 1971 and the replacement of Gorton by McMahon [as Prime Minister] two days later.

A feature of Whitlam's policy was its focus on Australian rather than territory interests. When he denounced Barnes for carrying 'gradualism to the point of imperceptibility', he insisted that Papua New Guinea's destiny was an Australian issue:

> The Minister will protest ... that the inhabitants of the Territory should decide for themselves, that they fear independence. The Minister's exploitation of a reluctance which he himself and his immediate predecessors have fostered sedulously is a tactic which reflects little credit upon him ... It is devious and dishonest to try to hold New Guineans responsible for developmental shortcomings which in fact are our own.[40]

He never sought Papua New Guinean support for this position, nor did he pretend to have it. After his Goroka speech, Guise told him that he agreed — but only in private.

Where Whitlam led, Gorton followed. The trigger for the U-turn was Whitlam's visit, Gorton's visit, and the conclusions Gorton drew from them, including the fact that Whitlam's policy played well in the newly attentive Australian media.[41] Gorton's interest in the place had been slight until the Bougainville crisis. Taken together, however, the Bougainville and Gazelle protests implied that peace was most fragile precisely where economic development was most advanced. Australian subsidies accounted for more than half of the Territory's budget, so economic development was essential for any degree of self-sufficiency, let alone self-government. Yet economic development was evidently going to antagonise the people most affected by it, destabilising the polity as a whole.

A new policy was required, and Gorton did not hesitate. Changes were announced in July 1970 and extended in 1971. These implemented most of what Whitlam had proposed, so that bipartisanship was restored — on Whitlam's terms. When Barnes's successor, Andrew Peacock, announced in October 1972 that self-government would be in place by December 1, 1973, Whitlam gave his full support:

> I would like to express also what I believe is a general view that the Minister has done our country a service in the comradeship and co-operation which he has achieved with the Government of Papua New Guinea.

The Gorton Reforms

It was not easy to teach Barnes to perform an about-face. Christine Goode heard that Gorton met Barnes after another embarrassing duel with Whitlam and told him, 'It's not good enough — doesn't go far enough.'[42] Expecting rebellion in his own Liberal Party, Gorton's only reliable supporters were in the Country Party, including Barnes. That explains the retention of a minister whose policies had to be reversed.[43]

Hay knew that he and Gorton would agree, but he could not address him without being disloyal to his own minister. Late in 1969, when the House of Assembly created another Select Committee, Hay flew to Canberra to beg the department to concede more authority to ministerial members. Not only did Barnes and Warwick Smith reject that approach, they would not refer it to Gorton.[44] Happily, there were back channels. Hay and Gorton were old boys of Geelong Grammar, whose headmaster contrived that Gorton invite Hay to dinner. Hay grabbed his chance to advise Gorton that Papua New Guineans must be given real responsibility. That was exactly what Gorton wanted to hear, and he used Hay's ideas to draft a letter to Barnes.[45] By the time the Select Committee arrived, Gorton was ready to urge it to move faster towards fuller autonomy. He was also ready to instruct the department to draw a map of how to get there.

Goode was one of the public servants who would steer new policies through the department. Arriving in 1968, she identified the dominant figures under Warwick Smith as Gerry Gutman in the Economic Division and John Ballard in Political Development. In Special Projects, she helped the other mover and shaker, Besley, to draft the Governor-General's speech to the House of Assembly (only one of her sentences survived). By the end of 1969, she was Personal Assistant to Warwick Smith, preparing Cabinet submissions on devolution.[46]

In Port Moresby in July 1970, Gorton announced what he believed were major changes. Like Whitlam, he did not claim Papua New Guinean support but hoped that the Select Committee would 'want to be associated' with his ideas.[47] He proposed that 'less should be referred to Canberra for decision and more should be retained for decision by the Administrator's Executive Council and by the Ministerial members'. The instruments for this shift included the selection of a spokesman for the AEC in the House, where he could be questioned. Gorton promised not to veto ordinances on subjects for which ministerial members were responsible. He also announced a transfer of executive powers through a device in the Papua New Guinea Act that allowed the Minister for Territories to define the functions of ministerial members.

> The powers to be transferred were substantial: education — primary, secondary, technical but not tertiary — public health, tourism, cooperatives, business advisory services, workers' compensation, industrial training, posts and telegraphs, territory revenue including taxation … price control, coastal shipping, civil defence, corrective institutions, registration of customary land, town planning and urban development.[48]

Gorton was leading the ministerial members to water, but would they drink?

He also replaced key personnel. Warwick Smith was replaced by Hay, whose post was filled by Leslie Johnson. Johnson had quit, but Gorton enticed him back by promising to end Warwick Smith's reign. As part of the same general post, Greenwell replaced Ballard as Assistant Secretary in the Legal Branch. Barnes found it hard to expound the new line, but he was loyal to Gorton and survived with his leader.[49]

The value of these reforms was less than Gorton hoped. First, the Administration continued to absorb Australian specialists, Australian practices and Australian values. Bringing Papua New Guineans into quasi-policy-making roles would not reverse that trend. Second, these reforms depended on energetic ministers, cooperative departments and an independent Administrator's Council. But if these had existed, the Territory would have already been autonomous. The Secretary to the AEC noticed that Australian public servants remained in charge of their departments, legally and practically.[50] Alan Kerr agreed. Public servants were baffled by the extra-legal powers attributed to ministerial members, several of whom spoke no English and some of whom were illiterate.[51] ToLiman was rare in being literate, fluent in English, industrious in his portfolio and supported by a helpful Director of Education. But he was quite unable to fulfil his competing obligations to his constituents, to his colleagues and to parents who wanted a school for their children.[52] In other cases, there was a poor fit between portfolio and department so that ministerial members were involved in a fraction of a department's activities. Browbeaten in the House, remote from their electors, surrounded by experts in arcane procedures, they were deeply insecure.[53]

The Gorton reforms made equally little impact on the AEC. The Council comprised the Administrator, two assistants, the Director of District Affairs, seven ministerial members and — Hay's nominee as AEC spokesman, which dismayed the department — the planter Tom Leahy.[54] At the end of his term, Hay wrote this tepid report card on the reformed AEC:

> the important decisions affecting the Territory are discussed and opinions of all the members are heard and debated. The predominant part is played by the elected members. The Administrator acts very much as a Chairman … no votes have been taken … conclusions have been arrived at by consensus.
>
> The AEC is not responsible to this House but it is responsive to it. Its responsiveness would be more obvious if the House had more time to devote to its affairs. As it is it has invariably been the practice to refer major matters for endorsement by the House.

AEC members were reluctant to represent the Administration, as they were allowed little room to manoeuvre. Even in private, they offered little criticism of the Administration. 'In fact,' concluded Hay, 'in Council meetings there were no serious disagreements on these matters with the policies pursued by the Colonial power.'[55]

In brief, Gorton stole Whitlam's policy clothes and surely intended to transfer powers, but decolonisation needed more than top-down reforms. If he and Barnes had remained in office, the movement to self-government would have continued, but devolution would still have been hampered by a House whose insecure members were overawed by officials, and by a self-doubting Cabinet. As Greenwell saw it, Barnes told Parliament that

> All initiatives for constitutional change would be subject to House of Assembly endorsement. That policy statement was the basis of Australian Government policy throughout the Barnes/Peacock period and was never quite forgotten during the Morrison period.[56]

So the House and the Council enjoyed a de facto veto over constitutional change, but evinced little interest in taking control. From Gorton, they gained the shadow of authority, but power would remain with the department that provided most of the revenue and an Administration used to conveying instructions. The machinery of self-government needed two more elements before there was real change in the distribution of power. The missing elements were officials to create a road map and Papua New Guinean leaders to drive along it.

Footnotes
1. Ted Wolfers, 'January-April 1967', in Moore with Kooyman, *A PNG Political Chronicle 1967-1991*.
2. Hay interviews, National Library of Australia.
3. Denoon, *Getting Under the Skin*.
3. 69/2160, undated minute by A. G. Martin, cited in ibid.
4. Eg., Heinz Arndt, *Asian Diaries*, Asia Pacific Monograph 2, Chopmen, Singapore, 1987, Chapter 12.
5. A451/2 68/4769, M. A. Besley's review, October 16, 1970.
6. A 451/2 68/4769, M. A. Besley's letters to UPNG, December 1969.
7. Ibid.; M. A. Besley's review, August 1970.
8. Cf. Susan Carruthers, *Winning hearts and minds: British governments, the media, and colonial counter-insurgency, 1944-1960*, London, Leicester University Press, 1995.
9. Eg., Crocombe, 'Communal Cash Cropping among the Orokaiva', *New Guinea Research Bulletin*, IV, 1964; and 'The M'Buke Cooperative Plantation', *New Guinea Research Bulletin*, VII, 1965.
10. A 452/1 71/2146, Social Change Advisory Committee Background Paper, October 1, 1968, referring to their 1964 *Follow Up Study on Mental Health of the Indigenes of TPNG*
11. A 452/1 71/2146, M. A. Besley's note, November 6, 1968, enclosing the SCAC's 'Notes on the Bougainville Situation'.
12. Ibid.; Confidential Minute by Hay, as Secretary of the Department, December 2, 1970.
13. A451/2 68/4769, M. A. Besley's review, October 16, 1970.
14 Philip Fitzpatrick, *Bamahuta: Leaving Papua New Guinea*, Pandanus Books, Canberra, 2005.
15 Donald Horne, *Time of Hope*, Sydney, Angus & Robertson, 1980.
16 Jim Byth, interview, Melbourne, 2000. See also Fitzpatrick, *Bamahuta*.
17. Interview, John Langmore.
18. Interview, Ross Garnaut. McCasker, who arrived in 1965, had been on the Vernon Committee reviewing Australian economic policy, but fell foul of John Stone and was therefore in exile in Konedobu.
19. Rachel Cleland, *Pathways to Independence: Story of Official and Family Life in Papua New Guinea from 1951 to 1975*, Perth, 1983.
20 Michael Hess, '"In the Long Run ...": Australian Colonial Labour Policy in the Territory of Papua and New Guinea', *The Journal of Industrial Relations*, March 1983.
21. Geoffrey Dabb, in 'Hindsight'; Interview, John Greenwell.
22. Interview, Greenwell, and Dabb, in 'Hindsight'.
23. Greenwell, Interview.
24. Interview, Tos Barnett.
25. In defending one client in 1964, Dabb attacked the basis for a common form of charging procedure: Ebulya (1964) P&NGLR 200. See also Daera Guba (1973) 130 CLR 353 and Teori Tau (1969) 119 CLR 564.
26. Dabb, in 'Hindsight'
27. Interview, John Ley.
28. Interview, Peter Bayne.
29. Nick O'Neill in 'Hindsight'.
30. Fenbury's plea to the 1965 ICJ conference is reproduced as 'Kot Bilong Mipela' in New Guinea.
31. Dabb in 'Hindsight', citing Morris and Read, 1974.
32. Interview, Ross Garnaut.
33. Ian Howie-Willis, *A Thousand Graduates: conflict in university development in Papua New Guinea, 1961–1976*, Australian National University, 1980.
34. Interviews with Ulli Beier. See also Ulli Beier, *Decolonising the Mind: the impact of the University on culture and identity in Papua New Guinea, 1971-74*, Pandanus Books, Canberra, 2005.
35. Whitlam, in 'Hindsight'. Beazley wrote the friendly preface to the Barnes biography; Loraine Nott's *CEB: Exploits of an Uncommon Man*, Pioneer Press, Warwick, 1989.
36. Hank Nelson, 'The Talk and the Timing', in D. Denoon (ed.), *Emerging from Empire? Decolonisation in the Pacific Islands*, Department of Pacific and Asian History, ANU, 1997.
37. Interviews with Morrison.

38. Whitlam, in 'Hindsight'.
39. Whitlam had the statement included in *Hansard*, October 10, 1972, pp. 2298–3000.
40. Nelson, 'The Talk and the Timing'.
41. Christine Mary Goode, 'Preparation and Negotiation — The Transfer of Power from Australia to Papua New Guinea 1970-1975', UPNG thesis, 1975; and interview with Paul Kelloway.
42. Goode, 'Preparation and Negotiation', p. 40.
43. Ian Hancock, *John Gorton: He Did It His Way*, Hodder, Sydney, 2002.
44. Hay's interviews, National Library of Australia.
45. Ibid., citing Gorton's minute of February 2, 1970.
46. Interview with Christine Goode.
47. Ballard to Newman, June 18, 1970, telex.
48. Johnson, 'Westminster in Moresby'.
49 Interview, John Greenwell.
50. Interview, Paul Ryan.
51. Interview, Alan Kerr.
52. ToLiman to Administrator; Interview, Ebia Olewale.
53. Mark Lynch, 'Communication and Cargo'.
54. Tom Leahy, *Markham Tom: Memoirs of an Australian Pioneer in Papua New Guinea*, Crawford House, Adelaide, 2002; Interview, Pat Galvin.
55. Hay's interviews, National Library of Australia.
56. Interview, John Greenwell; and Greenwell to Kerr, December 1976.

PART 2: DECOLONISATION

Chapter 6

Gearing Up

The Arek Select Committee

A generation later, it is hard to imagine a time when decolonisation seemed neither inevitable nor perhaps achievable. But, in 1969, the pace of parliamentary politics in Papua New Guinea was still leisurely. Weeks before Whitlam's visit and Gorton's U-turn, the Member for Ijivitari in Papua's Northern District, Paulus Arek, took the initiative. A graduate of Sogeri High School, Arek was more articulate and more experienced than most members. When he proposed another Select Committee, the House agreed, expecting that this, like Guise's Committee, would merely tinker with the status quo. Its membership reinforced that impression. Having proposed the Committee, Arek was (by convention) its chair. Seven of the 14 members (the Australians Tom Leahy, Wally Lussick and John Middleton, the Highlanders Tei Abal, Sinake Giregire and Matiabe Yuwi, and the Tolai Matthias ToLiman) belonged to the new and conservative United Party. Two more were officials, and the other five were aligned with Pangu (Arek, Donatus Mola, Ebia Olewale, Michael Somare and Oala Oala-Rarua).[1] Ninkama Bomai from Gumine in the Highlands warned that 'if you people really want to ruin the Territory you can introduce self-government, but we people in the Highlands do not want it in our area. [You] should inquire into our thoughts on these matters.' Arek assured him that they would do just that.[2]

The committee embraced precedents from previous committees and the Australian connection. They elected Deputy Administrator Leslie Johnson as Arek's deputy and agreed that he recruit an executive officer from Canberra. They asked members of previous committees (Johnson and Abal) for advice on how to manage consultations.[3] When Johnson quit (Chapter 5), a shaken Arek asked Barnes to bring him back to help draft the report.[4] Like the Gunther and Guise Committees, therefore, they first consulted Canberra. The political scientist Robert Waddell was sad but not surprised when Arek explained that 'we will find out from the Department of Territories what powers they would be prepared to delegate.'

> Although such an approach no doubt displayed a firm grasp of realpolitik, it seemed strange … that the committee should have to find out what Canberra was prepared to concede before they discovered what the people of Papua New Guinea wanted.[5]

As late as their visit to Canberra, their ambitions were modest. According to Bruce Juddery in the *Canberra Times*,[6] even Somare would not agree to independence: he just wanted more decisions made in Konedobu. Lussick, speaking for Arek, merely wanted decision-making to be more accessible to the people. On May 23 in the Melbourne *Age*, Arek summed up the confusion, conceding that the people did seem to want 'a basically incompatible form of constitutional advance'. Most did not want self-government for several years, yet they did want more full ministers with more power and more financial control. Perhaps the clearest expression of the committee's intention was Ebia Olewale's, commenting on demonstrations in Rabaul and Bougainville. The protestors were not hostile to the police or even to the Administration, he insisted, but resented Canberra's tight control. In his inaugural lecture at the University of Papua New Guinea, Charles Rowley expanded the critique: the local public service, he insisted, 'is effectively though not formally an extension of the Commonwealth Public Service, dominated by Australian values and methods. The real executive is located in Australia.'[7]

Cautious schizophrenia reflected the mood of meetings when the committee consulted the electors. In Rabaul, 1,500 people heard the Mataungans call for immediate self-government, demanding that 'all powers now held by Canberra should be surrendered to Papua-New Guinea immediately', and that there be a presidential form of government. As well as a presidency, however, they wanted regional governments, so that Highlanders could opt out of self-government.[8] That proviso acknowledged a strong Highland sentiment. In the Western Highlands 'on behalf of 37,000 people,' Kaibelt Diria insisted that they 'did not want self-government for another three generations'.[9]

Constitutional terms were used so loosely that it is difficult to determine what was meant. Somare and others sought devolution, but they avoided emotive terms ('independence' and even 'self-government') lest they offend audiences. Even in Rabaul and Bougainville, few people demanded 'independence' but they did want power to devolve, either to Konedobu or to regional bodies. As before, Canberra was fully informed, and learned that the people 'do not yet understand the way the present system of government works and the implications of future change. There is evident a desire for more political education.'[10] Every indication suggested another report seeking minor adjustments.

Overseas travel shifted some opinions. In March 1970, the committee formed two groups to see the world. Arek, Giregire, ToLiman, Middleton, Olewale and Littler went east to the Solomon Islands, Fiji, American Micronesia, Samoa and Tonga. Those who flew west to Ceylon, Ghana and Kenya were Abal, Yuwi, Mola, Somare, Oala-Rarua, Lussick, Leahy and Morrison.[11] Before they set out, they welcomed a new executive officer. Alan Kerr from the Department of Territories was well travelled, having escorted Members of the House and other Territory delegates through Africa on their way to UN meetings[12] in a campaign to introduce Papua New Guineans to Africans and Asians.

Kerr travelled with the Africa party, and observed that African politicians made a great impression. Africans equated self-government with the winning of an elected majority in the colonial assembly. The visitors were shocked to realise that they had enjoyed precisely such a majority since 1964 but had never thought to build on it. Kerr was also impressed by Somare's determination that his rival, Tei Abal, should hear and grasp all the comments of the Africans.

African insights were reinforced by Australian Government statements that change would have to be accepted, if not embraced. When Gorton delegated powers, the contrast between Australian and Territorial opinion was overt: the Australians wanted haste while the Select Committee lagged. Waddell summed up the tension neatly, if unkindly:

> Papua New Guinea was going to be treated like Henry Ford's early customers and be offered any kind of constitution provided it was parliamentary, unicameral and unitary.[13]

It would need deft wording to reconcile Australian policy with Territory sentiment. Happily, the committee was up to the task.[14] Their final report assumed that each House would last four years: 1972 to 1976 and 1976 to 1980. Their constituents felt 'that internal self-government should come about *no sooner* than during the life of the 1976-1980 House'. This anxiety was acute in the Highlands, whereas some other people did believe that 'the time is now ready for internal self-government'. To square the circle, the committee observed that 'the rate of political development and awareness ... is accelerating', so that Territory and Australian opinion might be expected to converge. In that case, 'the majority of the people of the Territory may request that the country move to internal self-government before the end of the next House of Assembly [ie,. before 1976]'. And they expected that a change of government in Australia would result in 'internal self government becoming a reality before the majority of the people are prepared to accept it'.

The committee listed popular views that were hard to reconcile. They saw little interest in independence but 'some desire for self-government'. There was a strong desire for regional government but equal interest in a central presidency. People valued Australian patronage but they also wanted to reduce official membership of the House and to increase the number of elected members. Perhaps rashly, they invited suggestions for the country's name and solemnly recorded not only the plausible Paguinea, Papua-New Guinea and Niugini, but the unlikely Melanesia, Taronesia, Paradise, Pangu — and even Bougainville.[15] Alan Kerr heard a man promise to accept Niugini — if it were pronounced Papua!

To synthesise these views and reconcile them with Australian policy, the committee proposed a program of development towards self-government. For the first time, they sketched a timetable, such that self-government would be achieved during the life of the next House (1972–76). To that end, they wanted to dilute the official membership, with no more than four official and three nominated members, as against 82 open and 18 regional seats (instead of 69 and 15). The Administrator's Executive Council should expand to include 10 ministers beside the Administrator and three other officials. The wider ministry would comprise 17 ministers, who would elect the Deputy Chair of the AEC. The Deputy Chair would be, in effect, the Territory's Chief Minister.[16]

These propositions were put to the House, together with a name (Niugini), a crest and a flag. After three days of debate, the House adopted the report, except the name Niugini. In September, the recommendations were accepted, though Tammur reckoned that the report 'only tells us what the Australian Government thinks this country should have'. He moved that self-government be granted by the end of 1972, but allowing regions to opt out. The motion was lost, 51 to 14. The next day, Arek explained that defence and external affairs would remain Australian responsibilities, and there would be shared control of police and internal security. He also expected 'some sharing arrangements' for 'the Public Service, judiciary, trade, banking and perhaps some areas of civil aviation'.

Because Canberra leaned on the committee, and the committee massaged the House, the territory had accepted the goal of self-government, at least in name. By January 1971 Whitlam found that the prospect of self-government was accepted by 'the most significant sections of the population'. The compromise did not, of course, satisfy him. He insisted that speed was essential in order to hold Papua New Guinea together, so he reckoned that the Minister should set target dates, that official members should leave the House at once, and that Territory ministers should begin to exercise real responsibility. These were more steps than the politicians would accept: on March 18 the House threatened to seek UN intervention if a Labor government tried to impose self-government.

As Goode suggests, the harmony between the committee, the Administration and the Territories Department embodied cooperation in drafting the report. The man in the middle was Alan Kerr, who formed warm relations with committee members. After his committee work, he returned to the department as assistant secretary for constitutional and political matters, and was one of the key intermediaries between Konedobu and Canberra in the transfer of powers.

The Gearing-Up Program

The Select Committee report delighted Barnes, who objected to timetables only if they were imposed from outside. He had no complaint about the House fixing dates, especially as they implied only gradual change. After the Territory's election of early 1972, he expected 'a cohesive group of Ministers' to emerge, supported by a majority in the House. In that case,

> the Commonwealth would in practice regard this group as constituting a government, with the authority of the Administrator gradually becoming confined to matters remaining within Commonwealth responsibility.

Further powers would be handed over as the House felt able to accept them, and the Papua New Guinea Act would be amended to acknowledge 'the attainment of full internal self-government'.[17] Australia had certainly changed course and so had Papua New Guinea's leaders. But the Territory would still need budget support; timid ministers would still rely on department heads; and self-government would be more shadow than substance.

Time, tide and the department did not wait for the Select Committee. Planning began when Territories officials began talks with (among others) the Prime Minister's Department, the Attorney-General's Department and Treasury. By June 1970, they were exploring 'the implications of early self-government'.[18] A revealing shift occurred between two drafts. The first pointed out anxiously that 'more work will be required on several matters, some of which require quite exhaustive examination', and the purpose of the draft report was

> not to advocate the early achievement of self-government, rather it aims at pointing up for Ministers those implications of early change which may be useful to Ministers when considering a related submission concerning changes in the constitutional arrangements.

The next draft deleted the need for exhaustive study and reworded the purpose:

> neither to advocate nor to argue against the early achievement of self-government. Rather it aims at pointing up for Ministers the more obvious implications of an early change.

The paper first delineated 'self-government', as a situation in which Australia

> 'has ceased to have any executive part in the administration of the Territory in relation to its internal affairs'. This assumes that internal security would be the responsibility of the local authorities, but that … [Australia would] retain responsibility for the external affairs and defence of the Territory.[19]

However defined, 'self-government' aroused passions. 'It is widely held to be a stage in development at which Australia and Australians would withdraw.' In order to dispel that notion, it was important to insist that Australian officers and Australian aid would continue.

> If the early achievement of self-government is contemplated it will be important to regard it and to express it as a move towards greater local responsibility but in continuing association with Australian men, money and assistance.

Whatever course Cabinet adopted, all policies should lead to 'greater involvement of indigenes in the social, political and economic affairs of the Territory', while the nervous were assured of continuing Australian involvement and commitment.[20]

Self-government was a stage, but on what road? Many people in the Territory imagined it as 'a lengthy period on the road to independence', but in recent African experience the stage lasted only a few months or was bypassed. It was an opportunity 'to draw up a constitution, arrange for self-determination, and make the necessary administrative changes for independence'. Australia's problem in Papua New Guinea was the reverse. If there was 'little pressure' to move forward, 'a lengthy period of self-government … might provide difficulties'. Australia would still be

> internationally responsible for acts of the local authorities whether or not it was in control of them; similarly it could be held responsible by the United Nations 'Committee of Twenty-Four' in regard to Papua … [and] Australia could find its own relations with Indonesia affected by acts of the local authorities.

Although prolonged self-government would not appeal to Australia, it might be needed to allay opposition in the Territory. Some dangers to Australia might be removed if the people had (by referendum) chosen this status instead of independence. That status ('self-government in free association with an independent state') was recognised by the UN, following the precedent of Cook Islands and New Zealand. As this was the only occasion when that 'freely associated', semi-independent status was mooted, it is worth seeing how the officials regarded it. They saw its benefit to Australia as the fact that people of the Territory would have chosen it, that 'Australia's responsibilities would have been delimited', and that her 'international responsibility would be reduced'. But there was an alarming downside:

> no matter what the constitutional position may be, Australia will always have a close interest in whatever happens in Papua and New Guinea and no matter how reluctant an Australian Government of the future may be to intervene to prevent chaos or in protection of its own interests, the possibility cannot be ruled out that it would feel compelled to do so even if the Territory had attained full independence.

Prolonged self-government or 'free association' were not outcomes that Australia should seek, but possibilities that might have to be endured.

Whatever self-government proved to be, there were obstacles on the road. One was the difficulty of winning the agreement of Australian departments and agencies with Territory interests. These included the Army and the Navy (still separate), specialist agencies in the Attorney-General's and Prime Minister's Departments, Civil Aviation, Shipping and Transport, Public Works, Interior and National Development. Several instrumentalities would also be affected, from broadcasting to airlines, banks and CSIRO scientists. The intimate involvement of Australian departments and programs is suggested by the fact that more than 100 pieces of legislation would have to be amended or withdrawn, from Air Accidents to Whaling (see Appendix).[21] Cooperation was by no means assured. An interdepartmental meeting in June discovered, for example, that Defence and Foreign Affairs were peeved to have been marginal to discussions: sensitivities would have to be stroked.[22]

Pat Galvin was the leading Territories officer involved in the Interdepartmental Committee that developed the cabinet submission on 'the Implications of Early Self-

Government'.[23] Alan Griffith and Bill Worth (both from Prime Minister and Cabinet) helped in 'ventilating issues and digging out entrenched positions'. By contrast, Galvin thought that Foreign Affairs representation was variable and low-key. Foreign Affairs wanted to represent itself as (and maybe to be) more progressive, the White Knight — but without mastering the detail of the issues. They did not like the way Papua New Guinea had been handled, and the time and resources it required of them in the UN General Assembly and elsewhere. Defence was more involved in the committee, and deputed helpful people to it. Most other departments expected little change in arrangements. Bureaucrats were not the only possible hurdle: Galvin believes that Gorton waited until McMahon was out of the Cabinet room before bringing this submission forward; it then passed without opposition. The UN could be difficult, as it would have to approve the outcome of devolution (Chapter 8).

Not least of the obstacles to swift devolution was the Administrator, who compiled a long list of prerequisites for self-government.[24] One political and constitutional requirement was a constitutional framework, though not necessarily a written constitution. A more problematic precondition was 'adequate and stable political leadership': although experienced leaders were emerging, the base was narrow. A stable and seasoned judiciary and public service were also necessary: if Australian office-holders stayed until localisation (which Hay predicted for the 1980s), all would be well, but this could not be assumed. Again, the forces of law and order were adequate only 'on assumption that leadership will be largely expatriate', and there were unresolved issues over the armed services (see below).

Hay urged the same caution in respect of economic issues. The level of aid was adequate — 'provided Australia accepts continuance of aid obligations and [the] Territory accepts some shortfall in full financial autonomy'. An adequate local tax base would emerge with Panguna copper mine, but banking and currency institutions were a long way off, and foreign investment needed encouragement. There was also a social prerequisite, in the form of new citizenship legislation, to retain expatriate public servants and foreign capital.

But Hay's most worrying concern was 'national unity and mutual confidence'.

> In the absence of any strong feeling of unity, some means would have to be found to create a degree of mutual confidence between the main groupings.

Proportional representation in Cabinet might serve as an interim measure, pending a full inquiry before independence, to determine 'whether the various parts want to remain together'.

He concluded that Australia would have to support Papua New Guinea 'more or less indefinitely' with finance and manpower. Australia would not control

> policies on major issues such as land, human rights and freedoms, the constitution, administration of the law, and so on, although it could expect a good deal of broad and some particular influence on economic policies.

One way to read his analysis is that self-government was feasible only if Australia and Australians continued to perform most of their present functions. Papua New Guinea's 'position would be more akin to that of French territories in West Africa than to that of British territories' — meaning more dependent financially and politically.

Fully aware of these cautionary remarks, the Territories Department completed a draft for Cabinet, beginning with a review of the Territory's status and the powers of the Territories Minister and the Administration. The ship of State was crewed by a public service of 14,240 Papua New Guineans and 7,085 expatriates (of whom one-quarter were permanent). Other Commonwealth departments and statutory bodies employed significant numbers; and 3,500 police and 3,500 soldiers maintained order. Obvious impediments to development and devolution were acute shortages of skilled Papua New Guineans: only a handful had professional credentials.

Australia had argued that change would not be imposed, but the majority of people — especially in the Highlands and the Sepik — were likely to resist early devolution. For these people, self-government looked like 'government by coastal Papuans and Tolais'. On the other hand, the Mataungan Association insisted that 60,000 to 90,000 Tolais were more than ready for self-government. The implications of self-government were widely misunderstood, either as access to 'cargo' or as the withdrawal of Australians, or in some places (and by some expatriates) as reverting to pre-colonial conditions. Fragmentation was a distinct possibility: some Sepiks, Highlanders and Bougainvilleans might try to secede if self-government was granted; but Mataungans might try to secede if it was withheld. Another unpleasant prospect was the chance that early self-government would slow the pace of economic development.

To achieve the goal of 'a peaceful and well ordered Papua and New Guinea well disposed towards Australia', the authorities must walk the tightrope between moving too soon or too late, between the minority who wanted self-government and the majority who did not yet find it attractive, many of whom assumed that Australia would proceed at the slowest pace. These difficulties could be reduced by 'pressing authority on to native members of the House of Assembly and native public servants' and by devolving decision-making to local and district levels. That approach would meet resistance but it was necessary in any political scenario. The department presented itself as proposing the middle way, moving 'along a course that might avoid the worst of either of the extremes.'

> This middle course would involve pushing the devolution of political authority on to the people's elected representatives — and on native leaders at all levels — just as fast as (or indeed a little faster than) it could be readily digested or would be understood in the more conservative areas. The intention would be to achieve self-determination as soon as practicable in a climate in which the people of the Territory would feel that Australia was anxious to promote their autonomy yet continue to assist them

Changing arrangements for governance needed legislative and administrative action in Australia. Until the moment of self-government, the Papua New Guinea Act barred the conferring of powers on Papua New Guinean Ministers by acts of the House of Assembly, which complicated the mechanics of transfer and necessitated a good deal of enabling legislation. [25]

Barnes had committed the department to preparing a program for 'movement to full internal self-government in the period 1972–76', although implementation would depend on the leaders and the policies adopted by the House of Assembly. So the department must plan that program.[26]

The head of the Division of Government and Law was John Greenwell, a successful lawyer before he joined the Public Service, and a clear thinker in constitutional and political affairs. He picked up on the Select Committee's proposal that constitutional change be 'geared to' achieving internal self-government during the life of the next House. First, what did internal self-government mean? For Greenwell, it meant the Papua New Guinea Government having responsibility for internal affairs, while Australia retained Defence and Foreign Affairs (possibly including trade, foreign aid and investment, and immigration). Next, a timetable had to be laid down. '*For the purpose of this programme only*, December 1975 has been chosen arbitrarily as the date for the granting of full internal self-government' (as matters turned out, this was serendipitous). The program had two aims. One was to define what had to be done, when it had to be done, and the interdependence of activities and agencies. The other was to protect the Australian Government by providing a contingency plan in case the transfer of powers happened faster than anyone expected.

Back from the Select Committee, Kerr was also involved in the 'Gearing-Up Program'. He describes it as a matrix, tabulating every event that had to occur between then and independence. The matrix listed the dates when the Australian Parliament would meet, when bills had to be ready for it, when the House of Assembly was due to meet, when acts of self-determination had to be made, when the UN Committee of 24 met and so on.

> These events were listed across the top of the matrix … Down the side were listed every possible function of government that we could think of — I think we got to 193.[27]

Lest the planning get ahead of the politics, before the Gearing-Up Program was referred to Papua New Guinea, Greenwell was careful to set its legal context.[28] The authority for the program was a Cabinet decision of May 18, 1970, which endorsed the draft program for presentation by Peacock to the leaders of the next House 'as a basis for initial discussions'. As Peacock had reminded everyone, 'The decision to accept self-government is one for the House of Assembly to speak about' or to resolve how the popular will should be measured. Australia wanted to encourage movement towards self-government, and (with a view to promoting unity) to involve non-government party leaders, so that Australia's position would be, 'as far as possible, accepted by all sections of political opinion in the Territory'. While the program embodied more determination than before, it had not departed entirely from the gradualist tradition:

> Some years ago it was legitimate to see in Home Rule a step of the greatest significance ... But proceeding from the present plan the constitutional change is of far less importance ... self-government will be largely though not entirely legislative recognition by the Australian Parliament of a state of facts which [already] exists.

Security Issues

Underlying every other consideration was the need to ensure peace and order. Internal security was problematic even before Gorton's fateful call-out of the troops. When Cabinet discussed self-government in June 1970, therefore, it directed Territories and Defence to mount a study of security. Cabinet often referred complex problems to interdepartmental committees, to ensure that they were thoroughly analysed and their ramifications explored. Such a committee might grind slowly, but it did grind exceedingly small.[29]

To that end, the departments commissioned 17 separate studies. Their overall purpose was to propose a program for transferring responsibility for internal security, to explore comparable episodes of decolonisation (by consulting the British), to advise on the timing of the transfer of responsibility, to review the organisation and capabilities of the police, and to propose procedures 'for a request by local authorities for the assistance of the defence forces (either locally based or Australian-based) in the event of domestic violence or the threat of such violence'.[30]

Sources for the study of the Territory's internal security were limited. Although the British were asked for information on the management of security while Kenya, Uganda, Singapore and Fiji were moving to independence,[31] Papua New Guinea was unlike a typical British colony. Fiji was likely to be the closest analogy, and Territories procured records of the Fiji constitutional conferences, and abstracted a checklist of items to address.[32]

A Territory Intelligence Committee (TIC, which evolved into PICNIC, the Papua New Guinea Intelligence Committee) collated patrol reports from *kiaps*, added clippings from the newspaper, and kept them under lock and key in a windowless room. The TIC was a subcommittee of the Australian Joint Intelligence Committee. (At self-government, the police special branch was separated out and given two staff seconded from ASIO.) The TIC could collect only information that was widely known.[33] No one who worked for them or read their summaries felt safer.[34] In discussion with other Departments, Territories revealed that there were two branches of the intelligence agency: the Intelligence Branch itself, which would become Papua New Guinea's Internal Security Intelligence Organisation, and a Security Branch, which serviced the Internal Security Committee. The Intelligence Branch evidently employed 100 people — including one Papua New Guinean.[35]

Despite this limitation, an officer of the department circulated a progress report and overview towards the end of 1971.[36] He noted, 'A general decline in respect for law and order and the authority of the government coupled with a rapid increase in the number of crimes reported', and expected further deterioration. There were two flashpoints. One was the Gazelle Peninsula, its problems caused (he thought) by 'strains imposed on a relatively static society by rapid economic development and the imposition of a technologically superior culture, land problems, educational opportunities and a high population growth'. That analysis blended the colonial psychiatry of the day[37] with empirical anthropology.

The second flashpoint was the Highlands. During the first half of 1971, there was a marked increase in reports of tribal fighting, with 22 deaths, 140 injuries and 800 arrests. Two police squads had restored some order, but the trend was worrisome. The violence was mainly intertribal, and it was acute in and around Mount Hagen in the Western Highlands. Although the hostility was not aimed at the Administration, here too 'it seems unlikely that the general state of law and order will improve' before independence.

Bougainville was not seen as a flashpoint although separatist sentiment persisted. A conciliation campaign had followed Lapun's and Bele's appeal and Gorton's intervention (Chapter 4), but secessionism was expected to revive after the 1972 election. The forecast was prescient. To prevent secession by force

> would impose intolerable strains on the internal security forces … and would almost certainly be unsuccessful. The only practicable method of preventing secession would be by political means.

Irian Jaya was another trouble spot. Melanesian opponents of Indonesia's annexation had carried out raids on isolated posts and patrols. If Indonesian troops launched large-scale operations against them, fighting was almost certain to spill across the border.

It was 'highly probable' therefore that there would be disorder 'on a scale beyond the capacity of the police force to deal with', and 'the assistance of the defence forces to restore order will be essential'. The police strength was 240 officers and 3,400 other ranks, expected to rise by 500 in five years. That strength included 11 'special duty squads' — riot police — of whom eight were in the Gazelle, two in the Highlands and one in Port Moresby. The Police Commissioner reckoned that his forces could deal with one large disturbance at a time (such as the 12,000-strong Mataungan rally in 1970) or one medium and one small riot. In view of the number and size of the risks, this was worrying. Recalling the Administrator's Executive Council's appetite for forceful measures, the department's fear of being drawn into actions provoked by a self-governing Cabinet was not unreasonable.

To complicate matters, officials still did not know how much the Pacific Islands Regiment (PIR) was entitled to assist the civil power. Territories assumed that there was

> no limitation on the power of the Defence forces to provide logistic, administrative and transport assistance, nor for units of the military forces to be used to deter unlawful activities by their mere presence *provided at all events that this did not require their involvement in violence.*[38]

It was the proviso that caused concern: if the military was barred from violent action, how strong would be its deterrent effect?

Towards the end of 1971, the IDC proposed to define internal security as 'co-extensive with the state of law and order' — a broad enough view to accommodate any likely crisis.[39] If troops were called out, they would probably be from one of the seven PIR rifle companies. In theory, each company mustered 120 men, but in practice this would be closer to 80. Groups of about 30 could also be drawn from the support companies, giving a maximum of 'about 600 fully trained men readily available'. If the crisis was protracted, other commitments would reduce this total. Unfortunately, it was not clear that troops would really be available at all. Although the Australian Departments of Defence and Territories had agreed that the PIR and the police would train jointly for riot control, and that their equipment would be compatible, the IDC discovered that joint training with the police had simply not happened:

> the Army held the firm view that the PIR could not under the present law carry out duties in aid of the civil power except with its normal weapons (i.e., rifles). The PIR is therefore unwilling to carry out training with batons and shields.

Greenwell agreed with the IDC that ultimate responsibility for internal security should remain with the Commonwealth for the time being: normal law enforcement might devolve to a self-governing Papua New Guinea, but not responsibility for emergencies.[40] This was the situation put to the first Interdepartmental Committee early in 1971.[41] The British view (with which John Ballard was most familiar) was that the period of internal self-government should be as brief as possible. A short period of self-government would minimise Australia's risks, although 'politics might dictate otherwise'. Papua New Guinea's circumstances might very well 'dictate otherwise': for this reason, the Secretary of the Territories Department would have preferred 'an evolutionary approach' to devolution, possibly dividing self-government into stages. To shield Australia from Papua New Guinea's troubles, the IDC urged Australians at all costs to avoid suggesting that the Papua New Guinea Government 'had a right to seek Australian help in internal security matters after independence'.

The United Party was expected to win the 1972 election. Tos Barnett, who observed them closely, doubted that they could have played a leading role in decolonisation, as they were 'pathetically dependent' on whoever advised them.[42] This helps explain why the Canberra discussions expected little contribution from Papua New Guineans. In May 1971, 'the Administration' was renamed 'the Government', while ministerial members became 'ministers',[43] but real change would need a change of personnel. In the nicest possible way, the Australians who had introduced elections were introducing self-determination. Like democracy, it was installed from the top down.

Appendix: 'Commonwealth Acts which, or some of the provisions of which, extend to the Territory of Papua and New Guinea'[44]

Air Accidents (Commonwealth Liability) Act 1963
Air Force Act 1923–65
Air Navigation Act 1920–66
Air Navigation (Charges) Act 1952–69
Airports (Surface Traffic) Act 1960–66
Aliens Act 1947–66
Approved Defence Projects Protection Act 1947–66
Atomic Energy Act 1953–66
Australian Coastal Shipping Commission Act 1956–69
Australian National Airlines Act 1945–66
Australian Security Intelligence Act 1956
Banking Act 1959–67
Banking (Transitional Provisions) Act 1959
Broadcasting and Television Act 1942–69
Citizenship Act 1948–69
Civil Aviation (Carriers' Liability) Act 1959–66
Civil Aviation (Damage by Aircraft) Act 1958
Commonwealth Employees' Compensation Act 1930–69
Commonwealth Motor Vehicles (Liability) Act 1959
Commonwealth Police Act 1957–66
Continental Shelf (Living Natural Resources) Act 1968
Copyright Act 1968
Courts-Martial Appeals Act 1955–66
Crimes Act 1914–66
Crimes (Aircraft) Act 1963
Defence Act 1903–66
Defence Forces Retirement Benefits Act 1948–69
Defence (Re-establishment) Act 1965–68
Defence (Special Undertakings) Act 1952–66
Defence (Transitional Provisions) Act 1946–66
Defence (Visiting Forces) Act 1963
Designs Act 1906–68
Diplomatic Privileges and Immunities Act 1967
Evidence Act 1905–64
Explosives Act 1961–66
Export Payments Insurance Corporation Act 1956–66
Extradition (Foreign States) Act 1966–68
Extradition (Commonwealth Countries) Act 1966–68
Fisheries Act 1952–68
Flags Act 1953–54
Geneva Convention Act 1949
Genocide Convention Act 1949
Gift Duty Act 1941–66
Gold Mining Industry Assistance Act 1954–68
Income Tax Assessment Act 1936–69
Insurance Act 1932–66
International Organisations (Privileges and Immunities) Act 1963–66
Judiciary Act 1903–69

Jury Exemption Act 1965
Lighthouses Act 1911–66
Marriage Act 1961–66
Matrimonial Causes Act 1959–66
Meteorology Act 1955
Native Members of the Forces Benefits Act 1957–68
Naval Defence Act 1910–68
Navigation Act 1912–68
New Guinea Timber Agreement Act 1952–53
Overseas Telecommunications Act 1946–68
Papua and New Guinea Act 1949–68
Papua and New Guinea Bounties Act 1926–37
Papua and New Guinea Loan (International Bank) Act 1968
Papua and New Guinea (Validation of Appointments) Act 1953
Passports Act 1938–66
Patents Act 1952–69
Patents, Trade Marks, Designs and Copyright Act 1939–53
Petroleum Search Subsidy Act 1959–69
Petroleum (Submerged Lands) Act 1967–68
Pollution of the Sea by Oil Act 1960–65
Privy Council (Limitation of Appeals) Act 1968
Re–establishment and Employment Act 1945–66
Removal of Prisoners (Territories) Act 1923–68
Repatriation Act 1920–69
Repatriation (Far East Strategic Reserve) Act 1956–66
Reserve Bank Act 1959–66
Royal Style and Titles Act 1953
Science and Industry Research Act 1949–68
Seamen's Compensation Act 1911–68
Seamen's War Pensions and Allowance Act 1940–69
Service and Execution of Process Act 1901–68
State and Territorial Laws and Records Recognition Act 1901–64
Statutory Declarations Act 1959–66
Submarine Cables and Pipelines Protection Act 1963–66
Trade Marks Act 1955–66
Trading with the Enemy Act 1939–66
Treaty of Peace (Bulgaria) Act 1947
Treaty of Peace (Finland) Act 1947
Treaty of Peace (Germany) Act 1947–66
Treaty of Peace (Hungary) Act 1947
Treaty of Peace (Italy) Act 1947
Treaty of Peace (Japan) Act 1952–66
Treaty of Peace (Roumania) Act 1947
War Crimes Act 1945
War Damage to Property Act 1948
War Gratuity Act 1945–66
War Service Estates Act 1942–43
War Service Homes Act 1918–68
War-time (Company) Tax Assessment Act 1940–66
Weights and Measures (National Standards) Act 1960–66
Whaling Act 1960–66
Wireless Telegraphy Act 1905–67
World Health Organisation Act 1947–63

Footnotes
1. Christine Goode, 'Preparation and Negotiation – The Transfer of Power from Australia to Papua New Guinea 1970–1975', UPNG thesis, 1975.
2. Robert Waddell, 'May–August 1969', in Moore with Kooyman, *A PNG Political Chronicle 1967–1991*.
3. A452/1: 69/4055, Leslie Johnson reports to Administrator, August 15, 1969.
4. Department of Territories press release May 7.
5. Waddell, 'January–April 1970', in Moore with Kooymans, *A PNG Political Chronicle 1967–1991*, p. 100–1.
6. Bruce Juddery in *Canberra Times*, February 19, 1970
7. Waddell, 'September–December 1969', in Moore with Kooyman, *A PNG Political Chronicle 1967–1991*, p. 97.
8. Territory press releases, April 28 and 29, 1970.
9. Department of Territories press release, May 20, 1970.
10. Asst. Sec. (Govt.) to Minister, April 28, 1970.
11. M. R. Morrison to Territories, March 12, 1970.
12. Interview, Alan Kerr.
13. Waddell, 'May–August 1970', in Moore with Kooyman, *A PNG Political Chronicle 1967–1991*, p. 115.
14. 'Final report from the Select Committee on Constitutional Development', reproduced in B. Jinks, P. Biskup and H. Nelson (eds), *Readings in New Guinea History*, Sydney, 1973, p. 412.
15. Asst. Sec. (Govt.) to Minister, May 14, 1970.
16. This, and information in the next five paragraphs, comes from Goode's 'Preparation and Negotiation'.
17. Hank Nelson, 'The Talk and the Timing'.
18. A452 T29 70/3045.
19. Quoting the Papua New Guinea Public Officers (Employment Security) Ordinance, section 10(6)
20. A452, T29, drafts of cabinet submission.
21. June drafts, appendix A and B.
22. Notes from Interdepartmental Committee, June 3, 1970.
23. Interview, Pat Galvin.
24. Telex, Hay to Warwick Smith, June 5, 1970.
25. Goode, 'Preparation and Negotiation', p. 7.
26. A452 T29 1971/2739, Greenwell's Minute of August 16, 1971. The Select Committee had submitted its final report on March 4, and Barnes had addressed Parliament on April 27.
27. Alan Kerr, in 'Hindsight'.
28. A452 T29 1973/976, Minute by FAS (Government and Law) John Greenwell, June 29, 1972.
29. Nancy Viviani and Peter Wilenski, *The Australian Development Assistance Agency – A Post Mortem Report*, Royal Institute of Public Administration, Monograph 3, 1976.
30. A452 T29 1971/3088, Draft Outline Report, December 1, 1971, unsigned but written by G. Cowap.
31. A452 T29 1971/3088, Secretary of Territories to British High Commissioner, undated.
32. A452 T29 1971/2739, N. Potter's Minute, March 24, 1971.
33. Interview, Pat Galvin.
34. Several personal communications. See also Fitzpatrick, *Bamahuta*.
35. A452 T29 1971/3088, IDC on Internal Security after Self-Government, September 16, 1971.
36. A452 T29, drafts of cabinet submission, mid-1970.
37. C. G. Rosberg and John Nottingham, *The Myth of 'Mau Mau': nationalism in Kenya*, New York, 1966.
38. A452 T29 1971/3088, draft letter to Attorney General's Department, undated (but mid-1971).
39. Ibid.; Draft IDC report, December 1, 1971.
40. A452 T29 1971/3088, First Assistant Secretary's Minute, December 7, 1971.
41. Ibid.; 1970/4428, IDC meeting on January 26, 1971.
42. Ibid.; March 20, 2001.
43. Goode, 'Preparation and Negotiation', p. 58.
44 A 452 T29 70/3045.

Chapter 7

New Men, New Visions

Andrew Peacock and Michael Somare

Early in 1972, two political surprises changed the pace and the nature of devolution, bringing in new men, new vision and new energy. Prime Minister Gorton was alienating his Liberal colleagues. When they had passed over Hasluck and selected this little-known war veteran, they imagined him to be a hawk in the war in Vietnam and a conservative at home. His economic and cultural nationalism shocked any Liberals who were not already offended by his autocratic style. Opposition gathered behind the Treasurer, the conspiratorial Sir William McMahon (Whitlam mocked him as 'Tiberius with a Telephone'). The feud reached its climax when Malcolm Fraser resigned as Minister for Defence and triggered a spill in the leadership of the parliamentary Liberal Party. When the party met, it was evident that Gorton had lost a great deal of support, so he yielded to McMahon as party leader and Prime Minister.[1] Since the Country Party supported Gorton (and had a history of thwarting McMahon), the new Prime Minister was more than usually suspicious of its leaders. He sacked Barnes as Territories Minister and replaced him on January 2 with Andrew Peacock — by telephone, naturally. The pretext for Fraser's exit was Gorton's handling of the call-out of the Pacific Island Regiment for a possible crisis in Rabaul. It was mere coincidence that a Territory issue ignited an Australian crisis. Gorton had little interest in Papua New Guinea, and McMahon even less: as Prime Minister, he showed no interest in the young Peacock or his portfolio.

Andrew Peacock, raised in a professional Melbourne family, studied law on his way to a career in politics. He was only 26 in 1965 when he became president of the Victorian Liberal Party. The next year, when Menzies retired, Peacock inherited his blue-ribbon seat of Kooyong. 'The colt from Kooyong' was so handsome, articulate, sociable, talented and ambitious that his continuing rise seemed inevitable. At 30, he was Minister for the Army. As Minister for Territories in 1972, he enjoyed an unusually free hand at an unusually critical time. Where Barnes was elderly and wooden, Peacock was young and silkily gregarious. Unique among ministers, he knew Papua New Guineans personally: he had met them — and of course remembered their names and their interests — when they were officer cadets and he was Army Minister. Barnes's off-the-cuff comments cast doubt on his commitment to devolution but Peacock embraced it wholeheartedly. This was not a policy that he had developed but it was he who animated it.

Peacock was delighted by the quality of his departmental officers. He knew little of them before he met them and — on the basis of Barnes's public persona — imagined a stuffy group, pursuing an unimaginative agenda. The extent and the direction of their policy ideas was a revelation.[2] The respect was mutual: John Greenwell reckoned that 'Peacock's charm and diplomacy were most effective' not only to make allies of Papua New Guineans but 'to dispel the bad attitudes which marked the Administration's relations with the Department, a hostility justified by past performance, notably Warwick Smith's'. The Minister could master a brief and advance an agenda gently but firmly.[3]

On his very first day in office, he flew to Port Moresby with Alan Kerr, the first of a score of visits that year. But when he landed, there were no politicians. The second House had risen and polling for the third would run from February 19 until March 11. Every politician was out on the campaign trail. Even when the winners (trailed by some incredulous losers) returned to Port Moresby, they had little time for Peacock. Instead, they got down to bargaining for office in the first of Papua New Guinea's now-famous bouts of horse-trading. Only in this final stage did Australian officials recognise the possibility of a Somare-led Cabinet. Only on April 20 were divisions called in the new House and the game was over. Even then there were rites to observe: the Administrator's Executive Council (the source of constitutional legitimacy) did not meet until May.

Meanwhile, Peacock was not a man to hang around. He and Kerr drove to the university at Waigani and talked for hours with anyone available. The students and staff were amazed that he came at all, let alone debated subjects such as self-government and independence. Barnes would never have gone there informally. His baffled visit to the Administrative College (Chapter 3) revealed only too clearly his unease with educated Papua New Guineans.

Like Barnes, Peacock welcomed target dates for constitutional advance, but he did not impose them. He cut the link between economic development and constitutional change, and he assumed that there would be a direct transition from self-government to independence.[4] He always emphasised that there was real power to be grasped: the new regime in the House would be 'in effect the first government of Papua New Guinea'. These statements did no more than restate the policy that Gorton and Barnes had announced, but Peacock's audiences could believe that the Government was 'looking forward, and fostering further constitutional change, rather than standing back passively'.[5] His tenure was brief and his policy initiatives few. He did amend the Papua New Guinea Act to increase the size of Somare's ministry;[6] he did accept the motion of the House to start internal self-government on December 1, 1973, or as soon as possible thereafter;[7] and (see below) he discussed details of the timing and the forms of the transfer of powers. But policy-making was not his key contribution. Papua New Guineans were bowled over when he sat with them, shared a beer or a meal or a party, and listened rather than lectured.

As matters turned out, his opposite number and collaborator was Michael Thomas Somare. The young teacher and journalist was a natural conciliator, preferring to build consensus on a compromise rather than insist on a position and confront opponents.[8] With these skills and a low-key manner, he built a multi-party coalition into a surprising majority, and held together an awkward amalgam of nationalists and separatists, radicals and managers. At the same time, he had to fence with a sometimes overbearing Australian Government. When Georgina Beier designed the cover for a study of Papua New Guinea politics,[9] she chose to show Gough Whitlam towering over the diminutive Somare, uncomfortable in Western attire — and another Somare in traditional finery looking self-possessed.

As late as the first sitting of the House, there was lively doubt about the composition of the de facto government. United Party and Pangu members displayed precocious mastery of manoeuvre. Before the opening of the House, each claimed the numbers for victory with such optimism that more adherents were claimed than there were members.[10] The United Party, with at least 40 members, nearly formed a majority on its own. Prudently, they kept their members together — and beyond the courtship of other party leaders — in Port Moresby's Salvation Army hostel. They were at a disadvantage, however, in having lost most of their European leaders, and there would be a new mood in the new House, in which the average age (35) of members was several years younger than that of the second House. The House also included several members, such as Father John Momis and John Kaputin, who possessed much better formal education than their predecessors. United had also lost its absolute grip on Highlanders, with the formation of the National Party, led by the canny Western Highlander Thomas Kavali and the flamboyant Iambakey Okuk from Simbu. Separatists and secessionists were bound to feel more comfortable with Pangu; and independents (lumped together with John Guise under the rubric 'coalition supporters') were also likely to lean towards Pangu.

The pivotal group was the People's Progress Party. If Pangu represented mainly public servants with a rather corporatist tendency, PPP was wedded to free enterprise and was in other ways more conservative. PPP's leader, Julius Chan, son of a Chinese businessman and his Melanesian wife, had studied in Australia for four years before a traffic accident triggered his premature return to the Territory. He joined the Department of Native Affairs as an auditor — and suffered blackballing by the Aviat Club — before taking over the family business in New Ireland in 1963. He won a seat in 1968 and, by 1970, he was parliamentary leader of the PPP. Unlike other successful politicians, Chan came across as a thoughtful, unemotional but clear speaker. In 1972, he was more interested in the quality of the new institutions than the speed with which they were realised. (Paulus Arek, the chair of the latest Constitutional Committee, felt more comfortable in PPP than in Pangu, but he and his colleagues were nonetheless committed to devolution.) After holding out until the last moment, the PPP group threw their weight behind Somare, and were rewarded with the main financial portfolios. At 33, Chan was Finance Minister and three years later became Deputy Prime Minister. Pangu and PPP had divergent values, and Chan saw business (including his own burgeoning companies) as quite compatible with office. Despite these differences, and occasional racist sniping at Chan, the coalition provided six years of stable government.[11]

The forging of an effective team was not all solemn negotiation. The most extrovert new minister was Iambakey Okuk, elected from Simbu to the surprise and annoyance of the United Party. He was a brave and effective campaigner, but new to government. When he resolved to sack the head of his department (Agriculture, Stock and Fish), it fell to Tos Barnett to take him aside and explain that he must do it formally and correctly, or not at all. Okuk was so enraged that he pulled a phone out of the wall and threw it — to the consternation of a Japanese delegation in the outer office, waiting politely for an interview.[12]

Peacock formed an instant and warm relationship with Somare, with whom he shared many traits. Somare told the House of Assembly, with pardonable exaggeration, that

> the appointment of Mr Andrew Peacock ... heralds a new era in Australian policies in Papua New Guinea. The Australian Government has drawn up a plan of movement towards self-government.[13]

Each was a fine communicator of mood; neither was a deep thinker nor burdened by awkward political principles. Somare was the perfect partner; but it is often overlooked that the whole coalition supported his push for early self-government and independence. The separatists (from Bougainville and the Gazelle) were at least as committed to national independence as they were to decentralisation, so they had to work within the coalition. John Guise must have regretted the timidity that cost him leadership, but as Somare's deputy and a mentor to younger Papuans he had no regrets about the road they travelled. It is difficult to imagine the United Party of 1972 becoming effective either as a government or as a partner in devolution.

Gough Whitlam and Bill Morrison

Peacock would have enjoyed completing the task that he embraced with such zest, but it was taken out of his hands. McMahon's government was no more united than Gorton's: at the end of 1972, for the first time in a generation, they lost an election. It fell to Gough Whitlam and Bill Morrison to complete the transfer of powers.

Whitlam was the first Prime Minister to take office with a vision for the Territory. He had first visited the territory as a RAAF navigator in 1945. Through his wife, Margaret, he was connected to Mick Leahy and claims to have learned from him, though it is impossible to imagine cosy chats between the urbane patrician and the rough prospector. As early as 1959 he took part with Hasluck in talks on the dependent territories of Melanesia. The next year, as Labor's deputy leader, he took several colleagues on a long tour of the territory while his party leader, Arthur Calwell, led a 'simultaneous but different itinerary'.

And he developed an alternative approach, although (Chapter 5) he was a solitary figure for some years. He and the Fiji-born and socially progressive South Australian Don Dunstan talked the Labor Party Conference of 1963 into 'a specific and advanced policy on PNG'. The rupture became overt in 1965 when Whitlam told a seminar in Goroka that the world 'will think it anomalous if PNG is not independent by 1970' (Chapter 5). His interventions reached a climax in 1969–70 with his headline-grabbing visit to Rabaul and the issue of 'Labor's Plan for New Guinea' in Port Moresby. The party accepted his vision just in time. Only in June 1971 did the National Conference declare that 'the Labor Party will ensure the orderly and secure transfer to PNG of self-government and independence in its first term of office'. During the 1972 election campaign, Whitlam spelt out his vision of Papua New Guinea's place in the context of Australia's interests. Labor had four commitments:

> First, to our own national security;
> Secondly, to a secure, united and friendly Papua New Guinea;
> Thirdly, to achieve closer relations with our nearest and largest neighbour, Indonesia;
> Fourthly, to promote the peace and prosperity of our neighbourhood.

Linking Indonesia and Papua New Guinea revealed the importance of Territory stability to Australia's relations with its more populous neighbour. A stable Papua New Guinea was threatened by 'immense and intense centrifugal forces'. Whitlam still maintains that Papua New Guinea's unity came under 'desperate and disparate challenges':

> I hear it asserted that my government was in error in pushing PNG into independence too soon ... I simply assert that, had we delayed PNG independence, even for another year, we would have put the country in the gravest danger of breaking up.[14]

The man Whitlam chose as Minister for Territories came from a radically different background from Peacock.[15] William Leonard (Bill) Morrison was destined for Labor as surely as Peacock was a born Liberal. The son of a butcher, his youth in the Sydney suburb of North Curl Curl was dominated by surf lifesaving. Teachers at North Sydney Tech introduced him to Dos Passos and other leftist literature — and to economics. A scholarship made him 'the first surfie to go to university', where he took Honours in Economics. Self-consciously working class among students from private schools, Morrison became deliberately abrasive, as rough as Peacock was smooth.

After university, he applied for every possible job: he was making sausages when he heard that he had been accepted as a cadet in External Affairs. In a 20-year diplomatic career, he served in London, Moscow and Washington, before moving to Bangkok and Kuala Lumpur. In Bangkok, the punctilious ambassador, David Hay, was offended by Morrison's flashy sports car, but became reconciled to his capable, if rakish, second secretary. Moving to Malaysia as Deputy High Commissioner, Morrison was impressed by the way the Government managed foreign aid, and was struck by the fact that a police field force could manage the country's border with more finesse than an army. He was there when Philippines forces invaded Malaysian Sabah. As Australians commanded Malaysian naval vessels, Australians were on the front line of Malaysia's counterattack: Gorton insisted that the vessels be recalled and the Australians removed. Morrison was in Kuala Lumpur when he met Whitlam and began discussing Papua New Guinea. He was already marked as 'political' in the diplomatic service. His opposition to the Vietnam War denied him promotion until Sir James Plimsoll succeeded Sir Arthur Tange as

Secretary of Foreign Affairs in 1965. When he announced that he would seek election to Parliament (in the Sydney seat of St George), Morrison was brought home to the 'purgatory' of the Aid Branch, the least prestigious section of the service.[16]

Elected to Parliament in 1969, he was active in parliamentary and party committees on foreign affairs. He was 44 in 1972 when he was appointed Minister for Territories. From his background, he brought a wealth of ideas about colonialism and decolonisation. He believed (with Whitlam) that it was safer to decolonise too fast than too slow: his Malaysian experience suggested that delay might allow radicals to hijack nationalist movements. In Papua New Guinea, Australia would have to take the initiative, since the ministerial members had obviously failed to change the distribution and exercise of power. A firm and short deadline would ensure movement towards devolution. He had formed a strong preference for police rather than soldiers to manage border disputes; he had seen the perils of military alliances and hoped to avoid a defence treaty that would bind Australia to Papua New Guinean adventurism. He had also matured into a determined operator, who seemed forthright to those who agreed with him but abrasive and abusive to those who crossed him.

Morrison was fortunate in the quality of the staff he inherited. As Secretary, the courteous and cautious Hay was the antithesis of the brusque minister. They had worked in Bangkok with roles reversed, and it is remarkable that such different men could cooperate. Hay was a meticulous supervisor of the complex affairs of the department, and sure-footed in dispelling the animus between Canberra and Konedobu. He knew what difficulties Leslie Johnson would endure as Administrator, and made every effort to ease them. Greenwell's legal expertise made him an excellent manager of the transfer of statutory powers and he and the affable Kerr were on good terms with the politicians and public servants of Konedobu. Don Mentz (the only officer who had worked in a Territory Administration) was well across the economic and financial issues. And some of the more acerbic officers had left: John Ballard and Gerry Gutman as well as Warwick Smith had moved on. Morrison was less impressed by the Territory public servants, with the important exception of Johnson, whose easy manner and sharp mind inspired general confidence. Morrison and Whitlam admired his rapport with Somare and others, and were pleased to inherit him as Administrator.

Unlike the courtly but tongue-tied Barnes, Morrison enjoyed an easy passage in Parliament. He recalls only two parliamentary questions on Papua New Guinea. When Peacock asked the first, he also sent a note that this would probably be his last, and so it proved. This silence was the more remarkable in view of the opportunities for debate, as so many pieces of legislation had to pass through Parliament unchanged (Morrison believes that 280 acts were amended). Within the Labor Party too, the old gradualism vanished. Papua New Guinea was once again a bipartisan issue, but now on the basis of decolonisation.

Morrison accepted that self-government should begin on December 1, 1973, but he wanted to speed up the transfer of powers: by that time 'all the powers would not only have been transferred but the Papua New Guinea Government would also already be exercising those powers'.[17] He was keen to begin shifting foreign affairs and defence powers as well, although these were explicitly reserved until independence. He always advised Papua New Guineans that the critical change in the exercise of powers was not independence but self-government, in order to 'demystify' independence. This approach meant that he wanted to shorten the gap between self-government and independence, when Australia would be responsible but not in control. He was most anxious lest self-government initiate 'a period of lethargy' that would 'encourage proponents of secession … to place pressure on the newly empowered self-governing House of Assembly'. Curiously, it fell to Hasluck — as Governor-General, opening the Australian Parliament — to declare that

> My Government will move with due speed towards the creation of an independent, united Papua New Guinea. Legislation will be introduced to provide for Self-Government on 1 December 1973 or as soon as possible thereafter.

Whatever he felt, Hasluck refrained from comment, just as he had while Barnes undermined his vision and Peacock undid it. The House of Assembly put up sterner resistance. On March 1, 1973, Matiabe Yuwi proposed a referendum on a date for independence, nominating 1974, 1976, 1978, 1980 or even later. This motion lost very narrowly (41 to 40). Unimpeded by the Australian Parliament or the Papua New Guinea House of Assembly, many powers of self-government were transferred several months before the target date.[18]

The Papua New Guinea Office and the Liaison Unit

The transfer of powers was impeded by the unique relationship between Australia and Papua New Guinea. Goode points out that legal control lay with the Minister and

> the point of coordination was the Department of Territories in Canberra rather than the Administrator and his Secretariat as was usual in British colonial practice.
>
> [Until self-government was achieved], the Papua New Guinea Act barred the conferring of powers on PNG Ministers by acts of the House of Assembly, which complicated the mechanics of transfer and necessitated a good deal of enabling legislation. [As an unfortunate result, the] transfer of power frequently entailed both detailed legislative and administrative action.[19]

When the Department of Territories dissolved, therefore, a complex and critical agenda remained. While 200 Territories staff transferred to the new aid agency, a smaller unit was mandated to complete the transfer of powers. Formally, the Papua New Guinea Office was a unit in the Department of External Affairs, responsible to Morrison as 'Minister Assisting the Minister of External Affairs for Papua New Guinea matters'. Greenwell was its first head and Kerr his deputy. Kerr dealt with the mechanics of transfer while Greenwell dealt with legal and constitutional matters, ensuring that the

Papua New Guinea Act fell down in stages, and that complementary legislation and provisions were ready to start up in Papua New Guinea. Their establishment of 40 staff shrank as functions were transferred. Once the task was well in hand, Kerr succeeded Greenwell and — like the Cheshire Cat — the office faded away. In 1974, Kerr and a few others transferred to the Department of the Prime Minister and Cabinet with vestigial responsibility.

The residual Canberra department created an outpost in Port Moresby. Confusingly, like its headquarters in Canberra, it was often called the Papua New Guinea Office. It was from this vantage point that Christine Goode took part in and recorded the shifting relations with the local government.[20] Patrick Galvin went to set the office up in January 1972, when it had nine staff. He was well equipped, having managed the Territories Department's International Relations, liaised with the UN, the South Pacific Commission and the OECD. He had also worked on Irian Jaya, aid and trade treaties, and he was well acquainted with senior officers in the Territory.[21] As the office expanded (to 70 staff by independence) and diversified its activities, it formed the kernel also of Australia's diplomatic representation.

Its counterpart in Konedobu was a much smaller unit headed by Tos Barnett and reporting to Somare. From teaching magistrates at the Administrative College, Barnett had gone to the university Law Faculty, where Vice-Chancellor Gunther noticed his skills and determined to use them elsewhere. An unwieldy committee of Australian men was pondering the transfer of powers. Gunther suggested, and Johnson agreed, that Barnett should manage this committee. He disbanded it at once and replaced it with three men: Ilinome Tarua, Brian Edie and himself. The Australian, Edie, was an industrious administrator. Tarua, from Kwato in Milne Bay, was one of the first Papuan lawyers. The trio advised Somare and other ministers on two main topics: 'issues involved in the transfer of powers and functions' and 'preparations to achieve independence'.[22]

They began placidly, expecting self-government in 1978 and independence even later.[23] Pangu's victory changed the pace of their work. It also introduced an odd difficulty. Barnett had helped Voutas in managing Pangu's election campaign, but Barnett's unit was answerable to the Administrator, not to Somare. In Voutas's view, therefore, Barnett was 'politically the enemy'. When he and others refused to talk to Barnett, the job became impossible. Barnett and Johnson suggested that the problem would disappear if the unit could be transferred whole to Somare. After an interview with the mandarin Tange, this proposal was accepted. Barnett's unit reported to Somare and only through him to Johnson. Barnett's main Australian counterpart was Kerr, while day-to-day matters were managed in the increasingly important Port Moresby-based Papua New Guinea Office. He had little respect for many public servants in Canberra, but he developed great respect for Greenwell and Kerr.

By July 1972, three months after they formed a government, Papua New Guinea ministers began talks on self-government with Peacock and Territories Department officials, using the Gearing-Up Program as the basis for discussions. Peacock explained that their purpose was 'to discuss in concrete terms the transfer of further powers'.

As a Constitutional Planning Committee had been created, and a date for self-government accepted, Peacock hoped to agree on

> a provisional or tentative timetable for the transfer of further powers and an agreed list of the administrative and legislative steps which have to be taken in order to give effect to that timetable.[24]

It was optimistic to suppose that the Gearing-Up Program would be accepted without debate or amendment. Somare used his opening address of the talks to explain his anxiety. He agreed that a long delay in handing over responsibility might sour relations between the two countries, and 'we are glad that our views on this issue seem to be shared by a progressive Minister ... and by his Departmental officers'. But he set out principles that should govern the discussions. First, his government would 'take the initiative in preparing the country to accept the idea of self-government and independence' and would not press for the legal handover until the House of Assembly expressed its will on the subject. Second, until that handover, 'there must be the maximum possible involvement of Papua New Guineans in the policy-making for, and the practical administration of' government. Thus 'all practical day to day administrative decisions must be made here' and, unless vital Australian interests were affected, 'the *policy* should be decided here also by my government'. Australian advice would be welcome, but 'we must get used to making our own decisions', so Australians would intervene only rarely. Third, the approach should involve Papua New Guinean ministers and officials as fully as possible.

Somare's fourth and final principle reflected a rather different mood. Taken aback by the thoroughness of the Gearing-Up Program, ministers realised that they were poorly briefed and they wanted to postpone discussions until they could master the issues. Somare confessed that his government could not yet formulate policies on critical matters such as development planning or even electoral arrangements. For this reason, he wanted the present meeting to be treated as preliminary.

This was a moment of recognition. The Papua New Guineans had approached self-government with more enthusiasm than anxiety. Only when they saw the thoroughness of the plan did they recognise that Australia might shed powers faster than Papua New Guinea could pick them up. Both sides agreed on the destination, but serious differences might emerge on how — and how fast — to get there.

Confident that both sides wanted the same outcome, the Australians began to sound out the UN. The Trusteeship Agreement required that independence be endorsed by the General Assembly after an Act of Self-Determination by the people of the territory. The form of this act was a matter of great importance. The Australian and Papua New Guinea Governments wanted the simplest possible mechanism — a single majority vote in the House of Assembly. But the UN could demand a plebiscite, or even separate plebiscites in New Guinea and Papua. UN compliance could not be taken for granted. There were precedents for separate referenda: before British Togoland joined the Gold Coast, and when the British Cameroons merged with Nigeria. France had opposed these assimilations of non self-governing territories (like Papua) with Trust Territories (like New Guinea). The prospect of a single plebiscite was alarming enough. Not only was Somare keen to avoid it, Whitlam feared (and Morrison was sure) that a referendum would be lost, with dire consequences for the Territory and the rest of Australia, which might not be able to disentangle itself.[25]

With some anxiety then, Peacock sent Greenwell to New York in June 1972 for talks with the Secretary-General and others.[26] He and Foreign Affairs worked closely, to great effect. Stanley Pearsall, Australia's representative to the Trusteeship Council, restated the position that self-government would be achieved at a pace determined by the House of Assembly, that the Chief Minister expected it in the lifetime of the present House, and that Australia would give every encouragement. The Australian delegation included three Papua New Guineans — Simon Kaumi (the Electoral Commissioner), Anton Parao (United Party) and Gavera Rea (Pangu) — who answered questions on the election, Bougainville, cargo cults and the fact that the United Party was limited mainly to the Highlands.[27]

Happily, a Visiting Mission of the Trusteeship Council, including members of the more radical Committee of 24, had overseen the 1972 election and described it as 'thorough, comprehensive and fair'. With the House's legitimacy endorsed, the UN was content that its majority vote would be sufficient. Opening the Session of the Trusteeship Council, the Secretary-General rejoiced that the Visiting Mission report

> confirms the uninterrupted march of this Territory towards the objectives of the Charter … a coalition Ministry has been formed and we are pleased to note the growing sense and form of unity for this new country and its now rapid movement towards self-government and independence.

Behind the formalities there was much camaraderie, suggesting that the Trusteeship Council was never likely to be a high hurdle. Australian diplomat Robin Ashwin congratulated the new President of the Trusteeship Council, the American W. T. Bennett:

> Mr President, we have seen you managing a visiting mission swimming in its underpants off the beach at Arawa in Bougainville. We have seen you ably conducting a meeting of some 70 male candidates for election to the House of Assembly at a Women's Training Centre in Kundiawa in the Chimbu.[28]

On December 7, ABC News reported that the Trusteeship Council, by acclamation, adopted a resolution expressing gratification about the schedule for full self-government.

Appendix: The Third House of Assembly and the First Cabinet[29]

David Hegarty's analysis alludes to the uncertainty of party affiliations:

> The actual number of members belonging to the parties was a little uncertain. A reasonable estimate showed Pangu twenty-four, PPP eleven, National Party seven, Mataungan Association three, Coalition supporters twelve, and the [United Party] forty-two.

Pangu
Michael Somare	Chief Minister
Paul Lapun	Mines
Ebia Olewale	Education
Albert Maori Kiki	Lands(later, Foreign Affairs and Trade, and Defence)
Gavera Rea	Labour
Reuben Taureka	Health
Boyamo Sali	Local Government

Coalition Members
John Guise	Interior
Paulus Arek	Information and Extension Services

New Guinea National Party
Thomas Kavali	Works
Iambakey Okuk	Agriculture, Stock and Fisheries
Sasakila Moses	Forests
Kaibelt Diria	Posts and Telegraphs

People's Progress Party
Julius Chan	Internal Finance
Donatus Mola	Business Development
John Poe	Trade and Industry
Bruce Jephcott	Transport

Footnotes
1. Ian Hancock, *John Gorton: I Did It My Way*.
2. Interview, Andrew Peacock.
3. Interview, John Greenwell.
4. Nelson, 'The Talk and the Timing'.
5. Goode, 'Preparation and Negotiation', pp. 66–7.
6. *House of Representatives*, August 16, 1972, p. 241.
7. *House of Representatives*, October 10, 1972, p. 2297.
8. Interview, Tos Barnett.
9. Rex Mortimer, Ken Good and Azeem Amarshi, *Development and Dependency: the Political Economy of Papua New Guinea*, 1979.
10. David Hegarty, 'January–April 1972', in Moore and Kooymans, *A PNG Political Chronicle 1967-1991*, p. 156.
11. *Australian Financial Review*, March 27, 1997
12. Interview, Tos Barnett.
13. House of Assembly, April 24, 1972.
14. E. G. Whitlam, in 'Hindsight'.
15. Interview, Bill Morrison.
16. According to Nancy Viviani and Peter Wilenski, *The Australian Development Assistance Agency*.
17. Bill Morrison, 'Draft Notes on the Timetable for Independence and the Transfer of Powers', in 'Hindsight'.
18. Goode, 'Preparation and Negotiation'.
19. Ibid. pp. 7–8.
20. Ibid.
21. Interview, Pat Galvin.
22. Ilinome Tarua, discussion by panel of constitution-makers, Port Moresby, March 28, 1996.
23. Interview, Tos Barnett. March 20, 2001.
24. Goode, 'Preparation and Negotiation', p. 75. The talks ran from July 27 to August 7.
25. Interview, Bill Morrison.
26. John Greenwell's files: the Trust Deed, Greenwell to Hay from New York, May and June 1972, on his soundings of UN officials on the form of the act of self-determination; Greenwell to Kerr, May 26, 1972, on a constitutional commission; Greenwell to Kerr, May 26, 1972, on Marianas; Greenwell to Hay, June 6, 7192, reporting Ambassador Plimsoll's views and the Secretary-General's speech.
27. Ibid., June 8, 1972.
28. Ibid., opening the 39th Session of the Trusteeship Council, May 25, 1972.
29. David Hegarty, 'January–April 1972', in Moore and Kooyman, *A PNG Political Chronicle 1967–1991*, p. 156.

Chapter 8

Creating a Constitution

Keen to decolonise Australia, Whitlam assured Somare that he endorsed the timetable that would confer self-government on December 1, 1973, and independence as early as 1974. He allowed little latitude in the timing, and none in the shape of independence. His policy speech ('It's Time') made 'a secure, united and friendly Papua New Guinea' a priority, an outcome essential to regional stability and Australia's fulfilment of the UN Trust. Twice in 1972, the UN General Assembly reaffirmed the need for unity and policies for 'discouraging separatist movements and promoting national unity'.[1]

Whitlam's government believed that speed was essential. Given enough time, the United Party might wean members of the coalition away from Somare and arrest the momentum to decolonise, or the forces of secession might rally. Whitlam laid it on the line: 'It is folly for anybody to believe that any section of Papua New Guinea would serve its interests by going it alone. For it would truly mean going alone.'[2] Haste was needed too, lest Australia find itself responsible for the actions of a government that it did not control. Morrison expected to have to prod Papua New Guinea's leaders, if they proved as stodgy as their predecessors. So a firm and short deadline was vital, and Somare's colleagues agreed, at least in principle (Chapter 7). A willing decoloniser was dealing with a willing successor. Surely nothing could impede the smooth and swift transfer of powers.

The Constitutional Planning Committee

But Papua New Guinea's peculiarities threatened this scenario. Apart from the need to create institutions from scratch (Chapters 9 and 10), the people had to be consulted and coaxed to accept citizenship in a nation-state. Then a turbulent parliament had to adopt a constitution; and the UN had to approve the processes of decolonisation.

Somare's team recognised that popular opposition, or even apathy, would jeopardise independence: a powerful Constitutional Planning Committee was essential to garner support. Somare was already alert (Chapter 7) to the risk of merely acting out Australia's scenario. According to the neat summary of his adviser, Tony Voutas,

> Suspicion that Australia would make all its constitutional decisions for it and continue to set the pace was a significant element behind … the setting up of the

Constitutional Planning Committee. Such a Committee would, it was hoped, more than counterbalance Canberra's planning and enable the PNG Government to establish its own priorities.[3]

As the CPC delved deeper, its members would demand more time. Whitlam and Morrison remained convinced that delay would jeopardise unity and decolonisation. And these rival visions were projected with increasing acrimony onto Papua New Guinea's government.

Somare proposed a committee of 15 respected parliamentarians:

Michael Somare, Chair ex officio	East Sepik	Pangu
Father John Momis, Deputy Chair	Bougainville	Pangu
Toni Ila	Lae	Pangu
Pikah Kasau	Manus	Pangu
Tei Abal	Wabag	United Party
Deputy Leader of the Opposition, promoted Leader, succeeded by:		
Anton Parao	Western Highlands	United Party
Angmai Bilas	Madang	United Party
Mackenzie Daugi	Northern	United Party
Sinake Giregire	Daulo	United Party
Matiabe Yuwi	Tari-Komo	United Party
Paul Langro	West Sepik	United Party
John Kaupa	Chuave	National Party
Paulus Arek	Ijivitari	People's Progress Party
Minister for Information, died, succeeded by:		
Boyamo Sali	Morobe	People's Progress Party
Stanis Toliman	Bogia	People's Progress Party
John Guise, Deputy Chief Minister	Alotau	Independent
John Kaputin, Minister of Justice	Rabaul	Mataungan

Arek's successor, Boyamo Sali, did not attend meetings, but Abal's successor, Anton Parao, became an active member. The selection of Momis as de facto chair reflected not only his reputation for articulate intelligence and integrity, but the pivotal importance of his Bougainville constituents. As a seminarian and priest, he was steeped in Bougainville's struggles with the mining company and the radical ideas of Paulo Freire gave him the language for his populism. The inclusion of four ministers underlined the CPC's crucial role, though two played little part in debates. The membership combined regional and party balance with personal distinction.

Cabinet appointed three full-time and several part-time consultants. The Kenyan political scientist Ali Mazrui declined his invitation. The most senior consultant was Jim Davidson, New Zealander by birth, Professor of Pacific History at the ANU and adviser to Samoa's constitution-makers. His protégé, David Stone, had analysed the Cook Islands Constitution before he joined the New Guinea Research Unit to study politics.

The Australian Ted Wolfers was the most experienced analyst of local politics. John Ley joined as counsel to the House of Assembly and he was joined later by Peter Bayne. All counted Papua New Guinean politicians among their friends; none identified with the Australian Government and most regarded Morrison — if not Whitlam — with suspicion verging on hostility. Seeing no indigenous advisers, the CPC selected the lawyer Bernard Narokobi. They were also advised by the Tanzanian Yash Ghai, Ronald Watts from Canada, Bill Tordoff of Manchester and Nigel Oram of the UPNG.

A clarifying crisis blew up in March 1973, when Mathias ToLiman, as Leader of the Opposition, accused the CPC of being the Government's rubber stamp. He told his (surprised) colleagues that they would be boycotting meetings until their demands were met. Evidently, he felt isolated from the CPC, some United Party members feared the radical influence of the CPC's consultants, and Tei Abal wanted more staff and facilities. After lengthy negotiations, ToLiman was promised regular briefings and Abal was allowed more facilities. Consultants were told (in Momis's neat phrase) to be 'on tap, not on top'. And Davidson's untimely death removed the consultant with the highest public profile.

That was the last time anyone accused the CPC of subservience. While the Government considered speed to be more important than perfection, the CPC came to see a constitution as a shield against all ills: it would set national goals, guide efforts to achieve them, guarantee rights and freedoms, prevent abuses of power and ensure local autonomy. Members began to talk of nation-building, which they saw as their own domain. 'True nation-building', they insisted, 'cannot be achieved by the central government imposing its will through bureaucratic processes. That would be a mere continuation of the old colonial system, an exchange of masters.'[4]

They reckoned that independence provided a chance to define:

> the philosophy of life by which we want to live and the social and economic goals we want to achieve. If the constitution is to be truly the fundamental charter of our society and the basis of legitimate authority it should be an instrument which helps achieve these goals ... The constitution should look towards the future and act as an accelerator in the process of development, not as a brake.

There was a whiff of utopianism in Narokobi's dream of overthrowing the State in favour of a confederation of villages:

> The rural wanples [communities] would be small democratic republics, like interpenetrating circles with common areas of culture and civilisation. They would work in cooperation ...
>
> At the same time, cities should re-organise themselves into communities ...
>
> Each wanples would tax itself, draw up its own budget and spend according to its ability. Certain property, including land, would be owned communally ... while other property would be owned by the family. Individuals would be left with minimum ownership.

Through moral training, each wanples would be prepared to defend itself through non-violence, even against the world.

The goals of this society would be:

a   Mutual Responsibility (Interdependence)
b   Community Solidarity ... Solidarity is comradeship. It is the wantok [kin] system.
c   Work
d   Mutual Faith
e   Participation
f   Culture and Civilisation
g   Non-violence[5]

The CPC declined to go far down that road but it was equally opposed to the Gearing-Up Program. In Greenwell's view, Canberra wanted no part in constitution-making, but it had to be involved in the transfer of powers. The CPC 'tended to fuse these two matters. Whilst they were not wholly separable the overlap was aggravated by the wide terms of reference.'[6]

Much more ambitious than its predecessors, the CPC ignored precedent. Guise and Arek, who had chaired earlier committees, were not asked for guidance. No one flew to Canberra to consult, nor did Australian advisers shape the agenda. Momis exercised real leadership and John Kaputin emerged as his alter ego. Momis's style was thoughtful and introverted: these qualities were complemented by Kaputin, who had a footballer's physique and a commanding presence. As one of the first Papua New Guineans to marry an Australian, Kaputin and his wife had attracted the displeasure of old-timer Australians and the suspicion of the security branch. Study in Honolulu allowed him to absorb some of the left-wing rhetoric of the 1960s, so — with Momis — he was happy to advocate the nationalisation of the country's mines. When the crunch came, he prized his membership of the CPC above his Cabinet post.[7] Both men advocated participation, decentralisation and redistribution. In effect, the CPC assumed two roles. One was to conciliate Highlanders and defuse separatism. The other was to draft a constitution for a unique polity. These roles would either divide the members of the CPC or alienate them from government.

In September 1972, the House aimed for self-government on December 1, 1973, giving the CPC 14 months to write a report, debate it in Parliament and draft a constitution. That was impossible, and a compromise was reached in May 1973 with Morrison and the Government: self-government would be introduced in two stages. The first, bringing minimal change, would arrive on schedule on December 1. The second would be some months later, when the new constitution would come into force. In the event, the final report arrived only in August 1974 and debate continued for another year. For the two years until the report surfaced, the CPC was harassed by both governments to hasten, and by the opposition to delay, while those with special interests tried to lobby them — and Momis's electors wanted him to entrench Bougainvilleans' rights.

Lines of accountability were always vague. The CPC was appointed by Somare, but the House laid down its terms of reference:

> To make recommendations for a constitution for full internal self-government in a united Papua New Guinea, with a view to eventual independence ... and to consider the mechanism for implementing the constitution ...

Lines were confused further when members began to claim a mandate directly from the people. Acting on Somare's advice to consult widely, they outperformed every earlier committee. They sponsored the formation of 200 discussion groups across the country, each serviced by officers of the Government Liaison Office. GLO officers would organise meetings, circulate papers, take minutes and report back to the CPC. Apart from their own issues, each discussion group was sent six detailed papers to discuss and respond to. Teams of CPC members, led by Momis or Kaputin, held open meetings in every subdistrict of the Territory (more than 100 in the end). The CPC also prompted individual and group submissions. Of 50,000 pro forma 'letter replies' distributed to the public, more than 2,000 were returned. So many were the responses that, said Mackenzie Daugi, 'in the end we abandoned the idea of analysing all submissions'.[8] And the more feedback they got, the more they treated the public as the source of their mandate.

No one had ever asked villagers such technical questions. The discussion paper on the courts and law officers, for example, asked:[9]

> Should judges and full-time magistrates continue to be independent of the Government and have their positions protected by our Constitution? How should they be appointed? Should the House of Assembly approve the appointment of judges?

> Who should have responsibility for major prosecutions — a Public Prosecutor whose position is safeguarded by the Constitution? If so, how independent of the Government should he be?

> Should the position of Public Solicitor be protected by the Constitution?

The responses to 13 specific questions were incorporated in the final report's chapter on 'The Administration of Justice'.[10]

The paper on the Public Service and the Ombudsman was even more sophisticated. The final paper, 'Human Rights, Emergency Powers and "Directive Principles"' (in effect, a philosophy of government), was not distributed until early 1974, while the final report was in draft. Some groups struggled. In the Southern Highlands, a well-attended meeting was baffled:

> because these people have no backgrounds of political. So I should say [the Adviser wrote] government must set up a political education in the village areas. Most of these questions were answered by teachers, clerks, medicals, and students.[11]

So progress was ponderous. The first interim report (tabled on September 27, 1973) was a very general statement. The House met just before Self-Government Day, December 1, when Momis tabled the second interim report. And at last, on June 27, Somare was able to present a draft to the House (the complete version was not printed for another three weeks).[12] The final report would dominate debate until independence — and even beyond.

The CPC Recommendations

The CPC judged that the people should develop their national identity and define national objectives. In this venture, members and consultants were 'excited, tickled, motivated, and inspired'.[13] They were also verbose. The final report filled 350 pages. It was, High Commissioner Critchley noted incredulously, longer than India's Constitution. One reason was the CPC's determination to spell out its intentions, rather than risk later interpretation. The CPC also specified rights and freedoms to be protected, and propounded five national goals expressing 'the needs and aspirations of our people in meaningful terms':[14]

> Integral Human Development Liberation and Fulfilment: All activities of the State should be directed towards the personal liberation and fulfilment of every citizen …;
>
> Equality and Participation: All citizens should have an equal opportunity to participate in, and benefit from, the development of our country;
>
> National Sovereignty and Self-Reliance: Papua New Guinea should be politically and economically independent and its economy should be basically self-reliant;
>
> Natural Resources and the Environment: The natural resources and the environment of Papua New Guinea should be conserved and used for the collective benefit of the people; and should be replenished in the interest of future generations;
>
> Papua New Guinean Ways: Development should take place primarily through the use of Papua New Guinean forms of social, political and economic organisation.

It would be difficult to dispute such motherhood sentiments. The most contentious proposals concerned citizenship, a topic that revealed the CPC's transformative ambition. Declaring their commitment to 'the indigenous people', they baulked at creating 'different classes of citizens', as in Malaysia and Fiji. The people must be able to share the country's wealth, but

> this redistribution of wealth would be made virtually impossible if we immediately made citizenship … freely available to foreign citizens who have lived here for some years during the colonial era.

Government should be Robin Hood. When governments in other new states tried to redistribute resources, however, 'constitutional provisions have limited their ability to acquire foreign-owned property' and obliged them to pay heavy compensation. The CPC wanted Papua New Guinea to enjoy 'sufficient flexibility to deal with the acquisition of foreign-owned property and payment for it'. Since Momis and Kaputin were demanding the nationalisation of mines, they must have known of the colossal compensation sums that such a policy implied.

The most novel idea was to dispense with a head of state. Surveying the roles of non-executive presidents and governors-general, they reckoned that most functions could be performed by Cabinet, or by the Prime Minister and Speaker of Parliament. All power would then be wielded by elected officers. That was entirely appropriate because 'it was from the people rather than from kings or chiefs that power was taken by the colonial rulers'.

Suspicious of central control and committed to human rights, the CPC took great pains to prevent authoritarian government. Apart from the last few years of Australian rule, people's rights and dignity had been 'suppressed or ignored'. To prevent any recurrence, the CPC proposed to entrench the rights listed in the Human Rights Ordinance 1971 (Percy Chatterton's initiative) so that only a two-thirds majority could amend them:

(1) the right to life;
(2) the right to personal liberty;
(3) freedom from forced labour;
(4) freedom from inhuman treatment;
(5) freedom from arbitrary search or entry;
(6) the right to protection of law;
(7) freedom of conscience, thought and religion;
(8) freedom of expression;
(9) freedom of assembly and association;
(10) freedom of employment;
(11) freedom of movement;
(12) the right to privacy;
(13) the right to stand for election to public office and to vote;
(14) freedom of information; and
(15) freedom from deprivation of property.

The libertarian thrust did not embrace non-citizens, whose freedoms might in some circumstances be curtailed.

Fearful of despotism, the CPC wanted to disperse power. Three Permanent Parliamentary Committees would preview bills. One would consider constitutional matters, foreign relations, trade and investment, defence, police and the Public Service. A second would oversee finance, industry and natural resources. The third would address social welfare, health, education and justice. The CPC was anxious to protect citizens' rights even during national emergencies, so the Government's emergency powers must be overseen by Parliament.

A further restraint was a Leadership Code to be enforced by the Public Prosecutor or the Ombudsman, to ensure the integrity of political, public service and judicial leaders:

> If Papua New Guinea is to have any chance of implementing its national goals and directive principles it must ensure that its leadership has a genuine commitment to these goals. [Therefore leaders must not threaten these goals] by collaboration with foreign or national businessmen, or [by] accepting bribes.

The code prohibited leaders and their families from:
— accepting loans from companies;
— accepting bribes;
— misapplying public funds;
— seeking an interest in a government contract;
— using confidential official information for personal advantage;
— holding shares or any other investment that could lead to a conflict of interest;
— in the case of ministers, holding a directorship;
— obtaining any paid employment other than that as a leader.

But the most immediately important proposals concerned decentralisation. Momis intended that elected provincial governments would transform administration:

> we realized that a host of institutions had been superimposed on our traditional system ... It was clear to us that, if we were to release the energies of our people, and if we were to enable them and their government to achieve a just, egalitarian self-reliant development we had to loosen the grip of these alien institutions.

Although several districts were interested in decentralisation, it was most urgent in Bougainville, where a Special Political Committee, led by Somare's emissary Leo Hannett, was channelling separatist sentiment into coherent proposals. In July 1973, the SPC demanded district government by November 1. The CPC favoured this outcome and a subcommittee was debating how it could be realised; but the Government's response — to create an area authority with limited powers — fell short.[15] In an attempt to revive negotiations, the CPC subcommittee began to meet Somare's staff (Voutas, Boyamo Sali and Gabriel Gris) and representatives of the SPC (Hannett, Moses Havini and Aloysius Noga) in September.[16] In November, Somare told the House that he would propose an Interim District Government.[17] The CPC's consultants, Watts and Tordoff — amazed by 'an administrative system so highly centralised and dominated by its bureaucracy'[18] — proposed structures and functions for provincial government, including an elected assembly and an executive headed by a premier. Provincial governments would receive grants from the centre, overseen by a National Fiscal Commission.

The Compromise Constitution

In brief, the CPC's thrust was to hedge the powers of the executive, entrench the rights of individuals and groups, distinguish between (indigenous) citizens and non-citizens, and disperse powers. The final report was populist and probably popular, but it did make enemies. While these ideas crystallised, two governments fumed. Morrison railed at the CPC as an interminable philosophy seminar funded by Australia, and he advised Somare to give them an ultimatum.[19] Ministers exercising their new powers were offended by the CPC's suspicions. They would have preferred a simple document, leaving complex matters to be decided by Parliament, or by the executive. Somare was ambivalent, but in March 1974 he seemed to agree, when he remarked that a constitution might not be essential before independence. Bill Kearney (Secretary of Law) and Joe Lynch (Parliamentary Draftsman) imagined an 'interim independence constitution'.[20] Lynch suspected that the CPC might make radical proposals that would 'cast too great a strain on society'. To sidestep protracted debates, he proposed a simple device: to adapt the Papua New Guinea Act to confer independence. This submission was drafted before Momis persuaded Somare that the final report was imminent.[21] Given the depth of these differences, the CPC should not have been shocked when Somare — presenting its final report — also tabled a 'Minority Report' by himself and Guise, allegedly prepared by Voutas.[22] The United Party also presented a paper.

All agreed that there should be an 'autochthonous' constitution, home-grown and validated by local — not Australian — law. Somare had asked for a constitution 'suited to the needs and circumstances of Papua New Guinea and … not imposed from the outside'. The CPC agreed:

> A 'home-grown' constitution should, as far as possible, be based on indigenous systems of and ideas about political institutions and procedures … the Committee believes that it should look to traditional values and procedures for inspiration.[23]

Ilinome Tarua explains that the House of Assembly, created by the Australian Government, could not therefore enact a home-grown constitution, although it was the obvious forum in which to debate it. One motion demanded a referendum, but this was defeated 52 to 28 when Somare insisted that the electors had given the House 'a mandate and power to make decisions'.[24] So the House was the arena where the thrust of the CPC report was blunted. The House then converted itself into a Constituent Assembly for the last lap.[25] The first discussions came in early 1974, when proposals were shown to Cabinet. From April to December, the House considered the draft final report and some of the final report itself. They first debated the CPC report as a whole, then considered each of its 15 chapters. The Constituent Assembly met 27 times in three months. There were literally hundreds of amendments to the draft constitution, many proposed by backbenchers.[26] The bulk of the debate was spread over three and a half months, to December 1974, although decentralisation was not discussed until March 1975. Early in 1975, the second and third drafts of the Constitution were discussed by parliamentary groups; and from May 23 to August 15 the Constituent Assembly debated the final (fourth) draft.

The minority report was published as a White Paper: an angry Momis retorted by calling the majority report the Black Paper.[27] Proposals in the United Party paper and from individuals were moved as amendments to the CPC report. Parties shattered and alliances formed. Most of the CPC formed a Nationalist Pressure Group (NPG) around Momis, Kaputin, Kaupa and Daugi, 'to preserve national resources and oppose alien influence'.[28] Its membership sometimes reached 28. The United Party shrank and Sinake Giregire — a member of the CPC — left to lead the new Country Party, a small but vocal group that generally supported the NPG. The radicalised allies lost most of their issues, but in an unstable House no outcome was secure.

Drafts by the Parliamentary Draftsman's team became contentious, Momis insisting that Lynch 'continually misunderstood clear drafting instructions'.[29] Lynch read these instructions as 'not necessarily final', and Somare supported him when he declared that 'instructions would be handed down by the executive', not by the House.[30] After four drafts, relations were so sour that the NPG and the Country Party wanted Lynch sacked, and debate adjourned pending a fifth draft. The startled Government arranged discussions between parliamentary leaders and advisers at which some issues were resolved — but new ones emerged. Kaputin denounced the Government's 'cynical attitude to the constitution, parliament and democracy'.[31] Eventually, Somare agreed that Lynch should follow the instructions of the House, and a committee oversaw the redrafting.[32]

The minority report differed from the majority in general and in detail. The Government took a different view of the size of Parliament, the role of regional electorates, citizenship and provincial government. It rejected group leadership, preferring a head of state elected by Parliament.[33] When it proposed that the House adopt a very brief constitution, containing only 'statements of essential principles', all hell broke loose. Momis and Kaputin were outraged; Somare was provoked to review Kaputin's appointment as Minister for Justice;[34] Momis, Pikah Kasau and Toni Ila, the three Pangu members of the CPC, were ejected from a party meeting.[35] Somare withdrew his invitation to Stone and Wolfers to attend debates.[36] Meanwhile, despite the CPC's desire to delay, executive powers were being transferred thick and fast. In March 1975, even the last — defence and foreign relations — were yielded and Papua New Guinea was de facto independent. In June, Somare was able to confirm September 16 as Independence Day.[37]

In the thick of the political action, passions were intense as the CPC ceased to be a cross-party alliance and took up the role of opposition. Provincial government was the most divisive issue and Barnett wanted it deferred beyond independence. Within the Government, the suspicion formed that some of the Bougainvilleans were resolved on secession and would not be satisfied with provincial government. Like many in Port Moresby, Barnett thought this structure 'totally unsuited' to most of the country and an extravagant dispersal of the country's administrative skills. Briefly, he thought that the issue had been deferred and he was appalled, when he recovered from a bout of cerebral malaria, to find it back on the agenda.

The small scale of the political class tended to magnify hostilities. For example, Momis wounded Moi Avei and other national advisers to Somare when he called them 'flowerpots' — merely decorative. But a Wolfers anecdote suggests how some Papua New Guineans could disagree without burning bridges.[38] On one magical occasion, he was Somare's guest on a harbour cruise, although they were on opposite sides of the political divide. As Somare and Barnett were completely estranged from the CPC and its advisers, Wolfers was decidedly nervous when Somare dropped anchor at Barnett's Loloata Island home. But when they arrived, Wolfers was astounded to find the arch-rebel Kaputin walking on the beach hand-in-hand with Christine Goode from the Papua New Guinea Office.

Relations among Papua New Guineans were usually gentler than among expatriates, and their wounds shallower. Stone and Ley were dismayed by the abandonment of the CPC ideals. In hindsight, Barnett describes them as 'paranoid about Australian influence'.[39] Stone suspected Australians in Somare's office and Ley detested Barnett and Kearney in particular. Conversely, the denigration of Barnett was sustained, even after he was knocked out of the game by malaria.

Despite personal and ideological disputes there was in reality a large area of agreement. The CPC proposed, the Government accepted (and the Constitution mandated) a unicameral Parliament, an independent judiciary and other liberal democratic checks and balances, including protection of human rights. The National Goals and Directive Principles were adopted without modification. Section 25 of the Constitution required all governmental bodies to give effect to the Goals and Principles 'as far as lies within their respective powers'. Where a law could be understood so as to give effect to the Goals and Principles, it should be understood and applied that way. Either Somare saw these as general statements that he could live with — or the goals and principles were vague enough to satisfy every point of view. There was agreement as well on the proposed Leadership Code — perhaps for the same reason.

The House did establish a Public Accounts Committee, but the Government looked askance at other permanent committees, perhaps seeing them as 'uncomfortably like an expensive proliferation of more powerful versions of the CPC; intended to act as permanent watchdogs'.[40] And, although the CPC disapproved, a conventional head of state was revived in stages. First, the White Paper proposed a head of state elected by Parliament. Then, in May 1975, the Government proposed (in the fourth draft) that the Queen be head of state, with a Governor-General elected by Parliament. The Constituent Assembly agreed. Bayne supposes that the Government retained the Queen as a symbol of continuity to allay villagers' anxieties.[41] The powers of the Governor-General were (and remain) severely limited. He or she 'shall act only with, and in accordance with, the advice of the National Executive Council'. Although he or she appoints a Prime Minister, it is Parliament that makes the nomination. Some of the constraints around a State of Emergency were also stripped from the CPC recommendations.

The House had supported the CPC's idea that fundamental provisions could be amended only by two-thirds of the members of Parliament, but the final draft allowed amendment by a simple majority. After heated criticism by Kaputin, the Government agreed to amend this provision on the floor of the Constituent Assembly. The outcome was a set of 'organic laws', which could be amended only with the support of specified majorities.

But citizenship was the most noxious issue, being personal as well as political. Most ministers would have been happy to privilege the indigenous people, but citizenship defined by ethnicity would pose serious procedural and moral — and political — problems. A few leading Papua New Guineans had married Australians. Kaputin and his Australian wife, among others, wanted to secure the rights of their children. There was also the more common awkwardness of ministers and members who held Australian citizenship. The CPC's first idea (that only people with two indigenous grandparents and no other 'real citizenship' would be automatic citizens) would bar ministers Chan and Jephcott, as well as Barry Holloway, the Speaker, and several United Party MHAs. The issue was inflamed when the CPC's ideas leaked to the press and prompted an intervention from Al Grassby, the flamboyant Minister for Immigration in Canberra. As the CPC understood him, Grassby assured Australians that

> if they give up Australian citizenship in order to become PNG citizens, they will be able to return to Australia at any time ... and almost certainly regain their Australian citizenship.[42]

Controversy festered for 18 months and the Constituent Assembly debated citizenship for six days, focusing on the qualifications for foreigners wanting to be citizens, and the situation of people of mixed descent.[43] Amendments allowed foreigners who had lived in the country for eight years to apply at once for naturalisation, and instituted a Citizenship Advisory Committee to assess their suitability.[44] The emotive concept of provisional citizenship survived until the fourth draft. Conversely, the Constituent Assembly agreed to extend (for 10 years) old laws that discriminated in favour of indigenous Papua New Guineans. The amendments also limited the protection of property provisions to 'automatic citizens' for five years. Another amendment enabled Parliament 'to confer a benefit, right or privilege' on automatic citizens only, for the first 10 years of independence. This compromise was a long way from the CPC's first strict ideas about indigeneity and citizenship, but the *Post-Courier* might have been right when it expected the deal to 'provide the cornerstone for the multi-racial society envisaged by the Chief Minister'.[45]

The treatment of provincial government astonished most observers. Some feared that provincial government would mean a proliferation of politicians, while others were anxious about the intransigence of Bougainvilleans. Under Ebia Olewale, as Minister for Provincial Affairs, officials doubted the practicality of the CPC proposals, but attitudes gradually softened. It was astounding then, when on July 30, 1975, after a failed attempt by Albert Maori Kiki to negotiate with Bougainvilleans, the Government moved in the Constituent Assembly to drop provincial government altogether. The stated reason was expense, but the decision was probably fuelled by anger and frustration among ministers. At any rate, in less than 20 minutes, members voted to withdraw these clauses. That prompted Bougainville's new Interim Provincial Government to threaten to secede as the Republic of the North Solomons. That decision was made 'with the support of, allegedly, some 200 elected traditional leaders'.[46] Hannett led the movement and (see below) Momis flew to the UN to argue Bougainville's case. The secession failed and provincial government was reconsidered a year later when Momis — reconciled with Somare and Minister for Decentralisation — reintroduced a version of the CPC scheme.

On August 15, 1975, with a month to spare, the Assembly adopted the Constitution. Months of argument and hundreds of amendments had produced a constitution that was only loosely based on the CPC report. Momis, at the UN, said correctly that 'the CPC was not responsible for the drafting of the Constitution as we have it today'.[47] In his view, Somare and the Australians had stripped it of most of its home-grown and creative features. Peter Bayne entered the debate rather late, when he succeeded Ley as Counsel to Parliament and de facto adviser to the United Party. He judged that the politicians in general were comfortable with institutions that were familiar, and were reluctant to venture into strange constitutional territory. They accepted the CPC view that the Constitution should provide a philosophy for government and for citizens (although the Preamble and the National Goals and Directive Principles were not justiciable). They were also happy to create statutory officers with some autonomy: Public Prosecutor, Public Services Commissioners and Judicial Services Commissioners. The outcome was a conventional Westminster-type constitution — with a few bells and whistles.[48]

Don Woolford put the same point less kindly.[49] For him, the CPC report

> was an imaginative attempt to make constitutional law conform with a distinctive and attractive view of Papua New Guinea. The government ... emasculated its report ... Basically, the committee was ... prepared to take institutional risks ... the government preferred the safety of the status quo. The conflict was at least partly one between visionaries and pragmatists. It was also one between those who thought power should be dispersed and those with whom power resided ...

On that view, the CPC was little more than a diversion, but that is to miss its real importance. The CPC served the purpose that nationalist movements provided in other colonies: its groups and meetings did raise political consciousness and did encourage a sense of national identity. The Constitution does provide national goals against which governments are still measured. It also met its immediate targets. Many participants were unhappy with the outcome but Somare considered that 'in the end, we developed a good Melanesian consensus'.[50] It is hard to disagree.

Discharging the United Nations Trust

The UN was more easily satisfied than Papua New Guinea's politicians (Chapter 7), but two significant groups resisted the Government's plan, and might appeal to the UN.

Before self-government there had been an abortive attempt to hold a referendum on Bougainville's destiny, but there was no chance that the UN would allow (much less require) a plebiscite for one part of a Trust Territory. A week before Papua New Guinea's independence, the issue came before the Trusteeship Council. The Australian Ambassador introduced the Papua New Guinea delegates — Ebia Olewale as Minister for Justice, Paulias Matane, the country's representative to the UN, Ralph Karepa and Rabbie Namaliu. The council reviewed the circumstances of the mandate and its previous decision of 1973, and heard the Bougainville petition from John Momis. Then they congratulated the Government and people of Papua New Guinea on their 'successful endeavours in preparing for independence' and stated their 'confidence that the unity of the country will be successfully maintained'. They congratulated Australia too, and 'the government and people of Papua New Guinea for the achievement of their independence'.[51] Adding to the convivial mood, Olewale thanked Australia for 'performing the enormous task well'. He was sure that Papua New Guinea's 'close and cordial relationship with Australia' would continue.

Momis's address was sombre: the people of Bougainville had a right to self-determination. For years they had been exploited as workers in Queensland and Fiji. Culturally and ethnically, Bougainville was part of the Solomons Group. 'Long neglected by the Australian Administration, Bougainville was "discovered" in the mid-1960s, when copper was found.' While the financial benefits went to Papua New Guinea, direct landowners suffered the loss of their land and an influx of foreigners. He insisted that, 'although the policies of the Somare government have been enlightened, in practice they are no different from those of the former Australian Administration', and the system of provincial government that could have reconciled Bougainvilleans had been abandoned. Olewale retorted that Momis's principle could result in 700 mini-states. Members of the council made their position clear when they attended the ceremonies at Port Moresby on Independence Day.

But the UN encounter was full of ironies. The second group who resisted national unity were Papuan separatists. In slightly different circumstances, Momis could have represented Papua New Guinea against a Papuan delegation, led by Olewale, their natural champion. In 1971, a Papua Action Group led by Olewale and Bert Counsel agitated for separation (Chapter 4). Their demands were brushed aside but, in 1972, Josephine Abaijah was elected to the House and formed Papua Besena (the Papuan tribe), whose first demand was a plebiscite on separation.

Abaijah's rhetoric played well around Port Moresby, but had little resonance further afield and none in the Southern Highlands, an anomalous part of Papua. Riots in Port Moresby in July 1973 dramatised the tensions between settled Papuans and Highlander migrants. They followed fiery speeches from Abaijah and her mentor, Dr Eric Wright, which allowed officials to represent them as xenophobic and nihilist. As far as possible, officials isolated her. When Morrison met Abaijah in August 1973, he was adamant

> that the UN had charged Australia to bring Papua New Guinea to independence as a single entity, and that Australia would deal only with the government of a unified PNG, and would neither deal with nor fund a separate segment.[52]

Olewale and other Papuan MHAs sympathised with Abaijah's program and weighed their options carefully. They came down on the side of national unity — but it was a close thing.[53]

Morrison's fears about referenda (Chapter 7) were removed when the UN accepted the resolution of the July 1975 meeting of the House of Assembly. His more serious fear was the High Court of Australia, because the legal case for Papuan separatists was much stronger than Bougainville's. Papua Besena might be incoherent, but a constitutional case brought before the High Court might vindicate their claim to Australian citizenship — and a status different to that of New Guinea. Morrison could only insist that the UN had charged Australia to bring Papua New Guinea, united, to independence, and that Australia would deal *only* with the government of a united Papua New Guinea. But, on the constitutional issue, he could only cross his fingers and pray that no one manufactured a case for the High Court. And that worked. Despite the peculiarities of Papua New Guinea's international status, therefore, and the exceptional ambition of the Constitutional Planning Committee, the outcome of the consultations and the constitutional debates was a united country with a rather conventional constitution.

Footnotes
1. Whitlam in 'Hindsight'.
2. Ibid.
3. Goode, 'Preparation and Negotiation', p. 73, citing Voutas.
4. Constitutional Planning Committee, *Final Report*, 1974.
5. Bernard Narokobi, 'We the People, We the Constitution', in Jean Zorn and Peter Bayne (eds), *Lo Bilong Ol Manmeri: Crime, Compensation and Village Courts*, UPNG, 1975, pp. 19–30.
6. John Greenwell to Allan Kerr, December 1976.
7. John Ley, in 'Hindsight'.
8. Daugi, Transcript of Discussion by Panel of Constitution-Makers, Port Moresby, March 28, 1996, p. 361, cited in Jonathan Ritchie, 'Making Their Own Law: Participation in the Development of Papua New Guinea's constitution, PhD thesis, Melbourne University, 2004.
9. *Post-Courier*, August 22, 1973.
10. CPC, Discussion Paper No. 4, 'The Courts and Law Officers'.
11. Noah Yalon, Adviser to the Komo Discussion Group, Southern Highlands District, n.d., PNG National Archives, cited by Ritchie, 'Making Their Own Law'.
12. *Post-Courier*, June 28, 1974.
13. Bernard Narokobi, 'The Constitutional Planning Committee, Nationalism and Vision', in Regan, Jessep and Kwa (eds) *Twenty Years of the Papua New Guinea Constitution*, p. 28.
14. CPC, *Final Report*.
15. News release No. 1980 B, *Talks on Special Authority*, August 16, 1973, PNGNA. 'Munkas supports Bougainville plan', *Post-Courier*, August 23, 1973.
16. Hannett, Havini and Noga flew to Port Moresby for talks on September 12 (District Commissioner, Arawa to Chief Minister's Office, September 11, 1973, PNGNA).
17. It was agreed that one Papuan and one New Guinean District would also receive district government (Don Woolford, *Papua New Guinea: Initiation and Independence*, UQP. Brisbane, 1977, p. 167).
18. Watts and Tordoff's report, April 1974.
19. Morrison, in 'Hindsight'.

20. Lynch to Kearney, March 28, 1974 (papers of C. J. Lynch), cited in Ritchie, 'Making Their Own Law'.
21. Barnett, 'Policy-Making in the Transfer of Powers from Australia', cited in Ritchie, 'Making Their Own Law'; Michael Somare, 'Transcript of Discussion by Panel of Constitution-Makers, Port Moresby, 28 March 1996', in Regan, et al., *Twenty Years of the Papua New Guinea Constitution*, p. 365.
22. The 'final' *Final Report* was tabled on August 15, 1974.
23. CPC, *Final Report*.
24. 'Referendum move beaten', *Post-Courier*, June 28, 1973. Somare, *Sana: An Autobiography*, Port Moresby, 1975, p. 103.
25. Ilinome Tarua, 'Autochthonous Constitution', in 'Hindsight'.
26. Lynch, 'Current Developments in the Pacific', p. 180.
27. Hegarty, 'May-August 1974', in Moore and Kooyman, (eds), *A PNG Political Chronicle 1967–1991*.
28. Downs, *The Australian Trusteeship*, p. 505.
29. Ley, 'The Challenges and Achievements of the Constitutional Planning Committee', in 'Hindsight'; James Griffin, 'January-June 1975', in Moore and Kooyman, *A PNG Political Chronicle 1967–1991*.
30. Lynch, 'Current Developments in the Pacific', p. 179.
31. *Post-Courier*, May 27, 1975.
32. Ley, 'The Challenges and Achievements of the Constitutional Planning Committee', in 'Hindsight'
33. *Government Paper, Proposals on Constitutional Principles*, Port Moresby, August 1974.
34. *Post-Courier*, July 5, 1974.
35. *Post-Courier*, July 4, 1974.
36. Somare to Momis, May 14, 1974, PNG National Archives, cited by Ritchie, 'Making Their Own Law'; Narokobi, 'The Constitutional Planning Committee, Nationalism, and Vision'.
37. *National Constituent Assembly Debates*, June 20, 1975.
38. Interview, Ted Wolfers.
39. Interview, Tos Barnett.
40. Ley, in 'Hindsight'.
41. Peter Bayne, 'The Constitution', typescript, 1985.
42. Second Interim Report
43. Graham Hassall, 'Citizenship', in Regan, et al., *Twenty Years of the Papua New Guinea Constitution*, p. 257.
44. James Griffin, 'July-December 1975', in Moore and Kooyman, *A PNG Political Chronicle 1967–1991*.
45. *Post-Courier*, July 24, 1975.
46. Griffin, et al., *Papua New Guinea: A Political History*, p. 214.
47. John Momis, 'The Constitutional Planning Committee and the Constitution', in Regan, et al., *Twenty Years of the Papua New Guinea Constitution*, p. 20.
48. Interview, Peter Bayne.
49. Woolford, *Papua New Guinea*.
50. Somare, 'Transcript of Discussion by Panel of Constitution-Makers, Port Moresby, 28 March 1996', p. 364.
51. PNG National Archives, DIES C13/2, part 2. Department of Chief Minister, Circular 716, undated, 'Discussion – United Nations Trusteeship Council'.
52. Interview, Bill Morrison.
53. Interview, Olewale, and Olewale in 'Hindsight'.

Chapter 9

A National Economy

Economic Strategy

Self-government offered a rare opportunity to review and overhaul economic policy, hitherto decided in Canberra. Ross Garnaut describes the economy rather well as 'a big lump of Australian public expenditure'. Public servants, the Panguna mine and service industries offered the only practical tax base.[1] Despite the misgivings of John Stone in the Australian Treasury,[2] the lump had grown since 1964 with the drive to create infrastructure. This spending deepened the Territory's financial dependence and complemented an extraordinary reliance on skilled Australian bank tellers, shop assistants, drivers and even labourers. And years of Australian subventions entrenched dependent attitudes. Mark Lynch, as Secretary to the Administrator's Executive Council, had to translate an economist's proposal to broaden the tax base by a Value Added Tax. This was difficult to render in Tok Pisin, except to say that the VAT was a tax on just about everything. 'There was a look of horror around the table and the debate did not get very far.'[3] Economic management remained an Australian domain. As late as the transition era, Pat Galvin attended a policy meeting in which Don Mentz of the Territories Department discussed economics with Bill Conroy, former head of Agriculture, now creating a Department of Foreign Affairs and Trade. Mentz and Conroy were old mates and old habits lingered. Conroy was flanked by two Papua New Guineans who said so little that Galvin thought they might as well be bookends.[4]

Outside the bureaucracy, however, development strategies were eagerly debated by politicians and academics. The debates were shaped by Walt Rostow's best-selling text, *Stages of Economic Growth: a Non-Communist Manifesto*, which argued that Britain's economic development should be understood as a succession of stages; that other industrial economies had passed through the same stages; and that every other nation should follow the same path. By 1970, two counterattacks had been mounted. Political economists — usually radical and pessimistic — articulated 'dependency theory', pointing to the political dimension of economic relations and the stubborn endurance of dependent relations between the world's developed metropoles and its underdeveloped peripheries. And a less radical approach grew out of E. F. Schumacher's *Small is Beautiful*,[5] advocating small-scale production using local material and local markets.

Both critiques were popular, and debate was sharpened by the belief that Papua New Guinea could learn from the errors of other newly independent countries. The 1973 Waigani Seminar, for example, heard animated papers for and against renegotiating the Bougainville Mining Agreement as well as papers canvassing broader questions of economic strategy.[6] Evangelical Tanzanians and 'Tanzaphiles' preached on Tanzania's 'African socialist' and allegedly self-reliant strategy.[7] An unusual UN Development Program team — Michael Faber's Overseas Development Group from East Anglia University — also impressed Somare. From Faber's prescriptions, Somare distilled eight aims that embodied a 'small is beautiful' strategy of national self-reliance, decentralised economic activity, gender equality and popular participation. In March 1973, he presented these as a philosophy of government.[8]

The rhetoric was seductive, especially for Pangu, but its realisation was frustrating. Each agency pioneering this strategy imploded — the Rural Improvement Program, the Village Economic Development Fund, and the South Pacific Appropriate Technology Foundation.[9] That neither surprised nor dismayed the Finance Minister, Julius Chan: he had never been a fan of adventurous economics, and his scepticism seemed to be vindicated when the Panguna mine (see below) reported vast profits while the small-scale ventures floundered.

Chan was a surprising figure to have such clout in a government led by Pangu and including self-conscious radicals. His officials found him able, courteous and attentive; but as an Australian citizen, and sometimes because of his Chinese heritage, he was suspect to economic nationalists like Kaputin and Momis. Under his leadership, a handful of young men developed economic strategies. At 28, Mekere Morauta became Secretary for Finance three years after graduating in Economics and a year after entering Treasury. Like Anthony Siaguru in Foreign Affairs and Rabbie Namaliu, private secretary to the Prime Minister, he was a product of the first year of the UPNG. He was supported by Ross Garnaut,[10] a Research Fellow in the New Guinea Research Unit drawn in to work on special projects until 1974 when he became Morauta's deputy in charge of General Financial and Economic Policy.

The other site of policy-making was the Central Planning Office, successor to Bill McCasker's Office of the Economic Adviser. To recreate this planning capacity, the Government sought an English-speaking economist who was not Australian but was familiar with Westminster traditions. The man who filled the bill as director was David Beatty,[11] who was home in Toronto after study in Cambridge and policy work in Tanzania. Unlike others who argued on the basis of Tanzanian rhetoric, Beatty did understand the Tanzanian economy and preferred more orthodox strategies.

The Central Planning Office was separate from the Department of Finance and was accountable not to Chan but to Somare. This division could have been paralysing; but Beatty, Morauta, Chan and Garnaut worked well together. The Cabinet Secretary (Paul Ryan, then Paul Bengo) chaired a daily meeting. Finance focused on strategy, and the CPO on forward planning. Beatty saw himself as 'the do-it guy while Garnaut provided the intellectual rigour'. They respected and consulted Sir John Crawford, 'the godfather of economic planning', who had taught most of them and who had helped to appoint Beatty. They also esteemed Anthony Clunies-Ross at the UPNG, who was rather more radical than they were.[12]

Another source of policy advice was the East Anglia Group, whose rhetoric (Beatty argues) was more radical than its bite. His judgment is not surprising: he had recommended Faber's appointment, having worked with him in Tanzania. Crawford detested the East Anglians but the Port Moresby team appreciated their innovative views on the informal sector. (By contrast, the Constitutional Planning Committee's economic nationalism alarmed the team, but the CPC had neither time nor the inclination to develop their ideas.) So the team pursued orthodox policies flavoured by dependency rhetoric. There really was Tanzanian influence in Papua New Guinea's economic strategy, but it had nothing to do with *ujamaa*.

It was just as well that the team was energetic, because machinery had to be built from scratch. They had to assist in the transfer of institutions while developing policy capacities as well as monetary policies. National currency was introduced on April 1, 1975, when the kina and toea replaced Australian dollars and cents. Chan and Somare campaigned energetically to instil pride in the currency — Chan even named his children Kina and Toea. Papua New Guinea was committed to a 'hard-currency policy' that implied fiscal discipline, small deficits and minimal debt. Meanwhile, the Panguna mining agreement was renegotiated, largely by Beatty and Morauta and (in Lapun's office) Stephen Zorn. Ok Tedi negotiations continued with Kennecott and began with the big Australian, BHP: these fell to Beatty, Garnaut and (in Somare's office) Namaliu. Australian aid had to be put on a secure footing, with Garnaut and Beatty advising Somare and Deputy Prime Minister Albert Maori Kiki. Meanwhile, John Langmore, Beatty and the Central Planning Office created the National Public Expenditure Plan as a framework for the planning and management of the budget.

Decisions were also needed for a sugar project at Ramu and the Frieda River mineral prospect, but an area of particular delicacy was the policy on foreign investment, addressed by a National Investment and Development Authority (NIDA) created in 1974 with Tom Allen as director.[13] For most of the Australian era, foreign (and especially Asian) investment was severely discouraged. A policy change in 1964 softened that stance, setting conditions on which Asian funds might be tolerated. These restrictive conditions implied the need to protect the Territory from a voracious lust to invest: it must be shown that the Asian capital was not readily available from other sources; each proposal would involve 'Asian know-how, otherwise unavailable'; it would expand the Territory's exports, train the people and involve the maximum domestic processing. The benefits to the Territory must include the retention of a good proportion of the profits, and the authorities would not countenance transfer pricing or other forms of tax minimisation. Four years later, another policy review chose to apply these constraints less strictly. Even then, every proposal would have to be approved by the AEC.[14] This timidity made sense, if at all, only in Australian terms. When a Secondary Industry Committee formed in 1970, it found that the Territory had little information and less control over investment policy, which needed clarification. All investment came through Australia, and it was not clear if any originated outside Australia.[15]

Allen's aim was to ensure that Papua New Guineans received fair value for natural resources and were not marginalised. Economic nationalists saw foreign investors as exploiters, bent on extracting resources at any environmental or cultural cost. To address this menace, some wanted a government takeover of foreign businesses. On the other hand, expatriates and others defended the status quo and minimal constraints, arguing that Papua New Guineans would need ages to acquire the skills and the capital to succeed. In between, the majority accepted that foreign investment should be encouraged but regulated.

South-East Asia and Latin America provided models for legislation to entice foreign investment into priority areas, subject to conditions such as local participation, technical training, further processing, environmental protection and appropriate technology. A very different strategy was implied by the Tanzanian model, which advocated village orientation and avoiding foreign domination. What emerged from the mix of local pressures and foreign models was 'fairly flexible foreign investment legislation, with a strong regulatory bias'. This flexibility would allow the Government to turn the tap towards tighter or looser control. Final decisions would rest with the Finance Minister, who might (or might not) delegate powers to NIDA's Board of bureaucrats and private sector leaders.

With independence, expatriate anxieties ebbed and the Government grew comfortable with foreign investment. Once enterprises were registered, Allen felt an 'air of relief' in government and among the affected companies. The teams negotiating major projects were highly professional, and, when it proved difficult to attract investors into priority areas, the Government began to send investment promotion missions to Australia, New Zealand, India and Europe. So the National Investment Strategy in 1976 set the seal on the transition from Dar es Salaam to Canberra. Local businesses were encouraged but the strategy emphasised foreign investment and technology in priority areas. It still talked of intervention but it released the brakes on investment in most projects and in most activities.

Land[16]

Riots in Bougainville and Rabaul were extreme manifestations of nationwide tension between people's ideas about land and the insistent needs of a cash economy. As a young lawyer in 1972, Ilinome Tarua managed land claims along the Papuan coast in Abau. When the Land Titles Commissioner rejected an application by villagers, Tarua was warned to expect a riot; but the Commissioner knew enough about land matters to bring in a police squad.[17] Independence would be vacuous if land issues were not addressed. Olewale recalls Albert Maori Kiki, the first Lands Minister, in one of Cabinet's first meetings, protesting that foreigners had deemed great tracts of land, which in the people's eyes had real owners, to be vacant. This was a grievance felt by every Papua New Guinean.[18]

It would be hard to overstate the importance of land issues. Ideas about the nature and the value of land are what most sharply divide Pacific Islanders from the settlers of

Australia and New Zealand. Australian settlers denied Aboriginal land titles through the doctrine of *terra nullius*, while New Zealanders recognised Maori titles; but in each case land was alienated. Although some land was alienated in the Pacific Islands, the scale was usually limited. As for the land that remained, most colonial governments merely codified the ways in which Islanders owned and inherited it, while the suppression of warfare stabilised land ownership and deepened people's attachment to particular territory. That attachment inhibits 'national' sentiment and shapes the ways in which Islanders imagine themselves: they were the owners of particular land long before they became subjects of a common sovereign or citizens of an independent state. It is significant that land has been the focus of two coups in Fiji, another in the Solomon Islands, secession from Vanuatu, and civil war in New Caledonia and Irian Jaya.

In 1970, the Administration made a last attempt to amend land laws. Gorton's 1970 ministerial arrangements gave authority in land matters to a ministerial member, but the land bills were devised secretly and introduced without him.[19] British advisers and Kenyan models shaped four bills, amounting to 400 pages of text. The officials expected that

> direct dealing between nationals would be facilitated and the messy tenure situation in the squatter settlements resolved. But expatriates were also expected to take leases or freeholds and capital investment would be greatly encouraged.

The bills came into the House in early 1971, and members might have approved them without grasping their significance until Percy Chatterton met the New Zealand historian Alan Ward, a visiting lecturer at the university and an authority on the ways in which Maori lost land. At Chatterton's request, Ward wrote seven pages of commentary. To anyone familiar with the dispossession of Maori and Hawaiians, the bills rang alarm bells and aroused 'the suspicion that the Administration was still hell-bent on launching a complete social revolution'. Ward criticised the bills and suggested another approach based on 'occupation licences'. Chatterton distributed the paper and it unleashed a barrage of criticism of the bills from the United Party as well as Pangu. Ward's paper became 'the catalyst for indigenous members to express the very serious anxieties they had held all along'. Public meetings demanded that the bills be shelved until self-government. In the face of this resistance, the bills were withdrawn.

After the 1972 election, therefore, a Commission of Inquiry into Land Matters was created, chaired by the dignified Sinaka Goava, a founding member of Pangu. Its nine other members came from every region: Father Ignatius Kilage, Edric Eupu, Posa Kilori, Cletus Harepa, Pokwari Kali, Boana Rossi, Donigi Samiel and Philip ToBongolua. The support staff included Nick O'Neill and Jim Fingleton (who had worked on land claims in the Public Solicitor's Office), Bill Welbourne and Philip Fitzpatrick.[20] For nine months, they heard submissions around the country.

Compared with the Administration's bills, the commissioners proposed less emphasis on creating individual title, that customary land be registered sparingly, and that ownership be vested in registered 'land groups' empowered to develop the land themselves or to grant rights of occupation to other Papua New Guineans. In short, they did not propose that customary tenure be converted to Australian forms of title, but hoped that new forms of tenure would evolve out of custom, along with a Papua New Guinean 'common law' on land. But it was easier to criticise the 1971 bills than to develop alternatives. Some of the commissioners' ideas were enacted as the Indigenous Land Groups Act 1975 and the Land Dispute Settlement Act 1975, but implementation was patchy.

More explosive than arguments about customary land was the crisis over freehold land in the Gazelle. When the commissioners visited Rabaul in 1973, tension was palpable. The Administration still protected freehold titles, with police if necessary. A few Tolai had bought freehold titles to plantation land, but land ownership was still mainly a race issue, and 'squatter' occupations were increasing. The New Guinean Planters Association hung tough: planters who were willing to sell demanded prices based on the assumption of a free market in land and strong prices for produce. These prices frustrated those Tolai who were prepared to buy. To resolve the impasse, the commissioners introduced another formula for valuation, based on the average income of the property, and they proposed compulsory acquisition. That approach opened the door to realistic negotiations, and tensions began to unwind.

The commission's final report in October 1973 noted that 1.4 million hectares of land had been alienated; 160,000 hectares had passed in freehold and 340,000 in leasehold to private interests, but most was held by the Crown. Resisting demands that all land be restored to the clans, the commissioners were persuaded (by Ron Crocombe) that the Government should retain much of it for public purposes. They proposed that the public ownership of all freehold land be asserted: former freeholders would be offered renewable leases. That strategy would give the Government control of alienated land and access to the added value, and would limit speculation. Unused land was also a constant provocation, so they proposed that holders make realistic proposals to develop it, or relinquish it without compensation.

So the failure of the 1971 land bills allowed an imaginative approach. To develop these ideas, a Policy and Research Branch was created in the Lands Department. But the momentum was soon lost. Fingleton (in the Policy and Research Branch) recalls that the policy issues were intractable and inertia returned to the Lands Department.[21] It would be hard to overstate the consequences of these imperfect resolutions.

Minerals

As in the 1930s, in the 1960s, Australian officials were depressed by the limited prospects of agricultural revenue and were dazzled by minerals. The Territories Department saw Panguna (Chapters 3 and 4) not just as a source of revenue but as a model for other resource projects. Panguna was operated by Bougainville Copper Ltd (BCL), whose major shareholder was Conzinc Riotinto Australia (CRA) in Melbourne, the board of which answered to the giant Rio Tinto in London. The agreement with CRA allowed the Government to buy equity but provided no royalties to landowners.

There would be no tax on income for three years, and for six or seven more years little tax would be paid. Because BCL was committed for renewable terms of 21 years, the deal promised revenue for at least a generation of independence. If self-government came in the late 1970s, Australia's short-term loss would yield Papua New Guinea's long-term benefit. But Bougainvilleans would endure loss of land and environmental damage while revenue went to a remote Papua New Guinea and skilled jobs to white artisans, and thousands of 'redskin' labourers would come to Bougainville.[22]

Even before the 1972 election, a member of the House asked pointedly if negotiators had taken 'advice from acknowledged experts'. Gerry Gutman assured him (tendentiously) that expert advice had been obtained and that 'the best possible deal was secured'.[23] When he resigned from the Public Service, Gutman publicised his view that the agreement gave more benefit to Papua New Guinea than comparable mines gave to Australia:

> Papua New Guinea's share of the equity ... has now a market value of about $160 million. A capital gain of over 500% in two years on investment financed by concessional loans ... does not look like a bad bargain, especially when that capital gain represents only a fraction of the total benefits accruing.[24]

This assertion was misleading since Australia's economy enjoys flow-on benefits from mining, while an undeveloped economy can benefit only through taxes or equity. Public opinion had also to be considered. The mood in Port Moresby was 'extremely delicate': even 'responsible circles' saw the agreement as unfair. So much was BCL distrusted that Somare agreed to cancel the formal opening of the mine and 'only after prolonged discussion with the Bougainvillean members' would he accept BCL money for Highland famine relief.[25] In the House, Momis moved to renegotiate the agreement. This idea was debated in and out of the House for weeks, and was approved in November. Meanwhile, Rio Tinto head office in London wanted Frank Espie to persuade the Minister for Territories to lean on Somare: Espie sensibly declined.[26] Rio Tinto argued that the agreement was sacrosanct but Beatty found contrary authorities and renegotiation became legally possible as well as politically necessary.[27]

The Minister for Mines, Paul Lapun, was a leader of Pangu and the separatist Napidakoe Navitu. He had criticised the mining laws for years and the issue was inflamed at Christmas 1972, when two Bougainvilleans were lynched by Highlanders after a car accident. But the Government was desperate for revenue and Cabinet wanted somehow to reconcile opponents of the mine.[28] So Lapun proposed that BCL and Australia explore changes to the agreement. If BCL balked, he 'would have to consider other possible courses of action'. To reassure other investors, he insisted that Panguna was a special case, negotiated by Australia: Papua New Guinea would honour all agreements that it negotiated for itself. Further, it was 'imperative that the people of Bougainville see the National Coalition government ... doing something to improve their lives'. Morrison naturally declined to become involved.[29]

The issue became critical when BCL announced its profits for 1973 — the first year of operation — as $A158 million. This was an astounding return on $400 million invested, made more odious by the fact that the Government received only $A29 million, mostly as dividends on its equity. BCL blamed exceptional metal prices. That was true[30] but irrelevant: profits on this scale demanded a political response. Sir Val Duncan, head of Rio Tinto and ultimate owner of BCL, invited Australia to buy Panguna as an independence present for Papua New Guinea. Garnaut calculated that the vast sum proposed would buy Rio Tinto itself;[31] but in any event, the Australians were not interested.

Chan came under pressure from Australian financial institutions, who demanded to know whether his government intended to renegotiate and, if so, whether all agreements were vulnerable. Chan's preference (he told Hay) was not to renegotiate at all, but if renegotiation did take place, 'there should be a firm statement … that it would not lead to the renegotiation of other agreements'.[32] The economic nationalists, sheltered from overseas pressures, felt no such constraint. In the end, a compromise was reached. Ministers consulted the American Stephen Zorn, as well as Beatty in the Planning Office, and Chan coaxed Garnaut and Anthony Clunies-Ross to devise a new way to tax mining. They researched the global market and knew precisely what this market would bear while BCL could only guess at Papua New Guinea's goals. Their anxiety peaked in 1974 when Momis and Kaputin demanded nationalisation, but the Cabinet had much narrower ambitions, centred on Garnaut and Clunies-Ross's Resource Rent Tax.[33]

Discussions began in 1974. When they stalled, Maori Kiki (as Deputy Chief Minister) stated that the Government's terms must be accepted or they would be enforced by law. That threat prompted a visit by Duncan himself. When his jet landed, however, 'there was no red carpet, no police band, not even a minister at the airport, simply BCL's own cars'. Duncan cooled his heels until Kiki explained that Somare was playing golf. On one view, Duncan was so disconcerted by this insouciance that he 'agreed where some of his own negotiators might not have … with the government's position'.[34] So the Government extracted more revenue, and sooner. A tax exemption on 20 per cent of profits was annulled, a tax holiday was cancelled, accelerated depreciation allowances were withdrawn, corporation tax was imposed and additional profits were taxed.[35] David had outmanoeuvred Goliath.

Or had he? For 15 years, Panguna was a material triumph: the Managing Director, Paul Quodling, reckoned that it created nearly half of Papua New Guinea's foreign earnings and 15–20 per cent of government revenue.[36] Without this income, independence would have rested entirely on Australian grace and favour. But the price was huge. O'Faircheallaigh points out that the environmental damage was calamitous 'because it raises starkly the question of power: power over land use, project design and environmental regulation, and over the distribution of benefits'.[37] Lapun would have agreed. He was rejected by his constituents in 1977 and, in the civil war of the 1990s, he lost his home. Even by 1988, he had regrets. 'When I was young they fooled me and now I am old and still alive to see the result of my decision I weep. Who cares for a copper mine if it kills us?'[38]

There were other continuities between the original agreement and its sequel. Most important — and ultimately fatal — was the fact that no one represented either Bougainville or the landowners. The new deal therefore did little to appease the province and offered nothing to landowners. Everyone seemed to believe that 'mining and its multiplier effects would promote nationalism rather than separatism'.[39] BCL was lucky: the Government's negotiating coup gave it a sense of ownership and renegotiation secured a generation of production.

Meanwhile, the American company Kennecott wanted an open-cut mine at Ok Tedi, to extract 25,000 tonnes of copper ore per day for 18 years. One hundred and sixty kilometres of road would deliver concentrate to barges to carry it to ships at the mouth of the Fly River. Kennecott angled for subsidies,[40] then presented its terms as an ultimatum. Faced with another corporate giant, in March 1975 Papua New Guinea rejected these terms. This was a well-researched response. Beatty, Garnaut and Namaliu had consulted Armine Bamfield, the guru of the mining consulting firm, Behre-Dolbeare. They needed to know how to drill the site to assess its value, before putting it on the market. Bamfield offered to do this for $20 million, and Cabinet agreed. Armed with this knowledge, they approached BHP in Melbourne (perhaps introduced by Peacock) and on Christmas Eve 1974 they helicoptered BHP's bosses over Mt Fubilan. Somare then took them to his home in the Sepik and the deal was done. When Kennecott pulled out, the Government managed the prospect until BHP took it over. In Richard Jackson's account, another Goliath was slain by David.[41]

As matters turned out, these victories were Pyrrhic. Revenues for 1973 did prove to be anomalous, so Panguna's revenues were never again as great. Jackson concedes that the deal with BHP for Ok Tedi was not quite as good as could have been extracted from Kennecott.[42] In the longer term too, Ok Tedi produced environmental damage at least as great as Panguna.

For better or worse, these sophisticated negotiations turned the country's back on a development strategy based on peasant agriculture or economic self-reliance. The negotiators created the framework for further mineral agreements and initiated a prospecting boom. In exchange for unprocessed ores, Papua New Guinea imported highly processed ideas.

Aid

For a generation, funds from Canberra grew in step with transfers to the Australian States. It would be inappropriate to continue these payments after independence, yet the Government would not survive the loss of half of its income. For several years at least, similar sums would be needed. They came in the new form of transfers from rich to poor countries: aid.

Australia's aid programs developed ad hoc from the 1950s, in step with her strategic interests.[43] By 1972, External Affairs managed the Colombo Plan and a few smaller projects, and allocated 150 officers to programs to spend one-quarter of Australian aid. Treasury deputed eight officers to handle relations with the World Bank, the Asian Development Bank and similar bodies; 135 staff in Education ran the Commonwealth Cooperation in Education Scheme; and 90 officers in Territories managed Papua New Guinea funds: this amounted to two-thirds of Australian disbursements overseas.

The Foreign Affairs approach was fixed in the 1950s. A developing country should ask Australia for experts or funds for a specific project. Australia would not initiate requests, nor did they tell recipients what was good for them.[44] Morrison had served in the unfashionable aid branch where he was dismayed by its amateurism: he lobbied to commit the Labor Party in 1971 'to reorganise the various Australian aid programs and to establish a mutual cooperation agency' when they came to power.[45] The creation of a professional and autonomous agency in the Whitlam Government was helped by the happy accident that the head of the Prime Minister's Office, Peter Wilenski, had a strong interest, and Whitlam was Minister for External Affairs for the first months of his government.

Those advantages were barely adequate to make headway against departments protecting their turf against the Government's aim of 'a unified administration to administer all aid'. In an ideal world for aid professionals, the agency would be a full department with its own minister. Existing departments preferred that the agency be subordinate – if it must happen at all. In September 1973, Cabinet compromised and created the Australian Development Assistance Agency as a statutory body.

The ADAA was born on the day of Papua New Guinea's self-government.[46] It therefore inherited the Territories Department's material responsibilities while constitutional issues were handed to the new Papua New Guinea Office. On November 30, 1973, the Department of Territories left its offices; the next day, the ADAA moved in. The new Director-General, Johnson, would sit in the chair of the last Secretary of the Department (Hay), and that was no coincidence. Johnson was selected partly to reassure Somare's cabinet that their needs would be considered with sympathy.[47]

But the succession was not smooth. The ADAA's 450 staff were drawn equally from Foreign Affairs and Territories, with a few from Education. (Treasury, resisting to the bitter end, refused to transfer either personnel or functions.) For several months, Johnson remained in Port Moresby, leaving leadership to the ranking bureaucrat, Max Loveday, from Foreign Affairs. Perversely, 'the Department which had so strongly objected to the Agency thus had the major say in its initial organisation and staffing'.[48] Until the passing of the Australian Development Assistance Agency Bill a year later, the agency operated as an office in Foreign Affairs — precisely the arrangement that everyone else had feared.

The anxiety of aid specialists was due to the Foreign Affairs tradition that aid was merely an instrument of foreign policy. The diplomats' view is summed up in the department's submission to a later tribunal:

> Aid lies with the framework of foreign policy and must be consonant with the Government's objectives in our relations with foreign countries. The amount and direction of our aid must be determined in the light of foreign policy objectives ...[49]

In this view, aid was best administered in discrete projects, whereas Territories staff were used to long-term budget support. Don Mentz, the most senior Territories officer in the ADAA, had many occasions to confront Loveday.[50] Since different sections of the agency occupied different buildings, there were few informal exchanges to soften the conflict. So aid policies were argued piecemeal by officials in a headless statutory body. When Johnson did arrive to referee shouting matches between Mentz and Loveday, he tilted towards budget support. Even then, the ADAA reported to Senator Willesee as Minister for Foreign Affairs, not to Morrison. That gave Foreign Affairs the upper hand — unless the Territories faction could reach Wilenski in the Prime Minister's office, or Whitlam himself.

The Papua New Guinea Government wanted a very gradual reduction of aid. Garnaut explored this scenario with officers of the Australian Treasury, where Stone had become the dominant personality. As head of the aid branch of Treasury during the 1964 World Bank mission, Stone had opposed the expansion of Australian transfers: his ideas now became more influential in Treasury. Garnaut told him that his views 'would mean the collapse of everything that has been built in Papua New Guinea', but Stone reckoned that the increased flows since 1964 were a terrible mistake: the sooner Papua New Guinea faced reality and slashed expenditure, the better.[51]

That put him on a collision course with Papua New Guinea, whose government saw that a radical reduction in the public sector would jeopardise stability.[52] They proposed instead to reduce the real level of aid by 2 or 3 per cent per annum — a very modest request while population was growing by 3 per cent and aid provided half of the budget.

Morrison was unsympathetic. His essentially political view of aid was revealed when he told his caucus colleagues that he was using it as a carrot to encourage movement towards independence.[53] But he also wanted to make Papua New Guinea's leaders confront harsh realities. In Malaysia, he admired the Economic Planning Unit that formulated development projects and invited donor countries to fund them. Based on this model, he proposed a two-part budget. Papua New Guinea would have sole control over its recurrent budget (funded mainly by domestic revenue). In a separate development budget, sectors would be identified (such as education, or health) which would attract funds from Australia and others. Details would be worked out between donors and Papua New Guinea.

Morrison drafted a letter to this effect for Whitlam to send to Somare, but he used an address to the 1973 Waigani Seminar to publicise his view that Australian aid should be a matter of 'cooperation and consultation'. Somare 'hit the roof' at this reversal of what he expected, and a network of academics sprang to his aid: Peter Drysdale and Nancy Viviani at the ANU, and Garnaut and Voutas in Port Moresby who insisted that funds on the large scale of aid to Papua New Guinea made responsible budgeting impossible if they came as projects.[54] The counterattack prevailed and Paul Kelloway and other officials spent 18 months 'getting Morrison off the hook' of his unpalatable commitment. The fig leaf was to call the process neither budgetary support nor project aid but 'program aid': Australia would nominate which budgetary section they wished to fund, but would have no control. After independence, this obfuscation was quietly shelved.[55]

Morrison was more helpful in a related matter. He observed that the fear of losing Australia's budget support gripped the Territory, and that opponents of independence were playing on this fear. He and Whitlam repeatedly stated Australia's long-term commitment to aid. What Papua New Guinea needed was not just money but forward commitment. The Australian Treasury preferred to consider aid (like all other proposals) on an annual basis. To overcome this obstacle, on February 15, 1974, Morrison persuaded Whitlam to assure Papua New Guinea of $500 million over three years, beginning in 1974–75. This was the occasion when he told caucus that he was using aid as a carrot.[56]

But a single gesture, however grand, could not close the issue. The size of the sum was hard to explain. Government funds flowed from so many taps — including Defence, Public Works and Civil Aviation — that it was impossible to name a lump sum to replace them. A serious disagreement centred on 'golden handshakes', the termination payments to Australian public servants (see Chapter 10). Critics demanded that this money was outside the $500 million: Morrison insisted that it had always been factored in as 'aid in one form or another'.

The climax of this dispute came just before independence, during the preparation of Australia's August 1975 budget. Somare, Chan and Maori Kiki met their counterparts at Kirribilli House in Sydney. Discussion raged through an afternoon, with Whitlam and his Foreign Affairs Minister, Willesee. But the key figure was absent: the Treasurer, Bill Hayden, was represented by the Assistant Treasurer. Hayden was sure that the Whitlam Government would stand or fall on the 1975 budget and he could not afford to let it blow out. He feared that if he attended he would be persuaded to exclude golden handshakes from the $500 million, and increase the overall commitment to Papua New Guinea. Such a concession would reopen debate on every other item in his budget. The case fell on ears that were not deaf but closed, and ministers were so shocked that their anger spilled over in public.[57]

> 'Australia has dumped us', Somare said bitterly [and] … reported that, when he asked Whitlam for a commitment after independence, Whitlam 'did not give an answer'. 'That's a big question mark', he was reported to have said.

Somare was sure that Andrew Peacock, who had made the initial commitment to golden handshakes, never intended that it count as part of the aid budget.[58] Hearing the ministers' outrage, Peacock travelled with them to Port Moresby, and began planning for a different form of commitment by the future Fraser Government. Meanwhile, the Papua New Guinea budget was in serious trouble. The first budget after independence had to cut government consumption expenditure by 10 per cent, a feat rarely achieved by any modern government.

That was not the only bruising encounter. Galvin recalls an incident in 1973 when the Australian Minister for Transport came with Morrison to negotiate the creation of Air Niugini as the government-owned carrier. The discussions went so well that Somare and Morrison had a few drinks before the formal reception. At the reception itself, Morrison took offence at a personal slight and declared that he was about to leave. Roland Kekedo was host of the reception: Morrison tried to punch him, Somare intervened and Kekedo floored him.[59]

A National Economy?

The management of Papua New Guinea's economy in the transition years was heroic: the country managed a budget cut of 10 per cent without panic, catastrophe or violence.[60] A more persistent hazard was slower to come into focus. A week after self-government an arms manufacturer arrived, asking about the small arms needs of ministers. He was the first in a queue of agents offering to sell aircraft, print currency, produce statues of the Chief Minister and so on. Some would visit ministers' houses with contracts ready for signature, and a few ingratiated themselves before it was clear that they were carpetbaggers.[61] In the next years, as the integrity of office-holders was tested, the Leadership Code was too weak, even in tandem with the Parliamentary Accounts Committee and the Auditor-General's office.

The Cabinet Secretariat had a mandate to marshall the facts of an issue before it came to Cabinet. A tragic exception occurred with the tabling of a strengthened Leadership Code. The leading public servants of the day — Morauta, Namaliu, Siaguru and Lepani, Papua New Guinea's 'Gang of Four' — persuaded Somare to introduce a tougher code. This was tabled in Cabinet without supporting argument. Chan and the PPP objected to the separation of ministers' business interests from their political roles. They combined with ministers who objected on procedural grounds (the absence of documentation) to defeat the proposal. The grand coalition fell apart, and Chan succeeded Somare as Prime Minister.[62]

But by then the institutions were built. While public attention focused on the CPC and its tussles with government, economic strategies and structures were quietly put in place. It was a matter of pride that there was low inflation, no balance of payments crisis, a hard currency and a resource rent tax. Ministers, their advisers and public servants created a coherent structure to regulate foreign investment and enterprise. Like every government before and since, they wrestled in vain with land issues, although they did defuse the Gazelle crisis. By good luck and very good management, they extracted more benefit from the mining sector than the Australians had.

But a paradox must be noted. This careful management and sophisticated negotiations undercut the village-centred and self-reliant rhetoric in which economic policy was couched in public. The decolonisation of the formal economy imported more values, institutions and procedures from the industrial world than had been introduced in 70 years of colonial rule.

Appendix: The 'Eight Aims' outlined by Michael Somare as a philosophy of government.[63]

1. A rapid increase in the proportion of the economy under the control of Papua New Guinean individuals and groups, and in the proportion of personal and property incomes that goes to Papua New Guineans.
2. More equal distribution of economic benefits, including movement towards equalisation of incomes among people and toward equalisation of services among different areas of the country.
3. Decentralisation of economic activity, planning and government spending, with emphasis on agricultural development, village industry, better internal trade, and more spending channelled to local and area bodies.
4. An emphasis on small-scale artisan, service and business activity, relying where possible on typically Papua New Guinean forms of economic activity.
5. A more self-reliant economy, less dependent for its needs on imported goods and services and better able to meet the needs of its people through local production.
6. An increasing capacity for meeting government spending needs from locally raised revenue.
7. A rapid increase in the active and equal participation of women in all forms of economic and social activity.
8. Government control and involvement in those sectors of the economy where control is necessary to achieve the desired kind of development.

Footnotes

1. Garnaut, in 'Hindsight'.
2. Interview, Garnaut.
3. Mark Lynch, in 'Hindsight'.
4. Interview, Pat Galvin.
5. E. F. Schumacher, *Small is Beautiful: A Study of Economics as if People Mattered*, New York, 1973.
6. M. Faber and D. Seers (eds), *The Crisis in Planning*, London, 1972; E. K. Fisk, 'Planning in a Primitive Economy: From Subsistence to the Production of a Market Surplus', *Economic Record*, 40 (1964), pp. 156–74. Jean Zorn and Pater Bayne (eds), *Seventh Waigani Seminar: Foreign Investment, International Law and National Development*, Butterworths, Sydney, 1975.
7. Michael Somare, *Sana*, pp. 78–9. See also Azeem Amarshi's chapters in A. Amarshi, K. Good and R. Mortimer, *Development and Dependency*.
8. N. Hughes, *The Eight Aims of the New Papua New Guinea*, Port Moresby, 1973, pp. 15.
9. Ray Anere, 'Economic Issues, 1975–1985', *Yagl Ambu*, 12 (March, 1988); T. K. Moulik, 'Crisis of Community Leadership', *Catalyst*, 3 (1985).
10. Interview, Ross Garnaut.
11. Interview, David Beatty.
12. Anthony Clunies Ross and John Langmore, *Alternative strategies for Papua New Guinea*, OUP, Melbourne, 1973.
13. Thomas Allen, in 'Hindsight'.
14. A452/1, 70/2960, ff. 34–32, summary statement.
15. Ibid., Administrator to Department, November 9, 1970, enclosing minutes of committee meeting.
16. Much of this discussion derives directly from Alan Ward's paper in the 'Hindsight' workshop.
17. Ilinome Tarua, in 'Hindsight'.
18. Ebia Olewale, in 'Hindsight'.
19. Alan Kerr, in 'Hindsight'.
20. Philip Fitzpatrick, *Bamahuta: Leaving Papua New Guinea*, Pandanus Books, Canberra, 2005.
21. Jim Fingleton, in 'Hindsight'.
22. Denoon, *Getting Under the Skin*.
23. ibid.

24. The *Age*, September 6, 1972.
25. 69/5655, Information paper 71/807 to AEC, October 18, 1972, and undated memo by Ross Burns. Ray Ballmer told A. W. Richardson about the cancellation on October 25.
26. 69/5655, Don Mentz, October 23, 1972, reporting a phone call from Espie.
27. Interview, David Beatty.
28. Ibid., and interview with Bill Brown.
29. 69/5655, Lapun to Hay, January 17, 1973; and memo dated January 23, 1973.
30. Copper soared from £450 per tonne at the end of 1972 to a record £1,135 a year later. Gold and silver prices enjoyed similar spikes. Prices slumped during 1974, but too late to avert renegotiation.
31. Interview, David Beatty.
32. 70/2960, Ministerial Schedule 397, Hay's minute of November 2, 1972.
33. Ciaran O'Faircheallaigh, *Mining and development: foreign-financed mines in Australia, Ireland, Papua New Guinea and Zambia*, London, 1984; Richard T. Jackson, *Ok Tedi: the Pot of Gold?*, Port Moresby, 1982.
34. Jackson, *Ok Tedi*, pp. 60–1; interview with Don Vernon, Melbourne, January 1998.
35. O'Faircheallaigh, *Mining and development*, p. 458. The Additional Profits Tax would yield 70 per cent on annual profits once BCL had earned 15 per cent on its capital.
36. Paul Quodling, *Bougainville: the Mine and the People*, Melbourne, CRA, 1990, 5ff. and p. 35.
37. Ciaran O'Faircheallaigh, 'The Local Politics of Resource Development in the South Pacific', in S. Henningham and R. May (ed.), *Resources, Development and Politics in the Pacific Islands*, Bathurst, 1992, p. 262.
38. Letter in the *Times of Papua New Guinea*, October 26, 1988, cited by John Connell, 'Compensation and Conflict: the Bougainville Copper Mine, Papua New Guinea', in John Connell and Richie Howitt (eds), *Mining and Indigenous Peoples in Australasia*, Sydney University Press, 1991.
39. Don Carruthers, 'Interview with James Griffin', *Weekend Australian*, June 9–10, 1990.
40. 71/2788, Kennecott — Preparation for Negotiations, August 1971.
41. Jackson, *Ok Tedi*, pp. 82-3; and interview with David Beatty.
42. Ibid.
43. Daniel Oakman, *Facing Asia: A History of the Colombo Plan*, Pandanus Books, 2004.
44. MacDonald, in 'Hindsight'.
45. The agency was abolished and replaced by March 1976. Nancy Viviani and Peter Wilenski, *The Australian Development Assistance Agency*. The quotation is from the ALP election platform.
46. Prime Minister's Office press release, September 18, 1973, cited in Viviani and Wilenski.
47. Don Mentz, interviewed in Canberra; Bill Morrison, interviewed in Canberra, April 2001.
48. Viviani and Wilenski, *The Australian Development Assistance Agency*, p. 14.
49. Foreign Affairs submission to the Royal Commission on Australian Government Administration, October 1974, cited in Viviani and Wilenski, p. 7.
50. Interview, Don Mentz.
51. Garnaut, in 'Hindsight'.
52. Ibid.
53. Morrison's notes for an address to the Party room, Morrison papers, National Library of Australia.
54. Viviani and Wilenski, *The Australian Development Assistance Agency*; interview with Morrison.
55. Interview, Paul Kelloway.
56. Morrison's notes for an address to the party room, Morrison papers, National Library of Australia.
57. Somare's comments occupied the whole front page of the next day's Melbourne *Weekly Times*.
58. James Griffin, 'July–December 1975', in Moore with Kooyman, *A PNG Political Chronicle 1967–1991*.
59. Interview, Pat Galvin.
60. Garnaut, in 'Hindsight'.
61. Lynch, in 'Hindsight'.
62. Moore with Kooyman, *A PNG Political Chronicle 1967–1991*. Garnaut believed that Critchley opposed the tougher code, assuming that it would destabilise the coalition, and pointing out that corruption was the normal way of doing business in South-East Asia.

Chapter 10

Creating a State

Decolonisation transformed a dependent Territory into a sovereign State, making people citizens instead of subjects. Sovereignty confers international equality and membership of global institutions. Some landlocked mini-states in Europe could leave it at that. Some insular mini-states in the Pacific and the Caribbean were experimenting with partial sovereignty, while Britain, France or the US continued to provide services.[1] Papua New Guinea was too large to behave like a mini-state and had opted for full independence so the new government had to provide schools and colleges, clinics and hospitals, roads and harbours, diplomats and soldiers, courts and police, agricultural, marketing and all other services to a scattered population. If it proved impossible to fund these on the desired scale, the Government needed a planning capacity to allocate whatever resources were available. It was easy to become a State internationally and in the abstract, but that would not satisfy the people, who needed concrete services. While a constitution was hammered out and economists built financial institutions, public servants were creating and staffing government agencies to fill the new offices in Waigani and deliver services.

Not unreasonably, many observers predicted catastrophe: under-qualified youngsters were rushed into key jobs in bodies that were brand new or were having their powers expanded. The quality of the new public service was uneven; but most of the new people in the new agencies performed as well as their Australian predecessors. Equally important — and more disconcerting — they outperformed their better-educated successors.

There were changes even at the top. When Johnson moved to Canberra, Tom Critchley succeeded him.[2] Like David Hay, Critchley was an experienced diplomat with recent experience in South-East Asia. This background (he assumes) commended him to Whitlam and Morrison as the man to oversee the moves to independence. His instructions were issued by the Minister for Foreign Affairs but were drafted by Morrison. They delineated three roles. As Australian High Commissioner *in* Papua New Guinea, he chaired the Executive Council and exercised Australia's residual powers. He was also Australia's High Commissioner *to* Papua New Guinea; and head of the Australia Office in Port Moresby (also known as the Papua New Guinea Office. Chapter 7). Conflicts between these roles should not have time to develop, since Australia still expected independence as soon as December 1974. In retrospect, Critchley would have liked four rather than three years between self-government and independence. But he believed that naming a specified date for independence was necessary to ensure a change of attitude among Australians and a real exercise of power by Papua New Guineans.

A National Bureaucracy

A shortage of skilled and experienced staff was an urgent problem. For decades, the Public Service Commission had enforced Australian standards to public service appointments and promotions, barring Papua New Guineans from most positions and opportunities. In an understandable but unfortunate reaction against that discrimination, Momis and Kaputin saw neo-colonial motives in any proposal to retain Australians, and demanded swift localisation. But a more effective spur to localisation was the 'golden handshake'.

The golden handshake — an inducement to permanent officers to take early retirement — was negotiated in turbulent times, with little concern for long-term consequences. When the Somare Government formed, the Public Service Board submitted its plans to expand the Public Service and localise personnel.[3] The plan was informed by the values of the previous House and the cautious ministerial members: they assumed an ever-increasing public service and leisurely localisation. Both elements appalled the new Cabinet with a precarious budget and a nationalist mandate. In September, Somare announced a new policy to merge departments, curb expansion — and cut the number of expatriates from 7,000 to 3,000 in three and a half years. This dramatic reduction should flow from natural attrition, without retrenchments.

Meanwhile, the Public Service Association had been negotiating with Territories over compensation for public servants who expected to be retrenched. Reaching an impasse in 1972, Peacock, as Minister for Territories, appointed as consultant the Adelaide businessman A. M. Simpson. His report — 'largely favourable to the Public Service Association position' — proposed that each retrenched officer receive a multiple of his or her superannuation contributions. This idea was adopted by the Australian Government, but not all Papua New Guinean ministers wanted seasoned officers to leave, nor could they see why the handshake was so generous. Dismay turned to alarm when platoons of public servants resolved to leave at independence: many contented officers could not resist the offer and the Government could not determine when they left. Least of all could ministers see the justice of deducting this sum ($60 to $70 million) from the aid budget.[4]

Alarmed by the evident skills shortage, Critchley wanted to create a special category of Australian public servants to help in a transition era.[5] He was also keen to build a training element into aid projects. Inspired by a successful project in Thailand, he wanted to link Lae to Moresby by road (a Unity Highway), the training component of which would strengthen the nascent Public Works Department. Australia's independence present was a suite of cultural institutions, which were important for national identity but marginal to the skills deficit.

The outcome of rapid localisation has been addressed by others, and is well summarised by Stewart Firth.

> The legacy of Australian administration was a large public sector of skilled people delivering services in education, health, transport, communications and policing.
>
> Tens of thousands of Australians did these jobs and left ... with handsome superannuation which counted as Australian aid. No PNG government could replicate the Australian way of doing things. It cost too much and depended on a highly educated bureaucracy.

It is widely agreed that, as well as 'the many impressive Papua New Guinean leaders' of the first generation, 'there were too many with too little knowledge of how to run a modern State'.[6] With the introduction of democratic institutions from the 1960s, the role of the *kiaps* was increasingly awkward. Papua New Guinean *kiaps* began to be trained and appointed, but that did not resolve the anomaly of an essentially Australian cadre of administrators operating in parallel with elected councillors and parliamentarians. The Department of District Administration continued and was added to the Chief Minister's Department, but most of the *kiaps* drifted away.[7]

Almost equally important in changing the nature of the Public Service, and much less often considered, is the unevenness of localisation: the Army and the police, for two important examples, were localised more swiftly than most of the civilian agencies, and the judges more slowly. Significant consequences flowed from this uneven pace.

The Uniformed Forces

The Department of Territories enjoyed little leverage in developing a national defence force: the Australian Army developed Papua New Guinea's armed forces with little civilian involvement. The Pacific Island Regiment descended from the Papuan Infantry Battalion, raised in 1940 (largely from Papua's constabulary). No similar force was raised in New Guinea, partly because of the terms of the mandate but also because the Administrator hesitated to arm New Guineans. The Japanese invasion trumped that concern, and two New Guinea Battalions were raised by the end of the Pacific War. These three battalions formed the Pacific Island Regiment of the Australian Army. Accusations of indiscipline were made and the PIR was disbanded in 1946 — 'a victory for those ... who saw native troops as a potentially dangerous, destabilising and unruly element'.[8]

By the 1950s, Australians were more anxious about *konfrontasi* with Indonesia than the possible risks of arming Melanesians. They reactivated the PIR in two battalions, created a Territory element in the Australian Navy in Manus, and revived the (mainly expatriate) Volunteer Rifles. Although there was no doubt about the PIR's courage under fire, a liaison officer deplored the absence of 'complete and instant obedience to the orders of a superior officer'.[9] Undaunted, the Army improved the soldiers' pay and conditions despite a prior agreement to keep parity with pay and conditions for the police. They also began to train officers. The first were commissioned in 1965 but — as in the civilian agencies — limited education barred many soldiers from officer training: in 1968, there were only six officers and six trainees. To prepare candidates to train in Australia, a Military Cadet School was opened in Lae.

Responses to demonstrators in 1969 (on Bougainville) and 1970 (in Rabaul) focused attention on relations between the Administration, the police and the PIR. The preparations for a call-out of the Army revealed unresolved issues. So seldom had Australians faced this issue that there were no precedents. (A few years later, after the 'Hilton bombing' in Sydney, Australians had to consult the history of British India to identify legitimate actions for the army.[10]) There were manuals for lending support to the civil power but the PIR had not seen them.[11] If the PIR had been involved, its approach would have been brusque: in Hay's gloss of the way soldiers dealt with such issues, 'You line them up, issue a proclamation, and if they don't disperse, you shoot'. Civilian sensibilities were very different. After an earlier riot in the Gazelle, for instance, Chief Justice Mann advised the authorities to assemble so much force that people would not risk defiance. That was also Hay's preferred approach. Since disorder was expected 'on a scale beyond the capacity of the police force to deal with' (Chapter 6), armed forces would surely be needed. Yet even at the end of 1971 officials did not know whether, or how, or how much the PIR would assist.[12] It was at this point that the Army revealed that the PIR simply would *not* train alongside the police.[13]

The PIR was listed in the Australian Order of Battle and paid by the Australian Department of the Army. Military planners had assumed that the Territory would be defended 'as if it were part of the Australian mainland' (as Hasluck put it) and that the PIR would remain part of Australia's forces. Many Australian officers worried about the pressure that Indonesia might bring to bear on Australia through Papua New Guinea. That assumption and that anxiety informed the demand for 'interoperability' — making sure that the PIR could use Australian Army weapons although they could not use the batons and shields of the local police. As far as possible, equipment and training were identical with Australia's. Australians even modified the standard rifle to suit the shorter stature of many PIR soldiers. Any move to reduce this interoperability would be unwelcome to Australian and to Papua New Guinean officers.[14] Such full integration into the Australian Army obviously inhibited it from morphing into a national force.

Perversely, while the Army stuck to its interoperable guns, Australia's strategic vision was undermining the case for integration. By 1972, *konfrontasi* was over, the setbacks of the Vietnam War had discredited the doctrine of 'forward defence', and the Government was rethinking its military obligations. Strategic disengagement was in the air, and the defence of Papua New Guinea shrank from 'vital' to a matter of 'abiding importance'.[15] The value of interoperability was disappearing — but not fast enough to affect events in Port Moresby.

The authorities did not develop a civilian department of defence until the very end of the colonial era, perhaps because there was no Canberra template for a strong department.[16] No civilian was ever involved in formulating policy. During a rare debate on defence in the

House of Assembly, in 1966, Paul Lapun moved a vote of appreciation for Australia's efforts, and this was carried without debate. A year later, the maverick Pasquarelli argued that a construction corps would be more useful than a PIR that he depicted as living in luxury. That heretical proposal died on the floor. Then in 1969, the House asked for a Defence Spokesman to be nominated from the House, and in that way to gain some control over defence. That request was refused because the PIR was intrinsic to the Australian Military Forces.[17] That honest answer begged the question of responsibility.

After the 1972 election, the position of Ministerial Spokesman for Defence was at last created, and supported by a three- or four-man civilian Defence Section. Somare was the first spokesman. While his stature lent importance to the role, he was already wearing so many hats that he could not devote much attention to military affairs. This arrangement therefore preserved the Australian Army's de facto control. The head of the Defence Section, N. L. Webb, seconded from the Australian Public Service, had correct relations with Somare, whereas the military commander enjoyed Somare's warm friendship. Outgunning Webb's civilians, the soldiers had a colonel as Director of Plans who consulted headquarters staff and enjoyed direct access to the Commanding Officer (Brigadier Aldridge, succeeded by Brigadier Norrie). Somare passed the defence role to Albert Maori Kiki in 1973, another high-profile leader, but one already busy as Deputy Chief Minister and Foreign Minister. So busy was the rest of the Cabinet that Ebia Olewale, for example, had no idea of the debates going on in and around Murray Barracks.[18]

When Morrison turned his attention to defence matters, he was dismayed by the size, the cost and the structure of the PIR: they seemed neither relevant nor affordable. Rather than allow the PIR to evolve into Papua New Guinea's Defence Force, he proposed a Police Field Force along the lines of Malaysia's, to patrol and manage the border in a non-provocative fashion. He believed that the Australian Army was over-ready to see the PIR as 'a short backstop to the police in the event of civil unrest'. Australians held combat positions, and that would embarrass Australia if the PIR deployed during internal disorder. For this reason, he wrote to Somare in August 1973, setting out procedures for consultation and warning that he 'should not assume that the PNGDF would be used prior to independence in any particular situation in aid to the civil power'. As Defence Spokesman and Foreign Minister, Kiki replied that his government was 'determined to look after its own security problems' and that soldiers should be used only as a last resort to maintain internal security.[19]

Morrison had raised these matters with Lance Barnard, the Minister for Defence, and in a meeting in January 1973 with Somare, Barnard, Johnson and the Chairman of the Chiefs of Staff, Admiral Victor Smith. He persuaded them that the police should be strengthened in order to handle internal disorder. They also accepted his more contentious proposal that a Police Field Force should be created. But the Chairman of the Chiefs of Staff opposed any reduction in the size of the PIR, and he resisted what he deemed to be civilian 'interference' in the PIR's internal security role.[20]

Australian and Papua New Guinean officers in Port Moresby predictably fought against a proposal that would disconnect the PIR from the Australian Army and (by training with police) blunt their professionalism. They simply ignored the decisions of the Canberra meeting. Since Barnard was over-stretched in an epic struggle to integrate the forces' supply departments, no attempt was made to enforce these decisions and Morrison's proposal lapsed. (He was not entirely alone. In the House of Assembly, Barry Holloway put forward the idea of a Special Services Unit. That concept was scotched at the same time as Morrison's.)[21]

Pat Galvin reckons that Morrison's proposal was never possible. The PIR was better — and more expensively — trained and equipped than the police. This was a rare institution in which 'Papua New Guineans were treated as equals; high performance was attained; and one outcome was a self-confident elite'. If that was not enough leverage, the Brigadier 'duchessed Somare shamelessly', so it was 'inconceivable that this outfit would consent to be down-sized or down-graded or integrated with any other agency'. Galvin also supposes that the head of the Department of Defence, Sir Arthur Tange, expected closer relations between the Papua New Guinean and Australian armed forces than proved to be the case after independence.[22]

Jim Nockels' bleak view is that the subversion of the agreement reflected 'the lack of capacity of anyone' in Canberra or in Port Moresby 'to centrally control this amorphous, humungous defence machine'. When Nockels came to Papua New Guinea as a civilian in defence planning, and saw that the existing arrangements were unaffordable, he revived the idea of a field force. He was promptly summoned before Brigadier Norrie, who threatened that

> if I didn't desist from sending notes back to Canberra suggesting that we might think of something different, and maybe a field force, he would personally have me escorted to the aircraft and sent back to Australia.[23]

As part of the campaign to defend Australian links, Papua New Guinean officers organised themselves in 1973 to address planning issues. The contest between civilians and soldiers for control over policy was quite lopsided. Before coming to office, Somare had argued that the Army was large enough with two battalions. By the end of 1972, he was denying any intention of reducing the size.[24] By weight of numbers, weight of argument and weight of inertia, therefore, a single security force was scuppered by soldiers who insisted on 'the discrete external defence function of a military force'.[25]

There remained the mechanics of creating a quasi-national defence force. The transition had been planned since the 1960s, and, in 1972, the Army created a Joint Force Headquarters in Port Moresby, based on Army Headquarters: there was no attempt to place the Joint Force 'under the command of … the head of the civil administration'.[26] The Papua New Guinea Defence Force was formed on Australia Day 1973, by renaming the Joint Force. Perversely (as Mench points out), the formation of the PNGDF as a national force required 'a very significant increase in senior and middle level Australian officers' for its headquarters.[27] It also entailed 'a dramatic expansion' in the number of officers and some inflation of rank levels.

When proposals came to Cabinet later in 1973, they resolved on a 3,500-man force, and equal status between the commander and the senior public servant in the

Defence Department. The first statement by Maori Kiki as Defence Minister, on Anzac Day 1974, justified a separate and expensive defence force by defining its three roles:

1 to defend the nation against external attack;

2 to assist the police in the maintenance of public order and security as a last resort if the police cannot reasonably be expected to cope;

3 to contribute as required to economic development and the promotion of national administration and unity.

There would be two battalions, an engineer company, a patrol-boat squadron and a landing-craft squadron, and appropriate support.

Morrison intended to transfer de facto control over defence long before independence. December 1974 was the target, but that had to be set back to March 1975, with provisos about the use of Australians in operations. In an era of ambivalent and divided responsibility, control was elusive. In July 1974, a force that had grown to 3,851, despite Morrison's instructions, still deployed 637 Australians. A year later, there were only 486 Australians, and Morrison was still anxious lest they become involved in an incident. But by the end of 1975 (after Morrison had enjoyed a stint as Defence Minister), there were only three Australians in combat positions.[28]

Powers were formally transferred in March 1975, but many steps were taken only at independence. The creation of a national defence force was a remarkable feat but — as Paul Mench points out — Papua New Guinea's assessment of her defence needs was almost identical to Australia's. That was due partly to decades of reliance on Australian officers, and partly to the arrival of independence too quickly to allow creative thinking. As a result, by 1974

> PNG defence solutions differed remarkably little from what Australia had planned and in some cases already developed and Australian defence planning had therefore, in great measure, been accepted by Papua New Guinean leaders ...
>
> [The Papua New Guinea Defence Force] ended up pretty much as if they had been designed completely by Australia and ... the elaborate processes of planning and consultation ... may be seen essentially as a legitimation of the Australian-developed defence forces.[29]

If Australia still saw the defence of Papua New Guinea as vital to her own interests, this continuity might have been justified, but there had been a seismic shift: no defence treaty was offered and the Papua New Guinea Government was too proud to ask for one. The Joint Statement of the Prime Ministers of Australia and Papua New Guinea, in 1977, was the end of a decade-long shift in Australia's strategic perceptions, so Papua New Guinea accepted full responsibility for her defence — with a defence force based on the assumptions of the 1960s.[30]

The PNGDF's dependence was profound. For one thing, the force needed continuing training. Again, policy-makers were constrained by the force's logistics requirements.[31] When Barnard inaugurated the PNGDF, he promised contributions to training, operational and technical assistance and equipment.[32] In reality, the PNGDF could develop *only* on the basis of a defence cooperation program with Australia. Papua New Guinea could deploy an effective force to put down secession in Vanuatu in 1980, but only because of the Australian drip.[33] As this support dwindled and Papua New Guinea's budget came under pressure, the effects on the PNGDF were corrosive. Its whole budget was consumed by wages, rations and other recurrent costs, so there was no money for repairs, for training in the field, or for patrolling. An army confined to barracks lost its edge and its discipline, long before it was put to the test of war in Bougainville.[34] As Anthony Siaguru put it, there was a huge military build up before independence, but

> when we've had to tighten our belt and live within our means, a lot of the soldiers and the defence force has been cut back regularly. Every year cabinet after cabinet cut back and made their soldiers lose more and more of their special entitlements and privileges.

A generation later, when the Eminent Persons Group advised retrenchment and retraining, the force was so ill-disciplined that 'there was a real danger that the military might have gone on the rampage'[35].

On the face of it, the Royal Papua New Guinea Constabulary was better prepared for useful roles in an independent country. Police traditions reached back to the very beginning of foreign control, as an armed constabulary. It was the only agency in which ambitious and determined men might expect adventure, relative affluence and independent authority (Chapter 3) before a comfortable retirement. During the 1960s, under officers such as Ray Whitrod, these men had begun to learn new roles as a modern police force — unarmed and professional — more like those of the Australian States and less like a colonial frontier force.

That metamorphosis was incomplete by the 1970s. The pioneering tradition was strong and, for example, when the Administration cracked down on the Mataungans, violent habits revived. Compared with the pull of the past, the attraction of the future was frail. The schooling of most policemen was too limited; too many expatriate officers left at independence; and facilities for training (such as their Gordon Barracks in Port Moresby) were cramped. In quantity as well as quality and training, the police were markedly poorer than the soldiers. Two hundred and forty officers and 3,400 other ranks included 11 'special duty squads' — in effect, riot police, who expected that they could manage one large disturbance at a time, or one medium and one small riot. As Critchley observed eroding efficiency and sinking morale, he urged Australia to top up the salaries of expatriates in order to retain them. He won that agreement, but too late: the police reached independence with few seasoned officers, and saturated by the values of the colonial past.[36]

The soldiers and police were better equipped for the 1950s than for the future. Together with the demise of the *kiaps*, these changes undermined the Government's control of town and countryside.

The Judicial System

Most Papua New Guineans experienced the judiciary as an integral facet of government, rather than as something independent or above it. In places where government control was new — especially the Highlands — *kiaps* still acted as judge and jury. Elsewhere, the formal courts often seemed equally subordinate to the *kiaps*. The Public Solicitor's Department could intervene, often successfully, but it could redress the power imbalance only in particular cases. Ian Downs, noting the legalism of proceedings, reckoned that episodes like the Varzin Case (Chapter 9) left the Tolai 'permanently embittered and with little faith in the courts'.[37] The same was true of Bougainvilleans when the Australian High Court upheld the Mining Ordinance against them.

Several members of the Constitutional Planning Committee, including Kaputin, Momis, Stanis Toliman and Angmai Bilas, had endured these frustrations personally and wanted the State to reform the courts, to reform the laws and to reshape the judiciary. Lest the structure be transferred and entrenched before they had reviewed it, Momis asked Morrison to delay.[38] As matters turned out, the Australians retained control only over the Supreme Court, but that was enough to allow Papua New Guineans to look into the judicial institutions and the values they embodied.[39] Kaputin, as Minister for Justice, summarised the most common complaints: the laws were too technical and better laws could improve people's lives; and the law restricted business and worked against Papua New Guineans. He said nothing about the need to prevent crime, but he did expect

> decreased tolerance of both poverty and privilege. For the underlying masses, development is apt to be a time of awakening hostilities, of newly felt frustrations, of growing impatience and dissatisfaction.[40]

A major defect of the court system was the absence of local tribunals. This meant (as Fenbury had pointed out in the 1950s) that many people relied on informal dispute-settlement — a 'completely unsupervised, and technically illicit legal system'.[41] He wanted local councils to have a law-enforcement arm, but Hasluck and Derham rejected that idea. They felt that a reasonable standard of justice would not be assured, and they did not believe that the resources could be found for supervision, so no action was taken.[42] Many later critics insisted that village courts should complement community structures on one hand, and superior courts on the other.[43]

Soon after self-government, attempts were made to fill this gap. In Kainantu, in the Eastern Highlands, for example, Village Courts started up spontaneously and forced the hand of the Government.[44] Geoffrey Dabb drafted a proposal and, in 1973, his draft legislation became the basis of the Village Courts Act, by which local courts would administer 'customary law'.[45] Under the supervision and control of District Court magistrates, these courts would resolve disputes within financial limits, impose limited penalties and be free to apply 'customary law' — although no one was willing to say what that was.

An immediate problem with the Village Courts was the impossibility of linking them through magistrates to the rest of the judicial system. The writers of the *Clifford Report* in 1984, for example, heard of Village Courts deteriorating in the absence of transport, facilities and visits by police and justice officials. That problem has not been addressed, and lack of supervision still accounts in large part for the defects of local courts. District Court magistrates cannot travel to do the job envisaged under the Act. Many Village Courts, therefore, 'have been colonised by the local power elite'[46] to the disadvantage of, for example, women. A Village Court system might have flourished if it had been introduced when funding was easier: its late creation exposed it to the tight budgets of independence.

When the CPC asked the people about the administration of justice, they demanded independent courts and an independent Public Solicitor. The CPC agreed that:

> the courts should be independent of the legislature and the executive … judges and magistrates should be sufficiently secure in their positions so that they can make their decisions without fear of personal repercussions.[47]

They were reluctant to give judges the same security of tenure as in Australia, since that might allow young judges to retain office well into their seventies. They proposed instead that a judge could be replaced after 10 years.[48]

For many years, all judges were likely to be expatriates. Only in 1972 did the University of Papua New Guinea graduate the first lawyers to join the Australian-trained Joseph Aoae, Buri Kidu and Bernard Narokobi. Scarcity led to dramatic career moves, such as Narokobi becoming Chair of the Law Reform Commission, and Ilinome Tarua thrust into drafting the Constitution. Buri Kidu quickly became head of the Prime Minister's Department and (though this was not part of the plan) Chief Justice soon after.[49]

The Bench would not be localised quickly if (by convention) a lawyer must work at the Bar for several years before elevation. That tradition generated tension between the desire for an independent judiciary and the likelihood that an expatriate Bench would show little interest in an indigenous jurisprudence. Morrison formed a poor opinion of the judges: he believed that they wanted to be transferred to Australian benches and he was sure that they did not deserve to be. By contrast, Papua New Guineans respected them so much that there was no pressure to localise the judiciary, which began almost by accident. In 1979, the Government resolved to deport Dr Ralph Premdas, a political science lecturer and adviser to ministers. Premdas appealed to the National Court to be allowed to remain in the country to organise an appeal. The court granted that request, to the dismay of the Minister for Justice. Nahau Rooney, once a member of Somare's kitchen cabinet, was a member of parliament from Manus. Articulate and energetic, she was unusual as a female parliamentarian and unique as a female minister. She reckoned that the Government, not the court, should decide who should be allowed to remain in the country, and she wrote to the Chief Justice saying so. The Supreme Court reacted by launching proceedings against her, describing her statements as contempt of court. Rooney was duly sentenced to eight months. When the Government released her on licence, five judges resigned.[50]

At much the same time, the Supreme Court handed down a custodial sentence of 10 weeks to Kaputin, who had become Minister for National Development. He had failed to comply with a court order to file the 1977 report of a company of which he was an office-holder.[51] What was astonishing in these events was the reverence paid to a court whose decisions astounded the Government as well as much of the public. In this crisis created by the judges' resignations, the Australian jurist Hal Wootton was willing to take over as Chief Justice, but the Government began a program of localisation with Buri Kidu as Chief Justice. The spur to localising judicial offices was the bench of judges, not the Government.

Kaputin and other reformers wanted to give greater scope, in theory and in practice, to 'customary law'. The criminal code of Queensland (adopted many years earlier) still prevailed. In 1963, a Native Customs (Recognition) Ordinance came into force, but custom was considered only in assessing an accused person's retaliation when provoked.

> Where an accused was perceived to be 'primitive' or 'unsophisticated', the courts were more prepared to extend the scope of the provocation defence and to give lesser sentences upon conviction.[52]

Encouraged by the CPC, the Constitution went further, asserting that custom had been adopted and must be applied as part of the underlying law. It stated that an Act of Parliament might provide for the proof and pleading of custom, regulate the manner or purposes for which custom may be recognised, applied or enforced, and provide for the resolution of conflict of custom.[53] The courts were charged to formulate appropriate rules, and to ensure that the underlying law developed as a coherent system.

But judges were not keen. When Narokobi was a judge of the National Court, he acted to recognise custom in relation to criminal matters, but he was rebuffed by the Supreme Court, where judges reckoned that customs had to apply throughout the country before they would be recognised. Since custom is necessarily local, such a test could never be met.

The issue was passed to the Law Reform Commission, created in 1975 with Narokobi as chair, assisted by Rooney, Francis Iramu, Meg Taylor and Charles Lepani. The commission moved to modernise and decolonise the more obviously colonial institutions. They proposed the abolition of the discriminatory Native Regulations, and these were duly repealed. Similarly, they recommended that the Police Offences Ordinances be replaced by a Summary Offences Act. When this was enacted in 1977, it abandoned the vagrancy law ('the offence of having no visible means of support'), although one commissioner did want this offence to remain so that police could arrest such persons and the court could order them back to their village.

> Together with the Arrest, Search and Bail Acts of 1977, these laws armed Papua New Guinea with updated and constitutionally valid legislation which was easy to understand and which provided a proper basis for the police to maintain law and order and act in an appropriate and lawful manner in dealing with suspected offenders.[54]

Beyond specific laws, the commission took its broader responsibility seriously. Working Paper 4, *Declaration and Development of the Underlying Law*, Working Paper 6, *Criminal Responsibility: Taking Customs, Perceptions and Belief into Account*, and especially its seventh report, *The Role of Customary Law in the Legal System*, did grapple with custom. Taking the opposite tack, however, was Lynch, the Parliamentary Draftsman, who combined the Criminal Codes of Papua and New Guinea into one document. Both derived from Queensland and Lynch introduced few changes. 'The opportunity to reform the Criminal Code so that it better reflected the world view of Papua New Guineans was lost.'[55]

This discussion implies that customary law could have been embraced if only the courts had taken their duties seriously. But the issue is more complicated than that. Dabb points out that the CPC imagined 'a body of customary law … waiting only for the tools needed to ascertain and apply it to solve many (some thought all) the questions about a legal system'.[56] If that were true, then research would uncover concepts and that were fundamental and widely followed. At the 1965 conference of the International Commission of Jurists, however, Justice Smithers observed that he had never seen field staff do their duty to record local customs, no doubt because 'the practices observed were but a wilderness of single instances.'[57] He approved of village dispute resolution, but insisted that 'decisions be reached … by reference to settled rules'. Without rules, it was impossible to ensure (or appeal, or even review) the fairness of decisions.

Fascinating 'single instances' were everywhere. Johnson was disconcerted to hear Siwi Kurondo in the second House of Assembly demand the retention of specific customs:

> We want no restrictions imposed to stop some of our ideas for looking after pigs. The women sleep with their pigs and I want this to be one of our customs that is continued.[58]

It is possible that 'customary law' — a single, consistent and discoverable body of ideas — simply does not exist. And if so, some of the critics of Papua New Guinea's Government are overstating their case. Early on, the Government 'lost interest in qualitative and substantive reforms', said Narokobi, or perhaps (according to David Weisbrot) it simply 'lost the will to reform'. In that respect, the Government merely reflects community values.

> The indignity of a wholly imposed legal system raises few hackles, and ... large numbers of expatriate judges, magistrates and lawyers playing a leading role in administering a foreign-based system of law and courts does not provoke the same emotional response that overt economic neo-colonialism does.[59]

The best analyst of contemporary 'customary law' issues, Sinclair Dinnen, observes important developments, for example in Bougainville, in resolving conflict. In the absence of the State during nine years of war, many local disputes were resolved by a creative 'mixture of "tradition" and newer structures'. In many parts of the country, informal dispute-resolution resources are used every day. These resources are concentrated in urban areas, along the highways and in areas of resource development rather than in less-developed regions.

Dinnen denies that the judicial system has broken down since independence:

> Often it is argued that the colonial system of order was very successful. Often there is an image of a system of *kiap* justice [but before self-government] that system itself was beginning to look shaky as it came under increasing resistance.[60]

Critics of the courts are not the only analysts who cherish a romantic view of colonial law and order. In reality, the Territory Administration was not always effective, even in its own terms, and colonial institutions (such as the *kiap* system) simply could not continue in a democratic society. By no means can all the defects of contemporary governance be attributed to decolonisation — or to the speed with which it was accomplished.

Footnotes
1. Robert Aldrich and John Connell discuss this phenomenon in *The Last Colonies*, Melbourne, Cambridge University Press, 1998.
2. Interview, Critchley. See also his National Library of Australia Oral History interview.
3. David Hegarty, 'September–December 1972', in Moore with Kooyman, *A Papua New Guinea Political Chronicle 1967–1991*.
4. Ross Garnaut, in 'Hindsight'. Garnaut suggested that this arrangement flowed from the Public Service Union's relations with the Labor Party. Morrison retorted that it was the result of Peacock seeking advice from Simpson, who, 'like all private sector people, are far more generous when it comes to using government money than they are with their own money'. The Simpson Report predated the Whitlam Government.
5. Critchley interview and Critchley's Oral History interview in the National Library of Australia.
6. Stewart Firth, 'Papua New Guinea: Why We Must Offer ex-Colony more than Words and Money', *Sydney Morning Herald*, March 27, 1997.
7. Philip Fitzpatrick, *Bamahuta*.
8. Paul Mench, *The role of the Papua New Guinea defence force*, Development Studies Centre Monograph 2, ANU, 1975, quotation from p. 20.
9. Ibid., p. 31: M. B. B. Orken, December 24, 1961.
10. Jim Nockels in 'Hindsight'.
11. Peta Colebatch in 'Hindsight'.
12. David Hay in 'Hindsight'. Draft IDC report, December 1, 1971.
13. A452, T29, 1971/3088, First Assistant Secretary's Minute, December 7, 1971.
14. Nockels, in 'Hindsight'.
15. Ibid., p. 55. See also Bruce Hunt's PhD thesis, 'Papua New Guinea in Australia's Strategic Thinking', University of New England, 2004.
16. Nockels, in 'Hindsight'.
17. Mench, *The Role of the Papua New Guinea Defence Force*.
18. Ibid.; and Interview, Ebia Olewale.
19. Morrison, 'The Transfer of Defence Powers', in 'Hindsight'.
20. Ibid.
21. Mench, *The Role of the Papua New Guinea Defence Force*, p. 76.
22. Interview, Pat Galvin.
23. Nockels, in 'Hindsight'.
24. Ibid.
25. Mench, *The Role of the Papua New Guinea Defence Force*, p. 76. (Morrison observes that 'the record of how the Australian military ignored the agreements reached at the meeting is contained in Walsh and Munster's *Secrets of State*'.)
26. Ibid., pp. 69–70.
27. Ibid., p. 73.
28. Morrison, 'The Transfer of Defence Powers', in 'Hindsight'.
29. Mench, *The Role of the Papua New Guinea Defence Force*, pp. 56, 92–3.
30. Hunt, *PNG in Australia's Strategic Thinking*.
31. Peta Colebatch, 'Transfer of the Defence Powers', in 'Hindsight'.
32. Mench, *The Role of the Papua New Guinea Defence Force*, p. 73.
33. Nockels, in 'Hindsight'.
34. Hank Nelson, in 'Hindsight'.
35. Anthony Siaguru, *The Great Game: Politics of Democracy in Papua New Guinea*, The Centre for Democratic Institutions Annual Address, June 18, 2001.

36. Interview, Critchley; and Sinclair Dinnen, *Law and Order in a Weak State*.
37. Ian Downs, *The Australian Trusteeship*, p. 173, cited by John Ley in 'Hindsight'.
38. John Ley, 'CPC's contribution to the constitutional provisions for the administration of justice', in ibid.
39. Morrison, in 'Hindsight'.
40. Cited by Dabb, in 'Hindsight'.
41. David Fenbury, *Practice Without Policy*.
42. Interview, John Greenwell.
43. Eg., William Clifford, Louise Morauta and Barry Stuart, *Law and Order in Papua New Guinea* (Clifford Report), IASER, Port Moresby, 1984; Sinclair Dinnen, *Law and Order in a Weak State*; Sinclair Dinnen and Alison Ley (eds), *Reflections on Violence in Melanesia*, Asia Pacific Press, Canberra, 2000.
44. Peter Bayne, in 'Hindsight'.
45. Dabb, in 'Hindsight'.
46. Dinnen, in 'Hindsight'.
47. CPC Final Report
48. Ley, in 'Hindsight'. So Sir Buri Kidu was not reappointed after his 10-year term.
49. O'Neill, in 'Hindsight', quoting Andrews, Chalmers and Weisbrot.
50. Stephen Pokawin, 'January–December 1979', in Moore and Kooyman, *A Papua New Guinea Political Chronicle 1967–1991*.
51. Ibid.
52. Nick O'Neill, in 'Hindsight'. O'Neil was Secretary of the Law Reform Commission.
53. Ibid., quoting Constitution of the Independent State of Papua New Guinea, 1975, schedule 2.1.
54. Ibid., quoting Law Reform Commission, *Report on Punishment for Wilful Murder*, Teport 3, October 1975.
55. Ibid.
56. Geoffrey Dabb, in 'Hindsight'.
57. Smithers, cited by Dabb in 'Hindsight'
58. Les Johnson, 'Westminster in Moresby'.
59. Narokobi and Weisbrot cited by Dabb, in 'Hindsight'.
60. Sinclair Dinnen, in 'Hindsight'.

Chapter 11

Defining the State

A new State must define itself, especially if its inherited shape owes everything to the convenience of colonial powers and nothing to cultural or economic compatibilities. Papua New Guinea's borders were so arbitrary and its internal links so frail that national sentiment mingled with parochial passions — and with pan-Melanesian solidarities. The 800 spoken languages measured not only people's isolation but the parochialism of each language community. English was spoken by a tiny elite of school-leavers; Tok Pisin was spoken mainly by men (and fewer women) who had lived away from home; *hiri motu* served as a lingua franca along the Papuan coast; but a national language was not the only element missing from national sentiment. Warfare had been suppressed in many parts of the Highlands only within living memory and in some places it was making a comeback. After four years of independence, the Government would have to declare a State of Emergency in all Highland provinces, in a vain attempt to bring tribal conflicts under control.[1]

Divisions between communities were real but porous. Every society engaged in trade and exchange, and people usually married partners from outside their close kin. That meant that suspicion of one's neighbours was mediated by cautious cooperation. Migrants to town sought out *wantoks* (who shared their language) and formed enclaves until jobs or other circumstances broadened their horizons. Parochialism did not rule out sympathy for others in similar troubles. Papua New Guinea therefore presented a shifting patchwork of loyalties and enmities, suspicions and empathies, mainly peaceful but sometimes erupting into violence.

Ebia Olewale's career suggests some of the complexities of ideas about affiliations.[2] Born in the Western District of Papua near the land border with Irian Jaya and the sea border with Australia, he went on from local schools to Sogeri High School near Port Moresby. That led to teacher training in Port Moresby. There he met Michael Somare and Albert Maori Kiki, who were at the Administrative College. As a trainee teacher, he revealed a flair for politics, organising protests against the dual wage decision (Chapter 3). After a spell of teaching in his home town, Daru, he was transferred back to Port Moresby, where he rejoined his friends and was one of the '13 angry young men' (Chapter 4) who addressed the Guise Committee so ungratefully in 1967. Shortly after that, he resigned his post, sailed to Daru and campaigned for election to the House as a Pangu candidate.

Defeating the sitting member (the docile ministerial member Robert Tabua), he joined the Pangu group in the House, although his ignorance of Tok Pisin (which was not then widely spoken in Papua) held him back: he told Ted Wolfers that he understood 'very little of what had passed'.[3] Across the Papua/New Guinea and party divisions he befriended another ex-teacher, Mathias ToLiman, who was struggling with the role of Ministerial Member for Education. Roles were reversed in 1972 when Olewale became a minister and ToLiman led the Opposition, but they remained close. ToLiman spoke to Olewale for the last time as he entered the Chamber in September 1972: 'Remember my high school in Toma', he said, then sat down and suffered a fatal heart attack.

Although Olewale aligned with Pangu, he did uphold Papua's separate status and its special relationship with Australia, and he helped to create Papua Action (Chapter 8). In the debate on Papua's status (Chapter 4), he worried that 'the drift toward unification had gone with Papuans largely unaware of it and without choice'.[4] Returned to the third House, he again aligned himself with Pangu — having resisted the siren song of Papua Besena and its charismatic leader, Josephine Abaijah. One influence on this delicate choice was the advice of his friend Paulus Arek, dying of cancer in 1973, that 'we must have a united country'. He was given the same advice by his older Papuan colleagues Oala Oala-Rarua, John Guise and Albert Maori Kiki. He was also anxious about what Australia would accept, and feared that separation might bring more problems than it solved.

In Somare's first coalition, as Minister for Education, Olewale still heard Abaijah's seductive appeal. Just as his colleague Paul Lapun had to balance his loyalties to Bougainville and to Pangu, Olewale had to live with dual loyalties. Opening the Port Moresby Show in June 1974, he 'questioned whether unity and independence were the only options available to Papuans'.[5] He empathised with Melanesians in Irian Jaya seeking to break away from Indonesia; and, briefly, he tried to annex the Torres Strait Islands to Papua New Guinea, also on the grounds of Melanesian solidarity.[6] Yet he could combine these sentiments with animus against provincial government in general, and Bougainvilleans in particular (see below). When Chan led the PPP out of the coalition in 1978, Olewale became Deputy Prime Minister. But even then — and even now — he wondered if national unity was the proper course: might not separate independence or Australian statehood have served them better? If Olewale juggled with contending loyalties, that made him an appropriate choice to negotiate the country's borders as Minister for Foreign Affairs.

National Unity and Decentralisation

There was general agreement that Australian rule was over-centralised, such that orders were transmitted from Canberra to the districts and even to patrol officers with little (if any) mediation in Konedobu. Proposed solutions ranged from Narokobi's anarchist vision in which villages would sustain and defend themselves, and land would be inalienable,[7] through plans to disperse decision-making to districts and subdistricts, to the division of Papua New Guinea into four regions.[8] Before the CPC reported, most of these options had been discarded and attention focused on the districts as counterweights to central government. The regional idea might play into the hands of Papua Besena; subdistricts were too numerous to be serious contenders; and insistent demands from Bougainville and Rabaul reinforced the CPC's interest in district-level affairs. The CPC therefore advised decentralisation for Bougainville particularly, and similar measures (in the name of provincial government) for the rest of the country.

For members of the CPC, provincial government was more than a governance proposal. Momis told the 1978 Waigani Seminar that provincial government was intended to

> fill the serious gap between the central government and the people and to transform the system of administration under which the colonial state had ruled us. [I]f we were to release the energies of our people, and if we were to enable them and their government to achieve a just, egalitarian self-reliant development we had to loosen the grip of these alien institutions.[9]

Meanwhile, with the help of Hannett's Special Political Committee, Bougainvilleans had channelled their manifold desires into clear-cut demands for autonomy.[10]

The Australian position was always clear. Like his political masters, Critchley wanted to protect Papua New Guinea's unity from secession and from decentralisation on the CPC model. No one yet knew how difficult it would be to create a state in Melanesia, but he did know how difficult it was to bring the machinery together in Waigani. He had general criticisms of the CPC's protracted debates, New-Age rhetoric, long-winded documents and ventilation of divisive issues. In particular, he opposed their approach to decentralisation. He suggested instead that Papua New Guinea experiment with less powerful area authorities, that they create local institutions very cautiously, and that powers conceded to Bougainville would be hard to deny to others. He was dismayed but not surprised when provincial government gave Bougainville's secessionists a base for an international campaign: fortunately, neither Papuans nor Mataungans had such a resource, so they were more easily contained.

That was not the only argument that swayed Somare's Government as events threw suspicion onto Bougainvillean intentions. Sending the Land Titles Commission to East New Britain, and despatching Rabbie Namaliu as District Commissioner, had defused tension in the Gazelle. By contrast, the renegotiation of the Bougainville Mining Agreement (conferring more benefit on the Central Government) did nothing to reconcile Bougainvilleans to the nation. Sending Hannett to the Special Committee did nothing to resolve outstanding issues and his dismissal exacerbated them.[11] Other emissaries to Bougainville also failed. Barnett and Gabriel Gris, for example, thought they had reached agreement on an Area Authority with enhanced powers, but they were roused in the middle of the night to learn that the deal was off.[12] Olewale led a last-ditch delegation in June 1975, also in vain.

At the end of July 1975, in an atmosphere of increasing suspicion against Abaijah on one hand and Napidakoe Navitu on the other, Cabinet decided not to risk provincial government at present and in its proposed form. According to Olewale,[13] Abaijah and her mentor, Dr Eric Wright, went to Bereina (in Mekeo country, Central Papua). Someone filmed Wright telling the chiefs how to blow up houses and bridges, and destabilise government. Cabinet was summoned to view the film, and saw Wright 'telling people how to destroy roads and bridges and houses', so they agreed to deport him.

Peter Bayne was talking to Namaliu in the House of Assembly when provincial government was due to be adopted. Somare walked in and said of the enabling clauses, 'They're off. We've taken them out of the Constitution.' Bayne learned that Cabinet had discovered attempts by some Bougainvilleans to win separate status from the UN. He also heard of people instructing a lawyer to draft a constitution for an independent Bougainville. True or false, stories like these might explain why Somare pulled out.

And it fell to the reformed separatist Olewale to manage this about-face. According to James Griffin, who deplored the decision, Olewale was the 'hatchet man', who gave the excuse that provincial government was unaffordable:

> PNG did not have 'this kind of money at this stage' ... However ... Olewale attacked the CPC and ... [singled out] Father John Momis. He did not admire, he said, the way the CPC 'took their document to be correct, without mistake in all its entirety': 'the man who conceived the idea of provincial government' was now a secessionist.

Griffin recalled Olewale's flirting with secession.[14] Certainly, Olewale had not forgotten Papua's interests. He weighed Papua's options with care, and asked two Papuan graduates — Renagi Lohia and Moi Avei — to examine the draft constitution to see what could be done for Papua. When they did not offer ideas, he fell back on his basic position that provincial governments would fragment the country.[15]

Ditching provincial government poisoned relations with Bougainville. A democratic government could hardly employ the *kiap* network, but who else would communicate with Bougainvilleans and monitor crises? One institution was the new National Broadcasting Corporation, amalgamating the Australian Broadcasting Corporation network and local radio services run by the Department of Information and Extension Services (renamed the Office of Information). These and the Government's Liaison Office were drawn into a Bougainville Task Force. The District Liaison Officer, for example, reported to the Director of the Office of Information on Bougainvilleans' (mainly cool) response to the Papua New Guinea independence celebrations.[16] A fuller account to the Bougainville Task Force noted 'significant numbers of Bougainvilleans at PNG independence celebrations' and reported that

> broadcast material is being prepared for Bougainville; more field officers [are] to be appointed to Bougainville districts; financial statistics [will be] prepared for [the] information of Bougainvilleans of central government largesse; etc, etc.[17]

Somare was keen to enlist the NBC as a protagonist as well as a reporter. For obvious reasons, he wanted to publicise the words of the Trusteeship Council when it congratulated his government for its 'successful endeavours in preparing for independence' and its statement that it trusted that 'the unity of the country will be successfully maintained'. The council conveyed to the Government and people of Papua New Guinea its 'best wishes for their national progress, unity and prosperity'.[18]

Somare told the chairman of the NBC of his anxieties about 'the current situation on Bougainville' and emphasised the Government's commitment to unity. Unity was 'a non-negotiable issue', and he sought the NBC's cooperation in helping the Government to communicate. 'I am cognizant of the danger of Radio Bougainville again being regarded as a propaganda radio station', but the Provincial Government seemed to him to be getting better coverage than the National Government. He particularly did *not* want a separate segment of government information (which he dismissed as *maus wara*, a Tok Pisin term for rubbish), but the integration of government information in routine broadcasting.[19]

In this first test of the NBC's independence, Chairman Sam Piniau proposed that the NBC would publicise the issue that 'finance is important to the people who favour secession'. He agreed that there should be 'a continuous flow' of information on Central Government spending in Bougainville and he thought that 'people generally are suspicious of the Bougainville leadership (unlike the Mataungan leadership)'. Then he suggested 'Fireside Chats' by Somare, Lapun and others proposed by the Task Force in order to

> direct attention of the listeners away from the current situation, and hopefully to build up the image of the Central Government through the Chief Minister and other ministers.[20]

But cooperation was difficult. A month later, Piniau withdrew the NBC from the Task Force as his suggestions were ignored, he valued the trust of his listeners and his relations with the Office of Information had soured.[21] The Chief Minister's office was appalled, and (with the help of the Office of Information) it drafted this letter for Somare to send to the NBC:

> Your attitude is quite unacceptable. You must be aware of the serious nature of events on Bougainville and the need for all of us to work together to improve the situation there. I demand the utmost cooperation between the NBC and the Office of Information … I expect the NBC to give every assistance to the communications programme currently being undertaken in the Bougainville Province.[22]

Although the NBC did rejoin the Task Force, NBC staff were reluctant to be pressed into service, whereas the Office of Information was happy in a partisan role.[23] Evidently, the Government inherited many attitudes — and tensions — that marked the Administration's relations with outlying districts.

Borders with Australia and Indonesia

Almost all Papua New Guinea's borders were problematic. Only to the north, towards remote Palau, did the open ocean form a natural limit. In the east, a rather arbitrary line split the Solomon Island chain, separating Bougainville from the British Protectorate. Bougainville was an obvious hot spot but the line itself was not likely to provoke trouble. To the west, however, the Indonesian province of Irian Jaya was separated by an unmarked and indefensible border. To the south, the border with Australia was so anomalous as to demand renegotiation.

Responsibility for foreign relations was shifting from Canberra to Waigani. There was limited experience to draw on, but the Director of Agriculture, Bill Conroy, a Somare family friend, had represented the Territory at marketing conferences. Somare agreed to combine Foreign Affairs and Trade with Albert Maori Kiki as minister and Conroy as its public service head. Conroy was assisted by Geoffrey Dabb. The leading Papua New Guinean was Anthony Siaguru, son of another Conroy friend in the Sepik and one of the first graduates. He enjoyed a swift induction as a trainee in Australia and attachment to the Australian Mission in Geneva. In 1975, he succeeded Conroy as Secretary.[24]

The Territory's western boundary was already under review as one sector of Australia's long border with Indonesia. Australian relations with Indonesia had been fraught through the years of *konfrontasi*, but they warmed with the inauguration of General Suharto's New Order. During 1972, the two governments were resolving residual border issues. Both were keen to involve Papua New Guinea in their confidence-building.

Until 1895, the British and Dutch had accepted the 141st meridian east, sight unseen, as the margin of their New Guinea territories.[25] When they realised that the Fly River was ignoring the meridian as it wound its tortuous way south to the Gulf of Papua, a new convention was agreed. The Fly was accepted as a Papuan river, but it did veer briefly into Dutch New Guinea so the convention gave Papua the land in the Fly River bulge. South of the bulge, a new meridian was pinned to the mouth of the Bensbach River. These were mere lines on maps until the 1960s when Australia and Indonesia surveyed this border. The surveyors endorsed the 141st meridian from the north to the Fly River, then followed the Fly meander and continued south along 141 01 10 to the sea.

In 1971, as the governments began to define seabed boundaries, Australia's position was vetted in Konedobu by the Administrator's Executive Council. When the negotiators turned to Irian Jaya and Papua New Guinea, the new constitutional formation meant that the AEC had to debate the issue (and it did so at length) before approving the negotiating position: and negotiations were handled by Philip Bouraga and Leo Morgan, beside two Australians (Webb and Dabb). Their Jakarta encounter resolved all issues except the Fly River bulge and the southern seabed.[26] That is where matters stood when there was a change of government in Australia. In the first days of his government, Whitlam acted as Minister for Foreign Affairs, keen to resolve all issues with Indonesia. In that context, he would 'follow up PNG-Indon[esia] sea & land boundary question[s]

… fully and promptly, involving Somare wherever practicable'.[27] Morrison ensured that Papua New Guinea was fully informed and Somare signed the agreement (on behalf of Australia) in February 1973.

An impediment to harmony was Indonesia's suspicion that the mouth of the Bensbach River had moved, taking the boundary with it. Until technical evidence disproved this idea, Indonesia felt that it had lost territory and sought territorial compensation in the Fly River bulge.[28] The real spur to this obscure dispute was the fact that 500 Irianese had fled east and enjoyed permissive residence in Papua New Guinea, where they had sympathisers. Indonesians suspected that some were aligned to the *Oposisi Papua Merdeka* (OPM), the umbrella group linking opponents of incorporation. The prospect of a copper mine on the border at Ok Tedi raised the spectre of population movements.[29] The Australians reckoned that Indonesia wanted

> acceptance of Indonesian sovereignty in West Irian … especially that of Papua New Guinea. In particular, they are anxious to avoid PNG support for West Irianese separatist movements in the border area.

They would really like an agreement like the one with Malaysia for their shared border, to secure the 'eradication of dissidents'. Papua New Guinean sentiment made such intimate cooperation unlikely, and divided the Australia-Papua New Guinea delegation that flew to Jakarta in October 1972. The Australians reported a 'marked divergence of view between the PNG Administration and Indonesia, particularly in relation to the significance of rebels and the action which should be taken'.[30] Realpolitik and sentiment had collided.

The critical point for the Indonesians was identified in an Australian Defence paper:[31] the nature of the regime that would control the border. Joint patrolling was one option, involving very close cooperation. Coordinated patrolling implied rather less intimacy. Instead of either approach, Defence proposed that Papua New Guinea merely agree to formal cooperation, and respond ad hoc to Indonesian complaints. Even in this scenario, however, Papua New Guinea would have to define 'procedures for handling fugitives'. Indonesia saw border-crossers as potential rebels and most Papua New Guineans saw them as refugees, so agreement was unlikely. The analysis concluded that Indonesia was unhappy with current arrangements

> and believed that Australia is not doing enough to prevent the use of PNG territory as a safe haven for dissidents from West Irian … [T]here is a very good case for Australia — and after independence PNG — to co-operate with Indonesia. Failure to do so could detract from the good relations we presently enjoy with Indonesia and which it is in our interests to foster between Indonesia and an independent PNG …

Australia saw the border as a security issue, while Melanesian solidarity was the lens through which Papua New Guineans saw it.

Whereas the Australian border would surely be easy to amend: both governments agreed that it needed to be changed. Torres Strait's shallow waters are full of islets and reefs. Queensland had annexed most of these before Federation,[32] and this was how Federal Australia came to acquire this border. So the uninhabited island of Kussa, less than a kilometre from the Papuan coast even at high tide, was Australian. The most northerly island inhabited by Australians — Boigu — was five kilometres from Papua. Torres Strait might look like a bridge, but little traffic crossed, and most of that flowed south. By the 1970s, 5,000 people lived in the islands, including 700 on the northernmost (Boigu, Saibai and Dauan), but more Torres Strait Islanders had moved to mainland Australia. Almost all migration flowed south from Papua into the islands, or from the islands to Queensland, and thousands of Papuans had kin or trade links to the Islanders.

In the event, it took years to hammer out a treaty. One hurdle was the Australian Constitution, which stated that a surrender of territory needed either the consent of Queensland's Government or a national referendum. While Queensland was governed by Sir Joh Bjelke-Petersen, an intransigent opponent of the Federal Government, especially when Labor ruled, Queensland's agreement was unlikely; and a referendum was unattractive because most referenda fail. An immovable obstacle was the Islanders. From Daru, Olewale saw them as fellow Melanesians who should be reunited with Papua New Guinea. The Islanders were less sentimental; they were fully aware of the advantages of Australian citizenship, and without their consent it was inconceivable that they could be transferred or evicted.[33]

Undeterred, in March 1974, Foreign Minister Maori Kiki proposed a single boundary. At the very least, the Australians should transfer uninhabited islands (conceding that Boigu, Saibai and Dauan would be Australian enclaves). Progress was slow while Canberra wondered how to deal with Queensland. Soon after independence, the Queensland position was set out in the Premier's statement to Parliament on October 7, 1975, and the Commonwealth position by Whitlam two days later. Peacock, as shadow Foreign Minister, feared that this 'festering problem' might develop into 'the greatest dispute between ourselves and our closest neighbour'. This was hyperbole, but the issue was important. As soon as the Liberals returned to power at the end of 1975, with Malcolm Fraser as Prime Minister and Peacock as Foreign Minister, they agreed to negotiate 'some revision'. They could accept a seabed boundary to the south of Boigu, Saibai and Dauan, but 'no Australian islands would be transferred to Papua New Guinea'. Ministerial talks agreed that Australia retain the inhabited islands, so long as their territorial sea was limited to three miles, and if other parts of the package were agreed. The uninhabited islands were another matter. That issue was resolved when Australian research concluded that these muddy islets had been Papuan all along.[34] When the seabed line was negotiated, therefore, to general relief, only nine uninhabited islets were identified as lying to the north of it (see Map 3).

These negotiations took place during global negotiations on the law of the sea. Australia and Papua New Guinea took part in the Third UN Law of the Sea Conference (UNCLOS) which extended the legal limits of states with coasts. The new Law of the Sea allowed a 12-mile territorial sea zone, and 200 miles of 'exclusive economic zone' for fisheries. It also encouraged countries to negotiate agreements on overlapping zones.

Negotiations resumed in July 1976, by which time Australia had conceded a seabed line south of Boigu, Saibai and Dauan. Negotiators readily agreed and Foreign Ministers Peacock and Maori Kiki endorsed this line in August — for seabed purposes, and so long as there was agreement on the rest of the Torres Strait settlement. Now the two outstanding issues were the status of uninhabited islands north of the line and whether that line or some variation of it would be the boundary for sea (not seabed) purposes.

The first election in independent Papua New Guinea was held in 1977. In a quixotic gesture, Maori Kiki quit his safe seat and ran against Abaijah. When he lost, Olewale succeeded him as Minister for Foreign Affairs, bringing cumbersome baggage.[35] In 1969, in connection with Irian Jaya, he had criticised 'Afro-Asian colonialism', and as minister he still sympathised with Irianese ambitions. (To mend the Indonesian fence, he was the first Foreign Minister to visit the newly annexed Indonesian province of East Timor.) He also reckoned that Torres Strait Islanders were Melanesian, so they should be added to the biggest Melanesian country. That could be accomplished, he thought, by shifting the border south to 10 degrees. Happily, his officials did not allow this dramatic idea to disrupt negotiations and the treaty was ready for signature in December 1978. Australia did not want a solid black line south of Boigu, Saibai and Dauan to imply a relocated 'border'. The solution was that a 'sea' (fisheries) line diverged north from the seabed line to form a 'hat' around those three islands. In exchange for the loss of these waters, Peacock proposed to share commercial fisheries in a 'protected zone'. The protected zone guaranteed 'traditional freedom of movement' and other traditional rights. Australia wanted this arrangement to win the support of the Torres Strait Islanders, but it would also benefit coastal Papuans. National authorities could exclude or regulate non-traditional use of resources. All this made for a complicated treaty, which was signed in 1978, but which did not come into force until 1985.

In retrospect, Olewale is relieved that his proposal for annexation failed. He concedes that the Islanders are better off as Australians — and, as Papua New Guineans, they would now be knocking at his door as kinsmen, demanding benefits.

Projecting Independence

An independent state must project an image, and the Government intended to revise old notions of relations between the various parts of the country, and between a united country and the rest of the world. Not before time: Papua New Guinea's global image was the artefact of missionaries and anthropologists. When Ulli Beier searched the well-stocked Ibadan University Library, all he found was J. H. Holmes's *In Primitive New Guinea*. In London, Anthony Forge gave him an ethnographer's view. It was only when they read Ted Wolfers's UN newsletters that they found political comment. Makerere University Library in 1972 had nothing at all.[36]

The Department of Territories had tackled the problem with evident ambivalence. Making no attempt to obliterate images of cannibals and Christians, Warwick Smith chose to contrast pre-colonial tradition with modernisation in the Australian present. An opportunity came in 1969, when the department organised a display for Expo '70 in

Osaka. Warwick Smith wanted 'to portray the Territory's main export commodities by contrasting them with subsistence farming photographs'. The display — *New Guinea: Progress in One Lifetime* — comprised 16 pairs of photographs, each contrasting a static past with a promising present:

haus tambaran	ANG House [the first skyscraper in Port Moresby]
subsistence	tea
subsistence	cocoa
subsistence	coffee
subsistence	copra
fishing, traditional	modern fishing
primitive children	schoolchildren
young tribesmen	university students
warriors	a *kiap* patrol
wood carving	Japan Lines ship
string bridge	road construction
village	airport
alluvial miners	CRA [at Panguna mine]
pigs [Melanesian]	cattle [European]
village elders	House of Assembly and councillors
witchdoctor	nurse and operating theatre[37]

This emphasis continued in a trade display in Vancouver that generated a gratifying number (40) of inquiries for rural products.[38] With self-government, image became the responsibility of Papua New Guinea's Department of Foreign Affairs and Trade, and the Office of Information. The transfer made little difference. Another trade display in New Zealand followed the same tradition: it was 'poorly thought out and inadequately equipped'. And the economic focus survived: at a Melbourne Trade Show in 1976, Somare proclaimed:

> Beneath the earth lie massive quantities of copper, the sea is rich in fish, and the timbe stands are some of the biggest in the world. This is Papua New Guinea today.[39]

The economic emphasis avoided the pitfalls of selecting social images. It was one thing to criticise exhibition visitors who asked about cannibals; it was quite another to define better imagery. At self-government, a Consulate-General opened in Sydney, with an information section. The role of that office was mainly to field Australian media requests and school children's needs for school projects. Some businesspeople were briefed, but Austin Sapias (the officer in charge) was frustrated to find that the information and display material were seriously dated. Before that problem was addressed, the office closed during an austerity drive.[40]

The problem was more than organisational. A year after independence, Caltex proposed to offer prizes for the best essays on 'national identity, national unity and self-reliance'.[41] The offer prompted discussion but no action. A few months later, the Minister for Information requested 'discussions and action' on a National Identity Campaign. Officers scratched their heads, suggested that they consult someone from the Education Department and someone else from the Institute of Papua New Guinea Studies, and lapsed into silence. If discussions were held, they left no trace.[42] Later that year, a production clerk complained that she had 'no idea' of production targets, nor could she find 'the aims of the Office of Information [for] the next few years'. She proposed to develop an office display, a domestic travelling display and overseas displays, but eight months later she had received no guidance, and plaintively tried to relaunch the topic.[43] Another year passed, and Siaguru reminded the office that it was obliged to prepare publicity, and asked what had been done. There is no response on file.[44]

If the office was negligent abroad, it was busy at home, where a domestic audience could perhaps be brought to a clearer perspective on national identity. From 1967, its officers were committed to propaganda in Bougainville, in favour of unity and the benefits of the Panguna mine. DIES agreed to translate BCL's educational booklet into Tok Pisin, and advised the company on its local publications and its ventures in film-making. DIES also publicised the company's scholarship program and — as the Bougainville situation deteriorated in 1969 — proposed an inquiry to develop a program to improve 'relations between the local people on the one hand and the Administration and BCL on the other' (explicitly tying the Government to BCL). Soon afterwards, the department agreed to publicise BCL's issue of shares to the public, and advised on publishing a newspaper.[45]

In fact, they were so busy defeating secession that little attention could be paid to the general idea of national unity and identity. Much energy was invested in displays at local shows, and publicising the kina and toea.[46] In 1977, it was politic to concentrate on shows in Goroka, Port Moresby, Morobe and Kokopo. Goroka was worth a particular effort:

a) for political reasons we are seen to be showing the flag of PNG in the Highlands, a densely populated region ... and always a thorn in the side of the Government.

b) We want to be seen to be recruiting from the Highlands areas and by participating in the Show ... we will be one step ahead of any criticism ...[47]

The Office of Information was not the only agency mandated to articulate national identity, and its failure mirrored the indifference of the whole government. Distracted by economic and constitutional crises and the fissiparous political system, the Government had little time or energy for such abstractions as identity and image. Many colonial assumptions, values and institutions therefore survived unexamined. They would eventually blow up into civil war.

Footnotes

1. Stephen Pokawin, 'January-December 1979', in Moore with Kooyman, *A Papua New Guinea Political Chronicle 1967–1991*, pp. 334–5
2. Interview, Olewale.
3. Ted Wolfers, 'May-August 1968', in Moore with Kooyman, *A Papua New Guinea Political Chronicle 1967–1991*.
4. Hegarty, 'May–August 1971', in ibid.
5. Hegarty, 'May–August 1974', in ibid., quoting the *Post-Courier* of June 17.
6. Interview, Olewale.
7. Bernard Narokobi, in G. Zorn and P. Bayne (eds), 7th Waigani Seminar, *Foreign investment, international law and national development*, 1973.
8. Hal Colebatch, in 'Hindsight'.
9. John Momis, opening address, Waigani Seminar, 1978.
10. John Ley, 'The Role of the CPC in Nation-Building', unpublished typescript.
11. Hegarty, 'September–December 1973', in *A Papua New Guinea Political Chronicle 1967–1991*.
12. Interview, Barnett.
13. Olewale, in 'Hindsight'.
14. James Griffin, 'July–December 1975', in *A Papua New Guinea Political Chronicle 1967–1991*.
15. Interview, Olewale.
16. DIES Archives, Port Moresby, C13/2, part 2, P. J. Somers, Ag. Government District Liaison Officer in Arawa, reports to Director, OI, September 18, 1975.
17. Ibid., Bougainville Task Force meeting, October 8, 1975.
18. DIES Archives, C13/2 Part 2, Bougainville Task Force, Department of Chief Minister, Circular 716, undated, 'Discussion — United Nations Trusteeship Council'.
19. Ibid., Somare to NBC, August 22, 1975.
20. Ibid., Chairman NBC to Director of Information, September 10, 1975, concerning his letter of September 9, about the Bougainville Task Force proposals.
21. Ibid., Chairman NBC to Director Office of Information, October 10, 1975.
22. Ibid., Philip Bouraga (Secretary to Prime Minister's Department) to Brian Amini, November 17, 1975, and draft latter dated November 25.
23. Ibid., Godfrey Wippon, Information Officer, Arawa, to Director, November 24; December 18, 1976, minutes of Task Force show that NBC has rejoined; Wippon's report of January 14, 1976. The Task Force continues to meet until June 1976 at least.
24. Anthony Siaguru, *The Great Game: Politics of Democracy in Papua New Guinea*, Address to Centre for Democratic Institutions, ANU, June 18, 2001.
25. A 452 T29, 1972/3835, Baird's brief for Morrison, January 3, 1973
26. A 452 T29, 1972/3835, Greenwell's memo, January 19, 1973.
27. A 452 T29, 1972/3835, Ellicott to Whitlam, December 8, 1972
28. A 452 T29, 1972/3835, Greenwell's memo, January 17, 1973.
29. A 452 T29, 1972/3835, Greenwell's minute, November 20, 1972.
30. A 452 T29, 1972/3835, Greenwell to Hay, December 1, 1972.
31. A 452 T29, 1972/3835, undated, unsigned paper handed to Greenwell on March 30, 1973.
32. Geoffrey Dabb, 'A Short History of the Torres Strait Border', in 'Hindsight', and Paul van der Veur, *Search for New Guinea's Boundaries*.
33. Interview, Olewale.
34. 'Status of the Islands of Kawa, Mata Kawa, and Kussa', 1978, Parliamentary Papers.
35. Interview, Olewale.

36. See Preface.
37. DIES 4/6/3, Part 2, Warwick Smith to Administrator, June 6 and 13, 1969.
38. Ibid., Department to Administrator, June 18, 1968.
39. DIES 4/6/3, Part 3.
40. DIES 4/5/7, Part 1, Consulate-General in Sydney, Austin Sapias, 1st Secretary (Information) reports for the quarter July 21 to October 22, 1975, on October 24.
41. DIES 4/2/20, Caltex to Brian Amini, October 15, 1976.
42. DIES, A5, National Identity Campaign, Assistant Director, Government Liaison to Assistant Director Production Division, both in the Office of Information, March 2, 1977.
43. DIES 4/6/1, Part 2, Acting Production Clerk to Director, March 28, 1977.
44. Ibid., Siaguru, Secretary for Foreign Affairs, to Office of Information, October 12, 1978.
45. DIES 5/6/23, Relations with BCL; Colin Bishop to Newby, May 29, 1967; G. A. Rudge to Director, September 9 and 11, 1969; Newby to Administrator, June 23, 1970; Newby to Chief of Division (Broadcasts), November 25, 1970; and October 1970.
46. DIES 4/6/2, Part 1.
47. Ibid., Assistant Director Sela to Director OI, May 17, 1976.

PART 3: THE LIMITS OF INDEPENDENCE

Chapter 12

Independence and its Discontents

Papua New Guineans handled the transition to independence with flair, despite their limited experience, the speed with which they had to act and the explosive agenda that they inherited. With great skill and some luck, they brought their country united to independence with new institutions, a new public service, a guaranteed income and a home-made constitution.

A Failing State?

The coalition that achieved these feats tottered in 1978 when Julius Chan took the PPP into opposition, and collapsed in March 1980 when the Leader of the Opposition, Iambakey Okuk, won a no-confidence motion, naming Chan as preferred Prime Minister. Chan had quit the coalition over the attempt to buttress the Leadership Code (Chapter 9) and disagreement on relations between private business and public office. Somare returned to office after the 1982 election but once again he was ousted in mid-term by a vote of no confidence, yielding to the ambitious young Western Highlander Paias Wingti. The pattern was now set, whereby coalitions are formed after an election but no government survives the fixed five-year parliamentary term. Votes of no confidence are the mechanism for replacing one opportunist coalition with another. By this device, Wingti was replaced by Rabbie Namaliu, who yielded to Wingti again, who was replaced by Chan, whose coalition collapsed in the wake of a bungled attempt to employ mercenaries (see below). After the 1997 election, Bill Skate — a gregarious accountant from Gulf Province, Governor of Port Moresby and cheerful opportunist — held a Cabinet together for nearly two years. Although many MPs lose their seats after one term, several leading players from the epic 1970s remain in public life 30 years later. It was Mekere Morauta who replaced Skate, and — this is where we came in, surely? — Somare himself took up the reins in 2002. He has supported and opposed most of his contemporaries, and has outlived or outlasted them all.

As governments cut corners and the Public Service became politicised, commentators adopted an increasingly sceptical tone. When saboteurs closed the Panguna mine and civil war shattered Bougainville in 1989, these military, political and fiscal crises sapped the optimism and the performance of government. War dragged on through the 1990s, soaking up funds and eroding morale. The Government's effectiveness — and the country's reputation — touched bottom. As public despair fuelled Christian revivalism, the Governor-General led a campaign that prayed for a clean government to emerge from the 1997 election.[1] Those prayers were ignored. In a desperate attempt to defeat the Bougainville Revolutionary Army before that election, members of Chan's Government engaged Sandline mercenaries.[2] Elements of the Defence Force defied the Government and arrested the mercenaries, with wide support from civilian protestors. Chan had to dismiss the mercenaries, step aside as Prime Minister, escape from Parliament in disguise and accept a judicial inquiry. The election of 1997, in which Chan lost his own seat, brought in a Cabinet led by the leading critic of Sandline, Bill Skate.

Paradoxically, military intervention did open the way for peace as rebels welcomed the Defence Force putsch. They agreed to talks, then to a truce, and finally to a settlement. But in every other respect Skate's term was the most turbulent in Papua New Guinea's history. As coalitions formed, fell and reformed around him, Skate appointed and sacked no fewer than three Deputy Prime Ministers, three Finance Ministers and three Governors of the Bank in two years. His image was battered when Australian television screened tapes in which he and his Police Minister discussed political bribes, and Skate boasted of having organised a gangland killing. His rather lame defence was that this was the whisky talking.[3]

A Commission of Inquiry into Sandline found that General Singirok's putsch had been unlawful, but it also unearthed improper Sandline payments to politicians and reported that the contract made by the Finance Minister (Chris Haiveta) had cut legal corners. The commission regretted that his 'credibility is brought into question': money that he transmitted from Switzerland was evidently part of a 'corrupt and improper payment'.[4]

Broader economic management was equally haphazard. The budget for 1999 was written not by the Finance Department but by Dr Pirouz Hamidian-Rad, formerly the World Bank's man in Port Moresby, now a consultant. Once the budget passed through Parliament, Skate resorted to Wingti's device of adjourning to avoid a vote of no confidence. Seven months passed before the Ombudsman compelled him to reconvene. Parliamentarians then resumed their desperate coalition-building while Skate tried to raise funds by recognising Taiwan as the Government of China. He then resigned, to jockey for the succession.[5]

In the tumultuous horse-trading, Mekere Morauta led one group, Speaker John Pundari another, and Skate a third. On the first day of the sitting, MPs voted for Skate's nominee as Speaker, which implied that he might win the next day's vote for Prime Minister. Politicking continued through the night though, as the Morauta team offered the leadership to Haiveta, prompting Skate to do the same. This manoeuvre so outraged Pundari that he changed camps (from Skate to Maorauta) for a third time: as MPs were driven to Parliament, he deflected his bus-load of supporters to the Opposition entrance. In Parliament, he proposed Morauta. Recognising defeat, Skate's team quickly crossed the floor to the winning coalition, giving 99 votes to Morauta and only five to the other nominee.[6]

Morauta, with more experience in public service than in Parliament, was welcomed by the Australian Government — lending colour to Skate's contention that he was Canberra's man.[7] No one doubted his integrity, however, and his Cabinet began to roll back tides of political appointments and clouds of mismanagement. A mini-budget was prepared with the aid of his old friend Ross Garnaut.[8] Cabinet dismissed several political appointees in the Public Service and the Army, reappointed respected public servants, and revived relations with China.[9] After what was really a parliamentary coup, however, Morauta's Cabinet was mainly Skate's (with 16 former Skate ministers) so the Prime Minister took control of as many portfolios as he could manage, to limit corruption by his colleagues.[10]

Parliament was not an engine for reform. Its most astute analyst was Anthony Siaguru, one of the 'Gang of Four' public servants who struggled to bring integrity to government in the 1980s, Member of Parliament and minister, then Commonwealth Deputy Secretary-General until he came home to organise the local chapter of Transparency International. He hailed Morauta (the 'ex oficio saviour of my country'), and yet even with

> Sir Mekere at the helm desperately trying to steer us in directions for the national good, the course is not at all certain when so many of the crew, as well as some of the passengers in cabin class, have their own ideas of where to go.

He noted the paradox that the country was 'overrun with democracy' but could not ensure good governance:

> [W]e have political parties, plenty of them! But they are essentially creatures of parliament ... Party members follow a dominant political personality ... and allow him to command their personal loyalty, unless of course better prospects appear. It reflects ... the kind of faction-operated politics of eighteenth-century Britain ... Our MPs are therefore not tied down by any constraints of commitment, either to political philosophies and specified policies on the one hand or the demands of toeing a party line on the other.

He blamed himself and all other electors who 'persistently vote for our local interests, which, in the main, run counter to the national needs and national priorities'. Once elected,

> what we want of him is to do his utmost to get into government and become a minister because that means easier access and opportunity to secure more goodies ...

> [Therefore] in the last election, in 1997, one-seventh of all seats were won by candidates with 8 or 9 per cent and less of the votes cast ... [and] some constituencies had over 60 candidates ...

> If choice is the criterion, we're absolutely overwhelmed by democracy. [One winner] represents 11 per cent of the electorate. Eighty-nine per cent are not represented … [so that people have become] more and more divided.

Siaguru hoped for salvation through electoral reform, strengthening the political parties.[11] But as he foresaw, the restoration of integrity is slow and faltering. Morauta himself offered one reason. At a recent seminar,[12] he cited his government's reform of the National Fisheries Authority. The Australians had praised the fisheries as evidence that 'good governance in the management of natural resources is possible'.

> Staff numbers were reduced from over 200 to about 50 professional officers. Clear management plans were set … Licensing powers were in the hands of an independent board and access agreements were negotiated … against clear criteria.

The reforms boosted exports to K350 million and direct employment from 450 to 6,000 and indirect employment to perhaps four times that figure, but in the two years since he lost office

> NFA has been wrecked by political meddling, bad management, misappropriation and other impropriety. NFA has again become a trading house of licences to foreign companies … Our marine resources are under threat and the security of our borders is at risk from indiscriminate licensing.

> The lesson: Reform can be very easily undone, without political commitment and strong, impartial administration.

Allan Patience describes very different obstacles to reform.[13] First, a girl of 10, who had been raped three times by a village man, came to the Village Court, which merely imposed a fine on the culprit, in effect treating the victim as no more than 'a juvenile prostitute'. That, said Patience, 'reflects very badly on a village society that fails to protect the young'. Second, there was discussion about an increase in electoral allowances for Members of Parliament, although everyone knew that 'these funds are used during elections to bribe voters'. Third, the new Governor-General, Paulias Matane, had taken an 'overly elaborate entourage' to London for an audience with the Queen. The expensive journey included a visit to Singapore to buy clothes. There were, asserted Patience, hundreds of other examples of inappropriate or immoral politics, including the mismanagement of forest resources,

> corruption in the public service, inadequate responses to HIV/AIDS, TB and other health crises, the flat economy, spiralling population growth rates, massive breakdowns in the delivery of basic and essential public services.

And these are the *friendly* critics! Other Australians are less charitable. Few resisted independence in 1975, but their ranks have swollen. Bill Hayden, who precipitated

Papua New Guinea's first financial crisis, called the country a 'social and political time bomb on our doorstep and the cause rests solely with Port Moresby'.[14] Peter Ryan never approved of the speed of Whitlam's decolonisation: as early as 1984, he declared that Papua New Guinea

> hurtles downhill into an ungovernable morass, for which the Australian taxpayer parts with some $A300 million a year. But it is 'unhelpful' and almost jolly bad form to mention it.[15]

The conservative ideologue B. A. Santamaria chimed in: 'A return to barbarism', 'Mayhem and massacre' and 'Nationhood squandered'.[16]

But many Papua New Guineans judge their governments even more harshly. Hank Nelson points to a dramatic change in people's recall of the Australian era. In the 1970s, people spoke of slights and misbehaviour by the *mastas*: now there is palpable nostalgia for days of equality, freedom and efficiency. This shift owes something to Papua New Guinea's youthful population, two-thirds of whom have no memory of Australian rule.[17] Some voices — including a Papuan pressure group — still seek incorporation into Australia, but others are simply despairing. Mal Smith Kela, a naturalised citizen, was elected Governor of Eastern Highlands Province. His work is extolled by Alois Francis, who insists that many of the country's problems are not attributable to Australia, but to mismanagement and corruption by today's bureaucrats and politicians.

> Imagine what it would be like if a State minister went out of his way to lead by example and collaborate with his departmental head to clean up their department.
>
> If he changed the attitudes of workers by coming to work early and set the example for bureaucrats to give 100 per cent commitment to their work …
>
> Eastern Highlands Governor Mal Smith Kela is one leader who is trying to do something positive …
>
> His government has for the first time in the last 15 years recorded a budget surplus. No government has done that before. No government has even shown the people the provincial government budget.
>
> The Governor does not hand cash to his constituents, like the governor of my own province, who unfortunately acts as an oil tycoon …
>
> Maybe, we need many Smith-Kelas to run our provinces and the country.

The *Post-Courier* caption was: 'Maybe we need white skins to run our country properly'.[18]

Despondency is widespread. The decline of law and order and the disruption of rural services[19] make many people ready to believe the worst. One vignette is described by Philip Fitzpatrick. A former *kiap* who now lives in Adelaide, he has worked with exploration firms and he records a conversation with a policeman in a mining camp.[20] The talk turns to independence:

> Well, we didn't have much choice about leaving [says Fitzpatrick], that was a political decision, and it wasn't just Gough Whitlam pushing that line, Michael Somare and all the other pro-Independence people were just as much to blame. The thing that bothered me was that we left with the job only half done.
>
> That's what my old man keeps telling me [the policeman replies]: he's quite bitter about it.

Fitzpatrick wonders if decolonisation might have been handled differently, as:

> pulling out as many expatriates as possible overnight seemed really dumb. I mean, what was wrong with declaring Independence and leaving all the expats where they were until properly trained Papuan New Guineans could take their place? What was the point of accelerating promotions amongst local staff, it was almost like deliberately setting them up to fail? They could have let the Tolais and the other advanced districts run themselves and still have had kiaps running the Highlands and the Sepik and the Western and Gulf Districts. None of the kiaps I knew minded having Michael Somare as a boss.
>
> One thing still bothers me though (says the policeman): why didn't the kiaps protest? My old man reckons the kiaps should have told the Australian Government they were wrong to think about leaving so early.

During the 25th anniversary celebrations of the Supreme Court in 2000, Bernard Narokobi welcomed Ebia Olewale, who had been Minister for Justice when the court began. If not for Olewale and other Papuan members, said Narokobi, there would not now be a united country. But Olewale is still ambivalent. Government services have withdrawn from most of his Western Province, and barely survive in Daru. Olewale and his family live in Port Moresby, part of a brain-drain from unserviced rural areas. He and others wonder if Papua might be easier to administer on its own: some cherish the Papuan claim to be Australians. While the level of corruption is hard for Olewale to believe, he is more distressed by the brazenness of those who practice it.[21]

When Morauta became Prime Minister, he echoed the apocalyptic mood and proclaimed that Parliament had 'a date with destiny':

> We have chosen order over chaos. We have chosen hope over despair. We have chosen pride in our young country over mindless pursuit of narrow interests. We have chosen

to give our children the chance of a decent life in their own country, in place of fearful descent into poverty, poor health and disorder.

More recently, Bire Kimisopa, Minister for Police and campaigner to bring back Australians, launched this jeremiad. At independence:

> we had everything going, the better roads, business was flourishing, law and order was kept at a minimum, our court system was functioning very well, education and health was doing better and unfortunately perhaps after 15 years, all of a sudden we're starting to see a complete deterioration of basically all government services. And that perhaps started with the way we've been running this country politically ... And ... once you start to change departmental heads, everyone down the systems was changed ...
>
> [I]t brought ... a whole heap of issues into the public service, especially cronyism ...
>
> [Of his own portfolio] the greatest fear that our people have is not the criminals but it's the police.
>
> [And the ultimate cause is economic.] The economy is growing roughly about 2%. The forecast for next year [is that] the population growth is far exceeding the GDP growth.[22]

As in this case, hyperbole is a feature of political discussion, but there is substance in the criticism. To begin at the top, Parliament is dominated by the executive, for reasons set out by Siaguru. Every candidate is de facto independent, and campaigning involves lavish gifts. (Violence has also become common in some Highland seats: but this is no cheaper.) Members enter Parliament so impoverished that 'their votes if not loyalties are sold' to the builders of coalitions.[23] Committed members attend closed camps in remote resorts or in Australia, while their leaders scour the countryside for the uncommitted.

The major leverage over backbenchers is 'electoral funds'. These 'slush funds' began on a small scale in 1983, but by 1999 the Government was paying half a million kina to each supporter every year. The excuse is the failure of provincial governments, but few members pass their funds to provincial treasuries, which therefore cannot deliver clinics or teachers or road repairs. The real rationale is that slush funds give the Prime Minister some control over backbenchers, except when his own position is under siege from motions of no confidence. These are now frequent — Namaliu survived eight during his three-year term.

In and out of office, parliamentarians are perpetually anxious. Half lose their seats after one term, and ministerial office is slippery, yet money must be raised to fund past and future campaigns. For corrupt behaviour, Leadership Tribunals have ousted a score of members: in the generous spirit of equal opportunity, some return from jail to be re-elected and even promoted to ministerial office. And in office, however briefly, ministers can sack public servants and appoint kinsmen.

The CPC hoped that provincial governments would be close to the people and provide a counterweight to the Central Government. In 1995, however, provincial government 'reforms' transferred real power from provinces to the centre.[24] Most parliamentary committees have also disappointed the hopes vested in them.

As Kimisopa conceded, the police are often seen as a threat. Meanwhile, the morale of the Defence Force has deteriorated so far that an Eminent Persons Group, appointed by Morauta, proposed retrenchments and retraining. The enraged soldiers rioted until the Government promised to shelve the advice. An endearing feature of the political culture is the freedom of public officials to denounce their institutions. Thus Colonel Kanene, Defence Attache at the Embassy in Indonesia, revives Morrison's radical questions (albeit unawares):

> The police force is in a mess, ill trained and lacks basic discipline ... Morale is at an all-time low, corruption is rife at all levels, and they have lost the respect of the people, especially when they go around burning homes and destroying property ...
>
> I suggest the Government should consider amalgamating the Papua New Guinea Defence Force ... with the police force.
>
> To be honest, the military has no role ... Our national security threats are internal and it is a police responsibility. The nation-building role is better left to the local contractors. To defend against external aggression? Well, who [is] the aggressor? ... If Indonesia attacks PNG, do we at least have enough troops to defend the Wutung border post for 30 minutes? This PNG Defence Force gets about K80 million every year to do what? If a situation like Bougainville arises, don't worry. It is a law and order problem and the [police] will deal with it.[25]

Other issues that dismay commentators include landowners negotiating directly with a well-resourced Malaysian timber company, so that (it is supposed) they win few benefits for themselves and less for the country.[26] All projects, from road construction to mining, entail interminable negotiations to compensate landowners. Provincial governance is uneven. The more affluent work well, with qualified staff and money to pay them; but poorer provinces flounder. Some provincial governments have been suspended for corruption or incompetence, provoking national politicians to ask if provinces are necessary. Conversely, the premiers of the island provinces wonder if they need a national government. In 1994, they told Port Moresby to leave them alone or they would consider secession. The crisis was literally overshadowed by a volcanic eruption that destroyed Rabaul and required relief efforts on a national scale.
But does this add up to 'a failed state'?

Probably, says Helen Hughes, the leading propagandist for a tougher Australian approach. In a report for the Centre for Independent Studies, she claims that

> Papua New Guinea is on the brink of collapse … [and] Australia could waste $2 billion in aid over the next five years unless PNG makes fundamental reforms … 'It's on the way to a dysfunctional state — a Haiti or a Congo or Idi Amin's Uganda,' she said. 'That's the sort of future it faces if it does not improve its economic performance.' The study says PNG needs to double or triple its growth rate if it is to step back from the brink of becoming a dysfunctional African-style state.
>
> The report says the most important change for agriculture and business would be to reform land tenure, introducing individual property rights …[27]

This is only the most newsworthy of many jeremiads, asserting that the State is either failing or has already failed. Elsina Wainwright deplores the violence of Port Moresby and the Southern Highlands, and the 'glorification of guns and gun culture'. The economy stagnates, governance is weak, corruption is rife, and HIV infections have increased dramatically.[28] Mark Dodd writes of 'lawlessness … leaving locals traumatized, foreigners closeted in fortified compounds and the country's economy and infrastructure in a mess'.[29] Susan Windybank and Mike Manning anatomise 'Papua New Guinea on the Brink'.[30]

Measuring Independent Papua New Guinea

Any evaluation of decolonisation must cut through the jungle of debate about Papua New Guinea's condition today. Critics often say (and always imply) that today's disasters are due to independence coming too early, too swiftly or too casually. Some of those who defend contemporary Papua New Guinea also attack the speed and manner of decolonisation. Opinions about decolonisation are therefore so intertwined with arguments about contemporary policy that it is impossible to tackle one without the other.

But critics do not specify the criteria against which they judge. Seldom do they follow Siaguru and propose constitutional solutions. Often — as with most of the critics cited above — denunciation dwells on economic performance and leads to free-market prescriptions. Always they imply that Papua New Guineans would be happier, healthier and wealthier if only their governments behaved more like Australians. But that is surely absurd. In colonies of settlement (Australia and New Zealand, North America), the colonists brought British laws and lawyers, viceroys and vicars: they also imported the values and expectations of the homeland.[31] Rulers and subjects might detest each other, but they did so on the basis of shared assumptions. These colonial regimes evolved predictably. The Australian settler colonies avoided many of the crises of the 20th century through the gradual pace at which powers devolved. Until the 1940s, they could rely on Britain's navy, capital, markets and migrants. Colonial governments experimented with industrial relations, tariff protection, minimum wages and female suffrage without risk and at their own pace.[32] Hasluck's notion that Papua New Guinea might enjoy an equally leisurely transition (Chapter 2) commanded no Australian support, and would not have appealed to Papua New Guineans. It was naïve politics, but an astute reading of Australia's history.

Commentators who demand a smooth transition to prosperity, social harmony and Western-style governance must be arguing from abstract principle rather than real models, because no country has ever behaved in this exemplary way. Wherever empires collapse or withdraw, similar problems arise. In the Americas, the Spanish republics took at least as long as the US — more than a century — to achieve good governance (abolishing slavery, bringing venal governors under control, and imposing limits on corporate capital). Few writers assert that African states are models of good governance after 40 years. A curious exception to this rule is Botswana, held up by Hughes as a model for Papua New Guinea.[33] But most of Botswana is desert. Since the 1890s, it has been a labour reserve for South Africa's mines, which explains its unusual economy and its distressing rates of HIV/AIDS. A cattle-keeping aristocracy guided decolonisation, and diamond mines fund its current account. It can be used as a model for Papua New Guinea only if we ignore its geology, geography, climate, social structure and political and economic history. And Tim Curtin suggests that Papua New Guinea's economy has outperformed Botswana anyway.[34]

Closer to home, every society in East Asia had to create new institutions in the wake of the Pacific War. The constitution forced on Japan, the dismantling of Manchukuo, the proclamation of the People's Republic of China, insurgent republics in Indonesia and Vietnam, revolution and war in Korea, all displaced colonial institutions with governments that were equally repressive. Almost as swift was the independence of India, Pakistan and Burma. India's democracy and China's development are admirable but hardly relevant. Many governments, including Singapore's and Malaysia's, revive or preserve the laws and agencies of colonial control to contain dissent and avoid accountability. This approach, defended as the application of 'Asian values', suggests the difficulty of combining open democracy with rapid economic development.

The latest analogy for Pacific decolonisation is the collapse of the Soviet Union. The socialist principles have withered in Mongolia, Kazakhstan, Kyrgyzstan, Tajikistan and Uzbekistan, but authoritarian rule persists.[35] Most of the post-Soviet regimes reimposed Soviet-style controls. Each has a major ethnicity, large minorities and Russian (and Russians) to help communication. Most people are Muslims, and ethnicity and citizenship compete for mass loyalties and provide a handy rationale for ruthless control. Uzbekistan's independence, for example, was certainly smoother than Papua New Guinea's: Islam Karimov led the country before 1991 and has since brooked no opposition. Kyrgyzstan's Parliament meets but a Security Council rules. The creation of effective post-Soviet governments generates the same temptations as the succession to colonial ones, while economic development, civil rights and honest resource management are at least equally problematic.

Are the states of the Pacific better models? We can rule out the unique Tongan monarchy. Samoa's independence constitution restricted the vote to title-holders. That flouted UN norms, but Samoans did it anyway. They adopted adult suffrage in 1991 but only chiefs can be candidates. Despite this self-definition and self-determination there is an unmet demand for accountability. Fiji is unique in other ways. Through the colonial era, the agency for ethnic Fijian affairs operated outside the rest of government. Commercial sugar-farming and urban commerce favoured Indo-Fijians, while ethnic Fijians were shielded from the market but exposed to their chiefs. Since the chiefs resisted devolution, independence was achieved only by entrenching communal institutions. With the support of the Great Council of Chiefs and the latent approval of the all-Fijian army, the chiefs moved smoothly from colonial rule to independence. That dispensation prevailed until 1987 when the chiefs were voted out. In short order, a military coup reversed the election, arguing that democracy was a 'foreign flower'.[36] A decade later a home-grown constitution restored democracy, but the new government was overthrown in another coup in 2000, after less than a year in office.

Samoan precedent emboldened constitution-makers to modify 'Westminster' principles. Not only did the Gilbert and Ellice Islands split in two (Kiribati and Tuvalu), but Kiribati elects its president. Officials in the Solomon Islands experimented before independence. Within a Governing Council, functions were exercised by committees of councillors and public servants, allowing full scope for Melanesian consensus. But in 1974, Islanders chose to revert to orthodox Westminster institutions.[37] In the Pacific, as elsewhere, decolonisation has not led directly to democratic harmony, equitable governance or economic development. In brief, there is no precedent for the ideal outcomes expected of Papua New Guinea.

Utopianism makes it hard to acknowledge Papua New Guinea's achievements. In his review article on child health, for example, Dr Trevor Duke feels obliged to adopt a defensive tone when he brings moderately good news:

> Civil turbulence is newsworthy and reinforces the political paradigm: tranquillity and slow progress are also part of the reality, but are not newsworthy … This current article does not seek to deny that some areas of the health service and other sectors crucial to child health have deteriorated, however, slow but important progress has occurred in many areas in the last 10 years [and especially since 1999].[38]

Against the grain, Tim Curtin offers a startling perspective on economic performance, drawn from his wide experience in Waigani. He now has time to assess Papua New Guinea's economy and its critics.[39] He begins by reviewing the assertion that population growth has outstripped economic growth. That claim relies on census figures for 1980 and 2000, but these must be inaccurate since the 2000 Census 'shows many more persons alive aged 20–29 than were alive aged 0–9 in 1980, and … more aged 35–39 in 2000 than had been alive aged 15–19 in 1980'. If the population figure is overstated, Gross Domestic Product per capita must be understated.

A second element of the calculation is GDP. Curtin notes that most critics take 1983 as their base year, although 1983 was exceptionally prosperous.[40] These and other issues, such as the choice of currency for these calculations, lead him to surprising judgments. Hughes and others assert that population growth 'equalled or exceeded' economic growth.

> [But in fact] over the whole period since independence, GNP per capita in Australian dollars (the currency in use in 1975) has increased by 3.5 per cent p.a., which is both better than implied by most commentators — and better than Australia's 2.5 per cent.

Amending suspect statistics might not be conclusive. A more realistic measure of wealth is food consumption, the core of poverty estimates. Here the difficulty is to put a value on people's subsistence production. Again, the arguments are too complex to repeat here, but the best-informed commentator, the agronomist Michael Bourke, estimates that 4.5 million tonnes of staples were produced in 2000, providing nearly 3,000 calories per day even without imported foods.[41] There are wide regional differences, but (as 2,200 calories is deemed sufficient for adults) there is no *national* food deficit. Curtin explains that the critics use estimates by the statisticians Gibson and Rozelle[42] rather than Bourke's surveys, so (like Chand) they reach the alarmist conclusion that '37 per cent of the population lived below the poverty line where the poverty line was set at an income level of K461 per adult'.[43]

None of this is academic. Many of those who assess Papua New Guinea's population, calorie intake or economic performance marshall their evidence to support particular policy prescriptions. Hughes is explicit about her advice. 'PNG must free up land ownership and farming' and the most important change 'would be to reform land tenure, introducing individual property rights to replace community ownership of land'.

The World Bank is just as explicit, denouncing the country's forestry projects, and even demanding the freezing of particular projects as a precondition for loans.[44] Hughes agrees that forestry and mining are poor options, and prefers the large-scale production of oil palm, which would generate annual economic growth of 7 per cent and double GDP every decade.[45] Bourke is not impressed. He cautions that Papua New Guinea 'would need to produce 4,700,000 tonnes of palm oil to totally replace crude oil and minerals'. Production on that scale that would require 1,500,000 ha of land, compared with today's 108,000 ha;[46] Curtin adds that Hughes's projected growth would, in 15 years, cover 7,000,000 ha: output would exceed world consumption and the price would collapse.

Curtin's prescription is also explicit: only forestry could replace mining income. Exports of forest products 'already contributed K415.8 million (5.3 per cent) to total exports of K7.79 billion in 2003' despite World Bank interference. If Papua New Guinea reached Sweden's level of output, 'logging exports could be worth K13 billion, nearly double total exports in 2003'. New Zealand's forests produced 10 times as much as Papua New Guinea's. Malaysia's forests yielded 40 times as much income as Papua New Guinea's, 'but the World Bank, Helen Hughes and others advise Papua New Guinea against even contemplating development of its largest resource'. Curtin concludes that Papua New Guinea

> could and should be a rich country, given its enormous human and natural resources, were it not all too often for 'stupid white men' (and women) in international aid

organizations and NGOs who have combined with others of that breed in its own bureaucracy to prevent exploitation of those resources.

Whatever the truth of these matters, we should be sceptical about the most apocalyptic commentaries, and yet many Papua New Guineans and Australians are willing to believe the worst. Papua New Guinea followed dozens of ex-colonies which beat a path to the UN. Many would envy her regular elections, peaceful changes of government, honest judiciary, free press, vigorous religious and workers' movements, uniformed forces with no political ambition, and good relations with neighbours. They might even envy her economy. Yet Papua New Guineans take little satisfaction in these feats. Evidently, many people's direct experiences make the doomsayers credible.

Olewale and Siaguru complain as citizens. Most of the critics analyse Papua New Guinea in the language of social science. But anyone who believes that these assessments are disinterested has not been paying attention. Consider Tim Anderson's denunciation of Helen Hughes as she lectures Australians who have paid to hear her:[47]

> [S]he exclaims that in PNG, 'there is just no economy, there's no life'.
>
> Who is to blame? A local corrupt elite, she says, which siphons off the surplus from aid and resource industries and fails to develop infrastructure and basic services. Not a word of blame for Ausaid, the army of 'development' consultants, or the mining and logging companies.
>
> The good news, she claims, is that Australia 'has taken the lead' in policy reform, through the 'enhanced co-operation program' and this may lead to a commitment to policies of 'broad based growth' and 'land reform' …
>
> The new element in the post-colonial era has been an aggressive drive to take land from ordinary PNG people — to destroy the customary title that guarantees their food security and social security …
>
> In this campaign, right-wing ideologues like Prof Hughes are central. Her argument … is that the community land ownership that covers 97% of PNG is the principal barrier to a 'development' which will lift millions of people out of poverty. It will also, rather conveniently, provide rapid access to PNG's vast resources for mining, logging and cash-crop companies.

Allan Patience is more measured in facing down the 'swelling chorus … asserting that PNG is a failed (or failing) state'. That critique

> permits certain smug and self-righteous Australian commentators — like Professor Helen Hughes — to paint PNG's systems of governance as riddled with corruption, incapable of delivering reasonable levels of service to the people, indifferent to

appalling collapses in law and order, unable to guarantee the security of the country, and hostile to the kind of civil society that would nurture a robust democracy.[48]

What is at stake is much more than a judgment of Australia's decolonisation and Papua New Guinea's independence. As they debate the shortcomings of the polity, the economy and the society, the protagonists seek influence over Papua New Guinea's policy-makers — and Australia's.

Footnotes
1. Bill Standish, *PNG 1999: Crisis of Governance*, September 21, 1999, Research Paper 4, 1999–2000, for the Australian Parliament's Foreign Affairs, Defence and Trade Group.
2. Sean Dorney, *The Sandline affair: politics and mercenaries and the Bougainville Crisis*, Sydney: ABC Books, 1998.
3. *Sydney Morning Herald*, November 28 and 29, 1997; *Post-Courier*, December 5, 1997; Hank Nelson, 'Crises of God and Man: PNG Political Chronicle 199799', *Journal of Pacific History*.
4. Neville Choi, 'Commission claims Haiveta received corrupt, improper money', *The Independent*, October 2, 1998.
5. Standish, *PNG 1999*.
6. MaryLouise O'Callaghan, 'PNG's night of the long knives', *The Australian*, July 15, 1999.
7. Standish, *PNG 1999*.
8. *The National*, August 11, 1999, for the full budget speech.
9. 'PNG', *Oxford Analytica Asia Pacific Daily Brief*, August 1999.
10. Garnaut, in 'Hindsight'.
11. Anthony Siaguru, *The Great Game*.
12. 'What will effects of the ECP be?', *Post-Courier*, December 7, 2004.
13. Allan Patience, 'Don't tolerate the intolerable', *Post-Courier*, October 25, 2004.
14. Bill Hayden, *Hayden: An Autobiography*, Sydney, 1996, p. 433.
15. Peter Ryan, cited by Standish, op. cit.
16. B. A. Santamaria, in *The Australian*, August 9, 1988, August 16, 1988 and March 7, 1989.
17. Hank Nelson, 'The talk and the timing'.
18. Alois Francis, letter in the *Post-Courier*, November 12, 2004.
19. Sinclair Dinnen, *Law and Order in a Weak State*.
20. Philip Fitzpatrick, *Bamahuta*, Pandanus Books, Canberra, 2005.
21. Interview, Ebia Olewale.
22. Transcript, *Sunday Profile*, ABC Radio, Sunday December 5, 2004.
23. In July 1982, the defeated Deputy Prime Minister, Iambakey Okuk, said, 'The voters have no rights at the moment. Once elected, the MP must decide what is best for his career', and added 'I can afford it. I can buy most of them.' Bill Standish, *Melanesian Neighbours: The Politics of PNG, the Solomon Islands and the Republic of Vanuatu*, Parliamentary Library, p. 62.
24. R. J. May, 'Postscript', R. J. May and A. J. Regan with Allison Ley (eds), *Political Decentralisation in a New State: The Experience of Provincial Government in PNG*, Crawford House, 1997, pp. 38695.
25. *Post-Courier*, November 22, 2004, 'We need to merge the Defence Force with the police'.
26. Colin Filer with Nikhil Sekhran, *Loggers, donors, and resource owners*, London and Port Moresby: International Institute for Environment and Development and Natural Research Institute.
27. ABC News, July 13, 2004.

28. Elsina Wainwright, 'Responding to State Failure — The Case of the Solomon Islands', *Australian Journal of International Affairs*, Vol. 57, No. 3, November 2003.
29. Mark Dodd, 'Problems Persist in Paradise', *Far Eastern Economic Review*, March 11, 2004.
30. Susan Windybank and Mike Manning, 'Papua New Guinea on the Brink', *Issue Analysis*, (Centre for Independent Studies), No. 30, March 12, 2004.
31. Donald Denoon, *Settler Capitalism: the dynamics of dependent development in the Southern Hemisphere*, Oxford, Clarendon Press, 1983.
32. William Pember Reeves, *State Experiments in Australia and New Zealand*, London, 1902; Donald Denoon and Philippa Mein-Smith, with Marivic Wyndham, *A History of Australia, New Zealand, and the Pacific*, Blackwell, Oxford, 2000.
33. Helen Hughes, *Can Papua New Guinea come back from the brink?*, Sydney: Centre for Independent Studies, 2004; Tim Curtin, *How poor is Papua New Guinea? How rich could it be?* ANU seminar paper, October 28, 2004.
34. Tim Curtin, *How Poor is Papua New Guinea?*
35. Robert Miller (ed.), *The Development of Civil Society in Communist Systems*; Barrett McCormick and Jonathan Unger (eds), *China After Socialism: In the Footsteps of Eastern Europe or East Asia?*, 1996.
36. Asesela Ravuvu, *The facade of democracy: Fijian struggles for political control, 1830–1987*, Suva, 1991; Brij Lal, *Another way: the politics of constitutional reform in post-coup Fiji*, Asia Pacific Press, Canberra, 1998.
37. Peter Larmour, *Legitimacy, sovereignty and regime change in the South Pacific: comparisons between the Fiji coups and the Bougainville rebellion*, Department of Political and Social Change, ANU, 1992.
38. Trevor Duke, 'Slow but steady progress in child health in Papua New Guinea', *Journal of Paediatric Child Health*, (2004), 40, pp. 659-63.
39. Curtin, *How Poor is Papua New Guinea?*
40. Hughes, *Can Papua New Guinea Come Back from the Brink?*; Satish Chand, 'PNG economic survey: transforming good luck into policies for long-term growth', *Pacific Economic Bulletin*, 19 (1) (2004), pp. 1–19.
41. R. M. Bourke, 'Agriculture in the Papua New Guinea Economy', seminar paper, ANU, August 2004.
42. J. Gibson and S. Rozelle, *Results of the household survey component of the 1996 poverty assessment for Papua New Guinea*, Port Moresby: Department of Planning, 1998; J. Gibson and S. Rozelle, 'Poverty and access to roads in Papua New Guinea', *Economic Development and Cultural Change*, 52(1) (2003); Hughes, *Can Papua New Guinea Come Back from the Brink?*; Chand, 'PNG Economic Survey'
43. Curtin, *How poor is Papua New Guinea?*
44. World Bank, *Project Appraisal Document on a proposed loan ... of US$17.36 million to ... Papua New Guinea for a forestry and conservation project*, World Bank, Washington, DC (Report No. 20641–PG, 2000); Colin Filer with Navroz Dubash and Kilyali Kalit, *The Thin Green Line. World Bank leverage and forest policy reform in Papua New Guinea*, Port Moresby and Canberra: NRI and ANU, 2000.
45. Hughes, *Can Papua New Guinea Come Back from the Brink?* Cited in Curtin, *How Poor is Papua New Guinea?*
46. Bourke, Agriculture in the Papua New Guinea Economy.
47. Tim Anderson, 'Pushing the new colonial agenda', *Post-Courier*, December 13, 2004.
48. Allan Patience, 'Failed and Vulnerable States,' Inaugural Lecture, UPNG, 2004, cites Helen Hughes, *Aid and the Pacific*, Sydney: CIS, 2003; Helen Hughes, 'Outlook for PNG Remains Bleak', The Canberra Times, April 1, 2004. See also Peter Bauer et al., *Aid and Development in the South Pacific*, Sydney: CIS, 2003.

Chapter 13

The Continuing Connection

John Guise held every high office except the one he most wanted. Speaker in the Second House, he was Somare's deputy in the third. For the rites of independence, he was Governor-General. In that capacity, he declared:

> Papua New Guinea is now independent.
>
> We have at this point in time broken with our colonial past and we now stand as an independent nation in our own right.

On the distinguished visitors' platform, Gough Whitlam thought the same of Australia since 'Australia was never truly free until Papua New Guinea became free'.[1] At this euphoric moment, when Australians celebrated the end of their own colonial narrative, they saw Papua New Guinea in cheerful terms. Its strategic significance was no longer acute: it was democratic, stable and well governed; and Panguna would make it economically self-sufficient. The country still relied on Australia and Australians for many services and for aid, but, despite Morrison's disapproval, funds came with no conditions. Australia was punctilious in respecting the country's sovereignty.

Compare this view with a recent statement by strategic analyst Hugh White. He welcomes Australia's 'more hands-on approach', but he wants more involvement:

> [T]o have a real chance of helping to pull Papua New Guinea out of its long, sad slide towards state failure, [Australians] are going to need to do a lot more, and to do it very differently ...
>
> We need to take a comprehensive approach that helps PNG address service delivery, central administration, economic development, constitutional issues, political processes and national identity.[2]

In the minds of some influential Australians, Papua New Guinea has become a political tragedy, an economic disaster and a strategic nightmare.

Two sets of pressures have transformed relations. One centres on aid. When much of the Third World became independent, the former colonies were assumed to be self-sufficient, or they would soon become so. Aid would not be needed for long, so it was delivered ad hoc. In time, delivery became more professional. The creation of AusAID's predecessor, ADAA (Chapter 9), like other Whitlam Government initiatives, was catching up with the practice of other developed countries. Even so, Morrison was not unusual when he imagined untied aid to Papua New Guinea as unfortunate and temporary.[3]

By the 1990s, however, aid had become normal globally. The World Bank took the lead. Its charter prohibits intervention in domestic politics, so the Bank focused on macro-economic issues; but its analysts noticed failures in programs designed to rescue countries from crises.[4] Appalled by repressive regimes, corruption and abuses of human rights, the Bank concluded that these were not merely human tragedies, but barriers to economic growth. Accordingly, they began to promote 'good governance' (democratic government, competent administration and market-friendly economics) in countries seeking their financial support.[5]

Individual donors followed suit, focusing on democracy, equity and participation — as well as economics. All began to impose conditions for their aid, and especially for their rescue packages. As bankruptcy stalked Cook Islands, for example, donors came to the rescue on condition that half the public service was retrenched and the other half took salary cuts. During Skate's difficult reign in Papua New Guinea, donors withheld funds pending the adoption of reforms (see below). As Macdonald points out, it is hard to say if donors' insistence on good governance is neo-colonial or benign. Either way, their effect is 'to make "them" appear to be more like "us"'.[6]

So it is hardly strange that there are limits to Papua New Guinea's options as a recipient of aid. What does make it unusual is the dominance of a single donor. Even without aid, Australia would loom large. In 1999, Standish reckoned that Australians had invested $A2.6 billion, and bilateral trade amounted to $A2.2 billion per annum.[7] To take a more concrete example, ex-*kiaps* are seen as the best intermediaries between outsiders and villagers, and resource companies employ them for liaison work with the people whose land they traverse — or excavate.[8]

But aid has become the central strand of this multidimensional relationship. Administered mainly by AusAID, it is a declining fraction of Australia's budget but a permanent feature of Papua New Guinea's. It exceeded $A300 million per annum through the 1990s while project aid displaced budgetary support. Garnaut, who lobbied for untied aid in the first place, insists that it was appropriate in the 1970s and perhaps later. He reckons that the defeat of the beefed-up Leadership Code in 1978 triggered the policy shift: untied aid was indefensible when news leaked out about the business interests of politicians. Project aid promised accountability. Whether or not it achieves this, project aid has undermined local control and damaged the morale of officers managing programs and services.[9]

The quality of public administration probably declined during the 1980s, but this was neither swift nor calamitous. For several years the new institutions of government functioned largely as intended. As one of the virtuous Gang of Four, upholding the integrity of government, Morauta conceded that efficiency and integrity might not last, but (at worst) they would inspire a later generation. And Cabinet rejoiced in low inflation, a healthy balance of payments, hard currency and the resource rent tax. Management deteriorated abruptly from 1989 with the closure of Panguna and civil war.[10] The mine provided one-third of foreign exchange earnings and one-fifth of government revenue. To survive this calamity, currency was devalued, 2,000 public servants were sacked and spending was slashed.

External help was needed but Australia was restrained. Aid was increased by a mere $20 million over two years. Australia's Foreign Minister, Gareth Evans, flew into Port Moresby: 'Before waiting to hear what Prime Minister Namaliu was doing [a lot] he remarked that PNG would have to tighten its belt.'[11] Papua New Guinea's leaders accepted that Australian aid should dwindle. (They could have pointed out that it had fallen from 0.3 per cent of Australian GNP in 1976 to 0.1 per cent in the 1990s.) In practice, Evans's curt advice recalled an ambush by the same government in 1985, when aid was cut abruptly for the next five years — and Hayden's sleight of hand in 1975.[12]

As the drumbeat of denunciations grew to a roar (Chapter 12), aid became conditional. By the end of the 1990s, instead of sending a cheque to Waigani, AusAID was funding 73 projects directly. Although each was no doubt well-conceived, collectively they marginalised Papua New Guinea's faltering institutions. AusAID treated local public servants as a lost cause and allowed them to be partly eclipsed by Australian consultants and by non-governmental organisations (NGOs).[13]

Australia is not the only possible benefactor. The World Bank has provided funds, for example, in a Structural Adjustment Program in 1996. However, Australia and the World Bank collaborated to suspend funds during the Skate era, pending specific reforms.[14] A particular complication was Dr Pirouz Hamidian-Rad (Chapter 12). The Bank declined to negotiate as long as he was a negotiator. Prime Minister Skate then tried to borrow commercially. Alas, European banks would not lend a cent: the country must rely on the World Bank and Australia. In spite of differences of emphasis, these two usually work together. When Morauta replaced Skate, for instance, Australia offered to relieve the liquidity crisis and asked the World Bank and the IMF to revive the Structural Adjustment Program.[15] The European Community, Japan, China and Taiwan might eventually become major donors, but so far they have not matched Australian support.

More broadly, Australia's aid 'increased in size, spread and significance just as the PNG state's capacities have declined'. As an Australian High Commissioner conceded, aid by itself is pointless: if an economy is poorly managed, 'in the long run no amount of aid will make much of a difference'.[16] That comment explains Australia's new enthusiasm for strengthening the agencies of government (and of civil society, which usually means the churches and politicians temporarily out of office). AusAID's priorities include 'promoting effective and equitable legal systems and strengthening the rule of law', and 'strengthening civil representation and participation to enable better scrutiny of policies and practices'. Another term for this approach is intervention.

Because of the dependence of one government on the other, relations between them would never be easy:

> Whatever Australia did, Papua New Guinean leaders would think Australians were patronising or interfering or neglectful or dominating. Australians would think PNG leaders were managing poorly, doing too little for development and enriching themselves at the expense of the population as a whole.[17]

One Australian body did find time to look broadly at this relationship. In 2002, the Senate Foreign Affairs, Defence and Trade Committee initiated an inquiry.[18] This bipartisan committee researched and debated for eighteen months before reporting. They endorsed existing aid programs, but also proposed a 'Pacific economic and political community'. The community could establish a common currency, labour market and budgetary and fiscal standards. Other proposals encourage closer cooperation and integrated services. Labour mobility would allow short-term workers to enter Australia. The twinning of Australian local councils and island communities, the exchange of public servants and an expanded volunteer program would complement official relationships, taking the emphasis away from the aid nexus.

On the most sensitive issue of the day, the senators reported that most of the submissions they had received 'recommended an end to the Government's policy of processing asylum seekers offshore — the "Pacific Strategy"'. That was a reference to Australia's agreement with Nauru and Papua New Guinea whereby asylum-seekers would not land in Australia (where they would gain legal rights) but would be interned in island camps while their requests for refugee status were processed. (Melbourne writer Jim Davidson claimed that the Government treated island nations 'as if they were simply client states: non-whites can be safely kept off-shore in ... our very own Bantustans'.[19]) This policy, observed the senators, fed the perception that 'Australia's domestic political considerations are more important than broader regional issues', so they wanted to end it.

An Eminent Persons Group tried to carry these ideas forward. When they toured the islands, however, island leaders feared that their sovereignty would be swallowed by a body that Australia would dominate. The only proposal to create a forum crashed on the reefs of sovereignty. The benefits of closer association were undeniable: but the loss of independence was intolerable.[20]

Meanwhile, the second set of pressures emerged. The terrorist assaults on New York and Washington, the massacre of holiday-makers in Bali and Australia's anxiety about terrorism gave prominence to a cadre of security specialists. Suddenly the world seemed more perilous, and Prime Minister John Howard incautiously (but revealingly) let a journalist describe him as America's deputy sheriff. The 'war on terror' threw sinister light on the (unrelated) collapse of the Solomon Islands Government in 2000 and helped to justify the intervention of an Australian-led force, the Regional Assistance Mission to Solomon Islands (RAMSI) to restore law and order. Unlike previous peace-monitoring, such as the Australian-led Peace Monitors in Bougainville, RAMSI has a mandate to disarm criminals and to strengthen the institutions of government. RAMSI deploys accountants and administrators alongside police and soldiers.

The ominous term 'arc of instability' was pressed into service to describe all Melanesia from Irian Jaya to Fiji. The phrase has a revealing history. It was coined in

Australia as a term to encompass civil strife in Indonesia, but it is no longer acceptable to refer so dismissively to that archipelago. Melanesians have inherited the term, even though most of their problems concern their stable (not to say stagnant) policies and performance rather than their frequent and peaceful changes of government.

However murky its origins, 'the arc of instability' is a lens through which some Australians now see Papua New Guinea as a security risk. A year of negotiations led to a bilateral Enhanced Cooperation Package to address these suddenly urgent problems. Seventy Australian public servants were posted to Waigani departments, and 200 police joined the RPNGC. These are not advisers but front-line officers. Australia was already funding retraining and retrenchment in the Defence Force, shrinking it from 3,300 to 2,000. Under the ECP umbrella, two Australian lieutenant-colonels will now 'work with the PNGDF'. Two more officers will follow.[21]

Allan Patience argues that these moves merely revive the security interest that he insists has always shaped Australia's relations with Papua New Guinea:

> the recent arousal of Australian interest in governance in PNG is directly related to the events of September 11, 2001, and the war on terrorism. And that interest ... is part of Australia's preoccupation with its own security.[22]

That perception is shared by James Laki, soldier and commentator, who reads Australian policies as 'driven by comments and observations by the Centre for Independent Studies and the Australian Strategic Policy Institute' and encouraged by the success of RAMSI, which some see as a dress rehearsal. He observes that Australia ignored the Solomon Islands crisis (they rebuffed Prime Minister Bart Ulufa'alu's plea for Australians to disarm the country's corrupt and partisan force) and the bizarre coup by George Speight in Fiji. After September 11, Australians were much more willing to intervene.

And what, he asks, is the role of Papua New Guinean politicians and public servants in the context of the ECP? Politicians will not control Australian officials.

> Does this mean Australia would be in control, just like the colonial days? Is it the public service, or some parts of it, that require capacity 'enhancement'? Some opinions from Australia suggest there is no 'legitimacy' to rule by the PNG Government ... If it is the political system that requires enhancement, then it would be interfering with the internal affairs of a sovereign country.[23]

These questions are much too complex to address here. Suffice to say that the equality of sovereign states that seemed axiomatic in 1975 has been abandoned. We seem closer to the paternalistic 1960s than to the optimistic 1970s: Australians enter Papua New Guinea quite freely while Papua New Guineans come to Australia mainly as students; the budget relies on Canberra's subventions; ministers display erratic interest in their portfolios and imperfect control of their departments; and Australians hold key posts in the economy, the bureaucracy and the uniformed forces.

It is now possible to address the criticism that Australians could and should have done very much better. Right-wingers pioneered this argument, but they have no lien on it. In his inaugural lecture at UPNG,[24] Allan Patience denounced

> the ham-fisted decolonization that Australia forced on PNG ... [and] The undue haste and unjustifiable comprehensiveness of Australia's withdrawal in 1976 — leaving PNG without the levels of infrastructure, capacity, and capacity-building necessary for a smooth transition to independence ...
>
> The grim fact is ... there never was a real, functioning 'state' capable of taking over in PNG once Australia withdrew ...
>
> And it's not just the hasty, Whitlamesque decolonization strategies that need a ... critique, but the whole miserable, lacklustre, complacent, lazy, ineffectual colonial period ... the insensitive paternalism of the Hasluck years, the sheer ignorance of the Barnes years, and the Whitlam-like hastiness of the Peacock years.

Nobody blames Papua New Guineans for accepting independence. On the contrary, they are portrayed as victims of a confidence trick by all-knowing, all-powerful Australians (especially Whitlam). These critiques rest on questionable assumptions: that the Pax Australiana extended across the whole territory, and that it was not unravelling. In that view, Australia could have stayed indefinitely and made ponderous preparations. It is also assumed that continuing Australian rule would have resolved, rather than exacerbated, problems of governance.

These assumptions are flawed. 'Tribal fighting' was reviving in the districts with the least exposure to Australian rule; those with the most economic development were the most truculent. Papua New Guineans made a better fist of dealing with resource companies than had the Australians, and brought peace to Rabaul and Bougainville, where Australian policy had fomented violence. Somare's coalition resulted from free and fair elections, and they wanted independence. After that election, independence was not Australia's call.

Although the general argument is wildly implausible, several specific suggestions deserve consideration. The most compelling is that Australia *should have localised the public service much earlier*. The necessary steps to have made that possible include removing the intransigent managers of the Public Service Commission and waiving the inflexible rules of the Commonwealth Public Service. The Administrative College and the university would have been created sooner; and ASOPA would have been overhauled to train Papua New Guineans in large numbers. These steps were affordable and achievable — but they were also unimaginable in Australia in the 1950s. Hasluck's purpose was to preserve social difference, even as he integrated the Administration into Australian systems of governance. That strategy was inimical to rapid localisation and the formulation of territorial standards.

Three territorial circumstances would have posed serious problems. A localised public service would have been dominated by cadets from coastal Papua and the New

Guinea islands, where primary education was most advanced. Educated people from the interior would have been as scarce as hen's teeth, and the public service could not have carried out its secondary but vital role of nation-building. The *kiap* system — the branch of government that touched most people — rested partly on the mystique of white skin. Coastal policemen and evangelists did wield authority outside their own communities, but they enjoyed only a reflection of the white men's authority. Finally, the scenario of swift localisation requires an exponential increase in the breadth of the school system, and much earlier secondary schooling. However, teachers were scarce in Australia at the time and the Director of Education, Bill Groves, could not recruit enough even for the schools that did operate.

It is also argued that *the legislature should have been localised much sooner*. But Papua New Guineans formed a majority of the House of Assembly from day one. It was not a stacked parliament that prevented self-determination. Devolution was impeded by the timidity of indigenous politicians, their inexperience in the face of esoteric rites in law-making and public administration, and the Territory's extreme financial dependence. These hurdles might have been vaulted by resolute actors, but to what effect? Until 1972, only a handful of leaders had the education, the experience — and the self-confidence — to challenge Australian advisors. The localisation of politics, like localisation in the public service, presupposes very different circumstances than actually prevailed.

Australian traditions inhibited participation either in law-making or in public administration. Despite interventions by David Hay and Tony Voutas, little deviation was allowed from Canberra precedents. Increasingly, Territory public service practices were brought into line with Australian rules. This uniformity could have allowed the fruitful transfer and exchange of public servants, but that was neither intended nor achieved. Conversely, the creation of an indigenous public service with its own salary structure was resisted fiercely (and understandably) by local public servants. Many Australian practices seem ludicrous in the local context (the Commonwealth and the Territory public services both worked from 7.45am to 4.06pm, five days a week) until we recall that the Territory public service was an Australian body, answerable through Australian public servants to an Australian minister. Its senior officers were all Australians until at least 1972. In government offices — though not in the House — adaptation could only have created confusion.

Should there have been *more time* between self-government and full independence? In very rare agreement, the CPC and Tom Critchley would both have preferred at least one more year. Against that view, Papua New Guinea did enjoy a much longer transitional period than was normal in Asia and Africa. One reason for Australia's insistence on speed was Morrison's expectation that he would have to apply pressure to make devolution work at all. That was a fair assessment of the inertia of the Ministerial Members, but Somare's coalition was very different. We cannot assess Morrison's, and Whitlam's, further argument that delay would have encouraged opposition and secession. Whitlam remains intransigent, although his tone is now defensive:

> I hear it asserted that my government was in error in pushing PNG into independence too soon ... I simply assert that, had we delayed PNG independence, even for another year, we would have put the country in the gravest danger of breaking up.[25]

Right or wrong, it was a considered and coherent position and one that Somare accepted.

What consequences might have followed from an extra year of self-government? Perhaps localisation of the public service would have been more measured. The House might have digested and accepted a few more of the CPC's proposals. It is (just) conceivable that the governments would have reached a more equitable agreement on aid and we might even hope that the roles of the Defence Force and the police would have been better conceived. But Papua New Guinea's leaders, lacking our perfect hindsight, might not have wanted or achieved these outcomes. They might even have made other mistakes.

Australia's insistence on *Papua New Guinea's unity* is worth reflection. In the 1970s, national unity was frail in the archipelago of ethnic and language communities. That is why the CPC was so passionately wedded to nation-building, and this concern is evident in Somare's anxiety about the national broadcaster. Was Australia's insistence on unity justified? It arose, after all, from Australia's own pursuit of regional stability and security, not from an assessment of local circumstances. Quite apart from the continuing distress of some Papuans and their determination to prove Papua's separate status, national unity has cost nine destructive years of civil war in Bougainville.

There is even a Pacific precedent (in the separation of the Gilbert and Ellice Group into Kiribati and Tuvalu) for splitting a colony. But most of Papua New Guinea's leaders have always insisted on unity, while 'Papua' and 'Bougainville' were (and are) no more coherent than Papua New Guinea. Ethnic coherence would have unravelled the Territory into a host of communities (like Narokobi's scenario, Chapter 8). This anarchic vision was abhorrent to Australians, and very few Papua New Guineans were willing to carry their parochial loyalties to the extent of ethnic autonomy. In any event, the question is moot. The UN saw Katanga's attempt to secede from Congo as evidence of a mining company's manipulation of political forces, and Biafra's populist attempt to leave Nigeria failed to win external support. After these events, UN endorsement of a fragmented Papua New Guinea was inconceivable.

It is hard to imagine plausible alternatives to the way that Australians did decolonise, but four sets of technical decisions are worth considering. A recurrent complaint of Papua New Guineans is the inadequacy of their material legacy: there were no railways, few all-weather roads and only obsolete ports (except in Bougainville). There were too few schools and clinics. Could the Territory have gained *better infrastructure*, more schools and colleges, a reliable transport system and better trained police if Hasluck had won bigger budgets? His shopping list (Chapter 2) hardly encourages that theory. Among other things he wanted to:
— double school enrolments;
— enrol 10,000 secondary scholars, 2,000 technical students and 2,000 teacher trainees;
— build or rebuild hospitals;

— provide more antenatal care;
— survey 40-50,000 people each year for tuberculosis;
— extend government influence to the whole population;
— extend Local Government Council coverage;
— increase the production of cocoa, coffee, rubber, logs and timber;
— create 7,500 land blocks; and
— double the mileage of roads.

This was an expansion of existing programs, with the same emphasis on general education and health. This was not the infrastructure that Critchley had in mind, or that Papua New Guinea's leaders now yearn for. That idealised public works program implies a different perspective than that which animated real policy-makers.

Another set of technical decisions led to a poorly designed *Defence Force and a constabulary* unsuited to modern policing. The inadequacies of the Defence Force stem from the Australian Army's autonomy and their failure to think through their strategic perceptions. Foreign policy analysts were keen to disengage from the Territory precisely when the army was determined to be embedded.[26] The defects of the police, on the other hand, do seem attributable to Australian political processes, the hasty departure of officers and the neglect of training.

Many decisions concerning *financial aid* could also have been handled more creatively. It was timely that Australia created a professional aid-management body, but several political decisions were calamitous. Hayden's deduction of golden handshake funds from the independence settlement was the most savage, but later decisions (Chapters 9 and 12) were equally high-handed and hard to accommodate.

With hindsight, we might imagine other benevolent scenarios — but that would be utopian. The young Papua New Guinean politicians and their officials had almost no experience in government. Australian public servants were not much older, and, in any case, the decolonisation project had no direct precedents. The achievement is even more remarkable when we recall the political context. The Whitlam Government was under siege and often in disarray while Papua New Guinea's novices were under fire from radicals in the CPC as well as conservatives in the United Party. In such a new, complex and emotional enterprise, of course there were mistakes and miscalculations; but there were fewer than we would expect in a project of this scale and complexity. The fact is that Papua New Guinea's governance was widely admired for more than a decade. Errors were made, but no plausible alternative would have produced much better outcomes, and they could have been much worse. The transfer of powers from Canberra to Waigani was an outstanding bureaucratic feat at both ends.

That brings us at last to the larger question: was an independent Papua New Guinea an appropriate goal? Separate destinies are implied in Alfred Deakin's view (Introduction) that 'A "White Australia" may exist … but a "Black New Guinea" the territory … must always remain'. If these neighbours were categorically incompatible, they must ultimately go their separate ways. That idea still underpins Australia's sense of itself. While most of the world gropes for regional associations, we represent ourselves as an isolate. When we think of ourselves as victims of distance (and Geoffrey Blainey's *Tyranny of Distance* is still a bestseller),[27] we ignore the links that bind our island neighbours to us – and us to them.

Until Federation, the idea of Australasia expressed the shared interests of colonists and colonial governors, relying on the Royal Navy for security, London for capital, Westminster for legitimacy and Christianity for salvation. For the makers of the Constitution, however, 'a continent for a nation' seemed to be the largest possible federation.[28] Papua and New Guinea did become Australian Territories, but not part of White Australia. While New Zealanders encouraged social assimilation in their dependencies, Australians insisted on social discrimination. Their decolonisations embodied the same contrast. Cook Islanders and New Zealanders invented free association and extended the matrix to Niue and Tokelau.[29] The effect, as well as the purpose, of New Zealand's decolonising was integration. Australia did propose something similar — but only for Nauru, whose 9,000 people would have settled in Australia.[30] When Guise asked about closer relations, the Government moved to cut Papua New Guinea loose (Chapter 4). New Zealand welcomed Islander immigrants: Australia made Papua New Guinea independent to avoid that outcome.

In the aftermath of the colonial era, an elastic region embraces the whole 'arc of instability': Australia is its core and its blind spot. Tens of thousands of Polynesians have moved to New Zealand,[31] but the longer road runs from Polynesia to Australia, via New Zealand. Thursday Island is another staging post: Torres Strait Islanders move south while Papua New Guineans cross from Daru for supplies and services, or to resettle.[32]

Within this lively region, most of its aid flows from Australia, and some from New Zealand. Several currencies are linked to the Australian dollar. Most of the social and natural science research on the islands is conducted in Australia or New Zealand. Peacemaking, peacekeeping and peace-observing depend on Australian logistics, and New Zealand's Pacific Policy relies on Australia's regional hegemony. Australians and New Zealanders cooperate in regional crises, most obviously when Bougainville peace talks were staged by New Zealand and endorsed by Australia.[33]

The system of separate, sovereign states obscures the social, economic and cultural networks, and obstructs the flow of capital, labour, technology and ideas. At the very least, the region needs a political forum such as the Australian senators proposed. The Pacific Forum meets rarely and casually, and the agenda of the Pacific Commission is technical, so neither can perform this role. In any event, their membership is too broad to focus on the issues of most importance to Papua New Guineans. Some meetings do occur between Australian and Papua New Guinean ministers, but conversations occur more often — and more unequally — between Australian bureaucratic patrons and Papua New Guinean clients. Especially as more Australians move into sensitive positions, Australia's relations with Papua New Guinea need an arena in which political issues can be raised, explored, argued — and resolved. We need to share technical services (in education, security, research, currency, agronomy, disease control, geology and meteorology for a start) and we need a political forum to oversee them. Decolonisation is not the end of a story but a new chapter.

Meanwhile, can we delineate this unique post-colonial relationship? Let us begin with a surprising continuity. In 2005, Australians acknowledged a labour shortage and one politician proposed that Papua New Guineans be admitted as seasonal workers. He made no headway at home, but the *Post-Courier*[34] summed up many Papua New Guineans' sense of grievance:

> Our bureaucrats and politicians have been talking to their Australian counterparts, pushing the concept of letting approved workers from PNG go to Australia for short-term working contracts.
>
> ... New South Wales parliamentarian and Kokoda Track champion Charlie Lynn reckons our people can do the jobs the Australians want filled ... We are Australia's nearest neighbours. They administered us for many years and pushed us into independence in a way that many would call 'rushed', perhaps premature. Mr Lynn knows well the sacrifices [of the Fuzzy Wuzzy Angels]...
>
> In essence, we deserve better treatment when a chance comes along, such as the current labour crisis in Australia ... we do have many thousands of moderately educated young people who could solve Australia's worries with fruitpicking and other seasonal industries.
>
> Australia, give our young people a chance. Lest We Forget.

Beneath the overblown rhetoric is the uncomfortable fact that Australians still enjoy easy access to Papua New Guinea, but the converse is not true: unlike (for example) Swiss or Canadians, Papua New Guineans cannot obtain working visas, though they can enter for schooling. Entry is not much easier than it was for Miss Tessie Lavau in the 1950s.

For 100 years, Australians have portrayed Papua New Guinea as Australia's dark Other. We suppose that we enjoy good governance, prosperity and social order where they endure mismanagement, poverty and chaos. From the other side of Torres Strait, Australia is also seen as the Other, often with admiration tinged with envy, and sometimes with resentment. Decades of de facto colonial rule have left such an emotive heritage that we cannot treat Papua New Guinea as if it were no more important than, say, Pakistan or Palau. The two countries rather resemble a divorced couple who find that their ties are too complex, too many and too sensitive to ignore. In brief, they need a neutral forum in which to meet, review the past and argue about the future, including the size and shape of the alimony.

The language of colonialism and independence is so limiting that policy-makers of the 1970s could see only two options: to be colonised or to be free. The reality has always been more nuanced: Papua New Guinea was substantially free in 1974 — perhaps more autonomous than under the ECP. That either/or choice resembles the language of the Family Court, in which a couple is either married or divorced. Australian rule over the Territory was not a marriage made in heaven, and it could never be consummated by full integration. Yet these countries are so close in so many ways that the divorce cannot easily be made absolute. Neither side was attracted to New Zealand's open marriage — 'free association' — with Polynesia. By default, independence was the only item on the agenda, but one political act could not undo ancient geography or modern history.

Some analysts condemn the colonial era while others denounce the manner and speed of decolonisation. Those views perhaps miss a more crucial point. Decolonisation is by no means complete and independence is a work in progress. What seemed like a divorce in 1975 is a trial separation, in which the two governments can negotiate a new way of living next to each other. As they grope towards a new relationship, it is more useful to understand the past than to moralise about it. If we do not understand the recent past, we are very likely to repeat it.

Footnotes
1. 'Freedom for Australia too', *The Australian*, September 16, 1975.
2. Hugh White, 'The deep mess of PNG demands long-term action', *Sydney Morning Herald*, December 15, 2004.
3. Barrie Macdonald, 'Decolonisation and "Good" Governance: Precedents and Continuities', in D. Denoon (ed.), *Emerging from Empire? Decolonisation in the Pacific*, Division of Pacific and Asian History, Canberra, 1997.
4. Peter Larmour (ed.), *Governance and Good Government: Policy and Implementation in the South Pacific*, Canberra: NCDS, 1995; World Bank, *Governance: The World Bank's Experience*, Washington, 1993; Barrie Macdonald, '"Good" Governance and Pacific Islands States', in Peter Larmour (ed.), *Governance in the Pacific Islands*, Canberra: NCDS, 1997.
5. World Bank, *Governance and Development*, Washington, 1992, p. 58.
6. Macdonald, 'Decolonisation and "Good" Governance'.
7. Bill Standish, *PNG 1999: Crisis of Governance*, Research Paper 4, 1999-2000, for the Australian Parliament's Foreign Affairs, Defence and Trade Group.
8. Eg., Glenn Banks, 'Mountain of desire: mining company and indigenous community at the Porgera Gold Mine, Papua New Guinea', PhD thesis, ANU, 1997; and Fitzpatrick, *Bamahuta*.
9. Interview with Ross Garnaut.
10. Ibid.
11. Stewart Firth, 'Papua New Guinea: Why we must offer ex-colony more than words and money', *Sydney Morning Herald*, March 27, 1997.
12. Ibid.; and interview with Ross Garnaut.
13. AusAID, *Papua New Guinea Program Profiles, 1999-2000*
14. AusAID, *International Development Issues*, 52, 1998.
15. Standish, *PNG 1999*.
16. David Irvine in an ANU seminar, cited by Standish.
17. Firth, 'Papua New Guinea: Why we must offer ex-colony more than words and money'
18. An inquiry into Australia's relations with Papua New Guinea and the islands of the south-west Pacific', for the Senate Foreign Affairs, Defence and Trade Group, August 12, 2003.

19. Jim Davidson, 'Land of the Long Black Cloud', *Australian Book Review*, March 2002.
20. See my 'Pacific Solutions', in *Times Literary Supplement* (5280), pp. 12-13 (June 11, 2004)
21. Sean Dorney, ABC, December 16, 2004.
22. Allan Patience, 'What is Australia really up to?', *Post-Courier*, July 5, 2004.
23. James Laki, 'A critical appraisal of the ECP', *Post-Courier*, October 13, 2004. Lt.-Col. Laki is a Senior Research Fellow at the National Research Institute
24. Allan Patience, 'Failed and Vulnerable States: Towards a Political Science of South Pacific Regionalism', Inaugural Lecture, April 30, 2004.
25. Whitlam in *Hindsight*.
26. Bruce Hunt, 'Papua New Guinea in Australia's Strategic Thinking', PhD thesis, University of New England, 2004.
27. Geoffrey Blainey, *The Tyranny of Distance: how distance shaped Australia's history*, Melbourne, 1968.
28. I develop this argument in *Historical Studies*, 'Re-Membering Australasia: A Repressed Memory'.
29. Karen Nero, 'The End of Insularity', in Denoon, *Cambridge History of the Pacific Islanders*.
30. Nancy Viviani, *Nauru: Phosphate and Political Progress*, Canberra, ANU, 1970; Nancy Pollock, 'Nauru: Decolonised, Recolonising, but never a Colony', in Denoon, *Emerging from Empire?*
31. Nero, 'The End of Insularity'.
32. *Sydney Morning Herald*, March 12, 2002.
33. Monica Wehner and Donald Denoon (ed.), *Without a Gun*, Pandanus Books, Canberra, 2002.
34. *Post-Courier*, March 9, 2005. Editorial, 'Australia, give our workers a fair go'.

Bibliography

Records of the Australian Department of Territories, series A451, held by the Department of Foreign Affairs and the National Archives of Australia, Canberra.
Records of the Papua New Guinea Department of Information and Extension Services (DIES), held by the Papua New Guinea National Archives, Waitgani.
John Greenwell's personal papers.
Bill Morrison papers, National Library of Australia.

'Hindsight: a Retrospective Workshop for Participants in the Decolonisation of Papua New Guinea', rspas.anu.edu.au/pah/publications/php

Alasia, Sam. 1997. 'Party Politics and Government in Solomon Islands'. Discussion Paper 7/1997. State Society and Governance in Melanesia Project, ANU.
Aldrich, Robert and John Connell. 1998. *The Last Colonies.* Melbourne: Cambridge University Press.
Amarshi, Azeem, Ken Good and Rex Mortimer (eds). 1979. *Development and Dependency: the Political Economy of Papua New Guinea.* Melbourne: OUP.
Anderson, Tim. 2004. 'Pushing the new colonial agenda'. *Post Courier.* December 13, 2004.
Andrew, Warwick, Don Chalmers and David Weisbrot. 1979. *Criminal law and practice of Papua New Guinea.* Sydney: Law Book Co.
Anere, Ray. 1988. 'Economic Issues, 1975–1985'. *Yagl Ambu,* 12 (March).
Arndt, Heinz, R. Shand and E. K. Fisk. 1969. 'An Answer to Crocombe — I, II, III'. *New Guinea,* June–July 1969.
Arndt, Heinz. 1987. *Asian Diaries.* Asia Pacific Monograph 2. Singapore: Chopmen.
Ballard, Chris. 1993. 'Stimulating Minds to Fantasy? A Critical Etymology for Sahul'. In M. A. Smith, M. Spriggs and B. Fankhauser (eds), *Sahul in Review.* Canberra: ANU.
AusAID, Canberra. *Papua New Guinea Program Profiles, 1999–2000.*
AusAID, Canberra. 1998. *International Development Issues,* 52.
Ballard, John A. (ed.) 1981. *Policy-making in a new state, Papua New Guinea 1972–77.* University of Queensland Press.
Banks, Glenn. 1997. 'Mountain of desire: mining company and indigenous community at the Porgera Gold Mine, Papua New Guinea'. PhD thesis, ANU.
and Chris Ballard (eds). 1997. *The Ok Tedi settlement: issues, outcomes and implications.* Canberra: NCDS, ANU.
Bauer, Peter T., Savenaca Siwatibau and Wolfgang Kasper. 1991. *Aid and Development in the South Pacific.* Sydney: Centre for Independent Studies.
Bayne, Peter. 1985. 'The Constitution'. Unpublished typescript.
and Hal Colebatch. 1973. *Constitutional development in Papua New Guinea, 1968–73: the transfer of executive power.* Port Moresby: New Guinea Research Unit, ANU.
Beier, Ulli. 2005. *Decolonising the Mind: The impact of the University on culture and identity in Papua New Guinea, 1971–74.* Canberra: Pandanus Books.

Belich, James. 2001. *Paradise Reforged: A History of the New Zealanders from the 1880s to the Year 2000*. Auckland: Penguin.

Bettison, D. G., C. A. Hughes, and P. W. van der Veur (eds). 1965. *The Papua-New Guinea Elections 1964*. Canberra: ANU.

Biskup, Peter, Brian Jinks and Hank Nelson. 1968. *A Short History of New Guinea*. Sydney.

Bourke, R. M. 2004. 'Agriculture in the Papua New Guinea Economy'. Seminar paper, ANU, August 2004.

Brown, B. J. and G. Sawer (eds). 1969. *Fashion of Law in New Guinea*, Sydney: Butterworths.

Brown, Paula. 1988. 'Gender and Social Change: New Forms of Independence for Simbu Women'. *Oceania*, XIX. p. 128.

Buckley, Ken and Kris Klugman. 1981. *The history of Burns Philp: the Australian company in the South Pacific*. Sydney: Burns, Philp.

Carruthers, Don. 1990. 'Interview with James Griffin', *Weekend Australian*, June 9–10, 1990.

—— and D. C. Vernon. 1990. 'Bougainville Retrospective'. In David Anderson (ed.), *The PNG-Australia Relationship: Problems and Prospects*, Canberra: Institute of Public Affairs.

Carruthers, Susan L. 1995. *Winning hearts and minds: British governments, the media, and colonial counter-insurgency, 1944–1960*. Leicester University Press.

Chand, Satish. 2000. 'PNG economic survey: transforming good luck into policies for long-term growth'. *Pacific Economic Bulletin*, 19 (1). pp. 1–19.

Chatterton, Percy. 1974. *Day That I Have Loved*. Sydney.

Choi, Neville. 1998. 'Commission claims Haiveta received corrupt, improper money'. *The Independent*, October 2, 1998.

Cleland, Rachel. 1983. *Pathways to Independence, Story of Official and Family Life in Papua New Guinea from 1951 to 1975*. Perth.

—— 1996. *Grass roots to independence and beyond: the contribution by women in Papua New Guinea 1951–1991*. Claremont, WA.

Clifford, William, Louise Morauta and Barry Stuart. 1984. *Law and Order in Papua New Guinea* (Clifford Report). Port Moresby: IASER.

Clunies Ross, Anthony. 1969. 'Economic Nationalism and Supranationalism'. Inaugural Lecture, UPNG.

Clunies Ross, Anthony and John Langmore, (eds). 1973. *Alternative Strategies for Papua New Guinea*. Melbourne: OUP.

Connell, John. 1991. 'Compensation and Conflict: the Bougainville Copper Mine, Papua New Guinea'. In John Connell and Richie Howitt (eds), *Mining and Indigenous Peoples in Australasia*. Sydney University Press.

Constitutional Planning Committee. 1974. *Final Report*.

Crawford, J. G. 1962. Emerging issues in New Guinea'. In Bettison, Fisk, West and Crawford, *The independence of Papua-New Guinea. What are the prerequisites?* Sydney.

Crocombe, R. G. 1964. 'Communal Cash Cropping among the Orokaiva'. *New Guinea Research Bulletin*, IV.

—— 1965. 'The M'Buke Cooperative Plantation'. *New Guinea Research Bulletin*, VII.

—— 1969. 'Crocombe to his critics'. *New Guinea*, September/October.

—— 1969. 'That Five Year Plan. For Papua New Guineans — token development'. *New Guinea*, December 1968–January 1969.

—— 1968. 'Bougainville Copper, C.R.A. and secessionism'. *New Guinea and Australia*, Vol. 3, No. 3.

—— Arndt, H. 1969. 'An answer to Crocombe — "Too many invidious and invalid comparisons?"'. *New Guinea and Australia*, Vol. 4, No. 2.

—— Shand, R. 'An answer to Crocombe. "In defence of nucleus estates"', in ibid.

—— Fisk, E. K. 'An answer to Crocombe. "How fast do you go?"', in ibid.

Crocombe, R. G. 'Crocombe to his critics: "The debate goes on …"', in ibid. Vol. 4, No. 3, 1969.

Curtin, Tim. 2004. 'How Poor is Papua New Guinea? How Rich Could It Be?' ANU seminar, October 28, 2004.
Dabb, Geoffrey. 'A Short History of the Torres Strait Border'. Partly reproduced in 'Hindsight'.
Daniel, Philip and Rod Sims. 1987. 'Papua New Guinea: a Case Study'. In Vincent Cable and Bishnodat Persaud (eds), *Development with Foreign Investment.* Beckenham.
Daugi, Mackenzie. 1996. 'Transcript of Discussion by Panel of Constitution-Makers'. Port Moresby, March 28, 1996.
Davidson, Jim. 2002. 'Land of the Long Black Cloud'. *Australian Book Review*, March 2002.
Deakin, Alfred. 1968. *Federated Australia: Selections from Letters to the* Morning Post *1900–1910.* MUP. Edited and introduced by J. A. La Nauze
Dening, Greg. 1980. *Islands and Beaches: Discourses on a Silent Land, Marquesas, 1774–1880.* University of Hawai'i Press.
Denoon, Donald. 1983. *Settler Capitalism: the dynamics of dependent development in the Southern Hemisphere.* Oxford.
—— Chris Ballard, Glenn Banks and Peter Hancock (eds). 1995. *Mining and mineral resource policy issues in Asia-Pacific.* Canberra: ANU.
—— 1985. 'Capitalism in Papua New Guinea'. *Journal of Pacific History*, XX 3–4. pp. 119–34.
—— with Kathleen Dugan and Leslie Marshall. 1989. *Public Health in Papua New Guinea, 1884–1984: Medical Possibility and Political Constraint.* Cambridge University Press.
—— (ed.) 1997. *Emerging from Empire? Decolonisation in the Pacific.* ANU, Division of Pacific and Asian History.
—— and Catherine Snowden (eds). 1979. *A Time to Plant and a Time to Uproot: A History of Agriculture in Papua New Guinea.* Port Moresby.
—— and Stewart Firth, Jocelyn Linnekin, Karen Nero and Malama Meleisea (eds). 1997. *The Cambridge History of The Pacific Islanders.* Melbourne.
—— 2000. *Getting Under the Skin: the Bougainville copper agreement and the creation of the Panguna mine.* Melbourne University Press.
—— and Philippa Mein-Smith, with Marivic Wyndham. 2000. *A History of Australia, New Zealand, and the Pacific.* Oxford: Blackwell.
—— 2004. 'Re-Membering Australasia: A Repressed Memory'. In *Australian Historical Studies*, 112. pp. 290–304.
—— 2004. 'Pacific paradoxes: Cooperation and colonialism in Australia's relations with the Islands'. *Times Literary Supplement* (5280). pp. 12–13. (June 11, 2004).
Diamond, Jared. 1997. *Guns, Germs, and Steel.* New York.
Dinnen, Sinclair. 2001. *Law and Order in a Weak State: crime and politics in Papua New Guinea.* University of Hawai'i Press.
—— and Alison Ley (ed.) 2000. *Reflections on Violence in Melanesia.* Canberra: ANU, Asia Pacific Press.
—— and Ron May and Anthony Regan (ed.) 1997. *Challenging the State: the Sandline Affair in Papua New Guinea.* ANU, NCDS.
Dodd, Mark. 2004. 'Problems Persist in Paradise'. *Far Eastern Economic Review.* March 11, 2004.
Donaldson, M. J. and Ken Good. 1988. *Articulated agricultural development: traditional and capitalist agriculture in Papua New Guinea.* Sydney.
Doran, Stuart. 1999. 'Western Friends and Eastern Neighbours: West New Guinea and Australian self-perception'. PhD thesis, ANU.
Dorney, Sean. 1990 (revised 2000). *Papua New Guinea: People, Politics and History since 1975.* Sydney: ABC Books.
—— 1998. *The Sandline affair: politics and mercenaries and the Bougainville Crisis.* Sydney: ABC Books.
Dove, J., T. Miriung and M. Togolo. 1974. 'Mining bitterness. In P. G. Sack (ed.), *Problem of Choice: Land in Papua New Guinea's Future.* ANU.

Downs, Ian. 1980. *The Australian Trusteeship: Papua New Guinea 1945-75.* Canberra: AGPS.
Duke, Trevor. 2004. 'Slow but steady progress in child health in Papua New Guinea'. *Journal of Paediatric Child Health.* Vol. 40. pp. 659–63.
Duncan, Ron. 1994. *Melanesian Forestry Sector Study.* Canberra: AIDAB [AusAID].
Earle, G. W. 1845. 'On the Physical Structure and Arrangement of the Islands of the Indian Archipelago'. *Journal of the Royal Geographical Society.* Vol. 15.
Epstein, T. S. 1968. *Capitalism, Primitive and Modern: Some Aspects of Tolai Economic Growth.* Canberra.
Epstein, A. L, R. S. Parker and Marie Reay (eds). 1971. *The Politics of Dependence: Papua New Guinea 1968.* Canberra: ANU.
Faber, Mike. L. 1974. 'Bougainville renegotiated. *Mining Magazine,* December 1974.
—— and Dudley Seers. 1972. *The Crisis in Planning.* London.
Farquharson, John. 1999. 'George Warwick Smith'. *Sydney Morning Herald,* December 31, 1999.
Fenbury, David. 1966. 'Kot Bilong Mipela. Better than Kot bilong gavment?' *New Guinea and Australia,* 4.
—— 1980. (2nd ed.) *Practice without Policy: genesis of local government in Papua New Guinea,* Development Studies Monograph 13. Canberra: ANU.
Filer, Colin with Navroz Dubash and Kilyali Kalit. 2000. *The Thin Green Line. World Bank leverage and forest policy reform in Papua New Guinea.* Port Moresby and Canberra: NRI and ANU.
—— with Nikhil Sekhran. 1998. *Loggers, donors, and resource owners.* London and Port Moresby: International Institute for Environment and Development and Natural Research Institute.
Firth, Stewart. 1997. 'Papua New Guinea: why we must offer ex-colony more than words and money. *Sydney Morning Herald,* March 27, 1997
Fisk, E. K. 1995. *Hardly Ever a Dull Moment.* History of Development Studies Monograph 5. ANU, National Centre for Development Studies.
—— (ed.) 1966. *New Guinea on the Threshold: Aspects of Social, Political and Economic Development.* ANU.
—— 1962. 'Planning in a Primitive Economy: special problems of Papua New Guinea'. *The Economic Record.* Vol. 38, No. 40, December 1962.
—— 1964. 'Planning in a Primitive Economy: from pure subsistence to the production of a market surplus', *The Economic Record.* Vol. 40, No. 90, June 1964.
—— 1971. 'Labour absorption capacity of subsistence agriculture'. *The Economic Record,* Vol. 47, No. 119, September 1971.
—— 1962. 'The economy of Papua-New Guinea'. In Bettison, Fisk, West and Crawford, *The Independence of Papua New Guinea,* Sydney.
Fitzpatrick, Peter. 1980. *Law and the State in Papua New Guinea.* London.
Fitzpatrick, Philip. 2005. *Bamahuta: Leaving Papua New Guinea,* Canberra: Pandanus Books.
Foot, Hugh. 1962. *Report on New Guinea, together with the relevant resolution of the Trusteeship Council.* United Nations Trusteeship Council, Visiting Mission to the Trust Territories of Nauru and New Guinea.
—— 1964. *A start in freedom.* London.
Francis, Alois. Letter in the *Post-Courier,* November 12, 2004.
Gammage, Bill. 1998. *The Sky Travellers: Journeys in New Guinea, 1938–1939.* Melbourne University Press.
Gardner, Robert and Karl Heider. 1968. *Gardens of War: Life and Death in the New Guinea Stone Age.* New York: Random House.
Garnaut, Ross and Anthony Clunies Ross. 1983. *Taxation of mineral rents.* Oxford: Clarendon Press.
—— 1974. *Taxing natural resource projects.* ANU.
Ghai, Yash and Antony Regan. 1992. *The Law, Politics and Administration of Decentralisation in Papua New Guinea.* National Research Institute Monograph 30. Boroko.
—— 1994. *Reflections on Self-Determination in the South Pacific.* University of Hong Kong.
Gibson, J. and S. Rozelle. 1998. *Results of the household survey component of the 1996 poverty assessment for Papua New Guinea.* Port Moresby: Department of Planning.

—— 2003. 'Poverty and access to roads in Papua New Guinea'. *Economic Development and Cultural Change*, 52 (1).
Glen, David. 2000. 'The Last Elusive Object'. MA thesis, ANU.
Goldsworthy, David. 1997. 'Menzies, Britain and the Commonwealth'. In Frank Cain (ed.), *Menzies in War and Peace*, Sydney.
Goode, Christine Mary. 1975. 'Preparation and Negotiation — The Transfer of Power from Australia to Papua New Guinea 1970–1975'. Thesis, UPNG.
Gore, R. T. 1965. *Justice versus sorcery*. Brisbane: Jacaranda.
Griffin, James T. 1990. 'Bougainville is a Special Case'. In Ron May and Matthew Spriggs (eds), *The Bougainville Crisis*, Bathurst: Crawford House.
—— 1970. 'Bougainville'. *Australia's Neighbours*, 68.
—— 1972. 'Bougainville – secession or just sentiment?' *Current Affairs Bulletin*, 48 (9).
—— 1973. 'Buka and Arawa: some black thoughts on a white history of Bougainville'. *Meanjin Quarterly*. Vol. 32, No. 4.
—— 1976. 'Kieta, Honiara and Port Moresby: hidden but not unknown'. *New Guinea*, 10 (4).
—— 1982. 'Napidakoe Navitu', in R. J. May (ed.), *Micronationalist Movements in Papua New Guinea*, ANU.
—— and Nelson Hank and Stewart Firth. 1979. *Papua New Guinea: A Political History*. Melbourne.
Groves, Murray. 1962. 'The Reign of Mr Hasluck'. *Nation*, May 5, 1962.
Hancock, Ian. 2002. *John Grey Gorton: He Did It His Way*. Melbourne University Press.
Hannett, Leo. 1969. 'Down Kieta Way, Independence of Bougainville'. *New Guinea and Australia*, 4.
—— 1975. 'The Case for Bougainville Secession'. *Meanjin Quarterly*, Spring 1975.
Hasluck, Paul. 1976. *A Time for Building: Australian Administration in Papua and New Guinea 1951–1963*. Melbourne University Press.
—— 1951. Address to the William McGregor Club, Sydney, November 20, 1951.
—— 1956. 'Australian Policy in Papua and New Guinea'. George Judah Cohen Memorial Lecture, University of Sydney.
—— 1956. 'Australia's Task in Papua and New Guinea'. Roy Milne Memorial Lecture, Perth.
—— 1960. 'Australian Policy in Papua and New Guinea'. House of Representatives, August 23, 1960.
—— 1961. Address to the Economic Society of Australia and New Zealand (NSW Branch), October 20, 1961.
—— 1962. 'The Future in Papua and New Guinea'. Public Service Association, Port Moresby, September.
Hastings, Peter. 1969. *New Guinea: problems and prospects*. Melbourne: AIIA.
—— 1971. *Papua New Guinea: Prospero's other island*. Sydney.
Hayden, Bill. 1996. *Hayden: An Autobiography*. Sydney.
Hess, Michael. 1983. '"In the Long Run …": Australian Colonial Labour Policy in the Territory of Papua and New Guinea'. *The Journal of Industrial Relations*, March 1983.
—— 1982. 'The Formation and Collapse of the Milne Bay District Workers Association'. MA thesis, University of Papua New Guinea.
Hirst, John. 2000. *Sentimental Nation: the Making of the Australian Constitution*. Melbourne.
Howie-Willis, Ian. 1980. *A thousand graduates: conflict in university development in Papua New Guinea, 1961–1976*. ANU.
Hudson, W. J. 1971. *Australia and Papua New Guinea*. Sydney.
Hughes, Helen. 2004. *Can Papua New Guinea come back from the brink?* Sydney: Centre for Independent Studies.
—— 2003. *Aid and the Pacific*. Sydney: CIS.
—— 2004. 'Outlook for PNG Remains Bleak'. *The Canberra Times*, April 1, 2004.
Hughes, N. 1973. *The Eight Aims of the New Papua New Guinea*. Port Moresby.

Hunt, Bruce. 2004. 'Papua New Guinea in Australia's Strategic Thinking'. PhD thesis, University of New England.
Inglis, Amirah. 1974. *'Not a White Woman Safe': Sexual Anxiety and Politics in Port Moresby, 1920–1934.* ANU Press.
International Bank for Reconstruction and Development ['World Bank']. 1965. *The Economic Development of the Territory of Papua and New Guinea.* Baltimore: Johns Hopkins Press.
Jackson, Richard T. *Ok Tedi: the Pot of Gold?* Port Moresby.
—— and Glenn Banks (eds). 2002. *In search of the serpent's skin: the story of the Porgera gold project.* Papua New Guinea: Placer Niugini.
Jinks, Brian. 1973. *New Guinea government: an introduction.* Sydney.
—— 1975. 'Papua New Guinea, 1942–1952: policy, planning and J. K. Murray'. PhD thesis, University of Sydney.
—— and Peter Biskup and Hank Nelson (eds). 1973. *Readings in New Guinea History.* Sydney.
Johnson, Leslie W. c. 1975. 'Westminster in Moresby: Papua New Guinea's House of Assembly, 1964–1972'. Annotated typescript in the possession of Christine Goode.
—— 1983. *Colonial sunset: Australia and Papua New Guinea 1970–74.* University of Queensland Press.
Kaputin, John. 1969. 'Rabaul. Truths as we know them …'. *New Guinea and Australia.* Vol. 4, No. 3.
Kiki, Albert Maori. 1968. *Ten thousand years in a lifetime: A New Guinea autobiography.* Melbourne.
Kimisopa, Bire. *Sunday Profile* transcript, ABC Radio. Sunday December 5, 2004.
Kituai, August. 1998. *My Gun, My Brother: The World of the Papua New Guinea Colonial Police.* Honolulu: University of Hawai'i Press.
Laki, James. 2004. 'A critical appraisal of the ECP'. *Post-Courier,* October 13, 2004.
Lal, Brij V. and Michael Pretes (eds). 2001. *Coup: reflections on the political crisis in Fiji.* Canberra: Pandanus Books.
—— and Hank Nelson (eds). 1995. *Lines across the sea: colonial inheritance in the post colonial Pacific.* Brisbane: Pacific History Association.
—— 1998. *Another way: the politics of constitutional reform in post-coup Fiji.* Canberra: Asia Pacific Press.
Langmore, John. 1972. 'A Critical Assessment of Australian economic policy for Papua New Guinea between 1945 and 1970'. Mimeo, Department of Economics, University of Papua New Guinea.
Larmour, Peter (ed.) 1997. *Governance and reform in the South Pacific.* ANU, NCDS.
—— 1992. *Legitimacy, sovereignty and regime change in the South Pacific: comparisons between the Fiji coups and the Bougainville rebellion,* Dept of Political and Social Change. ANU.
—— (ed.) 1995. *Governance and Good Government: Policy and Implementation in the South Pacific.* ANU, NCDS.
Latukefu, Sione (ed.) 1985. *Papua New Guinea: A Century of Colonial Impact, 1884–1984.* Port Moresby: NRI and UPNG.
Law Reform Commission. 1975. *Report on Punishment for Wilful Murder.* Report 3, October 1975.
Lawrence, Peter. 1964. *Road Belong Cargo: a study of the cargo movement in the southern Madang district.* Manchester University Press.
Lawson, John A. 1875. *Wanderings in the Interior of New Guinea.* London: Chapman Hall.
Leahy, Tom. 2002. *Markham Tom: Memoirs of an Australian Pioneer in Papua New Guinea.* Adelaide: Crawford House.
Ley, John. 'The Role of the CPC in Nation-Building'. Unpublished typescript, partly reproduced in 'Hindsight'.
Lynch, Mark. 1972. 'Communication and Cargo: some roles performed by Members of Papua New Guinea's House of Assembly, 1964–1972'. MA thesis, Sussex University.
Lynch, C. J. 1964. 'Towards a parliamentary ministerial system of government for Papua and New Guinea, with short critiques by O. OalaRarua and I. F. Downs, together with a reply by C. J. Lynch'. Port Moresby: Institute of Public Administration.

—— 1980. 'Current Developments in the Pacific: the Achievement of Independence in Papua New Guinea'. *Journal of Pacific History*, Vol. XV, No. 3.
McCarthy, J. K. 1968. *New Guinea: our nearest neighbour*. Melbourne.
McCarthy, J. K. 1963. *Patrol into yesterday: My New Guinea Years*. Melbourne.
McCormick, Barrett and Jonathan Unger (eds). 1996. *China After Socialism: In the Footsteps of Eastern Europe or East Asia?* New York: Armonk.
Macdonald, Barrie. 1997. 'Decolonisation and "Good" Governance: Precedents and Continuities', in Donald Denoon (ed.) *Emerging from Empire?: Decolonisation in the Pacific*, Canberra: Division of Pacific and Asian History.
Macdonald, Barrie. 1997. '"Good" Governance and Pacific Islands States'. In Peter Larmour (ed.), *Governance in the Pacific Islands*, Canberra: National Centre for Development Studies.
Maddocks, Ian. 1968. '"Udumu a-hagaia" (Motu, meaning open your mouth)'. Inaugural Lecture, University of Papua New Guinea.
Mair, Lucy. 1948. *Australia in New Guinea*. London.
Malinowski, Bronislav. 1922. *Argonauts of the Western Pacific*. London.
Mamak, Alexander and Ahmed Ali (eds). 1979. *Race, Class and Rebellion in the South Pacific*. Sydney.
Markus, Andrew. 1994. *Australian Race Relations 1788-1993*. Sydney.
May, R. J. 1998. 'Nugget, Pike, et al: the role of the Reserve Bank of Australia in Papua New Guinea's decolonisation'. North Australia Research Unit discussion paper. Darwin, ANU.
—— 2001. *State and society in Papua New Guinea: the first twenty-five years*. Adelaide: Crawford House.
—— and A. J. Regan with Allison Ley (eds). 1997. *Political Decentralisation in a New State: The Experience of Provincial Government in PNG*. Crawford House.
Mench, Paul. 1975. *The role of the Papua New Guinea defence force*. Development Studies Centre Monograph 2. ANU.
Menzies, R. G. 1969. *Afternoon Light: Some Memories of Men and Events*. Melbourne: Penguin.
Miller, J. D. B. 1965 (2005). 'Australia's Difficulties in New Guinea'. ANU seminar paper, November 1965, reprinted in *Journal of Pacific History*, 2005.
Miller, Robert (ed.) 1992. *The Development of Civil Society in Communist Systems*. ANU, 1992.
Momis, John and Eugene Ogan. 1972. 'A view from Bougainville'. In M. W. Ward (ed.), *Change and Development in Rural Melanesia*, Fifth Waigani Seminar.
—— 1971. 'Bougainville '71. Not discovered by CRA'. *New Guinea and Australia*, 6.
—— 1978. 'The Constitutional Planning Committee and the Constitution'. Opening address, Waigani Seminar.
Moore, Clive. 1985. *Kanaka: A History of Melanesian Mackay*. Port Moresby: IPNGS.
—— with Mary Kooyman (eds). 1998. *A Papua New Guinea Political Chronicle 1967-1991*. Bathurst, NSW.
Morris, Edward. 1898. *Austral English: a dictionary of Australasian words, phrases and usages ...* London.
Mortimer, Rex, Ken Good and Azeem Amarshi. 1979. *Development and Dependency: the Political Economy of Papua New Guinea*. Melbourne.
Moulik, T. K. 1985. 'Crisis of Community Leadership'. *Catalyst*, 3.
Munster, George. 1982. *Secrets of State: A Detailed Assessment of the Book they Banned*. Sydney.
Narokobi, Bernard. 1975. 'We the People, We the Constitution'. In Jean Zorn and Peter Bayne (eds), *Lo Bilong Ol Manmeri: Crime, Compensation and Village Courts*, UPNG. pp. 19–30.
—— 1983. *The Melanesian Way*. Suva: Institute of Pacific Studies.
—— 1983. 'A View from Papua New Guinea'. *Arena*, 65.
—— 1978. 'We the people, We the Constitution'. In Goldring, *The Constitution of Papua New Guinea: a Study in Legal Nationalism*, Sydney.
—— 2001. 'The Constitutional Planning Committee, Nationalism and Vision'. In Regan, Jessep, and Kwa (eds), *Twenty Years of the Papua New Guinea Constitution*.

Nelson, Hank. 1972. *Papua New Guinea: Black Unity or Black Chaos*. Melbourne: Penguin.
—— 1997. 'Frontiers, Territories and States of Mind'. In D. Denoon (ed.), *Emerging from Empire?*
—— 1997. 'The Talk and the Timing'. Ibid.
—— 1997. *Decolonisation in the Pacific Islands*. ANU, Department of Pacific and Asian History.
—— 2003. 'Our Great Task'. In *Meanjin*, Vol. 62, No. 3. pp. 123-35.
—— 2000. 'Crises of God and Man: PNG Political Chronicle 1997–99'. *Journal of Pacific History*.
Nott, Loraine. 1989. *CEB: exploits of an uncommon man*. Warwick, Qld: Pioneer Press.
Oakman, Daniel. 2005. *Facing Asia: A History of the Colombo Plan*. Canberra: Pandanus Books.
O'Callaghan, Mary-Louise. 1999. *Enemies Within : Papua New Guinea, Australia and the Sandline Crisis: the inside story*. Sydney: Doubleday.
—— 1999. 'PNG's night of the long knives'. *The Australian*, July 15, 1999.
O'Faircheallaigh, Ciaran. 1982. *Host countries and multinationals: case studies from Ireland, Papua New Guinea and Zambia of negotiations with mining corporations* Department of International Relations, ANU.
—— 1984. *Mining and development: foreign-financed mines in Australia, Ireland, Papua New Guinea and Zambia*. London: Croom Helm.
—— 1992. 'The Local Politics of Resource Development in the South Pacific'. In S. Henningham and R. May (eds), *Resources, Development and Politics in the Pacific Islands*, Bathurst.
Ogan, Eugene, 1974. 'Cargoism and Politics in Bougainville 1962–1972'. *Journal of Pacific History*, 9.
—— 1972. 'Business and Cargo: Socio-Economic Change among the Nasioi of Bougainville'. *New Guinea Research Bulletin*, 44.
—— 1989. 'Some Historical Background to the 1989 unrest in Bougainville'. Seminar paper, Department of Political and Social Change, ANU, June 1989.
Oliver, Douglas. 1973. *Bougainville: a Personal History*. Melbourne.
Ongka. *Ongka: A self-account by a New Guinea big-man*. (Translated by Andrew Strathern.) 1979. London.
Oram, Nigel. 1976. *Colonial Town to Melanesian City: Port Moresby 1884-1974*. ANU.
Parker, R. S. 1971. 'Shaping parties in New Guinea'. *Dissent*, 21, Spring 1971.
Pasquarelli, John. 1998. *The Pauline Hansen Story by the man who knows*. French's Forest, NSW: New Holland.
Patience, Allan. 2004. 'Failed and Vulnerable States: towards a Political Science of South Pacific Regionalism'. Inaugural Lecture. UPNG. April 30, 2004.
—— 2004. 'What is Australia really up to?' *Post-Courier*, July 5, 2004.
—— 2004. 'Don't tolerate the intolerable'. *Post Courier*, October 25, 2004.
Penders, C. L. M. 2002. *The West New Guinea Debacle: Dutch Decolonisation and Indonesia, 1945–1962*. Adelaide: Crawford House.
Pollock, Nancy. 1997. 'Nauru: Decolonised, Recolonising, but never a Colony'. In Denoon, *Emerging from Empire?*
Quodling, Paul. 1990. *Bougainville: the Mine and the People*. Melbourne: CRA.
Ravuvu, Asesela. 1991. *The facade of democracy: Fijian struggles for political control, 1830–1987*. Suva, Fiji.
Reed, Stephen. 1942. *The Making of Modern New Guinea*. Philadelphia.
Reeves, William Pember. 1902. 'State Experiments in Australia and New Zealand'. London.
Regan, Anthony, Owen Jessep and Eric Kwa (eds). 2001. *Twenty Years of the Papua New Guinea Constitution*. Sydney.
Ritchie, Jonathan. 2004. 'Making Their Own Law: Popular Participation in the Development of Papua New Guinea's Constitution'. PhD thesis, Melbourne University.
Rimoldi, Max and Eleanor. 1992. *Hahalis and the Labour of Love: a social movement on Buka Island*. Oxford.
Rosberg, C. G. and John Nottingham. 1966. *The myth of 'Mau Mau': nationalism in Kenya*. New York: Praeger.

Rowley, Charles. 1965. *The New Guinea Villager: a Retrospect from 1964*. Sydney.
Ryan, Peter (ed.) 1972. *Encyclopaedia of Papua and New Guinea*. 3 vols. Melbourne.
Sack, Peter. 1974. *Problem of Choice — Land in Papua New Guinea's future*. ANU Press.
—— (ed.) 1982. *Pacific constitutions: proceedings of the Canberra Law Workshop VI*. Canberra: Law Department, Research School of Social Sciences, ANU.
—— 1973. *Land between two laws: early European land acquisitions in New Guinea*. Canberra: ANU Press.
Salisbury, R. F. 1962. *From Stone to Steel: economic consequences of a technological change in New Guinea*. Melbourne.
Santamaria, B. A. *The Australian*. August 9, 1988; August 16, 1988; and March 7, 1989.
Schumacher, E. F. 1973. *Small is Beautiful: A Study of Economics as if People Mattered*. New York.
Shearston, Trevor. 2000. *Straight Young Back*. Pymble, NSW: HarperCollins.
Siaguru, Anthony. 2001. *The Great Game: Politics of Democracy in Papua New Guinea*. The Centre for Democratic Institutions Annual Address, June 18, 2001.
Sinclair, J. P. 1966. *Behind the Ranges. Patrolling in New Guinea*. Melbourne.
Somare, Michael. 1975. *Sana: An Autobiography*. Port Moresby.
—— 2001. 'Transcript of Discussion by Panel of Constitution-Makers, Port Moresby, 28 March 1996'. In Regan et al. (eds), *Twenty Years of the Papua New Guinea Constitution*. p. 365.
Souter, Gavin. 1965. *New Guinea: the last unknown*. Sydney.
Spriggs, Matthew and Donald Denoon (eds). 1992. *The Bougainville Crisis: 1991 update*. Bathurst: Crawford House Press.
Standish, Bill. *Melanesian Neighbours: The Politics of PNG, the Solomon Islands and the Republic of Vanuatu*. Parliamentary Library. p. 62
—— *PNG 1999: Crisis of Governance*. September 21, 1999. Research Paper 4, 1999–2000, for Australian Parliament Foreign Affairs, Defence and Trade Group.
Tomasetti, W. E. 1970. *Australia and the United Nations: New Guinea trusteeship issues from 1944-1966*. New Guinea Research Bulletin 36.
Turner, Mark. 1990. *Papua New Guinea: The Challenge of Independence*. Melbourne: Penguin.
van der Veur, Paul. 1966. *Search for New Guinea's Boundaries, from Torres Strait to the Pacific*. ANU.
Viviani, Nancy. 1970. *Nauru: Phosphate and Political Progress*. Canberra: ANU.
—— and Peter Wilenski. 1976. *The Australian Development Assistance Agency — A Post Mortem Report*. Royal Institute of Public Administration, Monograph 3.
Voutas, A. C. 1970. 'Elections and Communications'. In Marion Ward (ed.), *The Politics of Melanesia*, Waigani Seminar papers.
Waigani Seminars:
- 1st – *New Guinea people in business and industry*, 1967.
- 2nd – *The history of Melanesia*, 1968, edited K. S. Inglis.
- 3rd – *The indigenous role of business enterprise*, 1969.
- 4th – *The politics of Melanesia*, 1970, edited by M. W. Ward.
- 5th – *Change and development in rural Melanesia*, 1971, edited by M. W. Ward.
- 6th – *Priorities in Melanesian development*, 1972, edited by R. J. May.
- 7th – *Foreign investment, international law and national development*, 1973, edited by G. Zorn and P. Bayne.
- 8th – *Education in Melanesia*, 1974, edited by J. Brammall and R. J. May.
- 9th – *The Melanesian environment*, edited by J. H. Winslow.

Wainwright, Elsina. 2003. 'Responding to State Failure — The Case of the Solomon Islands'. *Australian Journal of International Affairs*, Vol. 57, No. 3, November 2003.
Wallace, Alfred Russel. 1874. *The Malay Archipelago: the land of the Orang utan and Bird of Paradise*. London.
—— 1876. *The Geographical Distribution of Animals*. London.

Ward, R. G. (ed.) 1972. *Man in the Pacific Islands: essays on geographical change in the Pacific Islands.* Oxford.
Waterson, Albert. 1972 'An Operational Approach to Development Planning'. In M. Faber and D. Seers (eds), *The Crisis in Planning.*
Wedega, Alice. 1981. *Listen My Country.* Sydney.
Wehner, Monica and Donald Denoon (eds). 2002. *Without a Gun: Australians' experiences monitoring peace in Bougainville, 1997–2001.* Canberra: Pandanus Books.
White, Hugh. 2004. 'The deep mess of PNG demands long-term action'. *Sydney Morning Herald,* December 15, 2004.
White, O. 1965. *Parliament of a thousand tribes: A study of New Guinea.* London.
Willey, Keith. 1965. *Assignment New Guinea.* Brisbane: Jacaranda Press.
Windybank, Susan and Mike Manning. 2003. 'Papua New Guinea on the Brink", *Issue Analysis,* No. 30. (Centre for Independent Studies.), March 12, 2003.
Woolford, Don. 1977. *Papua New Guinea: Initiation and Independence.* Brisbane: UQP.
World Bank. 1993. *Governance: The World Bank's Experience.* Washington.
—— 2000. *Project Appraisal Document on a proposed loan ... of US$17.36 million to ... Papua New Guinea for a forestry and conservation project.* Washington, DC. (Report No. 20641–PG, 2000.)
Worsley, Peter. 1957. *The Trumpet Shall Sound: a Study of 'Cargo' Cults in Melanesia.* London.
Zorn, Jean and Peter Bayne (eds). 1975. *Lo Bilong Ol Manmeri: Crime, Compensation and Village Courts.* UPNG.

Interviews

Tos Barnett, Port Moresby, March 18 and 20, 2001.
Peter Bayne, ANU, Canberra, May 25, 2001.
David Beatty, Toronto, August 2001.
Ulli Beier, Port Moresby, 1973.
Bill Brown, Sydney, August 1998.
Jim Byth, Melbourne, January 1998.
Tom Critchley, Sydney, March 4, 2001. See also his National Library of Australia Oral History interview with Michael Wilson, November 25, 1993.
Ron Crocombe, New Delhi, December 2003.
Sir Frank Espie, Adelaide, February 11, 1998.
Pat Galvin, Prahran, Melbourne, September 7, 2001.
Ross Garnaut, ANU, Canberra, 2001.
Christine Goode, Canberra, June 15, 2000.
John Greenwell, Canberra, October 27, 2000.
D. O. Hay, interviewed for National Library of Australia, 1973.
Leslie Johnson, interviewed for National Library of Australia, 1994.
Paul Kelloway, Lyons, ACT, November 2000.
Alan Kerr, Canberra, November 2000.
John Langmore, New York, August 2001.
Mark Lynch, Sydney, June 2004.
Don Mentz, Canberra, August 1998.
Bill Morrison, Canberra, February and April 2001.
Sir Ebia Olewale, Canberra, February 2001.
Andrew Peacock, Washington, 1997.
Stephen Pokawin, Port Moresby, August 2003.
Paul Ryan, Mosman, Sydney, January 22, 2001.
Don Vernon, Melbourne, January 1998.

Index

Abaijah, Josephine   125, 159, 160
Abal, Tei   39, 49, 58, 59, 62, 64, 67, 87
    on the Arek Select Committee   85
    on Constitutional Planning Committee
    113, 114
Abau, *Papua*   131
Abe, Dirona   39, 49
Abel, Cecil   54, 55, 67
Abel, Charles   54
Aboriginal Australians   32
Administration   32, 42, 96
    and attempted reforms   81–82, 101, 119
    and courts   76
    and events in Buka   15
    and House of Assembly   37–39, 46, 57, 95
    and mining disputes   61
    becomes the Government   96
    Central Advisory Committee for the Education
        and Advancement of Women   10
    restriction on   42
Administrative College   xiv, 47, 54, 107, 159, 191
    course for Native Magistrates   45
    name change issue   58
    Peacock's visit   101
Administrator   17, 47, 52, 82, 105
    see also Hay, David; Murray, J.K.
    Council 43,55,70,81–82,88,95
    see also Administrator's Executive Council
    Department of   21, 43
    of New Guinea   8 10
Administrator's Executive Council (AEC)   63, 81,
    82 95, 101, 128, 163
Africa
    after self-government   92, 180
    decolonisation   27, 30, 36, 180
    New English Writung   77
    study tour to   86–87
agricultural extension   11

agriculture   12, 26, 28, 30, 38   *see also* crops
aid   *see* AusAID; World Bank
Aike, Michael   45
Air Niugini   139
airlines   90
Alasia, Sam   16, 199
alcohol   35, 47
Aldridge, *Brigadier* Robert   147, 199
Allen, Ross   62
Allen, Thomas (Tom)   130, 131, 141
Anakapu, Pen   54
ancestral rites   45
Anderson, Tim   183, 199
Anglican Church   14
anthem for PNG   59
ANZUS   27
Aoae, Joseph   44, 76, 152
American Micronesia   86
apartheid   xv, 31, 73
Arawa people   60
Arawaki, Bin   22, 35
archaelogists   12
'arc of instability', *Melanesia*   189–190, 195
Arek, Paulus   66, 85, 86, 88, 102, 113, 115, 159
Arek Select Committee   85–88, 89
armed services   *see also* defence forces
    and self–government   91, 147–148
army
    and civil war   xv
Army's Directorate of Research and Civil Affairs
    see Directorate of Research and Civil Affairs
Aruno, Pupene   66
Ashton, Oriel   49, 67
Ashwin, Robin   109
Asia
    and Australia   32, 130
Asian Development Bank   136
Associated Country Women of the World   10

Asiba, Gerai 54
asylum-seekers 189
Auditor-General's office 140
AusAID 183, 187, 188, 194, 199
   see also project aid
Australasia 2
Australia
   and Asia 32, 131
   and land alienation 132, 183
   as colonial power xv, 3, 4
   Federation of *1901* 2, 27
   increased aid *2004* xv
   non-Europeans in 9, 31
   policy making 2, 4, 27, 56, 87, 183
   study tour to 23–24, 86
Australian aid 3, 91 128, 130, 136–140
   see also AusAID
   aid with no conditions 186
Australian Attorney-General's Department
   in PNG 30, 89
Australian Auditor-General 30
Australian Broadcasting Commission
   in PNG 31
Australian Department of the Army 146
Australian Department of Civil Aviation
   branch in PNG 30, 90
Australian Department of Defence 90, 91
   Army branch in PNG 30
   Navy in PNG 30
Australian Department of External Affairs 31, 104, 106,136
Australian Department of External Territories 4, 8
Australian Department of Foreign Affairs 4, 30, 90, 91, 137
Australian Department of Foreign Affairs and Trade xvi
Australian Department of National Development
   in PNG 30, 90
Australian Department of Public Works 90
Australian Department of Shipping and Transport
   in PNG 30, 90
Australian Department of Territories 25, 30, 40, 44, 65, 76, 85, 95, 136. 137, 166
   and mining negotiations 46
   disolved 106
   under Morrison 105
Australian Department of the Prime Minister and Cabinet 107

Australian Development Assistance Agency 137, 187
   Bill *1974* 137
Australian Executive Council 61
   see also Administrator's Executive Council
Australian Government 45
   and the development of independence 52–65, 78–82, 186–188
Australian Health Department 10
Australian High Court
   see High Court of Australia
Australian Joint Intelligence Committee 94
Australian Journal of Politics and History 77
Australian Meteorological Bureau
   in PNG 30
Australian Migration Act 9
Australian Military Forces 147
Australian National University 11, 12, 44
   New Guinea Research Unit 72, 74, 76, 113
   Research School of Pacific Studies *see* Research School of Pacific Studies
Australian Navy 145
Australian Prime Minister's Department
   in PNG 30, 89
   Public Service Board 30
Australian School of Pacific Administration 73
Australian Stratigic Policy Institute 190
Australian Territories 3, 30, 195
Australian Territorial Administration (anticipated) 73
Australian Treasury 43, 89, 128, 138, 139
Australians working in PNG xv, xvi, 3, 73
authoritarianism 44
autocracy xv
Aviat Club, *Port Moresby* 18, 76
Avei, Moi 161
Awol, Brere 64, 67
Azanifa, Boino 66

Ballard, John 41, 81, 96, 105, 199
Baloiloi, Leatani 22
Baluan Council, *Manus* 21
Bamfield, Armine 136
banking 88, 90, 91
baptism 45
Barnard, Lance 147, 150
Barnes, Charles 40–41, 42, 45, 53, 54, 61, 79
   and Gorton 80, 82

and Moral Rearmament 63
and the courts 76
and the transfer of power 88, 191
Barnett, Thomas (Tos) 45, 75, 96, 103, 107, 121, 122
Barrett, Donald 49
Barton, *Sir* Edmund 3
Batton, Ilomo 54
Bayne, Peter 76, 114, 122, 124, 161
Beatty, David 129, 130
Beazley, Kim *MP* 63, 79
Beckett, Jeremy 18
Behre-Dolbeare, *consulting firm* 136
Beier, Georgina 77, 102
Beier, Ulli 77, 166, 199
Bele, Raphael 61
Belshaw, Cyril 11
Belo, Yano 66, 95
Bengo, Paul 129
Bennett, W.T. 109
Bensbach River 163, 164
Besley, Tim 41, 73
Big Men 16–17, 18, 35
Bilas, Angmai 66, 113, 151
Binandere people 78
Biritu, Ugi 48
Bjelke–Petersen, *Sir* Joh 165
Bloomfield, William 39, 48
Boigu Island 165
Bokap, Daniel 66
Bomai, Ninkama 66, 85
Bonggere, Karigi 66
books 47, 199–208
borders 159, 163–166
Boroko
  1960s 74
  1970s xiv
Boroko United Church 74
Botswana 180
Bougainville xv, 14, 15, 38, 44, 65, 71, 160–162
  see also Buka; Panguna copper mine
  borders 163
  civil war 173, 193
  Interim Provincial Government 124
  Mining Agreement 129, 133, 160
  North 58
  peace talks 195
  separatist issues 95, 119, 121, 125–126
  Special Political Committee 119
  unrest 61, 71, 80, 86, 95, 123, 131, 191
Bougainville Copper Limited (BCL) 61, 133–136
  profits *1973* 134
Bougainville Revolutionary Army 172
Bougainville Task Force 161
Bougainvilleans 4, 60, 78, 151
  consultation with 70, 123–124, 161
  in Canberra 46
Bourke, Michael 182, 199
Bouraga, Philip 163
British African territories 30, 94, 108
British Navy 27, 195
British New Guinea *see* New Guinea — as British Protectorate
broadcasting 70, 76, 90, 161
Brokam, Nicholas 38, 39, 48, 57
Bryant, Gordon 79
Buchanan, Dennis 58, 67
budget, *PNG* 27, 39, 46, 56, 89, 130, 138, 187
  for defence 150,
  1999 172
Buka people 7, 17
Bully Beef Club 54
Bulmer, Ralph 72, 77
Bunting, *Sir* John 57
bureaucracy *see* public servants
Burns Philp *company* 11
Butovicius, Al 78
Byth, Jim 73

Cabinet 187–188
  emergent 43
  1970s 4, 92, 140
Calwell, Arthur Augustus 79, 103
Campbell, *Brigadier* Edward 71
Canberra, *ACT* xiv, xv, 23, 32
  see also Australian Government
  visit to 86
cannibalism 8, 166
cargo cults xiv, 14–15, 21
Carter, W.F 49
Casey, Noel 66
Casey, Richard Gardiner (Baron Casey of Berwick) 32
cash-cropping 15, 17
cassowaries 12

Catholicism 14
   see also Holy Spirit Regional Seminary
      Marist Mission, *Bougainville* 15, 45
ceiling fans xiv
celibacy 45
censorship 73
Centre for Independent Studies 190
Central Planning Office 129, 130
Central Policy and Planning Committee 43
Ceylon 86
Chan, *Sir* Julius 4, 64, 66, 110, 123
   and currency 130
   blackballed from club 18, 76, 102
   Deputy Prime Minister 102
   Finance Minister 1, 102, 135, 139
   in Opposition 171
   Prime Minister 140, 172
Chaney, Fred 39, 52
Chatterton, Percy 37, 49, 57, 58, 66, 118, 132, 200
Chauka, Lukas 21, 22, 24, 35
child health 181
China 173, 180
Chinese in PNG 62
Christianity 13–14, 166, 172, 195
Church and State 44, 45, 47
Chimbu 54
citizenship question 52, 91, 117, 123, 195
Citizenship Advisory Committee 123
civil aviation 88
civil defence 81
civil unrest 86
   see also Bougainville — unrest;
      Highlands — law and order problems;
      Port Morseby — riots
civil war xv, 172
   see also Bougainville — civil war
Cleland, *Sir* Donald 9, 17, 25, 42, 47, 70
Cleland, *Lady* Rachel 10, 74, 200
clothes 47
Clunies-Ross, Anthony 130, 135, 200
cocoa 28
coffee 28
   role of Big Men 11
colonialism 1, 10, 14, 25, 32, 73, 78, 79, 105
   in African writing 77
   in Australia 179, 195
   residues xiv
commerce 14

Commission of Inquiry (into governing the Gazelle) 63
Commission of Inquiry into Land Matters 132
Commission of Inquiry into Sandline 172
Commonwealth Acts concerning Papua New Guinea 97–98
Commonwealth Cooperation in Education Scheme 136
Commonwealth Department of Works
   see Australian Department of Works
Commonwealth Government *see* Australian Government
communication *see* broadcasting; media reports
communism 32
conflict between generations 77
Connolly, Peter *QC* 63
Conroy, William (Bill) 49, 128, 163
Constituent Assembly 120, 121, 122
constitution xv, 27, 53, 56, 91, 112–126, 143, 195
   see also Select Committee on Constitutional Development
   adopted 124
   amendments to 123–124
constitutional change 82, 90, 92, 94, 101
Constitutional Committee 102
Constitutional Planning Committee 4, 108, 112–119, 126, 130, 151, 194
   achievements 124
   compromise constitution 120, 124
   consultants 114
   interim report 117
   minority report 121
   recommendations 117–119
   second interim report 117
consultants 188
Contact Club, *Port Moresby* 74
Conzinc Riotinto (CRA) 45, 59, 60, 61, 70, 133
Cook Islands 53, 90, 187, 195
   Constitution 113
cooperatives 11, 15, 17, 35, 81
copper 45, 125
   see also Panguna copper mine
copra 11
Coral Sea coast, *Port Moresby* xiv
corruption xv, xvi, 173, 176, 178, 187
Council of Social Service 74
Counsel, Bert 64, 125
Counsel, Virgil 67

Country Party, Australia   80, 101
Courts   *see also* High Court of Australia; Territory Supreme Court
    Local and District   17, 35, 76
    procedures   47
    reputation   76
CRA   *see* Conzinc Riotinto
Crawford, *Sir* John   12, 74, 76, 129–130, 200
crime   xv, 76, 94, 151
Criminal Code   154
Critchley, Tom   117, 143–144, 150, 160, 192, 194
Crocombe, Ron   74, 133
Crocombe, Marjorie   53
crops   11
    see also cash cropping; coffee; copra; palm oil
cultural change   72
cultural institutions   144
currency   181, 195
    institutions   91
    introduction of   130
Currie, George   44
Currie Commission   44
Curtin, Tim   181
'customary law'   152, 154

Dabb, Geoffrey   75, 76, 154, 163
Dae es Salaam
    University   76
Daru   54, 159, 195
Dauan Island   165
Daugi, Mackenzie   113, 121
Davidson, *Professor* Jim   61, 113
DDT   36
de Murville, Couve   30
Deakin, *Prime Minister* Alfred   2, 194
decentralisation   119, 120, 124, 160–162
decision making   xv, 86, 92, 124
decolonisation   36, 59, 73, 79, 82, 86–96, 105, 112, 140, 143, 175, 179, 181, 191, 195
    1975   xv, xvi, 1
defence force   xv, 27, 56, 70, 121, 145–151, 172, 194
    see also army
    Australians with   190
    Joint Statement *1977*   149
    loss of morale   178
Defence Section   147
democracy   35–48, 54, 70, 96, 180, 187

demonstrations   86, 146
Denoon, Donald
    arrival in PNG   xiv
    books   201
Deparment of Agriculture, Stock and Fish   103
Department of District Affairs   63
Department of District Administration   16, 145
Department of Finance   129
Department of Government   63
Department of Native Affairs   102
Department of Shipping and Transport
    see Australian Department of Shipping and Transport
'dependency theory'   128
Deputy Public Solicitor   76
Derham, Professor David   35, 74, 75, 151
Derham Report   40
Development Bank   63
Development Capital Guarantee Declaration   40
development funding   46, 74, 92, 187–188
development strategies   128
devolution   4, 53, 56, 81, 82, 86, 92, 192
Dialogue, journal   44, 45
Dickson, Merari/Murari   17, 35
didimen   17
Dinnen, Sinclair   155
diplomacy   27
Director of District Affairs   82
Director of Education   59, 82
Director of Native Affairs   23
Directorate of Research and Civil Affairs
    (DORCA)   31
Diria, Kaibelt   49, 86, 110
discrimination   18
District Commissioner   9, 16, 21
    criticism of courts   76
District Courts   152
District Liasion Office   161
District Officers   42
Division of Government and Law   93
doctors   36
Dodd, Mark   179
DORCA   *see* Directorate of Research and Civil Affairs
Downer, *Sir* Alexander   9
Downs, Ian   39, 43, 46, 47, 49, 57, 58, 151
drama   *see* plays
Drysdale, Peter   138
Duba, Kaura   66

Duncan, *Sir* Val 135
Dunstan, Don 103
Dutch New Guinea 163
Dutch withdrawl 36
Dutton, Warren 67

East Anglia Group 129, 130
East New Britian 58, 160
East Timor 166
Eastern Highlands 35
Ebei'al, Tegi 66
economic crisis xv
economic development 43, 53, 80, 101, 179
    and democracy 180
Economic Division 81
economic issues 3, 11–13, 26, 28, 43, 91, 28–140
    see also budget; development funding; marketing; taxation
economic management 172
economic policy 129–140, 179, 194
economists 76, 128
Edie, Brian 107
education 3, 13, 17, 28, 58–59, 192
    see also schools
    and subsequent treatment 18
    at missions 14
    goals for 26, 28
    in Australia 8, 18, 22
    of parliamentarians 37, 47
    primary 44, 81
    secondary 44, 81
    technical 81
    tertiary 44, 45
Education Department 47
    Director of 47
Ehava, Gabriel 22
elected members *see* parliamentarians
elected provincial governments proposal 119
elections 37, 62, 96, 166, 183
    learning about 23, 109
    1972 4, 88, 95
    third xv
electoral education patrols 37
electoral reform 174
Elijah, Elliott 54
Ellis, Tom 43, 49, 61, 62, 63, 67
Emanuel, Jack 58, 62

emergency powers 58
Eminent Persons Group 150, 178, 189
enabling legislation 93
Endekam, Katigame 67
Enga 75
English language 37, 57, 59, 158
    New English Writing Studies 77
Enhanced Cooperation Package, *2004* xv, 190
environment 117, 131
environmental damage 135, 136
Epstein, Scarlett 12, 63
equal pay 47
Eri, Vincent 77, 78
Espie, Frank 70, 134
espionage 71
Eupu, Edric 48, 132
evangelists 10
    British xiv
    Polynesian xiv
Evans, *Senator* Gareth 188
Everett, Norman 66
exchange 12
Executive Council 56
expatriates 57, 59, 91, 122, 131, 144
exploration
    by Europeans 2
Explosives Bill, *1964* 38
Expo '70 166–167
exports 3
external affairs 56

Faber, Micheal 129
faliure of state? xv, 178–179
Faifax Harbour, *Port Moresby* xiv, 1
family planning 71
feathers 12
Federal Governemtn *see* Australian Government
Fenbury, David 21, 43, 74, 76, 151
Fenton, *kiap* 63
Fielding, Will 58, 67
Fiji 2, 86, 94, 117, 132, 180–181
    Great Council of Chiefs 181
Finances 43, 186–189, 194
    see also banking; currency; economic issues
financial institutions 143
Fingleton, Jim 132, 133
Fingleton, *Father* Wally 44

Firth, Stewart   145
Fisk, Ernest   12, 202
Fitzpatrick, Philip   73, 132, 176
flag of PNG   1, 59
Fly River   136, 163
Foley, Stanley   67
Food and Agriculture Organisation   28
food consumption   182
Foot, *Sir* Hugh   30, 37
Foot Committee   44
foreign investment   91, 130, 131, 188
foreign owned property   118
foreign relations   121, 194
forestry   174, 182
Forge, Anthony   166
fortified compounds   179
France
    in the Pacific   2
    see also New Caledonia
Francis, Alois   175, 202
Fransee, John Malcolm   79, 101, 165
Fraser Government   139
free press   183
Freire, Paulo   113
Frieda   130

Galloway, Ronald   67
Galvin, Patrick   41, 90, 91, 107, 128, 148
Gam, Rauke   66
Gang of Four   187
Gardens of War   xiv
Garnaut, Ross   77, 128, 129, 138, 173, 187
Garrett, Jason   67
Gazelle Peninsula   11, 13, 57, 60, 63 71, 160
    instability in   95, 133
    land disputes   133
'Gearing-Up Program'   93–94, 107–108, 115
Geelong Grammer, *school*   80
gender equality   129
German New Guinea
    see New Guinea — as German Colony
Germany
    in the pacific   2
Ghai, Yash   114
Ghana   86
Gilbert and Ellice Islands   181, 193
Gilmore, Graham   49

Giregire, Sinaki   38, 39, 48, 59, 66, 85, 113, 121
    overseas study tour   86
Glen, David   2
Goava, Sinaka   54, 132
gold   2, 11
Goods, Christine   80, 81, 88, 107, 122
Gordon Barracks, *Port Moresby*   150
Goroka   xvi, 12, 79, 103, 168
Gorton, *Sir* John Grey   4, 58, 61, 63, 79, 80–82, 85
    and Cabinet   91
    and land matters   132
    and the Liberal Party   101
governance   xvi, 16–18, 21, 35, 72, 73, 92, 180, 187, 194
government   28, 32, 70, 154, 171
    see also Australian Government; House of Assembly
    heads of departments   70
    Liasion Office   161
    ministerial members   81
    reform of   54, 85, 88, 92, 124, 178–179
government agencies   143, 161
Govenor-General of PNG   1, 59, 81, 122, 172
graduates   xv, 77
Grassby, Al   123
Great War
    see World War 1
Greenwell, John   75, 81, 82, 91, 101, 105
    as head of Papua New Guinea Office   106, 109
Griffin, James   46, 60, 161, 203
Griffith, Alan   91
Gris, Gabriel   119, 160
Gross Domestic Product (GDP)   181
Grove, Donald   67
Grove, William   49
Groves, *Dr* Bill   17, 192
guest worker proposal   196
Guise, John   39, 46, 47, 48, 52, 53, 66, 115, 159
    and the making of government   54, 76, 80, 112
    as Governor-General   186
    as Speaker   57, 59, 186
    house   38
    in the Somare government   103, 186
    speaks on *Guest of Honour*   76
Guise Select Committee   52–59, 85, 159
Gulf of Papua   163
Gulf Province   59
Gumine, *Highlands*   85

gun culture 179
Gunther, *Dr* John 17, 35, 36, 39, 42, 44, 47
    Assistant Administrator 36, 49
    Director of Health 36
    Select Committee 35–37, 55, 85
    Vice-Chancellor 44, 77, 107
Gunther Committee's Interim Report 36, 37
Gutman, Gerry 41, 76, 81, 105, 134

Hahalis people 15, 17
Hahalis Welfare Society 15, 44
Haivera, Chris 172
Hamidian-Rad, *Dr* Pirouz 172, 188
Hanaham people 15
Hannett, Leo 44, 61, 77, 78, 119, 160
Hanuabada 54
Harepa, Cletus 132
Hasluck, *Sir* Paul Meernaa Caedwalla 9, 17, 23,
    24–32, 151, 179, 203
    and land tenure 35–36
    and policy-making 43, 70, 74, 75, 193–194
    and Public Service 47
    as Govenor-General 106
    Minister for Territories 24, 42
    paternalism 79, 191
    relations with Cabinet 28–29
Hastings, Peter 25
Havini, Moses 119
Hawaiian
    dispossession 132
Hay, David 42, 58, 59, 60, 62, 70, 79, 143, 192
    and Gorton 80, 81
    and Bill Morrison 104, 105
Hayden, Bill 139, 174–175, 188, 194
health services 28, 36, 81, 174, 194
    see also child health; doctors; hospitals
Henderson, Frank 49, 67
High Court of Australia 61, 62, 126, 151
higher education
    see education-tertiary
Highlanders xiv, xv, 36, 55, 115
Highlands 85, 86, 87
    appeal for plebiscite 125
    law and order problems 151–152
    mapping of 2
    police rule 35
    producion in 12
    tribal fighting 95

Highlands Highway 16
Hindsight: a Retrospective Workshop for Participants
    in the Decolonisation of Papua New Guinea
    xvi, 83
Hitter, Eritus 22
HIV/AIDS 179, 180
Hohao 78
Holloway, Barry 47, 48, 55, 57, 74, 123, 148
Holt, Harold Edward *MP* 25
Holy Spirit Regional Seminary 44
Horne, Donald 73
hospitals 17, 28, 36
House of Assembly xv, 4, 36, 38–40, 147
    see also Territory House of Assembly
    and Administration 38–40, 43, 65, 88
    and Andrew Peacock 101
    and people's rights 44, 54
    and self-government 63, 82, 87–88, 93, 108
    anti-colonial seperatists 64
    dress code 57
    Independent Group 58
    limits on debating 45
    manipulation of 65, 82, 192
    official members 40, 54, 87, 88
    second, *1968* 56, 57–59, 101
    Select Committee 80–81
    Standing Orders 45
Howard, *Prime Minister* John 189
Hughes, *Professor* Helen 178–179, 182, 183, 203
houses
    of public servants xiv
Hubert Murray Stadium, *Port Mosebey* 1
human rights 118, 187

Iangalo, Leine 49, 67
Ibadan University Library 166
identity issue 77, 166–168
    see also land and identity 77
Ielelina people 15
Ijivitari 85
Ila, Toni 113, 121
illiteracy 81
imports 3
indenture 74
independence 80, 89, 106, 166–168, 197
    achievement of xvi, 121
    and post-independence disillusion 77, 179–183
    celebrations 1

gradualism 79
instead of statehood 4
reservations about xv, 87, 91, 183
target dates 26, 79, 87, 112
Independence Day 121, 125
Indigenous Land Groups Act 1975 133
Indonesia 36, 145, 180
annexation 95
border with 163, 164
Embassy of PNG 178
industrial relations 74
infections xiv
Information and Extension Services, *PNG* 23
infrastructure 179, 193–194
Inglis, Ken 77, 78
Institution of Technology 14
intergration 53
Intelligence Branch 94
Intelligence Committee 15, 94, 96
intelligentsia 45
interdepartmental Committee on 'the Implications of Early Self-Government' 91
Interdepartmental Coordinating Committee 43, 96
internal security 56, 94–96
Internal Security Authorities 44
International Commission of Jurists 76, 154
interpretation 58
inter-racial 70
Iokea Village, *Papua* 7
Iramu, Francis 153
Irian Jaya 29, 95, 107, 132, 159, 163, 166
border-crossers 164
Iwoksim, Wesani 67
Iuri, Poio 48, 66

Jackson, Richard 136
James, Meanggarum 48, 66
Japan
post war 180
Japanese occupation 62
Japlik land 62
Jephcott, Bruce 110, 123
Johnson, Leslie 37, 38, 49, 58, 63, 64, 65, 67
and Arek Select Committee 85
and Gorton 81
and Morrison 105
Director-General of ADAA 137

Johnson, Peter 66
Johnston, W.J. 21
Joint Force Headquarters, *Port Moresby* 148
Juddery, Bruce 86
Judicial Services Commissioners 124
judicial system 26, 74, 76, 151–155
judiciary 1, 27, 88, 91, 152, 183
June Valley xiv

Kainantu, *Eastern Highlands* 151
Kakun, Mangobing 66
Kali, Pokwari 132
Kambipi, Taimya 66
Kaniniba, Micheal 66
Kapena, Toua 66
Kaputin, John 102, 113, 115, 121, 122, 123, 151, 153
Karava, Ehava 48
Karepa, Ralph 125
Kasaipwalova, John 77, 78
Kasau, Pikah 113, 121
Kauage 77
Kaumi, Simon 109
Kaupa, John 113, 121
Kavoli, Thomas 102, 110
Kearney, Bill 120
Kekedo, Roland 139
Kela, Mal Smith 175
Kelloway, Paul 138
Kennecott, *company* 130, 136
Kanene, *Colonel* 178
Kenu, Wegra 39, 49, 57
Kenya xv
Kereku, Damien 63
Kerema District, *Papua* 7
Kerr, Alan 86–87, 88, 101, 105, 106
kiaps 16, 17, 18, 73, 145, 176, 192
and patrols 44
courts 17, 35
in Parliament 46–47, 58
patrol reports 94
Kidu, Buri 76, 152, 153
Kieta 46
Kiki, Albert Maori 47, 54, 78, 110, 123, 139, 166
and Olewale 159
Defence Minister 149
Deputy Prime Minister 130, 135, 147

Foreign Minister 147, 163, 165
Lands Minister 131
Kilage, *Father* Ignatius 45, 132
Kilori, Posa 132
Kimiropa, Bire 177, 178
Kiribati 181
Kiwais people 7
Kofikai, Sabumei 66
Kokoda Track 196
Kokopo 168
Konedobu xiv, 17, 22, 32, 41
 and policy-making 43
 offices of Administration 41, 42, 70
 protest at 47
konfrontasi 145, 146
Korea 180
Korobosea xiv
Kovave magazine 78
Kurondo, Siwi 48, 57, 66, 154
Kwato Mission 35, 54, 74

Labor Party, *Australia* xv, 73, 79
 Conference, *1963* 103
 Conference, *1971* 104
labour 189
 see also indenture; manpower planning
 for Australia 2, 189
 for plantations 3
 from Bougainville 125
 relations 47
Labour Department 74
labourers xiv, 13
Lae 16
lagatoi ships 12
Laki, James 190
Lalor, Peter 43, 75
Lambert, C.R.(Esky) 31
land and identity 13, 132
Land Dispute Settlement Act 1975 133
land disputes xv, 13, 61, 63–64, 125, 131–133
land management 27, 71
land register 62, 81, 132–133
Land Registration (Communally Owned Land) Ordinance 36
land tenure 13, 28, 35, 45, 91, 133, 179, 182, 183
Land (Tenure Conversion) Ordinance 36
Land Titles Commission 13, 36, 131

landowners
 and developers 178
Lands Department
 Policy and Research Branch 133
Langmore, John 74, 76, 130
Langro, Paul 62, 67, 113
Lapun, Paul *MP* 22, 38, 39, 45, 48, 57, 58, 60, 61, 147
 and uneven funding 64
 in Second House of Assembly 67
 in Third House of Assembly 110
 minister for Mines 134, 135
 on Bougainville 95
latrines 16
Lavau, Tessie 7, 8–10, 18, 21, 196
law and order 56, 63, 91, 94, 151–155
 see also fortified compounds; judiciary; Legal Branch; police; Public Solicitor's Office; Supreme Court
 African precedents 76
Law Department 74
Law Reform Commission 152, 153
Leadership Code 119, 122, 140, 171, 187
Leadership Tribunals 177
Leahy, Mick 79, 204
Leahy, Thomas (Tom) 55, 57, 58, 66, 82, 85, 86, 103
legislation requirements 93, 97–98, 107
Legislative Council 35, 38, 47
 Native members 17–18, 21, 25, 35
 1951 17
Lemay, *Bishop* 45
Lepani, Charles 153
Levy, Keith 48
Lewis, James 37
Ley, John 75, 76–77, 124
Liberal Party, *Australia* xv, 80, 101
literacy question 54
literature studies 77
Littler, Charles 67, 86
local councils
 and law-enforcement 151
local government 32
 and the Mataungan Association 63
 Buka 14
 Councils 17, 28, 35, 37, 62
 Port Moresby xiv
logging
 see forestry

Lohia, Renagi   161
Lokoloko, Tore   62, 66
Loloata island   122
London Missionary Society   14
louvered windowes   xiv
Loveday, Max   137, 138
loyalty   27, 42, 177
Lualul Village, *New Ireland*   22
Lue, Joseph   60, 62, 67
Lugabai, Michael   45
Lus, Pita   48, 57, 66
Lussick, Walter (Wally)   58, 67, 85, 86
Lutheran Church   14
Lynch, Joe   120, 121
Lynch, Mark   128, 154
Lynn, Charlie   196

McCarthy, J.K   38, 49, 204
McCasker, Alan   74
   Economic Adviser   43
McCasker, Bill   129
McEwen, *Sir* John   40
McKinnon, James   66
McMahon, *Sir* William   53, 79, 91, 101
Macmillan, *Sir* Harold   36
Madang   22, 44
Maddocks, Ian   16, 37
Maino, Anani   66
Makerere University   xiv, 166
malaria   2
Malaysia   104, 117, 178
   Economic Planning Unit   138
Maloat, Paliau   21, 22, 48, 57, 66
Maneke, John   67
Manlel, Paul   49
Mann, *Chief Justice Sir* Alan   75, 76, 146
Mano, Kiotago   37, 48, 66
manpower planning   71
Manus Island   21, 36, 145
Maori
   dispossession   132
Marcos, Imelda   1
Mariga Village, *Bougainville*   22
marketing   27
Markham River   16
Marshall Lagoon   54
Martin, Frank   49
Mason, Noel   49

Matane, Paulias   125, 174
Mataungan Assiciation   62, 92
Mataungans   58, 63, 65, 76, 150
   demonstrations by   86
Matibri, Suguman   48
Mawby, Maurice   61
May, Ron   74
Mazrui, Ali   113
Meanggarum, James   57
Media reports   60, 78
Medical College, *PNG*   47
Mek, Leo   45
Melanesian societies   xiv
Melanesians   31, 32, 73, 103
   and the Administration   16–17
   in Australia   3, 165
   perceptions of   78
   stereotypes   7–8
Melbourne Trade Show 1976   167
Melo, Tambu   48
Melpa people   12
Members of Parliament
   see parliamentarians
Mench, Paul   149
mental health   71
Mentz, Don   105, 128, 137, 138
Menzies, *Sir* Robert Gordon   23, 31
mercenaries   171, 172
Middleton, John   58, 67, 85, 86
migration   52, 159
Mileng, Stahl   22
Military Cadet School, *Lae*   146
Miller, J.D.B   53
millenarian ideas   13–15
Milne Bay   17, 22, 35, 54, 74, 107
mineral rights   47, 133–136
mining   3, 182, 183
   laws   134
   negotiations   46, 60, 178
   royalties   45, 46, 133
   regulation of   45
Mining (Bougainville Copper Agreement) Ordinance 1967   60
Minister for External Affairs   32
Minister for National Development   153
Minister for Territories   31
   see also Australian Department of Territories
Minister for Transport   31

Ministerial Spokesperson for Defence 147
Ministers
    and the Constitution 120
    and their Departments 190
Mirau, Gaudi 48
Miriung, Theodore 45
mismanagement xvi, 173, 174
missionaries 3, 13–15
    see also evangelists
    and elections 37, 57
    and independent thinking 44, 78
    on Legislative Council 17
mission hospitals 17
mission schools 58
modernisation 13, 32
Mo, Makain 48
Mola, Donatus 58, 67, 85, 110
Momis, *Father* John 44, 102, 113, 114, 115, 121, 122, 160
    and BCL 134
    at the UN 124, 125
Ministers for Decentralisation 124
Mona, Louis Sebu 66
monetary policies 130
moral issues 45
Moral Rearmament 63
Morauta, Mekere 129, 130, 171, 172, 173, 178, 187
Morgan, Leo 163
Morobe 22, 38, 168
Morrison, William Leonard (Bill) 4, 79, 82, 104, 137, 138, 192
    and aid delivery 187
    and defence matters 147, 149
    and the Constitution 120, 125, 126
Minister Assisting for Papua New Guinea matters 106
Moses, Sasakila 110
Moses, Uawi Wauve 66
Motu
    language xiv
Mouk village 21
Mt Fubilan 136
Mt Hagen, Western Highlands 22, 95
Murray, *Colonel* J,K 17, 25
Murray Barracks 147

Namalia, Rabbie 77, 125, 129, 130, 160, 161, 171
    as Prime Minister 188
name proposal 87, 88
Narokobi, Bernard 76, 114, 152, 153, 154, 159, 176, 205
Nasioi people 15, 60
Natera, John 44
nation-building 59–60, 114, 117, 145, 192, 193
National Broadcasting Corporation 161, 162
National Executive Council 122
National Fiscal Commission proposal 119
National Fisheries Authority 174
National Goals and Directive Principles 122
National Identity Campaign 168
National Investment and Development Authority (NIDA) 130
National Investment Stategy 131
National Party 102
National Public Expenditure Plan 130
national unity 59, 70, 91, 117, 126, 159–162, 167
nationalisation proposal 118
National Pressure Group (NPG) 121
Native Customs (Recognition) Ordinance 153
Native Land Commission 13, 35
Native Regulations 3, 10, 153
'Natives' 9–10
    and Citizens 18
    educated 44
natural resources 117
Nauru 189, 195
Navitu Napidakoc 134, 160
Nelson, Hank xvi, 3, 5, 78, 175, 205
Neville, Ronald (Ron) 49, 58, 67
New Britain 12
New Caledonia 132
New Guinea
    as British Protectorate 2, 3, 75
    as German colony xvi, 3, 11, 62
    as the 'last unknown' 8
    attempted annexation 2
    occupation of *1914* 10
New Guinea magazine 77
New Guinea Association, *Canberra* 24
New Guinea Islands 17, 64
New Guinea National Party 110
New Guinean Planters Association 133
New Guineans xvi, 17, 55
    as Australian protected persons 18, 53

New Ireland 102
New Zealand 2, 131, 195
　　and the Cook Islands 53
Newby, L.R. 23
Newman, A.P.J 49, 67
Niall, Horrie/Horace 38, 49
Nigeria 76, 77
Nimanbor, Parick 66
Niue 195
Nuigini
　　see name proposals
Nockels, Jim 148
Noga, Aloysius 119
Nombri, Karl 54
non-governmental organisations (NGO's) 188
Nugintz, Mek 66
Nwokolo, Ikenna 63, 76

Oala-Rarua, Oala
　　see Rarua, Oala Oala
Occupational Health and Safety 74
O'Faircheallaigh, Ciaron 135, 206
Office of Information 162, 167, 168
Office of the Economic Adviser 129
Ogut, Kup 22, 35
Ok Tedi copper mine 1, 130, 136, 164
Okuk, Iambakey 102–103, 110, 171
Okuyufa Village, *Eastern Highlands* 22
Olewale, Ebia 47, 54, 67, 85, 86, 110, 126, 159–160, 183
　　and border issues 165, 166
　　and Bougainville 160
　　and land issues 131
　　and Papua Action Groups 125, 159
　　at the UN 125
　　Deputy Prime Minister 159
　　in Third House of Assembly 159
　　Minister for Justice 125, 176
　　Minister for Provincial Affairs 123
Oliver, Douglas 14, 16, 70
O'Neill, Nick 62, 132
Oposisi Papua Merdeka (OPM) 164
Opperman, *Sir* Hubert Ferdinand 53
Oram, Nigel 76, 114
Order in Council 79
Organisation for African Unity 29
Ou, Pena 66
Owen Stanley Range xiv

Pacific Commission 195
Pacific economic and political community, *proposal* 189
Pacific Forum 195
Pacific Islands regiment 79, 95–96, 101, 145, 146–147
Pacific War (1941–45) 3, 8, 11, 31, 145, 180
　　Port Moresby xiv
'Pacific Strategy' 189
Palau 163
Paliwala, Abdul 76
palm oil 182
Pangial, Momei 48, 64, 66
Pangu party 41, 57, 58, 63, 64, 102, 107, 110, 134, 159
Panguna copper mine xv, 59, 62, 78, 91, 130, 133–134, 186, 188
Papua xv, 64
　　see also territory of Papua
　　annexation of *1907* 10
　　Northern District 85
Papua Action 159
Papua Besena (the Papuan tribe) 125, 159
Papua New Guinea Act, 1966 79, 88–89, 93, 101, 106, 120
Papua New Guinea Defence Force, *1973* 148, 150
Papua New Guinea Intelligence Committee (PICNIC) 94
Papua New Guinea Office 106–107, 137
Papuan Infantry Battalion 145
Papuan Pocket Poets 78
Papuans xiv
　　as Australian citizens 18, 53
Parao, Anton 109, 113
Parker, Robert 61
Parliament, *Australia*
　　visit to 24
Parliament, *PNG* 38, 45–47, 85, 118
　　see also elections; House of Assembly; Westminster procedures
　　and Administrator 38
　　and the Constitution 120
　　instability of xv, 91, 121, 171, 178
Parliament House 1
parliamentarians
　　from Papua 64
　　insecurity among 82, 177
　　perception of xvi, 24, 174
　　qualifications 54

Parliamentary Accounts Committee 140
Parliamentary Executive (Interim Provisions) Bill 1965 47
parliamentary procedures 35, 47, 58
   see also Westminster procedures
parochialism 159
party politics
   in Australia 24
   in PNG 102, 173, 174
Pasom, Singin 48
Pasquarelli, John 37, 48, 147
paternalism 18, 39, 44, 72, 78, 190
Patience, *Professor* Allan xv, 174, 183–184, 190, 191, 206
Peacock, Andrew xv, 80, 82, 93, 100–103, 107–108, 139, 144, 165, 166, 191
Pearsall, Stanley 109
penicillin 36
People's Progress Party (PPP) 64, 102, 110
pigs 12, 16
Piniau, Sam 162
Pita, Simogen 22, 38, 39, 49
planning capacity 4
plantations 3, 10–13, 28
planters 3, 10
   on Legislative Council 17
plays 78
plebiscites proposal 108
Plimsoll, *Sir* James 104
Poe, John 67, 110
police 35, 60, 63, 88, 94, 95, 105, 150
   see also Royal Papua New Guinea Constabulary
   riot police 95, 96, 150
Police Commissioner 95
Police Offences Ordinances 154
policy making xv, 4, 40, 43, 108
   see also Australia — policy making
policy making
   attempted reforms 81–82, 87, 94, 113–125, 183
political change 41, 89
Political Development Division 81
political education 21–24, 41, 86
political gradualism 44, 70
politicians 187
   see also parliamentarians
   buisness interests 187
Polynesians 195, 197
Pople, Graham 48

Popondetta 77
population 3, 181
Port Moresby 16, 43, 78, 107
   members of parliament in 38, 102
   1972 xiv
   migrants in xiv, 125
   population xiv
   rain shadow xiv
   riots *1973* 125
   show 168
Portugeuse territories 30
Port-Courier, newspaper xv, 123, 175, 196
post-Soviet governments 180
Premdas, *Dr* Ralph 152–153
presidency proposal 87
price control 81
Prime Minister
   appointment of 122
Prime Minister's Department 152
   see also Australian Prime Minister's Department
project aid 187, 188
Prompt Theatre
   in Canberra 78
propaganda 72
prospectors 2, 136
protected persons 52
provincial governments 121, 160
   failure of xv, 123–124, 161, 177, 178
protein 3
Public Accounts Committee 122
public debate
   discouraged 45
Public Order Bill 58
Public Prosecutor 124
public relations 70
Public Relations Advisory Committee 73
public servants xiv, 81
   see also houses
   and higher education 45
   from Australia 190
   termination payments 139
   wages 71
Public Service 26, 28, 47, 143, 187–188
   discrimination in 18
   dominated by Canberra 86
   grades 47
   localisation 144–145, 191–192
   politicisation of xv, 171

reorganisation xv, 4
salaries 47
Public Service Association 144
Public Service Board 144
Public Service Commissioners 43, 47, 54, 58, 124, 144
    slowness of 70, 191
    Territory Commissioner 43
Public Solicitor 76, 152
Public Solicitors's Department 151
Public Solicitor's Office 43, 74, 75, 76, 132
Public Works Department 144
Pundari, *Speaker* John 172
Pyne, Eric 67

Queen as head of state 122
Queensland Government 165
Queensland University 77
quinine 36
Quodling, Paul 135

Rabaul xv, 4, 16, 58, 62, 79, 191
    demonstrations in 86, 101, 131
    Deputy Public Solicitor in 76
    Multiracial Council 62
    volcanic eruption 178
Rabaul Times, newspaper 8
race relations 9, 62
racism xiv, 9, 18, 32
    see also discrimination
Ramu 130
Rarua, Oala Oala 22, 24, 54, 62, 67, 86, 159
Rarupu, Eriko 48
Rea, Gavera 109, 110
Reeve, Harold 49
referendum proposal 64, 90, 108–109
reform
    see government — reform of
Regional Assistance Mission to Solomon Islands (RAMSI) 189
regional governments 86, 87, 121–124
Reluctant Flame, play 78
republic of the North Solomons, *proposal* 124
Research School of Pacific Studies 74
Reserve bank 30
resource development 155
Resource Rent Tax 135

responsible government
    see self-government
Rhodesia 30
rights of way 13
Rio Tinto 59, 133 135
    see also Conzinc Riotinto Australia
riots 59
Ritchie, Harry 67
Ritchie, James 67
roads 28, 178
Rooney, Nahau 153
Rorovana people 60
Rossi, Boana 132
Rostow, Walt
    Stages of Economic Growth 128
Rowley, Charles 72, 77, 86
Royal Navy
    see British Navy
Royal Papua New Guinea Constabulary 150–151
    Australians in 190
rubber 28
Rural Improvement Program 129
Rural Progress Associations 35
Russia
    in the Pacific 2
Ryan, Paul 129
Ryan, Peter 175

sago 12
Sahul lost continent 2
Saibai Island 165
Saiho Hospital 22
Saki, Yakutung 22
Sali, Boyamo 110, 112, 119
Salin, Aisoli 17
Salisbury, Richard 12
Sambubu, Timaeus 22
Samiel, Donigi 132
Samoa 86, 180
Sapias, Austin 167
Sauinambi, Nauwi 66
SCAC
    see Social Change Advisory Committee
scandals xv
    see also corruption
schooling
    see education
schools 28, 47, 58
    see also Geelong Grammer; Sogeri High School

Schumacher, E.F. *Small is Beautiful* 128
Scouting 8
Scragg, Roy 49
Seale, Herbert 67
secession question 4, 60, 92, 95, 124
Secondary Industry Committee 130
security issues 18, 63, 88, 94–96, 189–190
Select Committee on Constitutional Development 39, 52
Select Committee on Parliamentary Procedures 58
self-determination 25, 70, 90, 92
self-government 4, 26, 27, 28, 29, 30, 39, 86–87, 106, 192
 see also Arec Select Committee
 form of ? 53, 54, 60, 86
 internal 52, 89, 92, 101
 machinery 82, 88
 through gradual change 42, 79, 92
self-reliance 129
self-sufficiency 80, 186
seminaries 14, 77
Senate Foreign Affairs, Defence and Trade Committee, Australia 189
separatism 115
Sepik District 54, 57, 92
servants xiv, 7, 8, 78
Seventh Day Aventists 14
seventh state ? 53, 54
sexism 21
shells 12
shipping
 Australian xiv, 11
Siaguru, Anthony 129, 150, 163, 173, 177, 179, 183
Simbu 102
Simbu people 10
Simogun, Pita 17
Simpson, A.M. 144
Sinclair, *Dr* Alex 71
Singilong, Meck 66
Singirok, *General* 172
Siune, Waiye 48
Skate, Bill 171, 72, 173, 187, 188
skill shortages 92, 128, 144
Smith, George Warwick 40, 42, 45, 55, 56, 63, 81, 101, 105, 166, 167
Smith, *Admiral* Victor 147
Smithers, *Justice* 154

Snedden, *Sir* Billy Mackie 53
social activism 14
social change 70–73
Social Change Advisory Committee 71, 74
Sogeri High School 85, 159
Solomon Islands 16, 36, 86, 132, 181, 189
 borders 163
 crisis 190
Somare, Micheal Thomas xv, 4, 47, 54, 57, 58, 61, 62, 108, 121, 171, 207
 and Andrew Peacock 101–103
 and BCL 134, 136
 and defence planning 148
 and Olewale 159
 and separatists 64
 and Whitlam 112, 139, 164, 192, 193
 coalition government of xv, 4, 102–103, 192
 Eight Aims 141
 in Second House of Assembly 67
 in Third House of Assembly 110
 on Arek Select Committee 85, 86, 87
 on Constitutional Planning Committee 113, 120, 121
 on self–reliance 129
 speech at independence celebrations 1
Somare Government 129–140, 144, 160, 191
Souter, Gavin 8
South Pacific Appropriate Technology Foundation 129
South Pacific Commission 28, 29, 107
sovereignty 189, 195
Spanish African territories 30
Spate, Oskar 11, 44
Special Projects 81
Special Services Unit proposal 148
Speight, George
 coup in Fiji 190
Spender, *Sir* Percy Claude 31
squatter settlements xiv
State of Emergency 122, 159
statehood question 4, 158–159
Stone, David 113, 121, 138
strategic interests 2, 26
 see also Defence Force; Police
Structural Adjustment Program 188
'subsistence affluence' 13
Stuntz, John 39, 49
subsidies 80

subversion 44
sugar 130
Sukarno 36
sulfa drugs 36
Summary Offences Act 154
Supreme Court 75, 76, 151, 153
Swan, Trevor 11, 76
sweet potato 12

Tabua, Robert 22, 38, 48, 159
Talis, Yakob 67
Tamindei, Pita 48
Tammur, Oscar 57, 58, 63, 66
Tange, *Sir* Arthur 104,107, 148
Tanzania xv, 76, 129,130,131
Taora, Era 75
taro 12
Tarua, Ilinome 35, 107, 120, 131
Tasmania 2
Taureka, Reuben 54, 110
taxation 14, 62, 81, 128
    VAT 128
Taylor, Meg 153
teacher trainees 28
Teachers' College 47
    Students' Council 47
Tedep 62
Ten Thousand Years in a Lifetime, autobiography 78
terrain 2, 11
Territories Minister *see* Minister for Territories
Territory House of Assembly 4 *see also* House of Assembly
Territory Intelligence Committee (TIC) 94
Territory of Papua 3
Territory Supreme Court 62
terrorism 189
Tertiary Students' Federation 47
tertiary study *see* education — tertiary
Tetley, Keith 48
Thursday Isand 195
Tiaba, Handabe 37, 49
timber 28, 178 *see also* forestry
Titimur, Epineri 67
ToBaining, Vin 22
ToBongolua, Philip 132
Tok Pisin 16, 21, 37, 38, 57, 58, 70, 159
    as language of plays 78

Tokelau 195
Tolai people 4, 62, 63, 92, 133, 151, 176
ToLiman. Matthias 38, 39 48, 58, 63, 66, 81–82, 113, 151, 159
    on Arek Select Committee 85, 86
    Leader of the Opposition 114
Tololo, *Sir* Alkan 59
Tomot, Melchior 63
Tonga 86, 180
tools 12
Tordoff, Bill 114, 119
ToRobert, Henry 44
Torres Strait 1, 32
    navigation in 2
Torres Strait Islanders 166, 195
Torres Strait Islands 159, 164–165
tourism 81
town planning 81
trade 3, 11, 30
trade displays 167
trade unions 71
traditional owners 62
traditional values 77, 120
transfer of powers 101, 105 106, 115, 120, 194
Transparency International 173
travel 23, 81, 86
Trobriands 54
Trusteeship Council 161–162
Tsibim, Daniel
tuberculosis 28
Tuvalu 181

Uganda 76
    1972 xiv
Ulia, Kokomo 66
Ulli 78
Ulufa'alu, *Prime Minister* Bart 190
Umut, Stoi 48
undersecretaries 38, 48, 55, 58
Unexpected Hawk, play 78
[The] Ungrateful Daughter, play 78
unification issue 64–65
United Church 14
United Nations 26, 89, 193 *see also* Food and Agriculture Organisation
    administrative union 64
    Committee of 24 93, 109

Decolonisation Committee   29, 36, 39
General Assembly   29, 91 112
Overseas Development Group   129
Trusteeship Agreement   108
Trusteeship Committee   29, 108
Trusteeship Council   125
United Nations Trust   124–126
United Nations Visiting Mission *1962*   15, 21, 30, 37
United Party   xv, 4, 64, 85, 96, 102, 109, 112, 194
paper on the Constitution   120, 121
United States of America   27, 109
University of Papua New Guinea   xv, xvi, 14, 44, 86
Creative Writing   78
first graduates   129
history courses   78
Law Faculty   76, 77, 107, 152
network   77
Peacock's visit   101
Waigani Seminar   xiv, 45, 74, 77, 129, 138, 160, 181, 207
Unkles, Gerry   43
urban development   81
urbanisation   45
Urekit, Koriam Michael   48, 66
Uroe, Nathabial   67

Vanuatu   132, 150
Varzin Plantation   62, 151
Vietnam   180
Vietnam War   74, 146
Village Book   16
village courts   151–152, 174
Village Courts Act   152
Village Economic Development Fund   129
villages   16, 78
proposed confederation of   114–115
violence   xv, 177
Viviani, Nancy   138
Volunteer Rifles   145
Votes of no confidence   171
Voutas, Tony   38–39, 47, 55, 57, 58, 61, 62, 74, 107, 112, 119, 138, 192
in second House of Assembly   67
Voutas Committee   58
Vunamami, *East New Britain*   22
Vunapoladig land   62

W.R. Carpenter *company*   11
Wabag   76
Wabiria, Andrew   66
Waddell, Robert   85, 87
wages   28, 47, 74
Waigani   *see* University of Papua New Guinea — Waigani Seminar
Waiko, John   77, 78
Wainwright, Elsina   179
Wakefield, Edward Gibbon   2
Wallace, Alfred Russel   2
wantoks (kin)   38, 159
War in the Pacific   *see* Pacific War
Ward, Alan   132
Ward, Eddie *MP*   8, 31
Warebu, Muriso   48, 67
Wari, Turi   66
Waro, Kamona   54
Warwick Smith, George   41–41
Watkins, W.W.   49, 52, 55, 67
Watts, John   58, 67
Watson, Lepani   38, 48, 66
Watts, Ronald   114, 119
Wauwe, Uauwi   48
Webb, N.L.   147
Wedega, Alice   35
Weisbrot, Daid   154
Welbourne, Bill   132
Wentworth, William Charles (1790–1872)   2
West Papua   29, 36   *see also* Irian Jaya
Westminster procedures   37, 58, 65, 124, 195
Weston, A.B.   76
Wewak   54
White Australia policy   2, 3, 4, 31, 53, 54, 73, 79, 194
White, Hugh   186
White, Terry   70
White Women's Protection Ordinance   74
Whitlam, *Prime Minister* Edward Gough   xv, 1, 4, 29, 78–80, 85, 88, 102, 186, 192
and Bill Morrison   103–106, 113
border issues   163–164
timetable for independence   112, 191, 193
Whitlam, Margaret   103
Whitlam Government   137, 175, 194
Whitrod, Ray   63, 150
Wilenski, Peter   137, 138
Willesee, *Senator* Don   138, 139

Willey, Keith 7, 78
Wingti, Paias 171
Wolfers, Ted 55, 70, 114, 121, 122, 159, 166
women
    antenatal care 28
    discrimination toward 21, 152
    education of 10
    equal pay for 47
    role of 10
Woolford, Don 124
Wootton, Hal 153
work and leisure 12
workers *see* labour; labourers
World Bank 3, 13, 30, 43, 136, 172 182, 187, 188
World Health Organisation 28
World War I 3
World War II *see* Pacific War
Worsley, Peter 14, 18
Worth, Bill 91
Wright, *Dr* Eric 125, 161

yams 12
Yambanda, Beibi 67
young people 17
Yuwi, Matiabe 67, 85, 106, 113

Zorn, Stephen 130, 135
Zurecnuoc, Zure 48

www.ingramcontent.com/pod-product-compliance
Lightning Source LLC
Chambersburg PA
CBHW060930180426
43192CB00045B/2876